OXFORD STUDENT'S Science DICTIONARY

Chris Prescott

OXFORD
UNIVERSITY PRESS

To Ann, Peter, and David

OXFORD
UNIVERSITY PRESS

Great Clarendon Street, Oxford OX2 6DP

Oxford University Press is a department of the University of Oxford.
It furthers the University's objective of excellence in research,
scholarship, and education by publishing worldwide.
Oxford is a registered trade mark of Oxford University Press
in the UK and in certain other countries

First published 1999
Second edition 2006
Third edition 2008
Fourth edition 2013
Updated reprint 2015
This edition 2020

British Library Cataloguing in Publication Data

Data available

ISBN 978 0 19 277694 5
5 7 9 10 8 6

Printed in China

Paper used in the production of this book is a natural,
recyclable product made from wood grown in sustainable forests.
The manufacturing process conforms to the environmental
regulations of the country of origin.

The publishers would like to thank Andrew Delahunty for his
contribution to this edition.

You can trust this dictionary
to be up to date, relevant
and engaging because
it is powered by the
Oxford Corpus, a unique
living database of children's
and adults' language.

Contents

➤ **How to use this dictionary** **4–5**

➤ **Quick Reference** **6–9**

  ➤ Understanding the question 6

  ➤ Getting calculations right 7

  ➤ Plotting graphs accurately 7

  ➤ Formulas to remember 8–9

➤ **A–Z** **11–287**

Introduction

This new edition of the *Oxford Student's Science Dictionary* contains over 1,000 words and phrases for students aged 11 – 16 years. It has been significantly updated and now uses alphabetical order to make a wide range of clearly defined scientific terms accessible to young learners. It also brings together related words in a way which builds connections and a deeper understanding of all areas of science.

With words from the curriculum and detailed vocabulary associated with topics ranging from cell biology, ecology, inheritance and variance, to atoms and bonding, electricity, forces and motion, and a 'Quick Reference' guide at the start with useful tips and formulas, this book is designed to be a comprehensive tool for both the classroom and for revision at home.

Where a word has several meanings, different meanings are numbered and often other related words are listed. This is a great way to build and extend vocabulary. Example sentences provide additional information about the headword and show its usage in a sentence.

Additional panels bring words that are related to, or can be used in connection with, the headword and a large number of tables clearly present useful information that students need to learn. Formulas are highlighted throughout and illustrations with appropriate annotations help to explain concepts more fully. All of this makes the dictionary a key reference tool for use with textbooks, worksheets, revision guides, and tests.

During the writing of this dictionary I have received extensive advice from the staff of Oxford University Press and their readers. Dr Jeremy Marshall gave specialist help as an editor and lexicographer on the first edition. I wish to express my sincere thanks.

Chris Prescott
2020

How to use this dictionary

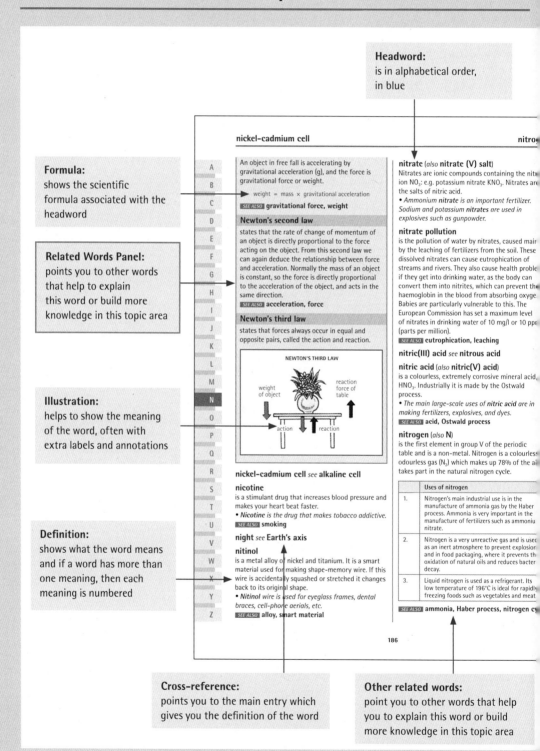

Headword:
is in alphabetical order, in blue

Formula:
shows the scientific formula associated with the headword

Related Words Panel:
points you to other words that help to explain this word or build more knowledge in this topic area

Illustration:
helps to show the meaning of the word, often with extra labels and annotations

Definition:
shows what the word means and if a word has more than one meaning, then each meaning is numbered

Cross-reference:
points you to the main entry which gives you the definition of the word

Other related words:
point you to other words that help you to explain this word or build more knowledge in this topic area

---

nickel–cadmium cell

nitro

An object in free fall is accelerating by gravitational acceleration (g), and the force is gravitational force or weight.

weight = mass × gravitational acceleration

SEE ALSO gravitational force, weight

Newton's second law

states that the rate of change of momentum of an object is directly proportional to the force acting on the object. From this second law we can again deduce the relationship between force and acceleration. Normally the mass of an object is constant, so the force is directly proportional to the acceleration of the object, and acts in the same direction.

SEE ALSO acceleration, force

Newton's third law

states that forces always occur in equal and opposite pairs, called the action and reaction.

NEWTON'S THIRD LAW

weight of object

reaction force of table

action   reaction

nickel–cadmium cell *see* **alkaline cell**

nicotine

is a stimulant drug that increases blood pressure and makes your heart beat faster.
• *Nicotine is the drug that makes tobacco addictive.*

SEE ALSO smoking

night *see* **Earth's axis**

nitinol

is a metal alloy of nickel and titanium. It is a smart material used for making shape-memory wire. If this wire is accidentally squashed or stretched it changes back to its original shape.
• *Nitinol wire is used for eyeglass frames, dental braces, cell-phone aerials, etc.*

SEE ALSO alloy, smart material

nitrate (*also* **nitrate (V) salt**)
Nitrates are ionic compounds containing the nit ion NO_3: e.g. potassium nitrate KNO_3. Nitrates are the salts of nitric acid.
• *Ammonium nitrate is an important fertilizer. Sodium and potassium nitrates are used in explosives such as gunpowder.*

nitrate pollution
is the pollution of water by nitrates, caused mair by the leaching of fertilizers from the soil. These dissolved nitrates can cause eutrophication of streams and rivers. They also cause health proble if they get into drinking water, as the body can convert them into nitrites, which can prevent the haemoglobin in the blood from absorbing oxyge Babies are particularly vulnerable to this. The European Commission has set a maximum level of nitrates in drinking water of 10 mg/l or 10 ppr (parts per million).

SEE ALSO eutrophication, leaching

nitric(III) acid *see* **nitrous acid**

nitric acid (*also* **nitric(V) acid**)
is a colourless, extremely corrosive mineral acid, HNO_3. Industrially it is made by the Ostwald process.
• *The main large-scale uses of nitric acid are in making fertilizers, explosives, and dyes.*

SEE ALSO acid, Ostwald process

nitrogen (*also* **N**)
is the first element in group V of the periodic table and is a non-metal. Nitrogen is a colourless odourless gas (N_2) which makes up 78% of the a takes part in the natural nitrogen cycle.

	Uses of nitrogen
1.	Nitrogen's main industrial use is in the manufacture of ammonia gas by the Haber process. Ammonia is very important in the manufacture of fertilizers such as ammoniu nitrate.
2.	Nitrogen is a very unreactive gas and is used as an inert atmosphere to prevent explosior and in food packaging, where it prevents th oxidation of natural oils and reduces bacter decay.
3.	Liquid nitrogen is used as a refrigerant. Its low temperature of 196°C is ideal for rapidl freezing foods such as vegetables and meat

SEE ALSO ammonia, Haber process, nitrogen cy

186

4

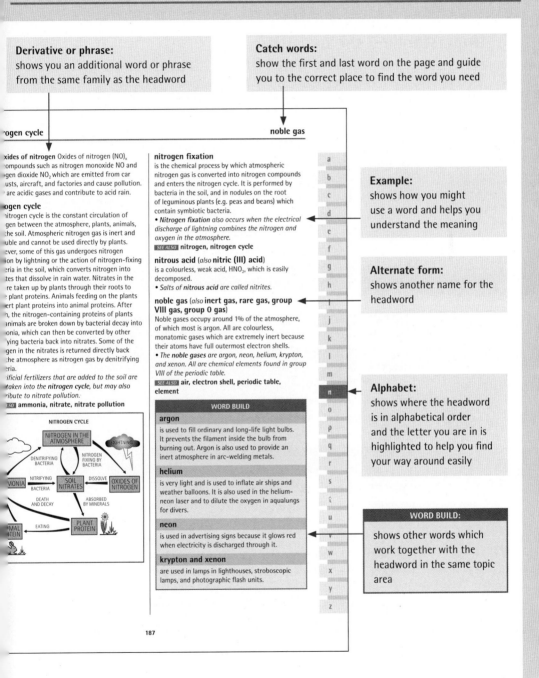

...ogen cycle

noble gas

...xides of nitrogen Oxides of nitrogen (NO)...
...ompounds such as nitrogen monoxide NO and
...gen dioxide NO_2 which are emitted from car
...usts, aircraft, and factories and cause pollution.
... are acidic gases and contribute to acid rain.

...ogen cycle
...nitrogen cycle is the constant circulation of
...gen between the atmosphere, plants, animals,
...the soil. Atmospheric nitrogen gas is inert and
...uble and cannot be used directly by plants.
...ever, some of this gas undergoes nitrogen
...ion by lightning or the action of nitrogen-fixing
...eria in the soil, which converts nitrogen into
...tes that dissolve in rain water. Nitrates in the
... plant proteins. Animals feeding on the plants
...ert plant proteins into animal proteins. After
...n, the nitrogen-containing proteins of plants
...animals are broken down by bacterial decay into
...onia, which can then be converted by other
...ying bacteria back into nitrates. Some of the
...gen in the nitrates is returned directly back
...the atmosphere as nitrogen gas by denitrifying
...eria.
...ificial fertilizers that are added to the soil are
...taken into the nitrogen cycle, but may also
...ribute to nitrate pollution.
SEE ALSO ammonia, nitrate, nitrate pollution

nitrogen fixation
is the chemical process by which atmospheric
nitrogen gas is converted into nitrogen compounds
and enters the nitrogen cycle. It is performed by
bacteria in the soil, and in nodules on the root
of leguminous plants (e.g. peas and beans) which
contain symbiotic bacteria.
• *Nitrogen fixation also occurs when the electrical
discharge of lightning combines the nitrogen and
oxygen in the atmosphere.*
SEE ALSO nitrogen, nitrogen cycle

nitrous acid (*also* **nitric (III) acid**)
is a colourless, weak acid, HNO_2, which is easily
decomposed.
• *Salts of nitrous acid are called nitrites.*

noble gas (*also* **inert gas, rare gas, group
VIII gas, group 0 gas**)
Noble gases occupy around 1% of the atmosphere,
of which most is argon. All are colourless,
monatomic gases which are extremely inert because
their atoms have full outermost electron shells.
• *The noble gases are argon, neon, helium, krypton,
and xenon. All are chemical elements found in group
VIII of the periodic table.*
SEE ALSO air, electron shell, periodic table,
element

WORD BUILD
argon is used to fill ordinary and long-life light bulbs. It prevents the filament inside the bulb from burning out. Argon is also used to provide an inert atmosphere in arc-welding metals.
helium is very light and is used to inflate air ships and weather balloons. It is also used in the helium-neon laser and to dilute the oxygen in aqualungs for divers.
neon is used in advertising signs because it glows red when electricity is discharged through it.
krypton and xenon are used in lamps in lighthouses, stroboscopic lamps, and photographic flash units.

a
b
c
d
e
f
g
h
i
j
k
l
m
n
o
p
q
r
s
t
u
v
w
x
y
z

NITROGEN CYCLE

NITROGEN IN THE
ATMOSPHERE

DENITRIFYING
BACTERIA

NITROGEN
FIXING BY
BACTERIA

LIGHTNING

...MONIA

NITRIFYING
BACTERIA

SOIL
NITRATES

DISSOLVE

OXIDES OF
NITROGEN

DEATH
AND DECAY

ABSORBED
BY MINERALS

...MAL
...TEIN

EATING

PLANT
PROTEIN

187

Quick reference

Understanding the question

Exam questions use 'command words' or words which direct the student to the answer the examiner is looking for. It is important that the student understands the meaning of the command word so they give the correct answer.

calculate (or **determine**)	Give a numerical answer based on a formula.
classify	Group things based on common characteristics.
compare	Identify similarities and differences.
complete	Add words, numbers, labels or plots to complete a sentence, table, diagram or graph.
deduce	Draw a conclusion based on general rules.
describe	Set out the facts or characteristics in a particular situation or experiment.
distinguish	Identify and understand differences.
draw (or **construct**)	Produce a diagram/drawing with sufficient detail and labels.
estimate	Suggest an approximate value with appropriate units.
evaluate	Consider all factors, then give an appropriate judgement or conclusion.
explain	Give a short answer (length indicated by number of lines for answer) with some supporting argument.
identify (or **name**)	Select and/or name an object, event, concept or process.
infer	Draw a conclusion based on observations.
investigate	Find out information by carrying out experiments.
label	Classify or add identifying words to diagram.
list	State a number of points or items without elaboration.
measure	Determine a numeric value.
outline (or **summarize**)	Summarize the essential points of something.
plot	Translate data into suitable graph or chart with labelled axes.
predict	Write down possible outcomes.
recognize	Identify facts, characteristics, or concepts that are needed to understand a particular situation.
show	Write down details, steps, or calculations to prove an answer.
sketch	Provide a simple freehand drawing.
suggest	Apply scientific knowledge from the syllabus to a new related situation.
state (or **write down**)	Provide a concise answer with no supporting argument.

Getting calculations right

Top tips for things to remember in scientific calculations:

- Write down the equation you are going to use (if it is not already given).
- If necessary rearrange the equation.
- Ensure that the quantities you put into the equation have the correct units. For example, you may need to change grams to kilograms or centimetres to metres.
- Make sure you show the stages of your working. Even if your final answer is wrong you can still gain marks for the correct method of calculation.
- If you use a calculator make sure your answer is of the correct order. If possible round up the numbers and do a rough calculation in your head.
- If stated in the question give your final answer to the correct number of significant figures.
- Always give units with your final answer (if not already given).

Plotting graphs accurately

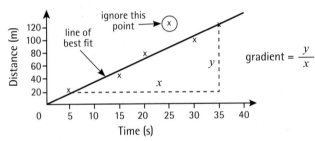

Top tips for things to remember when plotting graphs:

- Choose suitable scales so the graph takes up most of the available graph paper.
- Do not choose a scale where the small squares on the graph paper have to be counted and divided 'into halves' to represent a particular number.
- Label both axes with their name and unit of measurement.
- Plot points with a fine pencil.
- Draw a line of best fit. It does not have to go through all the points. Omit the points (outlier points) which obviously do not fit the pattern.
- The line of best fit does not have to go through the origin.
- To find a value on the y-axis which corresponds with an x-axis value, draw a vertical line from the x-value to the line of best fit. Then draw a horizontal line from where the vertical line touches the line of best fit, to the y-axis.
- Gradient (slope) of the graph is found by the amount it changes on the y-axis divided by the amount it changes on the x-axis.
- Make sure you label any coordinates accurately.

Formulas to remember

chemical equations

acid + base $\rightarrow$ salt + water

metal + acid $\rightarrow$ salt + hydrogen

metal oxide + acid $\rightarrow$ salt + water

metal hydroxide + acid $\rightarrow$ salt + water

metal carbonate + acid $\rightarrow$ salt + water + carbon dioxide

electricity: current, resistance, and potential difference

charge flow = current × time

resistance in series: $R_{total} = R_1 + R_2$

power = potential difference × current

potential difference = current × resistance

energy and efficiency

kinetic energy = $\frac{1}{2}$ × mass × speed^2

elastic potential energy = $\frac{1}{2}$ × spring constant × extension^2

gravitational potential energy = mass × gravitational field strength × height

change in thermal energy = mass × specific heat capacity × temperature change

energy transferred = power × time

energy transferred = charge flow × potential difference

efficiency = $\dfrac{\text{useful output energy transfer}}{\text{total input energy transfer}}$

forces and gravity

force = mass × acceleration

force = spring constant × extension

moment of a force = force × distance

weight = mass × gravitational field strength

pressure = $\dfrac{\text{force}}{\text{area}}$

magnification

$$\text{magnification} = \frac{\text{size of image}}{\text{size of real object}}$$

photosynthesis

$$\text{carbon dioxide} + \text{water} \xrightarrow[\text{sunlight}]{\text{chlorophyll}} \text{glucose} + \text{oxygen}$$

rates of reaction

$$\text{mean rate of reaction} = \frac{\text{quantity of reactant used}}{\text{time taken}}$$

$$\text{mean rate of reaction} = \frac{\text{quantity of product formed}}{\text{time taken}}$$

speed

distance travelled = speed × time

$$\text{acceleration} = \frac{\text{change in velocity}}{\text{time taken}}$$

momentum = mass × velocity

velocity = frequency × wavelength

work and power

$$\text{power} = \frac{\text{energy transferred}}{\text{time}}$$

$$\text{power} = \frac{\text{work done}}{\text{time}}$$

work done = force × distance

Aa

A *see* **ampere**

a *see* **amplitude**

abdomen
The abdomen is the body part that in most animals is between the thorax (chest) and the legs. It contains the digestive organs (alimentary canal).
• *An insect's abdomen is at the end of its body.*
SEE ALSO **alimentary canal, thorax**

abiotic factor
Abiotic factors are the non-living factors which influence the environment, including climatic factors and edaphic factors.
SEE ALSO **biotic factor**

> ### climatic factor
> Climatic factors include sunlight, rainfall, temperature, and humidity.

> ### edaphic factor
> Edaphic factors are the chemical and physical aspects of the environment, such as the oxygen content of water, the pH of soil, and the degree of air pollution.

A–bomb *see* **fission bomb**

abortion
is the expulsion of the fetus from the uterus before the 28th week of pregnancy.
• *Abortion may be induced or spontaneous.*
SEE ALSO **miscarriage**

absolute scale
(*also* **Kelvin scale, thermodynamic temperature scale**)
The absolute scale is based on the lowest possible theoretical temperature of absolute zero, which is zero on this scale. There are therefore no negative temperatures.

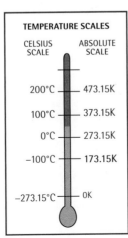

TEMPERATURE SCALES

CELSIUS SCALE	ABSOLUTE SCALE
200°C	473.15K
100°C	373.15K
0°C	273.15K
−100°C	173.15K
−273.15°C	0K

The relationship between the Celsius and absolute scales is:

$$\text{temperature (K)} = \text{temperature (°C)} + 273.15$$

• *The **absolute scale** was devised by Lord Kelvin (1824–1907), a Scottish physicist and mathematician.*

absolute zero
is the lowest temperature theoretically obtainable. It is 0K on the absolute scale. It is the temperature at which particles have their minimum amount of thermal energy and therefore have a minimum temperature and volume.
• *Absolute zero is equivalent to –273.15°C.*

absorption
is the passing of soluble food molecules through the walls of the intestines and stomach into the bloodstream.
• *Absorption normally occurs through villi.*
SEE ALSO **villus**

absorption of radiation *see* radiation

acceleration
is the rate of change of increasing velocity (or speed). If the velocity changes at a constant rate, then the object travels at constant or uniform acceleration. Acceleration, like velocity, is a vector quantity, as it has both size and direction.
• *Acceleration is often expressed in units of metres per second per second (m/s^2).*
SEE ALSO **force, vector quantity, velocity**

acceleration of gravity
is the acceleration which the gravitational pull of the Earth exerts on a freely falling object.
• *On the Earth's surface **acceleration of gravity** has a value of 9.8 m/s^2. This means that for every second, the object's velocity increases by 9.8 m/s.*

accommodation
is changing the thickness of the lens to focus on objects at various distances from the eye. When the ring of ciliary muscles contracts, the suspensory ligaments are loosened and the lens becomes fatter, to focus on nearby objects. When the ciliary muscles are relaxed, the suspensory ligaments are tightened, which makes the lens thinner, to focus on distant objects.
SEE ALSO **eye, lens**

accumulator *see* secondary cell

a b c d e f g h i j k l m n o p q r s t u v w x y z

accuracy

is the degree to which a measurement represents the actual value of the thing being measured. Experimental measurement is always subject to some error. Errors may arise due to human error or because of the inaccuracy of the measuring instrument itself.

• *It is important to minimize reading errors and to appreciate the accuracy of the measuring instrument you are using.*

acetic acid *see* ethanoic acid

a.c. generator *see* alternator

achromatic lens

An achromatic lens is one that corrects chromatic aberration by combining two lenses made of different kinds of glass, such that their dispersions cancel each other out but their refractions do not.

SEE ALSO **chromatic aberration, dispersion, lens**

acid

An acid is a chemical compound which produces hydrated hydrogen ions $H^+(aq)$ when in aqueous solution. All acids, when in aqueous solution, have certain general properties. They:

– turn moist litmus paper from blue to red
– have a pH value of less than 7
– are electrolytes: in solution they contain ions
– react with metals like zinc and iron to form a salt and hydrogen gas
– react with metal carbonates to form a salt, water, and carbon dioxide gas
– neutralize bases and alkalis to form a salt and water.

SEE ALSO **amino acid, carboxylic acid, ethanoic acid**

mineral acid

Mineral acids are acids which are often strong and corrosive inorganic compounds. Most do not occur naturally but are made for laboratory and industrial use. They include sulfuric acid H_2SO_4, nitric acid HNO_3, hydrochloric acid HCl, and carbonic acid H_2CO_3.

organic acid

Organic acids are naturally occurring acids found in vegetables, fruit, and other foodstuffs. They are usually weaker acids but still have a sharp or sour taste. They include ethanoic acid (found in vinegar), citric acid (in lemons), lactic acid (in milk), and oxalic acid (in rhubarb).

➤ strength of acids

The strength of an acid depends on its degree of ionization in aqueous solution. Strong acids like sulfuric acid are fully ionized in water. Weak acids like carbonic acid are only partially ionized in water. Most of the ions formed recombine and remain as molecules. This is shown by the reversible sign in the chemical equation.

CORROSIVE

$$H_2SO_4(l) \xrightarrow{\text{water}} 2H+(aq) + SO_4{}^{2-} \ (aq)$$

$$H_2CO_3(l) \underset{}{\overset{\text{water}}{\rightleftharpoons}} 2H+(aq) + CO_3{}^{2-} \ (aq)$$

acidic oxide *see* oxide

acid radical

An acid radical is a group of atoms in an acid which becomes negatively charged when in solution.

• *Acid radicals cannot exist by themselves but can join with metal ions to form salts.*

SEE ALSO **salt**

Acid	Salt name	acid radical
hydrochloric	chloride	Cl^-
sulfuric	sulfate	$SO_4{}^{2-}$
sulfurous	sulfite	$SO_3{}^{2-}$
nitric	nitrate	$NO_3{}^-$
nitrous	nitrite	$NO_2{}^-$
phosphoric	phosphate	$PO_4{}^{3-}$
phosphorous	phosphite	$PO_3{}^{3-}$
carbonic	carbonate	$CO_3{}^{3-}$
methanoic	methanoate	$HCOO^-$
ethanoic	ethanoate	CH_3COO^-

acid rain

is rainwater which has a pH less than 5 due to dissolved gases such as sulfur dioxide and oxides of nitrogen. These gases are produced mainly by burning fossil fuels. Normal rainwater has a pH of 5.6 due to dissolved carbon dioxide. With dissolved sulfur dioxide and oxides of nitrogen, the pH can fall by up to 2 points, which is a 100-fold increase in acidity.

• *Acid rain damages leaves, washes essential nutrients out of the soil, and kills fish and other aquatic life in lakes and rivers.*

acquired characteristic

Acquired characteristics are physical characteristics which are acquired by an individual organism during its lifetime.
• *Acquired characteristics are not genetic and are not passed on to future generations, e.g. scars following wounds or the stunted growth of a plant growing in poor soil.*

acquired immune deficiency syndrome
see **AIDS**

actin *see* **muscle**

actinoid (*also* **actinide metal**)

Actinoids are a series of metallic elements of atomic numbers 90 to 103 inclusive. All are very rare metals and most are radioactive.
• *The actinoids after uranium are called 'transuranic elements' and are made in nuclear reactors.*
SEE ALSO **periodic table**

activation energy (*also* E^A)

is the amount of energy which colliding particles must have in order to start a chemical reaction and change reactant particles into products.
• *Activation energy is used in the breaking of chemical bonds.*
SEE ALSO **bond breaking**

activator *see* **promoter**

active immunity *see* **immunity**

active site

The active site is an area on the enzyme molecule to which the substrate attaches during the reaction. The active site is very specific and acts like a lock for a key. Only the specific substrate will fit the active site.
SEE ALSO **enzyme, substrate**

active transport (*also* **active uptake**)

is the movement of substances such as mineral salts through a membrane in living cells against a concentration gradient, i.e. from low to high concentration. It is a process which requires energy and occurs in the root hairs. The concentration of minerals in the soil is quite low in comparison to the concentration inside the root hair. Energy (supplied from the mitochondria of root hair cells) is used to move the mineral salts into the root hair. This is opposite to the direction they would normally take by diffusion.
SEE ALSO **mineral salt**

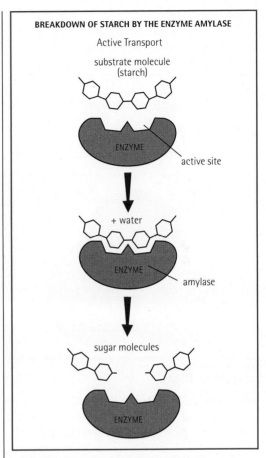

BREAKDOWN OF STARCH BY THE ENZYME AMYLASE

activity series *see* **reactivity series**

addition polymerization *see* **polymerization**

addition reaction

An addition reaction is a chemical reaction in which one molecule adds onto another.
• *Unsaturated molecules like alkenes undergo addition reactions.*
SEE ALSO **malkene, substitution reaction, unsaturated molecule**

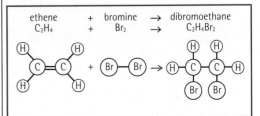

additive mixing

is colour mixing by adding light of different colours (i.e. different wavelengths) to produce an overall colour. For example, the three primary colours of light will join together to produce an overall white colour.
• *Additive mixing is the method used in colour television.*
SEE ALSO **colour, subtractive mixing**

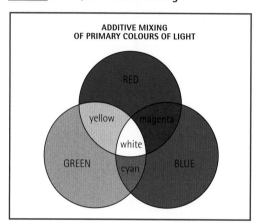

ADDITIVE MIXING
OF PRIMARY COLOURS OF LIGHT

RED

yellow   magenta

white

GREEN   cyan   BLUE

adenine *see* DNA

adenosine triphosphate (*also* ATP)

is a substance used as a store of chemical energy by living cells. Removal of one of its phosphate groups releases energy for biochemical reactions.
SEE ALSO **chemical energy**

adipose tissue

is a special tissue in which the body stores fats.
• *Adipose tissue occurs under the skin and around the muscles, heart, and kidneys.*
SEE ALSO **subcutaneous layer**

adolescence *see* puberty

adrenal gland

Adrenal glands are endocrine glands found above the kidneys which produce adrenalin. This prepares the body for action by increasing the rate of breathing, respiration, and release of glucose from the liver. It also constricts blood vessels in the gut, diverting blood to the brain and muscles where it is needed for action.
SEE ALSO **endocrine gland, hormone**

aeration *see* sewage

aerial (*also* antenna)

An aerial is the part of a radio system which is used to transmit or receive radio waves.
• *Transmitting aerials can be tall masts. Microwave aerials for receiving TV signals are usually dish-shaped.*

aerobic respiration

is respiration which uses oxygen (air) and which releases energy (i.e. is exothermic) and produces carbon dioxide and water.

$$glucose + oxygen \rightarrow carbon\ dioxide + water$$
$$C_6H_{12}O_6 + 6O_2 \rightarrow 6CO_2 + 6H_2O$$

• *These products are similar to combustion products, and aerobic respiration is sometimes referred to as 'slow combustion'.*
SEE ALSO **anaerobic respiration, respiration**

aerodynamic

describes the movement of solid objects through the air. Wind tunnels are used to test the air resistance of vehicles to see whether or not their shape is aerodynamic.
• *Aerodynamic objects are normally smooth and rounded.*

aerosol *see* colloid

afferent neurone *see* neurone

afforestation

is the planting of trees to create new forests.
SEE ALSO **deforestation, reforestation**

afterbirth

The afterbirth is the placenta, expelled by further contractions shortly after the birth of the baby.
SEE ALSO **placenta**

agglutination

is the clumping and sticking together of red blood cells due to the reaction of antigens with antibodies on their surfaces.
SEE ALSO **antibody, antigen**

agranulocyte *see* lymphocyte

AIDS

is caused by HIV (human immunodeficiency virus), which is transmitted through the exchange of body fluids, often during sexual intercourse. This disease damages the immune system of the body by making the lymphocytes (white cells in the blood which fight disease) inactive. The body becomes vulnerable to infection, especially by pneumonia, brain infections, severe diarrhoea, and an unusual type of skin cancer called Kaposi's sarcoma. At present AIDS cannot be cured, although there are drugs to fight the virus and prevent it from being transmitted to others.

SEE ALSO **HIV**

air

is a mixture of gases, the most important of which are nitrogen, oxygen, and carbon dioxide. The gases are extracted by liquefying the air. This is done by repeatedly compressing it, and then rapidly expanding it, which lowers its temperature. The components are then separated by fractional distillation.
• *Air is the main source of oxygen, nitrogen, and noble gases.*

SEE ALSO **carbon dioxide, nitrogen, noble gas**

Component	Percentage by volume	Boiling point in °C
nitrogen	78.08	−196
oxygen	20.95	−183
argon	0.93	−186
carbon dioxide	0.03	−78
neon	0.0018	−246
helium	0.0005	−269
krypton	0.0001	−157
xenon	0.00001	−108

air pollution (*also* atmospheric pollution)

is the release into the atmosphere of toxic substances which have a harmful effect on the natural environment. Most air pollutants are gases (or tiny smoke and lead particles) which are released into the troposphere.

Air pollutant	Chemical formula	Source
carbon monoxide	CO	exhaust fumes
sulfur dioxide	SO_2	burning fossil fuels (coal, oil, natural gas)
CFCs	–	used in refrigerants, aerosols
oxides of nitrogen	$(NO)_x$	exhaust fumes
lead particles	Pb	exhaust fumes
smoke particles	C	coal and wood fires

alcohol

Alcohols are organic compounds that contain the −OH functional group. They are usually colourless, flammable liquids which are good solvents and fuels. The most important is ethanol.
• *Alcohols form a homologous series with a general formula $C_nH_{2n+1}OH$.*

SEE ALSO **ethanol**

Name of alcohol	Value of n	Molecular formula	Structural formula
Methanol	1	CH_3OH	
Ethanol	2	C_2H_5OH	
Propanol	3	C_3H_7OH	
Butanol	4	C_4H_9OH	

Name of alcohol	Boiling Point (°C)	Uses
Methanol	66	making meths, solvent, fuel
Ethanol	78	alcoholic drinks, solvent/cosmetics, fuel
Propanol	97	solvent, aerosol, antifreeze
Butanol	118	solvent, perfumes (esters), flavouring (esters)

alcohol abuse

is the excessive consumption of alcoholic drinks, which contain the drug called ethanol. This is found in beer, wine, and spirits made from fruit and grain. It is a sedative which slows down the activity of the brain.
• *Alcohol abuse slows your reactions and increases the likelihood of accidents.*

SEE ALSO **ethanol**   »

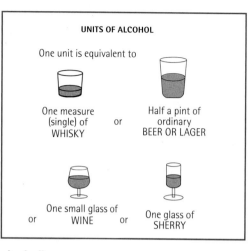

UNITS OF ALCOHOL

One unit is equivalent to

One measure (single) of WHISKY   or   Half a pint of ordinary BEER OR LAGER

or   One small glass of WINE   or   One glass of SHERRY

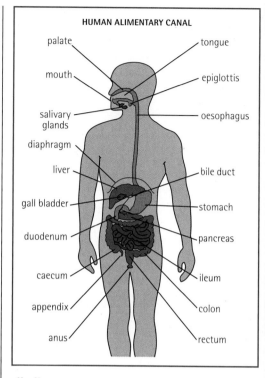

HUMAN ALIMENTARY CANAL

palate, tongue, mouth, epiglottis, salivary glands, oesophagus, diaphragm, liver, bile duct, gall bladder, stomach, duodenum, pancreas, caecum, ileum, appendix, colon, anus, rectum

alcoholism

is addiction to alcoholic drinks. It is caused by prolonged excessive drinking, which can cause physical damage, especially to the liver and stomach, and also mental deterioration. An alcoholic who stops drinking becomes depressed and anxious, and suffers withdrawal symptoms such as delirium and uncontrollable shaking.

algae *singular* alga

Algae are simple living organisms that can carry out photosynthesis and live in aquatic habitats or in moist situations on land. Green slime on paths and seaweed are common examples of algae.

• *Algae were once classified as plants but are now classified as protists.*

SEE ALSO photosynthesis, protoctist

alien *see* habitat

alimentary canal (*also* digestive tract, gastrointestinal tract, gut)

The alimentary canal is a tube in the body of animals in which food is moved along by the action of peristalsis. The muscular tissue of the canal squeezes the food along the canal, and the glandular tissue secretes the enzymes for chemical digestion.

• *In most animals the **alimentary canal** has two openings, the mouth (for ingestion) and anus (for egestion). In between, the processes of digestion and absorption take place.*

SEE ALSO peristalsis

alkali

Alkalis are water-soluble bases which produce hydrated hydroxide ions OH^-(aq) when in aqueous solution. All alkalis are soapy to touch and share several properties. They:
  – turn moist red litmus paper from red to blue
  – have a pH value greater than 7
  – are electrolytes: in solution they contain ions
  – produce ammonia gas when warmed with ammonium salts
  – neutralize acids to form a salt and water.

• *Potassium hydroxide solution KOH(aq), sodium hydroxide solution NaOH(aq), and calcium hydroxide solution Ca(OH)$_2$(aq) are **alkalis**, and so is ammonia solution NH$_3$(aq).*

alkali metal (*also* group I element)

Alkali metals are the elements in the first group in the periodic table, which all have a single valence electron.

• *Alkali metals all react with water to form alkalis (soluble metal hydroxides), hence their name.*

SEE ALSO alkali, periodic table, valence electron

➤ **physical properties of the alkali metals** show trends as we go down the group (see table). Francium is excluded, as it is an unstable radioactive element.

The melting points and boiling points are much lower than you would normally associate with metals. They have weak interatomic forces, so they are also relatively soft metals and can be cut with a knife. The freshly cut surface is silvery but this soon tarnishes. The first three elements in the group are less dense than water and will therefore float on water.

Element	Symbol	Atomic radius (nm)
Lithium	Li	0.15
Sodium	Na	0.19
Potassium	K	0.23
Rubidium	Rb	0.25
Caesium	Cs	0.26

Element	Melting point (°C)	Boiling point (°C)
Lithium	180	1,330
Sodium	98	892
Potassium	64	760
Rubidium	39	688
Caesium	29	690

Element	Density (g/cm^{-3})	Appearance
Lithium	0.53	silvery-white metal
Sodium	0.97	soft silvery-white metal
Potassium	0.86	soft silvery-white metal
Rubidium	1.53	soft silvery-white metal
Caesium	1.9	soft golden-coloured metal

➤ **chemical properties of the alkali metal** are very similar and they are all very reactive, being the highest metals in the reactivity series. This is because they have only one valence electron to lose to form the stable ion (Li^+, Na^+, K^+). Alkali metals are therefore good reducing agents. Because the elements are so reactive with oxygen and water, they are stored under oil to prevent reaction with the moist air. The metals all burn in air with coloured flames to form basic oxides. They all react violently with cold water to form hydrogen gas and an alkali. Alkali metals also react violently with non-metals like chlorine to form ionic compounds. Salts of alkali metals (nitrates, carbonates, sulfates, and chlorides) are white crystalline ionic solids which are water soluble.

Element	Lithium
Symbol of ion	Li^+
Flame colour	crimson red
Chemical reaction with oxygen	burns with red flame to form the oxide $4Li + O_2 \rightarrow 2Li_2O$
Chemical reaction with water	reacts with cold water to form the alkali and hydrogen gas $2Li + 2H_2O \rightarrow 2LiOH + H_2$
Chemical reaction with chlorine	burns to form the white chloride salt $2Li + Cl_2 \rightarrow 2LiCl$

Element	Sodium
Symbol of ion	Na^+
Flame colour	brilliant yellow
Chemical reaction with oxygen	burns with a yellow flame to form the oxide $4Na + O_2 \rightarrow 2Na_2O$
Chemical reaction with water	reacts violently to form the alkali and hydrogen gas $2Na + 2H_2O \rightarrow 2NaOH + H_2$
Chemical reaction with chlorine	burns to form the white chloride salt $2Na + Cl_2 \rightarrow 2NaCl$

Element	Potassium
Symbol of ion	K^+
Flame colour	lilac
Chemical reaction with oxygen	burns with a lilac flame to form the oxide $4K + O_2 \rightarrow 2K_2O$
Chemical reaction with water	catches fire and forms the alkali and hydrogen gas $2K + 2H_2O \rightarrow 2KOH + H_2$
Chemical reaction with chlorine	burns to form the white chloride salt $2K + Cl_2 \rightarrow 2KCl$

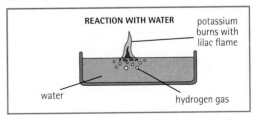

REACTION WITH WATER   potassium burns with lilac flame

water

hydrogen gas

➤ occurrence of alkali metals

Sodium and potassium salts are plentiful on the Earth's surface (sodium 2.7%, potassium 2.5% by mass in the Earth's crust). Lithium salts are found only in trace amounts, and rubidium and caesium are extremely rare. As the salts of these metals are water-soluble, there are high concentrations of these salts in the sea, especially sodium chloride.

Mineral	Main chemical constituent
common salt	NaCl (sodium chloride)
saltpetre	KNO_3 (potassium nitrate)
Chile saltpetre	$NaNO_3$ (sodium nitrate)

➤ extraction of alkali metals

is carried out by electrolysis of their molten chlorides. The molten metal collects at the steel cathode, and chlorine gas collects at the graphite anode.

$$\text{cathode } Na^+ + e^- \rightarrow Na \text{ (sodium metal)}$$

$$\text{anode } 2Cl^- \rightarrow Cl_2 + 2e^- \text{ (chlorine gas)}$$

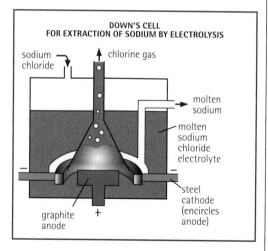

DOWN'S CELL FOR EXTRACTION OF SODIUM BY ELECTROLYSIS

sodium chloride — chlorine gas — molten sodium — molten sodium chloride electrolyte — steel cathode (encircles anode) — graphite anode

alkaline cell (*also* **nickel–cadmium cell**)

An alkaline cell is a common rechargeable cell which has a negative cadmium electrode and a positive nickel electrode. It is a dry cell as it has a non-liquid electrolyte of alkaline potassium hydroxide.

• *The chemical reactions inside an **alkaline cell** are reversible by connecting to an outside source of electricity (recharging), so it is a secondary cell.*

SEE ALSO dry cell, secondary cell

alkaline-earth metal (*also* **group II element**)

Alkaline-earth metals are the elements in the second group in the periodic table, which all have two valence electrons. They are called alkaline-earth because their oxides are alkaline, and because salts of calcium and magnesium are common in the Earth's crust.

SEE ALSO alkali, periodic table, valence electron

➤ physical properties of alkaline-earth metals

are similar for all the elements (except beryllium). The melting and boiling points are higher than the alkali metals (Group I) as there are two electrons per atom, so double the bonding strength. However, they are still lower than a typical transition metal. The alkaline-earth metals are noticeably softer than transition metals and have lower densities.

Element	Symbol	Atomic radius (nm)
Beryllium	Be	0.11
Magnesium	Mg	0.16
Calcium	Ca	0.2
Strontium	Sr	0.21
Barium	Ba	0.22

Element	Melting point (°C)	Boiling point (°C)
Beryllium	1,280	2,270
Magnesium	650	1,110
Calcium	838	1,440
Strontium	768	1,380
Barium	714	1,640

Element	Density (g cm^{-3})	Appearance
Beryllium	1.85	hard white metal
Magnesium	1.74	quite soft silvery metal
Calcium	1.55	soft silvery metal
Strontium	2.6	soft silvery metal
Barium	3.5	soft silvery metal

➤ chemical properties of the alkaline–earth metals

are very similar: they are all reactive metals whose reactivity increases down the group. They always form the stable M^{2+} ion (Be^{2+}, Mg^{2+}, Ca^{2+}) because they lose two electrons to form the stable inert gas configuration. All burn in air with characteristic flame colours to form basic oxides.

However, the alkaline hydroxides of group II are much less soluble than group I. Alkaline-earth metals react with non-metals, like chlorine, to form ionic compounds. Salts of alkaline-earth metals (nitrates, carbonates, sulfates, and chlorides) are white, crystalline, ionic solids. The solubility of the sulfates and carbonates decreases down the group.

Element	Magnesium
Symbol of ion	Mg^{2+}
Flame colour	white
Chemical reaction with oxygen	burns with brilliant white light to form $2Mg + O_2 \rightarrow 2MgO$
Chemical reaction with water	reacts with steam to form oxide and hydrogen $Mg + H_2O(g) \rightarrow MgO + H_2$
Chemical reaction with chlorine	burns to form the white chloride salt $Mg + Cl_2 \rightarrow MgCl_2$

Element	Calcium
Symbol of ion	Ca^{2+}
Flame colour	red
Chemical reaction with oxygen	burns with red flame to form oxide $2Ca + O2 \rightarrow 2CaO$
Chemical reaction with water	reacts with cold water to form hydroxide and hydrogen $Ca + 2H2O(l) \rightarrow Ca(OH)2 + H2$
Chemical reaction with chlorine	burns to form the white chloride salt $Ca + Cl2 \rightarrow CaCl2$

Element	Barium
Symbol of ion	Ba^{2+}
Flame colour	apple green
Chemical reaction with oxygen	burns with a yellow-green flame to form oxide $2Ba + O2 \rightarrow 2BaO$
Chemical reaction with water	reacts with cold water to form hydroxide and hydrogen $Ba + 2H2O(l) \rightarrow 2Ba(OH)2 + H2$
Chemical reaction with chlorine	burns to form the white chloride salt $Ba + Cl2 \rightarrow BaCl2$

➤ **occurrence of the alkaline-earth metals**
Calcium is the fifth most abundant element in the Earth's crust. Vast quantities occur as the rocks chalk, limestone, and marble. These deposits are formed mainly from the shells of dead marine animals. Magnesium is the eighth most abundant element in the Earth's crust. It is found mainly as the carbonate (magnesite $MgCO_3$) often joined with calcium carbonate (dolomite $CaCO_3 . MgCO_3$). The other alkaline-earth metals are much rarer.

Mineral	Main chemical constituent
Limestone	$CaCO_3$ (calcium carbonate)
Chalk	$CaCO_3$ (calcium carbonate)
Marble	$CaCO_3$ (calcium carbonate)
Anhydrite	$CaSO_4$ (calcium sulfate)
Gypsum	$CaSO_4 . 2H_2O$ (calcium sulfate)
Magnesite	$MgCO_3$ (magnesium carbonate)
Dolomite	$CaCO_3 . MgCO_3$ (mixed carbonate)

alkane (*also* **paraffin hydrocarbon**)
Alkanes are a homologous series of hydrocarbons with a general formula C_nH_{2n+2}. They are saturated molecules which only contain single covalent bonds.
• *Alkanes are the main hydrocarbons found in petroleum and natural gas.*

Alkanes (C_nH_{2n+2})			
Name	no.	Molecular formula	Structural formula
methane	1	CH_4	H | H–C–H | H
ethane	2	C_2H_6	H H | | H–C–C–H | | H H
propane	3	C_3H_8	H H H | | | H–C–C–C–H | | | H H H
butane	4	C_4H_{10}	H H H H | | | | H–C–C–C–C–H | | | | H H H H
pentane	5	C_5H_{12}	H H H H H | | | | | H–C–C–C–C–C–H | | | | | H H H H H
hexane	6	C_6H_{14}	H H H H H H | | | | | | H–C–C–C–C–C–C–H | | | | | | H H H H H H

➤ **properties of alkanes** Alkanes are fairly unreactive molecules as their C–C and C–H bonds are strong.

• *The first four members are gases. Higher members are liquids and eventually waxy solids. Alkanes burn in a plentiful supply of air to form carbon dioxide and water (steam).*

$$ethane + oxygen \rightarrow carbon\ dioxide + water$$
$$2C_2H_6 + 7O_2 \rightarrow 4CO2 + 6H_2O$$

alkene (*also* olefin hydrocarbon)

Alkenes are a homologous series of hydrocarbons with a general formula C_nH_{2n}.

• *Alkenes are unsaturated molecules with at least one carbon-carbon double bond. They are formed when petroleum fractions undergo cracking.*

Alkenes (C_nH_{2n})			
Name	no.	Molecular formula	Structural formula
ethene	2	C_2H_4	H H $C=C$ H H
propene	3	C_3H_6	CH_3 H $C=C$ H H
butene	4	C_4H_8	C_2H_5 H $C=C$ H H
pentene	5	C_5H_{10}	C_3H_7 H $C=C$ H H
hexene	6	C_6H_{12}	C_4H_9 H $C=C$ H H

➤ **properties of alkenes** Alkenes are chemically more reactive than alkanes because of the carbon-carbon double bond. Like alkanes, they burn in a plentiful supply of air to form carbon dioxide and water (steam).

$$ethane + oxygen \rightarrow carbon\ dioxide + water$$
$$C_2H_4 + 3O_2 \rightarrow 2CO_2 + 2H_2O$$

alkyl group

An alkyl group is a hydrocarbon radical (group of atoms) derived from an alkane by the removal of one hydrogen atom.

SEE ALSO **alkane**

CH_3 –	methyl
C_2H_5 –	ethyl
C_3H_7 –	propyl
C_4H_9 –	butyl

alkyne

Alkynes are a homologous series of hydrocarbons with a general formula C_nH_{2n-2}. Alkynes are unsaturated molecules with at least one carbon-carbon triple bond.

• *The first alkyne hydrocarbon is ethyne (acetylene) which is important as a fuel in 'oxyacetylene' torches for cutting and welding metal.*

SEE ALSO **homologous series, unsaturated molecule**

Alkynes (C_nH_{2n-2})			
Name	no.	Molecular formula	Structural formula
ethyne	2	C_2H_2	
propyne	3	C_3H_4	
butyne	4	C_4H_6	
pentyne	5	C_5H_8	
hexyne	6	C_6H_{10}	

allele (*also* allelomorph)

An allele is an alternative form of a particular gene. In a diploid cell there are usually two alleles of each gene (one from each parent). They occupy the same relative position (locus) on homologous chromosomes.

SEE ALSO **chromosome, diploid, gene**

dominant allele

A dominant allele is a gene that will always affect an individual's phenotype.

SEE ALSO **phenotype**

recessive allele

A recessive allele is a gene that only affects an individual's phenotype if it is part of a homozygous pair.

SEE ALSO **homozygous, phenotype**

Genotype (Genetic information)	Phenotype (Characteristics)	Description
BB	brown eyes	homozygous
Bb	brown eyes	heterozygous
bb	blue eyes	homozygous

B = dominant allele for brown eyes
b = recessive allele for blue eyes

allelomorph *see* allele

allergy

An allergy is a condition producing an unfavourable, and in some cases life-threatening, reaction to certain foods, pollen, or other substances. Allergies often produce a skin rash or cause sneezing, but in severe cases they can cause anaphylactic shock.
• *An allergy to pollen grains or dust in the air is called hay fever.*
SEE ALSO **eczema, pollen**

allotrope

Allotropes are solid forms of an element with different molecular structures. Diamond and graphite are allotropes of carbon. Other allotropic elements are oxygen (normal dioxygen O_2 and ozone O_3), sulfur (rhombic and monoclinic forms), and phosphorus (red and white forms).

➤ **allotropic** Allotropic elements have forms with different molecular structures.

Property	Diamond	Graphite
appearance	transparent	black, shiny
hardness	extremely hard	very soft
density	3.5 g cm^{-3}	2.3 g cm^{-3}
conductivity	non-conductor	conductor
burning in oxygen	very difficult	easy, to form carbon dioxide

alloy

An alloy is a mixture of two or more elements (usually metals except for carbon in steel). Common alloys and their uses are shown in these tables.
• *Alloys are often stronger than their constituent elements.*
➤ **alloys of aluminium** are light, fairly strong, and resistant to corrosion as they are protected by a thin oxide coat. They are used in the aerospace industry, buildings (e.g. window and door frames), overhead power cables, etc. Pure aluminium is a soft, light metal, but it can be strengthened by adding small

amounts of copper and/or magnesium to make the alloys called duralumin and magnalium. The new atoms present in these alloys prevent the aluminium atoms from sliding over one another and therefore strengthen its structure.
SEE ALSO **aluminium**

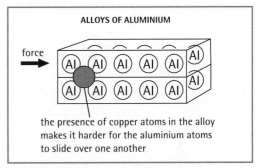

ALLOYS OF ALUMINIUM

force

the presence of copper atoms in the alloy makes it harder for the aluminium atoms to slide over one another

Non-ferrous alloy	Approximate composition
Cupronickel	75% Cu 25% Ni
Bronze	90% Cu 10% Sn
Brass	70% Cu 30% Zn
Solder	60% Sn 40% Pb
Pewter	70% Sn 30% Pb
Constantan	60% Cu 40% Ni
Magnalium	70% Al 30% Mg
Duralumin	95% Al 5% Cu/Mg
Amalgams	Hg/Sn alloys

Non-ferrous alloy	Uses
Cupronickel	'silver' coins
Bronze	medals, swords, statues
Brass	ornaments, electrical contacts
Solder	flux for metals
Pewter	mugs, ornaments
Constantan	thermocouples
Magnalium	aircraft frames
Duralumin	construction
Amalgams	fillings in teeth

»

Ferrous alloys (alloys of iron and steel)	Composition
Wrought iron	99% Fe
Cast iron	96% Fe 4% C
Mild steel (low-carbon)	99.5% Fe 0.5% C
High-carbon steel	98.5% Fe 1.5% C
Manganese steel	87% Fe 13% Mn
Tungsten steel	95% Fe 5% W
Stainless steel	>50% Fe 18% Cr 8% Ni

Ferrous alloys (alloys of iron and steel)	Uses
Wrought iron	garden gates (malleable)
Cast iron	engine blocks (dense)
Mild steel (low-carbon)	car bodies (easily shaped)
High-carbon steel	drills (tensile)
Manganese steel	helmets (impact resilient)
Tungsten steel	cutting tools (very strong)
Stainless steel	cutlery (resists corrosion)

alluvial deposit

Alluvial deposits are materials such as soil and silt which have been deposited by rivers.

• *Alluvial deposits are often very fertile.*

alpha decay *see* radioactive decay

alpha particle (*also* α)

An alpha particle is a positively charged helium nucleus which is ejected from certain radioactive nuclei. It is relatively heavy (with four times the mass of a proton) and so alpha radiation is the least penetrating form. However, because it is positively charged it attracts electrons from nearby atoms. It is therefore strongly ionizing.

alpha radiation

is formed by a stream of alpha particles.

alpha sulfur *see* sulfur

alternating current

is an electric current which reverses its direction of flow in periodic cycles. In Britain, mains electricity alternates at 50 cycles per second (frequency 50 Hz) and has a voltage of about 230 V.

SEE ALSO **root mean square value (RMS value), direct current, electric current**

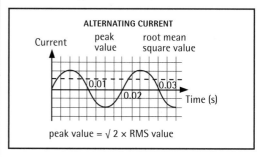

peak value = √ 2 × RMS value

alternator (*also* a.c. generator)

An alternator is a generator which produces electrical energy in the form of alternating current. The direction of the induced current changes at regular intervals, producing an alternating current. Increasing the speed of rotation increases the frequency of the alternating current generated.

SEE ALSO **alternating current, generator**

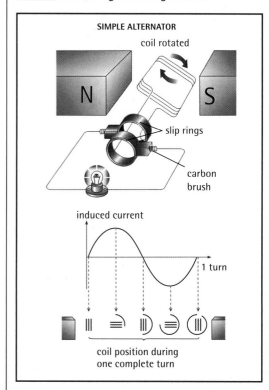

altimeter

An altimeter is an instrument used to measure height above sea level, e.g. in aircraft.

• *Atmospheric pressure decreases with height, so an aneroid barometer can be used as an **altimeter**.*
SEE ALSO **aneroid barometer**

aluminium

is a lightweight, silvery, non-corrosive, non-magnetic metal that is used to make many different objects. It is the most abundant metal in the Earth's crust. It is extracted from the ore bauxite by electrolytic reduction. Alloys of aluminium (duralumin, magnalium) are stronger than the pure metal.
• *Aeroplanes are made from **aluminium** alloys because they are light and strong.*
SEE ALSO **alloy, aluminium extraction**

aluminium extraction

is from its oxide ore bauxite (Al_2O_3) by electrolytic reduction. The ore is first purified by dissolving in alkali, and then recrystallized out as pure aluminium oxide (alumina). This is then mixed with cryolite (Na_2AlF_6), which lowers its melting point to about 900°C. The molten mixture is then electrolyzed. Molten aluminium collects at the cathode, and oxygen gas is given off at the anode.

$$cathode \ Al^{3+} + 3e^- \rightarrow Al$$
$$anode \ 2O^{2-} - 4e^- \rightarrow O_2$$

SEE ALSO **electrolytic reduction, extraction of metals, generator**

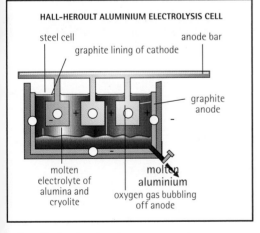

HALL–HEROULT ALUMINIUM ELECTROLYSIS CELL

steel cell
graphite lining of cathode
anode bar
graphite anode
molten electrolyte of alumina and cryolite
molten aluminium
oxygen gas bubbling off anode

alveoli *singular* **alveolus**

Alveoli are the tiny air sacs at the end of each bronchiole through which oxygen diffuses into and carbon dioxide diffuses out of the blood.

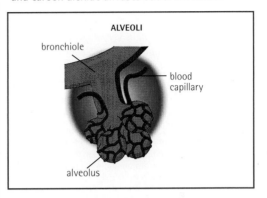

ALVEOLI
bronchiole
blood capillary
alveolus

AM *see* **amplitude modulation**

amino acid

Amino acids are the monomer units of all proteins and contain the —COOH and —NH_2 groups at either end of the molecule.
• *Amino acids undergo condensation polymerization by eliminating a water molecule which forms the peptide link between the monomers.*
SEE ALSO **monomer, peptide link, polymerization**

ammeter

An ammeter is an instrument used to measure the amount of electric current flowing through a particular point in an electrical circuit.
• *An **ammeter** must be connected in series.*
SEE ALSO **electrical circuit, electric current**

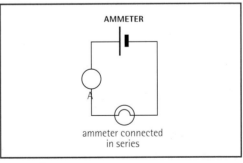

AMMETER
ammeter connected in series

ammonia

is a colourless, pungent gas, NH_3, that is less dense than air. It is the most soluble of all gases and dissolves in water to form an alkali called aqueous ammonia, NH3(aq). It is the only common alkaline gas and moist red litmus paper immediately turns

»

blue in the presence of ammonia. It neutralizes acids to form salts. For example:

ammonia + sulfuric acid → ammonium sulfate

$$2NH_3 + H_2SO_4 \rightarrow (NH_4)_2SO_4$$

• *Commercially **ammonia** is very important, with millions of tonnes being made each year by the Haber process, mostly for the manufacture of fertilizer.*

SEE ALSO **Haber process**

Uses of ammonia	
1	manufacture of fertilizers, especially by reaction with sulfuric and nitric acids to make nitrogenous fertilizers such as ammonium nitrate NH4NO3 and ammonium sulfate (NH4)2SO4.
2	manufacture of nitric acid by the catalytic oxidation of ammonia over heated platinum. Uses of nitric acid include making explosives (nitroglycerine, trinitrotoluene (TNT)) and azo dyes (by the reduction of various nitro compounds).
3	as a solvent in aqueous solution, especially as a degreasing agent since it dissolves grease and fat.

ammonite
An ammonite is a fossil of an extinct mollusc with a flat, spiral shell.
• *Ammonites lived at the time of the dinosaurs, around 250 million years ago.*
SEE ALSO **fossil, mollusc**

amniocentesis
is the taking of a sample of amniotic fluid from a pregnant woman for microscopic examination of the cells shed from the embryo's skin.
• *Amniocentesis can determine the condition of the unborn baby, including the presence of Down's syndrome.*
SEE ALSO **amniotic fluid**

amnion (*also* amniotic sac)
The amnion is the membrane that encloses the embryo in the uterus of mammals.

amniotic fluid
The amniotic fluid is the watery liquid inside the amnion that supports the embryo and protects it from knocks.
SEE ALSO **amnion**

amoeba *see* protozoan

amoebic dysentery
is a disease caused by the protist called Entamoeba. This may be present in contaminated food or drinking water. It lives in the intestine of its host and causes abdominal pain and severe diarrhoea.
SEE ALSO **protoctist**

amorphous
describes a solid which has no crystalline structure.
• *Amorphous materials include carbon black and plastic sulfur.*

ampere (*also* amp, A)
One ampere is equal to one coulomb of electric charge passing any point in a conductor in one second.
• *The ampere is the SI unit of current.*

amphibian (*also* Amphibia)
Amphibians are cold-blooded vertebrates which are semi-aquatic: the female always returns to the water to lay her eggs. Amphibians usually undergo metamorphosis. The larval form (tadpole) lives in water and has gills. The adult form normally lives on land and has lungs. Amphibians were the first vertebrates to occupy land (about 370 million years ago).
• *The class of amphibians includes frogs, toads, newts, and salamanders.*
SEE ALSO **metamorphosis**

amphoteric
describes a chemical compound that can act as an acid in one reaction but as a base in another.
• *Zinc oxide (ZnO) and aluminium oxide (Al_2O_3) are amphoteric oxides.*

amp hour
An amp hour is a quantity of electric charge equivalent to 1 amp flowing for 1 hour. It is equal to 3,600 coulombs.
• *Car batteries are often rated in amp hours. A 40 amp hour battery will deliver 1 amp for 40 hours or 2 amps for 20 hours.*
SEE ALSO **electric charge**

amplify
To amplify a sound is to increase its strength by giving it greater energy and making it louder.
SEE ALSO **loudness**

➤ **amplifier** An amplifier is an electronic device that increases the loudness of a sound or the power of an audio device or radio signal.

amplitude (*also* **a**)

is the height of a wave from its peak to its mean rest position. The size of the amplitude indicates the energy carried by the wave and represents for instance the loudness of a sound or the brightness of a light.

SEE ALSO **mean position, wave**

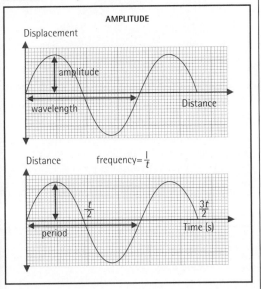

AMPLITUDE

amplitude modulation (*also* **AM**)

is a form of radio transmission in which the sound being broadcast is conveyed by variations in the amplitude of the radio carrier wave.

• *Amplitude modulation is used on long and medium wavebands.*

SEE ALSO **amplitude, carrier wave, frequency modulation**

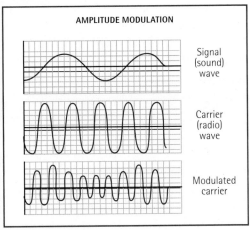

AMPLITUDE MODULATION

a.m.u. *see* **atomic mass unit**

amylase

Amylases are a group of closely related enzymes that break down starch, glycogen, and other polysaccharides.

SEE ALSO **enzyme**

anabolism *see* **metabolism**

anaerobic respiration

is respiration which takes place in the absence of oxygen (air) and in which food substances are only partially broken down. It produces lactic acid or alcohol and releases smaller amounts of energy and fewer ATP molecules than aerobic respiration.

$$\text{glucose} \rightarrow \text{lactic acid} \rightarrow \text{ethanol} + \text{carbon dioxide}$$
$$C_6H_{12}O_6 \rightarrow 2CH_3CHOHCOOH \rightarrow 2C_2H_5OH + 2CO_2$$

• *In humans, anaerobic respiration often occurs in the muscles during vigorous exercise when not enough oxygen is available.*

SEE ALSO **adenosine triphosphate, aerobic respiration, alcohol**

anaesthetic

An anaesthetic is a chemical that produces a temporary loss of sensation and of the ability to feel pain. Gaseous anaesthetics are inhaled using a mask, while volatile liquid anaesthetics are injected using a hypodermic syringe.

• *General anaesthetics should result in the patient becoming unconscious.*

SEE ALSO **drug, medicine**

analgesic *see* **drug**

analogue reading

An analogue reading is one which is given by an instrument which has a continuous scale. Measuring cylinders, thermometers, rulers, clocks with hands, and meters with a scale and a pointer are all analogue instruments.

• *Analogue readings are subject to reading errors.*

SEE ALSO **digital reading, reading error**

analogue signal

Analogue signals are signals (electrical impulses) which have a continuous variation of voltage with time.

• *An example would be the voltage output from a microphone. When analogue signals are*

»

a b c d e f g h i j k l m n o p q r s t u v w x y z

25

amplified, any background noise associated with the signal is also amplified, which causes signal distortion.

SEE ALSO **digital signal**

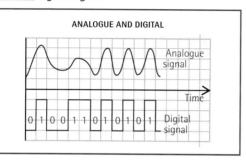

ANALOGUE AND DIGITAL

ancestor
An ancestor is the form of a plant or animal that lived in the past and from which it is descended.
• *Recent **ancestors** of people are grandparents.*

androecium
is the collective term for all the male parts (stamens) of a flower.
SEE ALSO **anther, filament, pollen**

androgen *see* **sex hormone**

aneroid barometer *see* **barometer**

angina pectoris *see* **high blood pressure**

angiosperm (*also* **flowering plant**)
Angiosperms are seed-bearing plants that produce flowers. The seeds grow inside a fruit which develops from an ovary inside the flower. There are two classes of angiosperms: monocotyledons and dicotyledons.
• ***Angiosperms** are the most common plants in the plant kingdom. They are also the most highly developed and inhabit a wide range of habitats.*
SEE ALSO **dicotyledon, monocotyledon**

angle of declination
is the angle between true geographic north and a line towards magnetic north. It varies depending where on the Earth's surface you are, and gradually changes with time, probably because of convection currents in the outer core of the Earth.

• *In 1659 the **angle of declination** was zero and it will be again in about a hundred years.*
SEE ALSO **Earth's magnetic field**

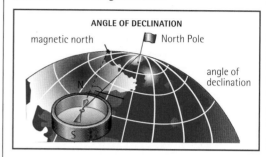

ANGLE OF DECLINATION

angle of incidence *see* **reflection of light**

angle of inclination (*also* **angle of dip**)
is the angle between a horizontal line and the direction of the Earth's magnetic field at a point on the Earth's surface. The angle of inclination is measured using a dip circle (see diagram).
SEE ALSO **Earth's magnetic field**

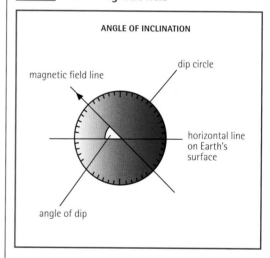

ANGLE OF INCLINATION

angle of reflection *see* **reflection of light**

anhydrous
describes salts which have lost their water of crystallization.
SEE ALSO **salt, water of crystallization**

animal charcoal *see* **charcoal**

animal hormone *see* **hormone**

animal kingdom (*also* **Animalia**)

The animal kingdom includes most multicellular organisms that cannot photosynthesize. Most animals have certain characteristics:
- heterotrophic nutrition
- movement, to be capable of searching for their food
- developed nervous system and sense organs, to be able to respond quickly to stimuli
- their cells do not have cell walls.

• *The animal kingdom can be split into two main groups, called vertebrates and invertebrates.*
SEE ALSO **invertebrate animal, vertebrate animal**

animal starch *see* **glycogen**

anion

An anion is a negatively charged ion that is attracted to the anode during electrolysis.
• *All non-metal ions and most radicals (except the ammonium ion) are anions.*
SEE ALSO **anode, cation, electrolysis**

testing for anions

Anion tests include testing for carbonates, halides (chloride, bromide, and iodide), and sulfates.
• *Testing for anions often involves a precipitation reaction.*
SEE ALSO **carbonate, halide, precipitate, sulfate**

annealing

is a type of heat treatment applied to metals (ferrous and non-ferrous) to soften them and remove stresses within so they are easier to work or machine, and less likely to shatter.
• *Annealing consists of heating the metal and then allowing it to cool very slowly.*

annelid (*also* **Annelida**)

Annelids are invertebrates which are segmented worms with round bodies, such as earthworms and leeches.
• *Each segment of an annelid is internally separated from the next and has stiff bristles (chaetae) which are used as sense organs.*
SEE ALSO **invertebrate animal**

annual

Annuals are plants that complete their life cycle in one year, during which they germinate, flower, produce seeds, and die.

• *Examples of annuals are sunflower and marigold plants.*

anode

The anode is a positive electrode to which the anions (negative ions) are attracted during electrolysis.
SEE ALSO **anion, cathode, electrode**

anodizing

is a method of coating objects made of aluminium with a protective oxide coating by electrolysis. Aluminium is more reactive than iron and soon forms a thin oxide coating (10^{-6}cm). However, unlike iron oxide (rust) it does not flake off but acts as a protecting film to prevent further corrosion.
• *Anodizing makes this oxide layer thicker (10^{-3}cm) by making the aluminium the anode of a cell in which dilute sulfuric acid is electrolyzed. Oxygen forms at the anode and reacts with the aluminium to make a thicker, more protective oxide coating.*
SEE ALSO **anode, electrolysis**

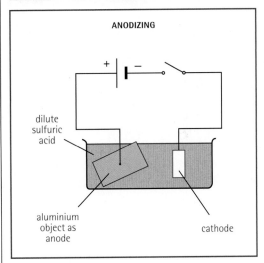

ANODIZING

dilute sulfuric acid

aluminium object as anode

cathode

anomalous expansion of water

occurs on cooling water between 4°C to 0°C, as the water expands instead of contracting. Above 4°C there is normal expansion with increased temperature. This means that water at 4°C has a maximum density. It is for this reason that the surface of a pond will not freeze until all the water is at 4°C. When it does freeze, the warmest water (at 4°C) is at the bottom, and the solid ice, being less dense than the liquid, floats on top. Even when the

»

surface water becomes colder, the denser, warmer water will not circulate. Fish can survive in the warmer water at the bottom of the pond.

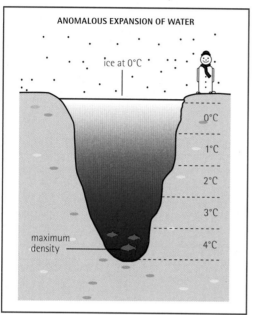

ANOMALOUS EXPANSION OF WATER

ice at 0°C

0°C
1°C
2°C
3°C
maximum density
4°C

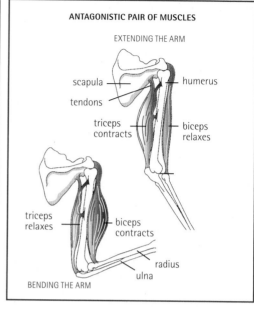

ANTAGONISTIC PAIR OF MUSCLES

EXTENDING THE ARM

scapula
humerus
tendons
triceps contracts
biceps relaxes

triceps relaxes
biceps contracts

radius
ulna

BENDING THE ARM

anorexia nervosa
is an eating disorder typically involving refusal to eat and an obsessive desire to become slim.
• *Anorexia nervosa is becoming increasingly common among girls and young women in affluent countries.*

ANS *see* autonomic nervous system

antagonistic hormones *see* hormone

antagonistic pairs
are muscles that work in pairs but have an opposite effect to each other, like the biceps and triceps. As one contracts, the other relaxes.
SEE ALSO biceps, triceps

antenna *see* aerial

anther
The anther is the pollen-producing part of a flower's stamen.
• *The anther normally consists of two lobes, each containing two 'pollen sacs' with the grains of pollen.*
SEE ALSO pollen, stamen

antibiotic
Antibiotics are substances obtained from microorganisms, especially fungi, that cause the destruction of other microorganisms such as disease-producing bacteria. Antibiotics do not kill viruses.
• *Common antibiotics are penicillin, streptomycin, and neomycin.*
SEE ALSO penicillin

antibody
Antibodies are 'defence proteins' found in the blood plasma. They are produced by the white blood cells called lymphocytes in response to antigens such as bacteria, toxins, viruses, etc.
• *Some antibodies prevent the action of toxins. Others kill bacteria by dissolving their outer membranes, or cause bacteria and viruses to clump together so that they cannot reproduce properly.*
SEE ALSO antigen, plasma

anticyclone
An anticyclone (or a high) is a region of high atmospheric pressure caused when air flows in

from above. As it descends, it becomes warmer and therefore can hold more water vapour. Clouds therefore disperse, and so anticyclones are associated with dry weather.
SEE ALSO **atmospheric pressure**

antigen
An antigen is any substance from whatever source that stimulates the production of antibodies.
• *Some antigens are present in the body from birth, including those which are used in determining blood groups.*
SEE ALSO **antibody, blood group**

antinode
An antinode is a point on a stationary (standing) wave where the amplitude of the vibration is at a maximum.
SEE ALSO **amplitude, stationary wave, wave**

antiseptic (*also* germicide)
An antiseptic is a chemical that kills or inhibits the growth of harmful microorganisms but is non-toxic to body cells.

antitoxin
An antitoxin is an antibody that neutralizes a toxin and prevents it from having a harmful effect.
• *An antitoxin is also described as an antigen, which is any substance that stimulates the production of antibodies.*
SEE ALSO **antibody, antigen, toxin**

anus *see* large intestine

anvil *see* ossicle

aorta
The aorta is the largest artery in the body, carrying oxygenated blood out from the left ventricle of the heart.
SEE ALSO **artery**

apoplexy *see* high blood pressure

apparent depth *see* refraction of light

appendicular skeleton *see* human skeleton

appendix *see* large intestine

aqueous humour
is a watery liquid secreted and absorbed into the front cavity of the eye. It is renewed about every four hours.
• *The cornea and lens obtain food and oxygen by diffusion through the aqueous humour.*
SEE ALSO **eye**

aqueous solution *see* solution

arachnid (*also* Arachnida)
Arachnids are arthropods which have four pairs of legs and no antennae.
• *Examples of arachnids include spiders, ticks, and scorpions.*
SEE ALSO **arthropod**

Archimedes' principle
states that when a body is partially or totally immersed in a fluid, there is an upthrust equal to the weight of the fluid displaced. The word 'fluid' is used because the principle applies to both liquids and gases. Objects surrounded in air (such as balloons) experience upthrust as well as objects immersed in liquids. A hot-air balloon rises up because of the upthrust from the surrounding denser cold air.
• *Archimedes' principle was named after the Greek mathematician Archimedes (287–212 BCE).*
SEE ALSO **fluid, upthrust**

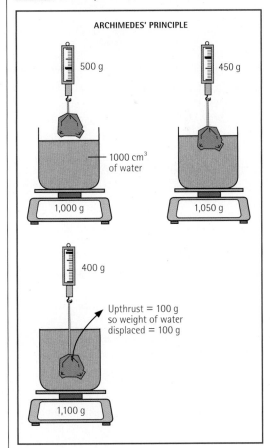

ARCHIMEDES' PRINCIPLE

500 g

450 g

1000 cm³ of water

1,000 g

1,050 g

400 g

Upthrust = 100 g so weight of water displaced = 100 g

1,100 g

argon *see* noble gas

arteriole

An arteriole is a small artery that carries blood to the capillaries.

SEE ALSO artery, capillary

artery

An artery is a wide muscular-walled blood vessel that carries blood away from the heart towards the body tissue.

• With the exception of the pulmonary arteries, *arteries* carry blood rich in oxygen (oxygenated blood) which makes them appear bright red.

SEE ALSO blood vessel, pulmonary artery, renal artery

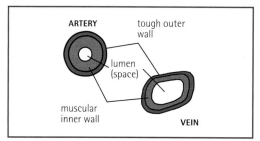

ARTERY   tough outer wall
lumen (space)
muscular inner wall
VEIN

arthropod (*also* Arthropoda)

Arthropods are the largest and most successful phylum of invertebrates and have segmented bodies, jointed legs, and a hard exoskeleton.

SEE ALSO invertebrate animal

artificial insemination (*also* AI)

is the deliberate introduction of semen (sperm) into the female's cervix or uterus (womb) by any method other than sexual intercourse.

• Artificial insemination is used as a fertility treatment for humans and is a common practice in animal breeding.

SEE ALSO fertility treatment, insemination

artificial satellite

Artificial satellites are man-made satellites that orbit the Earth, Moon, Sun, or a planet.

• Communication satellites are *artificial satellites*.

SEE ALSO communication satellite, satellite

artificial selection *see* inbreeding

asbestos

is a fibrous silicate which has its silicate chains interspersed with calcium and magnesium ions (see diagram). Asbestos is chemically inert and fire-resistant and was formerly used in fire-protective clothing and brake linings.

• *Asbestos* dust contains microscopic fibres that can irritate the lungs and cause the lung disease asbestosis, so its use is now very restricted.

SEE ALSO silicate

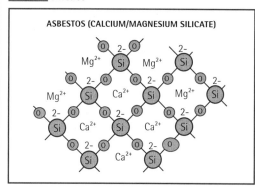

ASBESTOS (CALCIUM/MAGNESIUM SILICATE)

ascorbic acid *see* vitamin

asexual reproduction *see* reproduction

asphalt *see* bitumen

assimilation

is the use of absorbed food molecules in the processes of growth, tissue repair, and reproduction.

asteroid (*also* minor planet)

The asteroids are a large number of rocks orbiting the Sun in a belt between the orbits of Mars and Jupiter.

• Asteroids vary in size from a few km to about 200 km.

astronomical telescope

An astronomical telescope is a telescope that uses two convex lenses to produce a highly magnified, inverted, virtual image formed at infinity. To achieve this, the image of a distant object becomes the object of the second convex lens.

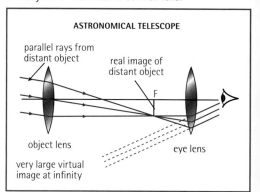

ASTRONOMICAL TELESCOPE

parallel rays from distant object
real image of distant object
F
object lens
eye lens
very large virtual image at infinity

atheroma *see* high blood pressure

atmosphere

The atmosphere is the air that surrounds the Earth and is held to it by gravity.

SEE ALSO air

WORD BUILD

troposphere

The troposphere is the lowest layer of the atmosphere, in which most weather occurs. Its average thickness is around 15 km (ranging from 7 km at the poles to 28 km at the equator). The temperature gradually decreases as we go higher in the troposphere.

stratosphere

The stratosphere is the second lowest layer of the atmosphere, up to around 50 km. Temperature increases slightly in this layer, as it is heated from below by infrared radiation from the Earth's surface.

SEE ALSO ozone, ozone layer

ionosphere

The ionosphere is the third lowest layer of the atmosphere, in which gases are ionized by absorption of the Sun's radiation. This layer is important for radio communication, as radio waves of certain wavelengths are reflected by its lower parts and so can travel great distances around the world.

exosphere

The exosphere is the highest region of the atmosphere, which begins at an altitude of about 400 km and thins out almost completely at about 1000 km.

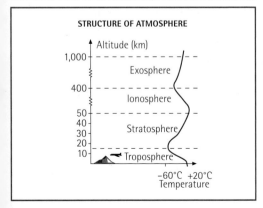

STRUCTURE OF ATMOSPHERE

primary atmosphere (*also* Earth's early atmosphere)

The primary atmosphere is the atmosphere for the first billion years of the Earth's existence. During this time volcanoes released gases like water vapour, carbon dioxide, and small proportions of methane and ammonia. The water vapour condensed to form the oceans. When the oceans formed, carbon dioxide gas in the atmosphere dissolved in the water and carbonates were precipitated producing sediments. This gradually reduced the amount of carbon dioxide in the atmosphere.

secondary atmosphere

The secondary atmosphere is the atmosphere that appeared about 2.7 billion years ago when algae first appeared and started to release oxygen into the atmosphere by photosynthesis. Over the next billion years plants evolved and the percentage of oxygen increased to allow animals to evolve. The amount of carbon dioxide in the atmosphere decreased due to photosynthesis by plants and also by the formation of sedimentary rocks and fossil fuels (coal, oil, natural gas). Methane and ammonia in the atmosphere were oxidized by the oxygen gas to produce nitrogen gas, carbon dioxide, and water vapour.

atmospheric pollution *see* air pollution

atmospheric pressure

is the pressure exerted by the air and is caused by the gravitational attraction of the air to the Earth. It acts equally in all directions and decreases with altitude.

• *Atmospheric pressure is measured using bars (1 bar = 10^5 Pa) or millibars (1 mb = 100 Pa).*

atom

An atom is the smallest particle of an element which can take part in a chemical reaction and remain unchanged. These particles are extremely small. They have a radius of around 10^{-10} m and a mass of about 10^{-22} g. During chemical reactions, atoms are rearranged but not created or destroyed (conservation of mass).

• *If a golf ball were magnified to the size of the Earth, then an **atom** would be the size of a marble!*

atom economy (*also* atom utilization)

is a measure of the extent to which the atoms of the reactants in a chemical equation end up in the desired product of the reaction.

• *Atom economy is an important consideration by chemical companies when making specific chemicals and reducing possible pollutants, wastage, cost, etc.*

SEE ALSO **chemical equation, product, reactant**

atomic bomb *see* fission bomb

atomicity

is the total number of atoms in a given molecule.

• *Glucose $C_6H_{12}O_6$ has an atomicity of 24.*

atomic lattice *see* metallic lattice

atomic mass unit (*also* a.m.u.)

An atomic mass unit is an arbitrary unit which is equivalent to $\frac{1}{12}$ of the mass of a carbon-12 atom. It is equal to 1.66033×10^{-27} kg. This $\frac{1}{12}$ of is roughly equivalent to the mass of a hydrogen atom. The table shows the relative atomic mass of elements.

Element	Chemical symbol	Approx A_r
aluminium	Al	27
bromine	Br	80
calcium	Ca	40
carbon	C	12
chlorine	Cl	35.5
copper	Cu	63.5
hydrogen	H	1
iodine	I	127
iron	Fe	56
lead	Pb	207
magnesium	Mg	24
nitrogen	N	14
oxygen	O	16
phosphorus	P	31
potassium	K	39
silicon	Si	28
silver	Ag	108
sodium	Na	23
sulfur	S	32
zinc	Zn	65

atomic number (*also* proton number)

An element's atomic number (or proton number) is the number of protons it has in the nucleus of its atom. Every element is defined by its proton number. If you change the proton number you change the element.

• *The atomic number of an element always equals the total number of electrons in the atom (number of protons = number of electrons).*

SEE ALSO **mass number**

atom utilization *see* atom economy

ATP *see* adenosine triphosphate

atrium *plural* atria (*also* auricle)

The atria are the two uppermost chambers of the heart which receive blood from the veins.

• *The atria have relatively thin muscular walls and force blood into the ventricles.*

attenuation

is the gradual decrease in strength of a wave as it loses energy when passing through a medium.

• *Attenuation is due to absorption and scattering, and results in a gradual decrease in the amplitude of the wave as its energy is converted to heat energy.*

SEE ALSO **amplitude**

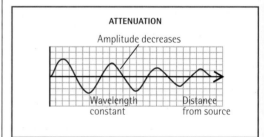

ATTENUATION
Amplitude decreases
Wavelength constant
Distance from source

audible sound

is sound within the human hearing range.

SEE ALSO **human hearing range, loudness**

auditory nerve *see* inner ear

auricle *see* atrium

aurora

Auroras are luminous phenomena that occur in the night sky especially around the poles. They result from the interaction of the solar wind with atoms and molecules high in the upper atmosphere, which are then attracted to the poles by the Earth's magnetic field.

SEE ALSO **solar wind**

WORD BUILD
aurora australis (*also* **southern lights**)
is the aurora which occurs above the South Pole.
aurora borealis (*also* **northern lights**)
is the aurora which occurs above the North Pole.

autonomic nervous system (*also* ANS)

The autonomic nervous system is that part of the nervous system that is not under voluntary control. It is controlled by the hypothalamus, which sends information via motor neurones to involuntary muscles (smooth and cardiac muscles) and to the glands of the body.

SEE ALSO **hypothalamus, neurone**

autotrophic nutrition *see* nutrition

auxin

Auxins are plant hormones which promote and regulate growth.

SEE ALSO **hormone**

Aves *see* bird

Avogadro's law (*also* Avogadro's hypothesis)

states that equal volumes of all gases contain the same number of particles at the same temperature and pressure. This means that one mole of any gas occupies a certain volume called the molar volume.
• *Avogadro's law is only true for ideal gases.*

SEE ALSO **ideal gas, molar volume, mole**

Avogadro's number (*also* Avogadro constant, L)

The Avogadro constant is the number of particles in one mole of substance. It has the value of 6.02×10^{23} as defined by the number of atoms in 12 g of the carbon-12 isotope. If you multiply one unit of relative atomic mass by Avogadro's number you convert it to grams.
• *The Avogadro constant is named after the Italian scientist Count Amedeo Avogadro (1776–1856).*

SEE ALSO **mole**

axial skeleton *see* human skeleton

axis *plural* axes

The axis of the Earth is an imaginary line through the Earth from the North Pole to the South Pole.
• *The earth rotates or spins around its axis towards the east, which is why the Sun, Moon, and stars rise in the east and make their way westward across the sky.*

axon

The axon is the part of the neurone that conducts electrical impulses away from the cell body of the nerve.

SEE ALSO **neurone**

a
b
c
d
e
f
g
h
i
j
k
l
m
n
o
p
q
r
s
t
u
v
w
x
y
z

Bb

bacillus *see* **bacteria**

backbone *see* **vertebral column**

background count
The background count is a measure of the natural radioactivity in a particular place.
SEE ALSO **natural radioactivity**

background radiation *see* **natural radioactivity**

backward reaction
The backward reaction is the direction from products back to reactants in a reversible chemical reaction.
• The **backward reaction** *goes from right to left in the chemical equation.*
SEE ALSO **forward reaction, reversible reaction**

bacteria *singular* bacterium
Bacteria are microorganisms which consist of a single cell without a nucleus, and with a type of cell wall unlike that of a plant cell. Some bacteria are pathogens (cause disease). Other bacteria are important in ecology as decomposers, and in biotechnology.
• *Bacteria in the soil are very important, as they are decomposers and help break down dead plant and animal remains and excrement.*
SEE ALSO **resistant bacteria, microorganism**

nitrifying bacteria
are microscopic bacteria present in all types of soil which convert ammonium compounds into nitrates, which can be used as nutrients by plants.

denitrifying bacteria
are microscopic bacteria present in all types of soil which release nitrogen back into the atmosphere.
SEE ALSO **nitrogen cycle**

WORD BUILD
bacillus
A bacillus is a rod-shaped bacterium. Many are responsible for food spoilage.

coccus
A coccus is a spherical bacterium. Such bacteria can join together in clumps (staphylococci) or in chains (streptococci).
• *A coccus is a type of bacterium that can cause sore throats.*

spirillum
A spirillum is a rigid, spiral-shaped bacterium that can cause syphilis.

vibrio
A vibrio is a comma-shaped bacterium that can cause cholera.

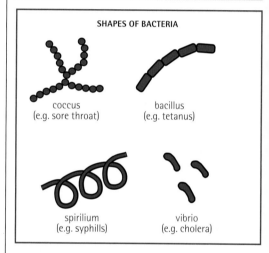

SHAPES OF BACTERIA

coccus
(e.g. sore throat)

bacillus
(e.g. tetanus)

spirilium
(e.g. syphills)

vibrio
(e.g. cholera)

bactericide
A bactericide is a substance that is used to kill harmful bacteria. Common examples are antibiotics, antiseptics, and disinfectants (chemicals which kill bacteria). Sterilization is also used to kill bacteria by heating.
SEE ALSO **irradiation**

bacteriophage (*also* phage)
A bacteriophage is a virus that infects bacteria. When inside the bacterium, it can cause the bacterial cell to disintegrate. Bacteriophages are used to control manufacturing processes which use bacteria, such as cheesemaking.
• *Bacteriophages play an important role in genetic engineering.*

bacteriostatic

describes a substance that slows down the growth and reproduction of bacteria without killing them.
• *Antibodies are bacteriostatic.*
SEE ALSO **antibody**

bacterium *see* **bacteria**

baking

is the use of baker's yeast mixed with flour and water (dough) to make bread. Flour contains starch which, when mixed with water, is digested by the yeast and produces bubbles of carbon dioxide gas. These get trapped inside the dough and make it rise. Flour also contains a protein called gluten. This forms sticky threads as the bread is kneaded and helps to trap the carbon dioxide. When the bread is baked, the yeast is killed, the alcohol evaporates, and the carbon dioxide escapes. The remaining starch and gluten give the bread its firm texture.
SEE ALSO **yeast**

balance

is the sense by which the brain detects the position of the head, so that it can coordinate the muscles to keep the body upright.
SEE ALSO **ear**

balanced diet

A balanced diet consists of food which contains carbohydrates, fats, proteins, minerals, and vitamins in the correct proportions to maintain good health. Poor diet can lead to malnutrition.
• *Balanced diets vary depending on the age, sex, body size, and level of activity of the individual.*
SEE ALSO **malnutrition, obesity**

balanced forces

are forces acting on an object which remains at rest or travels at a constant speed. For example, the balanced forces on an aircraft moving at a constant speed and constant height consist of equal drag and thrust and equal lift and weight respectively.

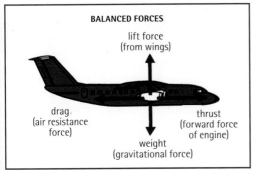

BALANCED FORCES

lift force
(from wings)

drag
(air resistance force)

thrust
(forward force of engine)

weight
(gravitational force)

ball-and-socket joint *see* **joint**

bar graph *see* **graph**

barium *see* **alkaline-earth metal**

barometer

A barometer is an instrument which measures atmospheric pressure.
SEE ALSO **atmospheric pressure**

aneroid barometer

An aneroid barometer is a type of barometer formed from a metal box with a thin, corrugated lid. The air inside this box is removed and the lid is supported by a spring. Changes in pressure cause the lid to move against the spring. This movement is magnified with levers to control a pointer.
• *Aneroid barometers are not as accurate as mercury barometers but are more robust.*

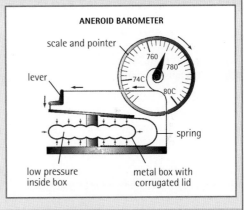

ANEROID BAROMETER

scale and pointer

760
780
74C
80C

lever

spring

low pressure inside box

metal box with corrugated lid

mercury barometer

A mercury barometer is a simple barometer which consists of a glass tube about 80 cm long which is completely filled with mercury. It is inverted and the open end is submerged in a dish of mercury. The mercury in the tube drops until the pressure of the mercury at the base of the tube is equal to the air pressure acting on the mercury in the dish. At sea level, atmospheric pressure is about 760 mm of mercury (equivalent to 101,325 Pa).

»

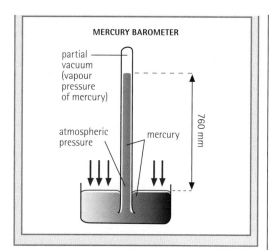

MERCURY BAROMETER

partial vacuum (vapour pressure of mercury)

atmospheric pressure

mercury

760 mm

Basic SI unit	Standard
second	Time taken for 9,192,631,770 resonance vibrations of an atom of caesium–133.
kelvin	1/273.16 of the temperature of the triple point of water.
ampere	Current that produces a force of 2×10^{-7} newtons per square metre between parallel conductors which are 1 metre apart.
mole	Amount of substance that contains the Avogadro number of particles (atoms, ions, or molecules).
candela	Monochromatic source of light of frequency 540×10^{12} Hz with a power of 1/683 watt per steradian.

basalt *see* rock (igneous)

base

Bases are chemical compounds that react with acids to form a salt and water. Simple bases are oxides and hydroxides of metals. Complex bases include many organic compounds containing the amine group ($-NH_2$), such as those found in DNA.

SEE ALSO **chemical compound**

base unit

A base unit of measurement is not defined in terms of other units, but has its own standard definition. For example, the metre is a base unit of length, but speed, which is measured in metres per second, is a derived unit.

• *There are seven **base units** in the SI system (see tables).*

Basic SI unit	Symbol	Quantity
metre	m	length
kilogram	kg	mass
second	s	time
kelvin	K	temperature
ampere	A	electric current
mole	mol	amount of substance
candela	Cd	luminous intensity

Basic SI unit	Standard
metre	Distance light will travel in a vacuum in 1/299,792,458 of a second.
kilogram	Mass of international prototype kilogram made of platinum-iridium alloy and kept at Sèvres, France.

basic oxide *see* oxide

basic oxygen process (*also* bop process)

The basic oxygen process is an industrial process to make steel. Oxygen gas is blown under high pressure into molten pig iron. This oxidizes impurities such as carbon and sulfur to gases, which then escape. Other impurities such as phosphorus and silicon are converted to acidic oxides, which are neutralized by adding a base such as calcium oxide. Very pure iron is then left, to which calculated amounts of carbon and/or other metals are then added to produce the various steel alloys.

SEE ALSO **oxide**

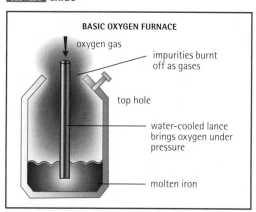

BASIC OXYGEN FURNACE

oxygen gas

impurities burnt off as gases

top hole

water-cooled lance brings oxygen under pressure

molten iron

bat

A bat is a flying mammal. Its wings are thin skin stretched between its fingers and its leg.

• *Most **bats** are nocturnal and their ears are enlarged and specialized for echolocation for hunting prey and avoiding obstacles.*

SEE ALSO **echolocation, mammal**

battery

❶ A battery is a number of electric cells connected together. Torch batteries often have two 1.5 V cells connected in series to give a battery of 3 V.
SEE ALSO **cell**

❷ A battery in a circuit gives potential energy to the electrons which come from it. It can only 'push out' electrons when the electrical circuit between both terminals of the battery is complete. The electrons travelling around the circuit lose all this potential energy. The energy may be given off as heat when it passes through a wire, or light as it passes through a bulb. The same number of electrons reaches the other terminal of the battery, so there is no loss in current. It is only the potential energy of the electrons that is lost.
SEE ALSO **potential energy**

bauxite *see* extraction of metals

beam

A beam of light is a group of rays of light moving in the same direction.
• *A beam of light comes from light sources such as projectors, torches, headlights, etc.*
SEE ALSO **ray**

beat

Beats are regular variations in loudness when two or more sounds of slightly different frequency are heard at the same time. A beat is the result of interference between the two sound waves, as the waves go alternately in and out of phase with each other. The closer together the frequency of the two sounds, the slower the beats.
SEE ALSO **interference, loudness**

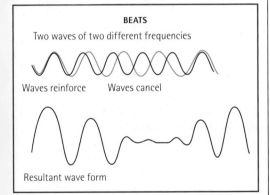

BEATS

Two waves of two different frequencies

Waves reinforce   Waves cancel

Resultant wave form

becquerel (*also* **Bq**)

A becquerel is the SI unit for measuring radioactivity, equal to the activity in a material in which one nucleus decays on average per second.
SEE ALSO **radioactivity**

bedrock (*also* **parent rock**)

is the lowest level of rock, which is usually the original source of the topsoil before weathering.
SEE ALSO **soil, subsoil, topsoil**

bee

A bee is a flying insect known for its role in pollination when collecting nectar from flowers. Bees use the nectar to make honey to feed to their larvae. It is stored in a wax honeycomb.
• *Most bees live in colonies. A colony of honeybees, for example, consists of workers (sterile females), drones (fertile males), and a single fertile female, the queen bee.*
SEE ALSO **pollination**

beetle

A beetle is an insect with hard wing casings covering its back.
• *There are over 300,000 different types of beetle in the world.*
SEE ALSO **insect**

berry

A berry is a fleshy fruit with a seed or seeds inside. Berries are often edible so animals help to disperse the seeds inside, as when they are eaten the seeds are not digested by the animal and pass through as excrement (with their own supply of manure).
• *Berries include grapes, tomatoes, and blackcurrants.*
SEE ALSO **fruit, seed**

beta decay *see* radioactive decay

beta particle (*also* β)

A beta particle is a high-energy electron emitted from certain radioactive nuclei. Beta particles can travel almost at the speed of light. They are much lighter than alpha particles and are more penetrating but have less ionizing effect.
SEE ALSO **alpha particle, radioactivity**

beta radiation

is formed by a stream of beta particles (electrons) emitted by certain radioactive nuclei.
SEE ALSO **beta particle**

beta sulfur see **sulfur**

biceps
The biceps is the flexor muscle in the upper arm which bends the forearm.
SEE ALSO **muscle**

bicuspid see **tooth**

bicuspid valve (*also* **mitral valve**)
The bicuspid valve in the heart consists of two flaps and prevents blood from flowing back into the left atrium.
• *The bicuspid valve opens to allow blood to flow from the left atrium to the left ventricle.*
SEE ALSO **atrium, ventricle**

biennial
Biennials are plants that require two growing seasons to complete their life cycle. In the first year food reserves are built up which are used in the second year for producing flowers and seeds.
• *Wallflower, foxglove, and carrot plants are examples of biennials.*

big-bang theory
The big-bang theory suggests that the universe was formed from a highly dense central mass (the size of an atomic nucleus containing all the matter in the universe) that exploded around 15 thousand million (15 billion) years ago.

bile
is a greenish-yellow fluid produced by the liver and stored in the gall bladder. The bile is released along the bile duct into the duodenum. It is alkaline and so neutralizes stomach acid.
• *Bile is not an enzyme but breaks up (emulsifies) fat droplets so that enzymes like lipase can work better.*
SEE ALSO **gall bladder, small intestine**

bimetallic strip
A bimetallic strip consists of two metals (usually brass and invar) with different linear expansivities, riveted together. On heating, the different metals expand by different amounts, which causes the strip to bend.
• *Bimetallic strips are used in thermostats, as they can open and close electric circuits at different temperatures.*
SEE ALSO **thermostat**

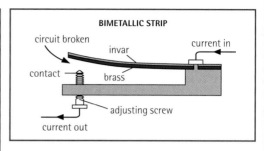

binary compound
A binary compound is a compound made up of two different elements.
• *Water (H_2O), carbon dioxide (CO_2), sodium chloride ($NaCl$), sulfur dioxide (SO_2), ammonia (NH_3), and methane (CH_4) are all binary compounds.*
SEE ALSO **compound**

binary fission
is a method of asexual reproduction in which the genetic material and cytoplasm of a single-celled organism divides equally to form two new cells. These 'daughter cells' are genetically identical to the parent cell and are therefore clones. Bacteria under favourable conditions multiply in this way every 20 minutes. Within less than 10 hours, one bacterium could multiply to over a million.
SEE ALSO **clone, reproduction**

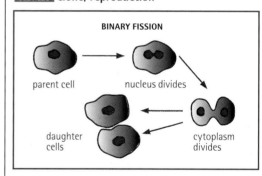

binding energy
is the energy required to cause a nucleus to decompose into its constituent neutrons and protons.

binomial classification
is the system of naming living organisms (and extinct organisms) using a two-part scientific (Latin) name. The first part of the name is the genus. The second part is the species. For example, the binomial name for a human is *Homo sapiens*.
• *Binomial classification was devised by the Swedish botanist Carl Linnaeus (1707–78).*
SEE ALSO **genus, species**

biodegradable

describes any substance which can be broken down by natural processes of decay.

• *Plant and animal waste products (including sewage) are biodegradable and are broken down by the actions of bacteria and fungi.*

biodiesel

is a biofuel made from plant material that absorbs carbon dioxide during photosynthesis. An example is rapeseed oil which can be used in place of diesel fuel in modified engines.

• *Biodiesel has a much lower carbon footprint than normal diesel fuel produced from the fractional distillation of petroleum.*

SEE ALSO **biofuel, carbon footprint, fractional distillation**

biodiversity

is the existence of a wide range of plants, animals, and microorganisms in a natural community or habitat. Disease, excessive hunting, invasion of new organisms into a habitat, and change of habitat (caused by intensive crop farming with no hedgerows, deforestation, factories, housing, landfill, etc.) can all have a profound effect on biodiversity.

• *Biodiversity is important to maintain stable systems in nature.*

SEE ALSO **community, habitat, microorganism**

bioenergetics

is how plants harness the Sun's energy during photosynthesis in order to make food.

• *Bioenergetics allows plants to be producers in food chains.*

SEE ALSO **food chain, photosynthesis, producer**

biofuel

is plant material or animal waste which can be used as a fuel resource.

• *When biofuel decomposes in the absence of air (anaerobically), it produces biogas.*

SEE ALSO **biogas**

biogas

is the gas which is produced from rotting organic matter. It contains approximately 50% methane and is a useful fuel for heating, cooking, and lighting.

• *Most sewage works and many landfill sites are now designed to collect biogas.*

bioleaching

is a biological extraction method for low-grade metal ores (called bio-ores) which uses soil bacteria. These bacteria oxidize metal sulfide ores producing sulfuric acid, which then reacts with other metal ores and releases a solution of metal ions (called the leachate). This leachate can then be electrolyzed to release the metal ion.

• *Bioleaching is a slow process but is used to extract copper from low-grade ores as most of the high-grade copper ores have run out.*

SEE ALSO **bacteria, bio-ore, electrolysis**

biological classification

first classifies living organisms into very large groups called kingdoms. The largest kind of subgroup within a kingdom is called a phylum. Each phylum is divided into classes, which are then subdivided into orders, which are divided into families. Every living organism belongs to a species. Each species belongs to a genus, and each genus to a family. This table shows the classification of a human being.

SEE ALSO **genus, phylum, species**

Kingdom	Animal
Phylum	Chordata
Class	Mammalia
Order	Primates
Family	Hominidae
Genus	*Homo*
Species	*sapiens*

biological oxygen demand (*also* B.O.D.)

is a measure of the extent of pollution in water. Polluting organic matter (agricultural waste, sewage, etc.) encourages the growth of microorganisms which use up the oxygen in water.

• *High biological oxygen demand values indicate severe pollution.*

B.O.D. (mg dm^{-3})	Significance
below 30	no pollution
30–80	mild pollution
above 80	severe pollution

biological pest control

This involves the use of organisms which are themselves harmless to crops but which feed on pests that damage crops.   »

• *Biological pest control reduces the need for chemical pesticides and so helps to cut down on pollution. Two common crop pests are mealy bugs and aphids. Special types of ladybird can be used to attack mealy bugs and a certain species of midge larva will eat aphids.*

SEE ALSO **pesticide**

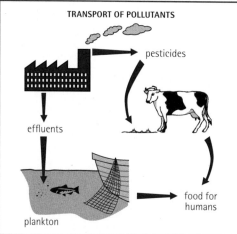

TRANSPORT OF POLLUTANTS

pesticides

effluents

food for humans

plankton

biology

is the scientific study of living things from the tiniest microscopic organisms to the largest whales.

biomass

is the mass of all the organisms at a particular trophic level in a food chain.

SEE ALSO **food chain, pyramid of biomass, pyramid of numbers**

bio-ore

A bio-ore is an ore that is used in bioleaching. Here the metal is extracted from its ore using soil bacteria.

• *Bio-ores are low-grade metal ores.*

SEE ALSO **bacteria, bioleaching, ore**

biosphere

The biosphere is a general term for the region of the Earth (including the air and sea) which may be inhabited by living organisms. Life exists where energy from the Sun can interact with air, water, and substances in the Earth's crust.

• *The biosphere is the sum of the world's ecosystems.*

SEE ALSO **ecosystem**

biotechnology

is the use of living organisms (containing enzymes) for the production of useful substances or processes.

• *Examples of biotechnology are brewing, baking, cheesemaking, sewage treatment, and genetic engineering, which can be used to modify bacterial cells to produce substances such as hormones (e.g. insulin), vaccines, etc.*

SEE ALSO **baking, brewing, cheesemaking**

biotic factor

Biotic factors are factors arising from the activities of living organisms (including humans) which influence the environment.

• *Biotic factors include availability of food, number of predators, competition from other organisms, disease, and the impact of human activities.*

SEE ALSO **abiotic factor**

biped

A biped is an animal that walks on two legs.

• *Birds are bipeds but the only mammals which are bipeds all the time is the human.*

SEE ALSO **bird, mammal**

bird (*also* Aves)

Birds are warm-blooded vertebrates with feathers, wings, and a beak. They evolved from reptiles around 150 million years ago. Their skin is dry and has no sweat glands. Cooling to maintain a constant body temperature is achieved by panting. Fertilization is internal and birds lay eggs with a hard shell.

• *Although all birds have wings, some (e.g. emu, ostrich, penguin) have wings that are not large enough to support their body weight, so they cannot fly.*

SEE ALSO **vertebrate animal**

birth (*also* parturition)

Birth is the process by which the fully grown fetus separates from its mother at the completion of pregnancy. The baby is pushed, normally head first, out from the vagina, still joined by the umbilical cord to the placenta. This is cut, and the stump forms the baby's navel.

SEE ALSO **fetus, pregnancy**

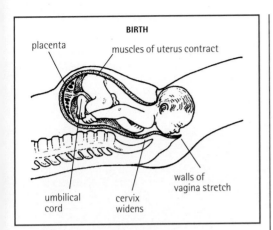

BIRTH

placenta · muscles of uterus contract · umbilical cord · cervix widens · walls of vagina stretch

Stages in a blast furnace	
1.	Coke burns with the oxygen in the air to produce heat and carbon dioxide gas. $C + O_2 \rightarrow CO_2$
2.	This carbon dioxide reacts with more coke to give carbon monoxide. $CO_2 + C \rightarrow 2CO$
3.	The carbon monoxide reduces the iron ore to molten iron, which trickles to the bottom of the furnace. $Fe_2O_3 \rightarrow 2Fe + 3CO_2$
4.	The limestone in the furnace decomposes to form calcium oxide. $CaCO_3 \rightarrow CaO + CO_2$
5.	The calcium oxide is a fluxing agent and combines with impurities such as sand in the ore to form molten calcium silicate or slag. This trickles down the furnace and floats on top of the molten iron. $CaO + SiO_2 \rightarrow CaSiO_3$

birth control see contraception

bisexual
❶ A person who is bisexual is sexually attracted to men and women.
❷ in biology, having characteristics of both sexes
SEE ALSO **hermaphrodite**

bitumen (also asphalt)
is a semi-solid, tarry substance left behind after distillation of petroleum.
• *Bitumen is commonly used in surfacing roads and in waterproofing felt for roofing.*

black hole
A black hole is a region of space where gravity is so strong that even light cannot escape.
• *A black hole is thought to be formed after a supernova.*
SEE ALSO **supernova**

black lead see graphite

bladder (also urinary bladder)
The bladder is a hollow muscular organ which stores urine before it is discharged.
• *Flow of urine from the bladder is controlled by a ring of muscle (urinary sphincter) between the bladder and the urethra.*
SEE ALSO **urethra, urine**

blast furnace
A blast furnace is a furnace for smelting iron ores such as haematite (Fe_2O_3) or magnetite (Fe_3O_4) or siderite ($FeCO_3$) to make impure iron, which is called pig iron. The furnace is charged from the top with the three raw materials: iron ore, coke, and limestone. The furnace is heated by blowing hot air in at the bottom.
SEE ALSO **pig iron, smelting**

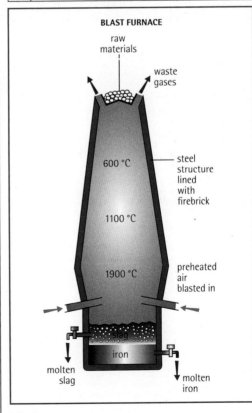

BLAST FURNACE

raw materials · waste gases · 600 °C · steel structure lined with firebrick · 1100 °C · 1900 °C · preheated air blasted in · slag · iron · molten slag · molten iron

blind spot
The blind spot is an area of the eye where the optic nerve and the retina meet.
• *There are no receptor cells in the blind spot.*
SEE ALSO **eye, retina**

blood

is a fluid in the bodies of animals that transports oxygen and nutrients to cells, and carries waste products from the cells to the organs for excretion. An adult human has about 5.5 litres of blood which travels around the body in the circulatory system. Blood has three main functions: transport, defence against disease, and the regulation of body temperature. The main components of the blood are shown in the table below.

SEE ALSO **circulatory system**

Component	Plasma
Size (mm)	-
Number (per ml)	-
Functions	Transports carbon dioxide, food materials, hormones, and waste products (urea) in solution.
	Liquid medium for floating blood cells, antibodies, and platelets.
	Transports heat around the body.

Component	White cells
Size (mm)	0.02
Number (per ml)	7,000
Functions	Help destroy bacteria and fight disease.
	Make antibodies.

Component	Red cells
Size (mm)	0.008
Number (per ml)	5,000,000
Functions	Transport oxygen.
	Transport small amount of carbon dioxide.

Component	Platelets
Size (mm)	0.003
Number (per ml)	250,000
Functions	Important in blood clotting.

blood clotting (*also* blood coagulation)

is the thickening of the blood into a clot at the site of a wound. First, the blood platelets separate and release a chemical (thromboplastin). This reacts with a protein in the plasma (fibrinogen) and causes it to harden into a fibrous substance called fibrin. Red blood cells and platelets get trapped in a mesh of these fibrin fibres, and so the blood clot is formed.

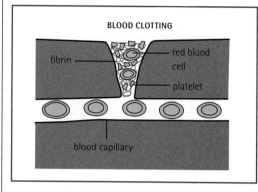

BLOOD CLOTTING

fibrin — red blood cell — platelet — blood capillary

blood group

Blood groups provide the main method of classifying blood, according to whether the antigens A or B are present in the red blood cells. Blood group A has antigen A only. Blood group B has antigen B only. Blood group AB has both antigens, and blood group O has neither.

SEE ALSO **antigen, rhesus factor**

blood pressure

is the pressure exerted by the flow of blood through the major arteries of the body. It is usually measured in mm Hg (millimetres of a column of mercury that the given pressure can support).

• *Normal* **blood pressure** *is 120/80 mm Hg. The higher value is the pressure when blood is being forced out of the heart, and the lower value is the pressure when the heart muscles relax so the heart fills with blood.*

SEE ALSO **high blood pressure**

blood serum *see* serum

blood transfusion

Blood transfusions must only be given to people of compatible blood groups whose blood can mix without agglutination of the red cells. People produce antibodies against those antigens which are not normally present in their blood, and this causes agglutination.

SEE ALSO **agglutination, antigen**

compatible blood groups		
Blood group	Can give blood to	Can receive blood from
A	A and AB	A and O
B	B and AB	B and O
AB	AB only	All groups (universal acceptor)
O	All groups (universal donor)	O only

blood vessel

Blood vessels are tubular structures through which the blood of an animal flows.

SEE ALSO **arteriole, artery, capillary**

B.O.D. *see* biological oxygen demand

boiling

is the rapid change in state from a liquid to a gas (or vapour), usually caused by heating. On heating, the particles in a liquid gain energy. Eventually they have sufficient energy to overcome the binding forces in the liquid, and spread away as particles of a gas.

boiling point

is the temperature at which all of a liquid changes into a gas (or vapour) because the vapour pressure of the liquid is equal to atmospheric pressure.
• *A pure substance has an exact **boiling point**. Impurities raise (elevate) boiling points.*

SEE ALSO **freezing point, melting point, vapour pressure**

bolus

A bolus is a ball of chewed food bound together with saliva and small enough to pass through the oesophagus.

bond *see* chemical bond

bond breaking

During chemical reactions, when bonds are broken, energy is absorbed in an endothermic process. If a chemical reaction is endothermic overall, then the energy required to break the old bonds is greater than the energy released in making bonds.

SEE ALSO **bond making, endothermic reaction**

bond energy

is the amount of energy required to break a particular bond in a compound. Exact values for particular bonds vary slightly, as they depend upon what other atoms are in the compound. However,

'average bond energies' are commonly used for calculating energy changes.

SEE ALSO **bond breaking**

(kJ mol^{-1})	Average bond energies
H–H	436
H–O	464
H–Cl	431
C–C	348
C=C	611
C≡C	835
O=O	496
Cl–Cl	242
C–H	435
C–Cl	339

bond making

During chemical reactions, when bonds are made, energy is given out in an exothermic process. If a chemical reaction is exothermic overall, then the energy released in bond making is greater than the energy used in breaking all the bonds.

SEE ALSO **bond breaking, exothermic reaction**

bone

is the hard connective tissue of which the skeleton of most vertebrates is made.
• *Bone contains collagen fibres and calcium salts.*

SEE ALSO **collagen, connective tissue, skeleton**

compact bone

is bone which has few spaces in it and is found in the outer layer of most bones.
• *Compact bone is made up of concentric rings of tightly packed bone cells.*

spongy bone

is bone that has spaces in it, which may contain bone marrow.
• *Spongy bone is light and is found in short or flat bones like the breastbone or sternum. It also fills the ends of large bones like the thigh bone or femur.*

SEE ALSO **bone marrow**

bone marrow

is soft tissue that fills the centre of spongy bone.
• *Bone marrow has a good supply of blood and makes red and white blood cells and blood platelets.*

SEE ALSO **bone**

bony fish see fish

bop process see basic oxygen process

Bourdon pressure gauge

A Bourdon pressure gauge is an instrument for measuring the pressure of a gas or liquid. It consists of a coiled, flattened tube which straightens out as the pressure increases. The movement of the coiled tube is made to move a pointer across a scale to indicate the size of the pressure.

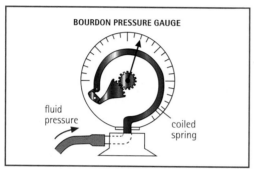

BOURDON PRESSURE GAUGE

fluid pressure

coiled spring

bowel see large intestine

Bowman's capsule

A Bowman's capsule is the closed end of a nephron, and is found in the cortex of the kidney where filtration takes place.
• *Each Bowman's capsule is shaped like a cup and contains a glomerulus.*
SEE ALSO **kidney, nephron**

WORD BUILD

filtration

occurs in the Bowman's capsules. The renal artery brings blood to each glomerulus, where the pressure builds up as the capillaries are narrow. This pressure pushes small molecules out of the blood capillaries and into the Bowman's capsule. Only small molecules can pass out of the capillaries (water, glucose, amino acids, urea, minerals, and vitamins). These make up the glomerular filtrate which passes through the rest of the kidney tubule. The larger molecules like proteins and blood cells remain in the capillaries of the nephron. This filtration under pressure is also called 'ultrafiltration'.

glomerulus

A glomerulus is a tangle of blood capillaries located in each Bowman's capsule of the kidney.

Boyle's law

states that the volume of a given mass of gas at a constant temperature is inversely proportional to its pressure:

pV = constant

This is only true for an ideal gas. In terms of kinetic theory, when the volume of gas is halved, then there will be twice as many collisions on the walls of the container, if the mass remains the same. Therefore halving the volume of a gas doubles its pressure.
• *Boyle's law was named after the Irish physicist Robert Boyle (1627–91).*
SEE ALSO **ideal gas, kinetic theory of gases, pressure of a gas, temperature of a gas, volume of a gas**

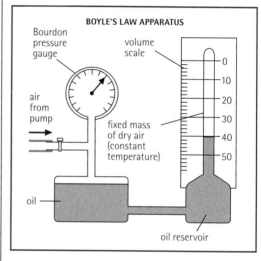

BOYLE'S LAW APPARATUS

Bourdon pressure gauge

volume scale

air from pump

fixed mass of dry air (constant temperature)

0
10
20
30
40
50

oil

oil reservoir

Bq see becquerel

brain

The brain is the main organ in the central nervous system which coordinates and controls most nerve activity. It is protected by the cranium and is surrounded by three linings called meninges. It is made up of millions of nerve cells which are arranged in various sensory and motor areas.
• *The main parts of the human brain are the highly developed cerebrum, and the cerebellum, medulla oblongata, and hypothalamus.*
SEE ALSO **central nervous system, cranium, meninges**

WORD BUILD

cerebrum

The cerebrum is the largest and most highly developed area of the forebrain and it controls most physical activity and all intelligent action such as speech, learning, decision-making, imagination, etc. The cerebrum is composed of two cerebral hemispheres.

cerebral hemisphere

The cerebral hemispheres are the two halves of the cerebrum which form the main sensory and motor areas of the brain.

cerebellum

The cerebellum is the front part of the hindbrain which coordinates and controls muscle movement and balance.

medulla oblongata

The medulla oblongata is the posterior part of the brain which controls all reflex actions and involuntary actions like the heartbeat, breathing rate, blood pressure, etc. It is under the overall control of the hypothalamus.

hypothalamus

The hypothalamus is the master controller of all unconscious activity and is situated at the base of the brain. It controls the autonomic nervous system and the action of the pituitary gland. It also controls water and temperature regulation and so is important in homeostasis.

pituitary gland (*also* master gland)

The pituitary gland is at the base of the brain and controls the production of hormones by the endocrine glands.
SEE ALSO endocrine gland, hormone

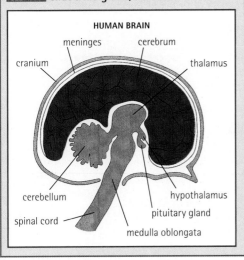

HUMAN BRAIN

meninges — cerebrum
cranium — thalamus
cerebellum
spinal cord — hypothalamus
pituitary gland
medulla oblongata

brain case *see* cranium

braking distance (*also* stopping distance)

is the distance required for road transport vehicles to come to rest in emergencies. When a force is applied to the brakes of a vehicle, work is done by the frictional force between the brakes and the wheel which reduces the kinetic energy of the vehicle. The greater the speed of the vehicle, the greater the braking force needed to stop the vehicle in a certain distance. Large deceleration can lead to brakes overheating and loss of control.
• *Braking distance is affected by weather conditions (e.g. wet and/or ice) and poor condition of the vehicle (e.g. brakes and/or tyres). It also depends on the driver's reaction time, which can be affected by distractions (e.g. mobile phones), tiredness, drugs, and alcohol.*
SEE ALSO force, friction, kinetic energy store

brass *see* alloy

breastbone *see* rib cage

breathing (*also* ventilation)

is the movement of air in and out of the lungs. It involves the physical movement of the diaphragm and intercostal muscles.
• *A relaxed adult has a breathing rate of about 16–18 times per minute.*
SEE ALSO diaphragm, intercostal muscle

breech birth

A breech birth is when a baby is born bottom first. In about four per cent of births the baby fails to turn around in the uterus to face the cervix before labour pains begin.

brewing

is the use of brewer's yeast to convert sugar solution into alcohol by a fermentation reaction.
• *In brewing the main sugar (from germinating barley seeds) is maltose and the important enzyme in the yeast is zymase.*
SEE ALSO fermentation, yeast

brine

is a concentrated solution of sodium chloride (common salt).
SEE ALSO sodium chloride

brittle

describes a material that does not bend easily. Ceramic material like pottery is strong but is also very brittle.

»

• **Brittle** *materials are likely to snap or break into small pieces if they are dropped on the floor.*
SEE ALSO **ceramic**

bronchiole
A bronchiole is a terminal air tube in the lungs.

bronchus *plural* bronchi
A bronchus is a branch of the trachea leading to a lung.
SEE ALSO **trachea, lung**

bronze *see* alloy

Brownian motion
is the random motion of particles in water or air caused by collision with the surrounding molecules.
• **Brownian motion** *was first observed by Robert Brown in 1827 when studying pollen grains on the surface of water.*

bryophyte
Bryophytes are primitive plants, liverworts, and mosses, with simple stems, leaves, and roots. They live in damp conditions as they need water for reproduction. The male bryophyte produces sex cells which must swim to the female to fertilize it.
• *After fertilization, the female* **bryophyte** *grows a capsule that contains spores, which, when released, grow to become the new plant.*
SEE ALSO **spore**

bubble chamber *see* radiation

buckyball *see* fullerene

bud
A bud is the part of the plant which contains new leaves or flowers.
SEE ALSO **flower, leaf**

budding
is a method of asexual reproduction used by simple animals like hydra, which grow a new group of cells out of the side of the parent body. This 'bud' breaks off to form a new individual. In colonial animals such as coral, the new individual remains attached though it is self-contained.
• **Budding** *also occurs in certain fungi such as yeast.*
SEE ALSO **reproduction**

buffer solution
A buffer solution resists changes in pH when an acid or an alkali is added or when the solution is diluted.

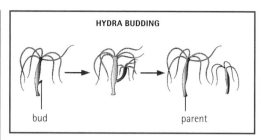

HYDRA BUDDING

bud — parent

Living organisms are very sensitive to pH changes, so blood and tissue fluids contain important natural buffers.
• **Buffer solutions** *are normally weak acids and the salts of such acids (or weak alkalis and their salts).*
SEE ALSO **acid, alkali, pH**

bug
A bug is an insect with sucking mouthparts.
• *The bedbug sucks blood and the aphid sucks plant sap.*
SEE ALSO **insect**

bulb *see* stem

bulimia
is an eating disorder typically involving excessive eating followed by self-induced vomiting.

buoyancy
is the result of the upward force on an object (upthrust) which is floating or suspended in a fluid (liquid or gas).
• **Buoyancy** *is the reason a boat floats on water. The upward force from the water balances the weight of the boat.*
SEE ALSO **principle of flotation, upthrust**

burette
A burette is a long, vertical, graduated glass tube with a tap at one end which is used in titration to add controlled volumes of liquids.
SEE ALSO **titration**

burning *see* combustion

buzzer
A buzzer is an electrical device which makes a buzzing sound when it is part of an electrical circuit.
• **Buzzers** *convert electrical energy into sound energy.*
SEE ALSO **electrical circuit**

Cc

C *see* **carbon, centre of curvature, heat capacity**

c *see* **specific heat capacity**

cactus *plural* cacti
A cactus is a fleshy plant with prickles or spikes and no leaves. Cacti have thick stems to store water and extensive rooting systems that enable rapid absorption of water over a wide area after rainfall.
• *Cacti are plants that can grow in very dry habitats like deserts.*
SEE ALSO **habitat**

caecum *see* large intestine

caesarean birth (*also* caesarean section)
A caesarean birth is the surgical removal of the baby from the uterus. This is carried out with difficult births such as awkward breech births, or when the placenta covers the cervix, or with large babies and a narrow vagina, or multiple births, etc.
SEE ALSO **birth**

caffeine
is a drug found in coffee, some soft drinks, and tea. It is used medicinally in the treatment of asthma.
• *Caffeine in coffee and tea might stop you sleeping well at night as its effect on the body is to stimulate metabolism.*
SEE ALSO **drug, metabolism**

calciferol *see* vitamin

calcium *see* alkaline–earth metal

calculation of energy change *see* chemical energy

calculations from chemical equations *see* chemical equation

calculations of heat energy *see* heat energy

calibrate
To calibrate an instrument is to mark it with a standard scale of measurements.
• *Rulers are calibrated on a standard scale so that all measurements using rulers are comparable.*

calorie
A calorie is the energy needed to raise the temperature of 1 gram of water by 1°. It is equal to 4.18 joules. Calories are used to measure the energy contained in food. A 15-year-old boy requires an average 2,500 calories per day while a 15 year old girl requires an average 2,100 calories per day.
• *Eating more calories than you require for your activities can make you overweight.*
SEE ALSO **energy, joule**

calorific value
is a measure of the heat given out per unit mass of fuel during complete combustion.
• *Calorific values are often used to measure the energy content of foodstuffs as well as fuels (1 calorie = 4.18 joules).*
SEE ALSO **combustion**

calorimeter
A calorimeter is an apparatus for measuring the amount of heat produced in a chemical process.

calyx
is the collective name for all the sepals of a flower.
SEE ALSO **flower, sepal**

cambium
The cambium is a thin layer of living tissue in woody plants, between the xylem on the inside and the phloem on the outside.
• *Cambium cells are able to divide and make more xylem and phloem, and so form a meristem.*
SEE ALSO **meristem, phloem, vascular tissue**

camera
A film camera contains a convex lens which forms a small, inverted, real image on the photographic film. When you press the shutter, a hole opens through which light passes onto the film. The size of the hole is called the aperture and is controlled by a diaphragm. The aperture size and the shutter speed (0.1 s to 0.001 s) determine the overall exposure. In dull conditions the shutter speed is longer and aperture larger than in bright conditions. To focus the image, the lens can be moved backwards or forwards. In the latest digital cameras, the image is captured by a charge-coupled device (CCD) or complementary metal-oxide semiconductor (CMOS) image sensors, both of which convert light into electrons.
SEE ALSO **image, lens**

»

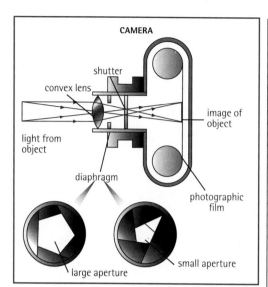

CAMERA

shutter
convex lens
image of object
light from object
diaphragm
photographic film
large aperture
small aperture

camouflage
describes the colouring of an animal to help it blend in with its background so that it is hard to see.
• *Insects are often camouflaged on leaves and twigs to avoid being eaten by predators.*
SEE ALSO **predator, prey**

cancer
is the result of changes inside cells that lead to cell division and uncontrolled growth. The result of this uncontrolled growth is called a tumour.
• *Cancers can be treated with radiation and drugs.*
SEE ALSO **carcinogen, cell division, tumour**

canine see **tooth**

cannabis
is a genus of flowering plants which contain hallucinogenic drugs that affect the brain. It is also called marijuana, grass, hash, dagga, or dope.
• *Medical cannabis is a broad term for any sort of cannabis-based medicine used to relieve symptoms of a disease.*
SEE ALSO **drug, medicine**

capacitance (*also* F)
is the ratio of the electric charge on one of the metal plates of the capacitor to the potential difference between the two metal plates. The relationship is:

$$\text{capacitance (F)} = \frac{\text{charge on conductor (C)}}{\substack{\text{potential difference between} \\ \text{conductors (V)}}}$$

• *The unit of capacitance is the farad (F) or coulomb per volt.*
SEE ALSO **capacitor, potential difference**

capacitor (*also* **electrical condenser**)
A capacitor is an electrical device designed to store small quantities of electric charge. Typically it consists of two parallel metal plates separated by an insulating material called a dielectric. This may be air, paper impregnated with oil or wax, plastic film, or ceramic. The capacitance of a capacitor depends on the dielectric used. The capacitance increases if the size of the plates increases, or if the distance between them becomes less.
• *Capacitors are used in many electrical and electronic circuits. Besides storing charge, they can be used to block direct current while allowing alternating current to pass. They can also be used for time delays, as it takes time for a capacitor to charge up.*
SEE ALSO **capacitance, electric charge**

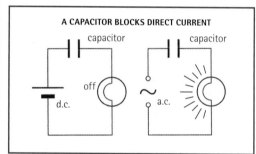

A CAPACITOR BLOCKS DIRECT CURRENT

capacitor   capacitor

off
d.c.   a.c.

capillarity
is the tendency of water to rise into small, very narrow spaces.
• *Clay soils have small air spaces and good capillarity , and dry out slowly. Sandy soils have poor capillarity and dry out quickly.*
SEE ALSO **soil**

capillary
Capillaries are the narrowest type of blood vessel. Capillaries branch off from arterioles and take oxygen and dissolved food to all cells. This diffuses through the thin capillary wall into the tissue fluid surrounding each cell. Capillaries also take waste material from the cells. These capillaries join to form venules.
• *Capillaries can be constricted or dilated according to tissue requirements.*
SEE ALSO **arteriole, blood vessel, venule**

car battery (*also* **lead–acid accumulator**)
A car battery is a secondary cell which contains electrodes made from lead and lead(II) oxide

immersed in a liquid electrolyte of dilute sulfuric acid. This is a wet cell.

• *A car battery consists of six cells each with an emf of 2V, so the total voltage of the battery is 12V.*
SEE ALSO **secondary cell, wet cell**

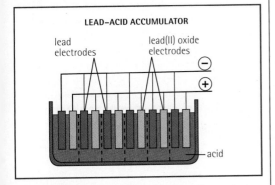

LEAD–ACID ACCUMULATOR

lead electrodes   lead(II) oxide electrodes

− +

acid

carbohydrate
Carbohydrates are a group of organic compounds with a general formula of $C_x(H_2O)_y$, and are important nutrients, especially for energy. Carbohydrates include all sugars, starch, glycogen, and cellulose.

• *Foods rich in* **carbohydrates** *include sugary foods such as jam, honey, sweets, and cakes, and starchy foods such as potatoes, rice, bread, and spaghetti. Vegetables and cereal foods contain cellulose.*
SEE ALSO **cellulose, glycogen, starch**

carbon (*also* C)
is the lightest non-metallic element in group IV of the periodic table and forms the basis of life chemistry.

• *Carbon is an element which forms allotropes (e.g. graphite, diamond).*
SEE ALSO **diamond, graphite**

carbonate
Carbonates are ionic compounds containing the carbonate ion CO_3^{2-} (e.g. calcium carbonate $CaCO_3$). All carbonates react with acids to form salts, water, and carbon dioxide gas. On heating, most carbonates (except those of group I) undergo thermal decomposition to form the metal oxide and carbon dioxide gas.

• *Most* **carbonates** *are insoluble in water (except group I carbonates).*

carbon black (*also* soot)
is a fine powdered amorphous (non-crystalline) form of carbon formed by burning hydrocarbons in insufficient air.

• *Carbon black is used as a pigment and filler (e.g. for rubber soles of shoes or rubber tyres).*
SEE ALSO **amorphous**

carbon capture
is the process of trapping gaseous emissions when burning fossil fuels and not allowing the gases (like carbon dioxide) to escape into the atmosphere. This helps to reduce global warming as carbon dioxide is a greenhouse gas.

• *Carbon capture can be used to remove gases formed in fossil fuel power stations which could be pumped deep underground to be absorbed into porous rock.*
SEE ALSO **carbon dioxide, fossil fuel, global warming**

carbon cycle
The carbon cycle is the constant circulation of carbon between the atmosphere, plants, animals, and the soil. Carbon dioxide is taken from the atmosphere during photosynthesis and incorporated into plant tissue. Animals feeding on plants then incorporate the carbon into their tissue. Respiration by both plants and animals returns carbon back into the atmosphere as carbon dioxide. Dead organic matter (plant and animal remains) undergoes bacterial decay, with respiration of the decomposers also releasing carbon dioxide. Some tissue in plants becomes fossilized into fossil fuels. Combustion of such fossil fuels releases carbon dioxide back into the atmosphere. The excessive use of fossil fuels contributes to global warming, as carbon dioxide is a greenhouse gas.
SEE ALSO **carbon dioxide, combustion, fossil fuel**

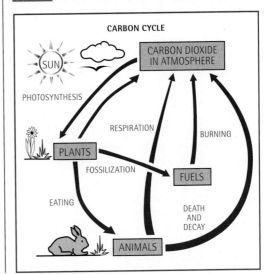

CARBON CYCLE

SUN

CARBON DIOXIDE IN ATMOSPHERE

PHOTOSYNTHESIS

RESPIRATION

BURNING

PLANTS

FOSSILIZATION

FUELS

EATING

DEATH AND DECAY

ANIMALS

carbon dating

By comparing the amounts of carbon-14 in dead material (like wooden artefacts, leather sandals, etc.) with the levels of carbon-14 in living material, we can measure the age of the dead material. It takes 5,600 years (the half-life of carbon-14) for the activity to halve. The proportion of carbon-14 in living material is kept constant, as food eaten contains carbon-14. On death this ceases, so the level of carbon-14 starts to fall. This method of **carbon dating** assumes that the levels of carbon-14 in living material have not changed over thousands of years.

carbon dioxide (*also* CO_2)

is the gaseous higher oxide of carbon, which forms when carbon or its compounds burn in a plentiful supply of air (oxygen). Carbon dioxide is present in very small amounts in the atmosphere (0.03%), but it is very important because it is used for photosynthesis in plants. The table shows the properties of carbon oxides.

• *Much* **carbon dioxide** *is dissolved in the seas and the lakes, or combined to form carbonates in the rocks.*

SEE ALSO carbon monoxide

Carbon dioxide	Carbon monoxide
Odourless, colourless gas	Odourless, colourless gas
Turns limewater milky	No effect on limewater
Non-toxic	Very poisonous
Acidic oxide (dissolves to form carbonic acid)	Neutral oxide
Does not support combustion	Burns with a blue flame to form carbon dioxide
Not a reducing agent	Reducing agent

carbon fibre

Carbon fibres are the black, silky threads of carbon formed by charring textile fibres at temperatures from 700°C to 1,800°C.

• *Carbon fibres are light and strong and are used to reinforce plastic resins to make high-strength composites for fishing rods, squash and tennis rackets, golf clubs, etc.*

carbon fibre composite

uses carbon fibres embedded in a resin material. Such composite materials are extremely strong and can also conduct electricity.

SEE ALSO composite material

carbon footprint

The carbon footprint of a product is the total amount of carbon dioxide and other greenhouse gases emitted over the complete life cycle of the product. Because of global warming it has become imperative to try to limit the emission of greenhouse gases like carbon dioxide and methane and therefore lower the carbon footprint as much as possible.

• *The* **carbon footprint** *of plant biofuels is much lower than the carbon footprint of fossil fuels. This is because when they are growing, biofuel plants photosynthesize, and take in carbon dioxide.*

SEE ALSO biofuel, carbon dioxide, fossil fuel

carbon monoxide (*also* CO)

is the gaseous lower oxide of carbon, which forms when carbon or its compounds burn in a restricted supply of air (oxygen).

• *Carbon monoxide is found in exhaust fumes of petrol or diesel engines and is very poisonous.*

SEE ALSO carbon dioxide

carbon neutral

describes a process or activity in which there is no overall release of carbon dioxide into the atmosphere. It is often achieved if the process or activity involves a plant material, which when grown took in carbon dioxide through photosynthesis. This carbon dioxide is often released when the material is burnt.

• *Carbon neutral processes lower greenhouse gas emissions and help to reduce global warming.*

SEE ALSO carbon dioxide, global warming, greenhouse gas

carboxylic acid (*also* **fatty acid**)

Carboxylic acids are organic acids that have a —COOH functional group. They are generally weak acids. This is because they exist mainly as molecules and do not form hydrogen ions as easily as mineral acids. However, carboxylic acids do exhibit normal acidic properties.

SEE ALSO acid, ethanoic acid, methanoic acid

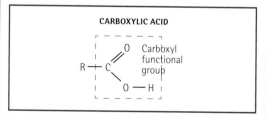

CARBOXYLIC ACID

R — C, O // Carboxyl functional group, O — H

carcinogen

A carcinogen is a substance that can cause a cancerous tumour to develop.

• *Carcinogens include tobacco smoke (nicotine chemicals), certain industrial chemicals, and ionizing radiation (such as ultraviolet radiation and X-rays).*

SEE ALSO **cancer**

cardiac cycle

The cardiac cycle is a cycle of events which makes one complete pumping action of the heart. First both atria contract and pump blood into their respective ventricles, which relax to receive it. Then the atria relax and take in more blood, while the ventricles contract to pump the blood out of the heart.

SEE ALSO **atrium, ventricle**

cardiac muscle *see* muscle

cardiac sphincter

The cardiac sphincter is a muscular ring between the oesophagus and the stomach. It relaxes to let food through.

• *Sometimes acid escapes from the stomach into the oesophagus if the **cardiac sphincter** is weak. The result is heartburn, which is a burning pain in the chest.*

SEE ALSO **oesophagus, stomach**

cardiovascular disease

is disease of the heart and/or circulatory system. It can be treated by drugs, mechanical devices (pacemakers) or organ transplants. Cardiovascular disease is a serious medical condition and should be monitored and treated appropriately.

- Drugs like statins are widely used to reduce blood cholesterol levels which slows down the rate of fatty material deposit inside blood vessels.
- Stents are mechanical devices to keep coronary arteries open and improve circulation.
- Artificial pacemakers are electrical devices to correct irregularities in heart-beat.
- In case of heart failure a donor heart, or heart and lungs can be transplanted.

carnivore

Carnivores are animals like cats, bears, dogs, and wolves which eat meat. These animals have well-developed canine teeth and are predators or carrion-eaters.

• *All **carnivores** are either secondary or tertiary consumers.*

SEE ALSO **consumer, predator**

carnivorous plants *see* **insectivorous plant**

carpel (*also* pistil)

A carpel is the female reproductive organ of a flower. Typically each carpel has a stigma, style, and ovary.

• *Some flowers have a single **carpel**; others have several clustered together.*

SEE ALSO **ovary, stigma, style**

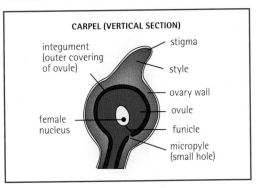

CARPEL (VERTICAL SECTION)

integument (outer covering of ovule) — stigma
— style
— ovary wall
— ovule
female nucleus —
— funicle
— micropyle (small hole)

carrier wave

A carrier wave is a continuously transmitted radio wave. It carries a signal which is combined with the carrier wave by amplitude modulation or frequency modulation.

SEE ALSO **amplitude modulation, frequency modulation, radio waves**

cartilage (*also* gristle)

is a tough connective tissue which is softer than bone, as it does not contain as many mineral salts. Cartilage is found on the ends of bones where they meet in a joint. In some joints it is the main cushion between the bones.

• *Cartilage also maintains the shape of certain organs, like the nose or the ear flap (pinna), and forms the whole endoskeleton in some animals such as sharks.*

SEE ALSO **connective tissue, endoskeleton**

cartilaginous fish *see* fish

cast iron

is hard, brittle iron made from remelted pig iron mixed with scrap steel.

• *Cast iron is good for moulding into complicated shapes such as engine blocks.*

SEE ALSO **pig iron, steel**

catabolism *see* metabolism

catalysis

is the process of changing the rate of reaction by using a catalyst.

catalyst

A catalyst is a substance that increases the rate of a chemical reaction without itself undergoing any permanent chemical change. A catalyst is often very specific and may increase the rate of one particular reaction, but have no effect on another reaction. Most industrial catalysts are transition metals or their compounds.

• A *catalyst* works by lowering the activation energy.
SEE ALSO activation energy, chemical reaction, enzyme

Catalyst	Process and chemical reaction with catalyst
Iron (Fe)	Haber Process Nitrogen + hydrogen → (Fe) ammonia
Vanadium (V) oxide	Contact Process Sulfur dioxide → (V2 O5) sulfur trioxide
Nickel (Ni)	Hydrogenation of margarine Unsurated hydrocarbon → (Ni) saturated hydrocarbon
Platinum (Pt)	Catalytic converter Carbon monoxide → (Pt) carbon dioxide
Palladium (Pd)	Catalytic converter Hydrocarbons → (Pd) water + carbon dioxide
Rhodium (Rh)	Catalytic converter Nitrogen oxides → (Rh) nitrogen

catalytic converter

A catalytic converter is a device fitted to a car exhaust to convert harmful gases (carbon monoxide and oxides of nitrogen) into harmless gases (carbon dioxide and nitrogen). The catalysts are usually platinum and rhodium. Other catalysts such as palladium will also oxidize unburnt hydrocarbon fuel to water and carbon dioxide.

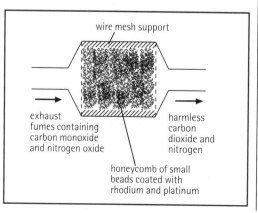

wire mesh support

exhaust fumes containing carbon monoxide and nitrogen oxide

harmless carbon dioxide and nitrogen

honeycomb of small beads coated with rhodium and platinum

carbon + nitrogen monoxide → carbon oxide + nitrogen dioxide

$$2CO + 2NO → 2CO_2 + N_2$$

(platinum converts CO to CO_2
rhodium converts NO to N_2)

catalytic cracking (*also* cat cracking)
see cracking

caterpillar

A caterpillar is the larva of a butterfly or moth. A caterpillar hatches from a tiny egg. When it has grown big enough it becomes a pupa (chrysalis).

• *Caterpillars* of the peacock butterfly eat nettle leaves.
SEE ALSO insect, larva, metamorphosis

cathode

The cathode is a negative electrode to which the cations (positive ions) are attracted during electrolysis.

• The *cathode* is always connected to the negative terminal of the battery or cell.
SEE ALSO anode, cation, electrode

cation

A cation is a positively charged ion that is attracted to the cathode during electrolysis. All metal ions and the hydrogen ion are cations. The table shows cations and anions in ionic compounds.
SEE ALSO anion, cathode, electrolysis

➤ testing for cations uses sodium hydroxide solution. The test involves adding a few drops of sodium hydroxide to a solution containing the cation (metal ion) and recording the colour of any metal hydroxide precipitate that forms.

• *Testing for cations* usually involves adding sodium hydroxide solution or the flame test.
SEE ALSO flame test, metal compound, precipitate

Name of cation	Cation	Colour of metal hydroxide precipitate
iron (II)	Fe^{2+}	green
iron (III)	Fe^{3+}	orange-brown
copper (II)	Cu^{2+}	blue
calcium	Ca^{2+}	white
zinc	Zn^{2+}	white (dissolves in excess sodium hydroxide)

celestial

describes anything to do with the sky or space. A celestial body is any naturally occurring object in space, which is seen from Earth.

• *Celestial bodies include stars, planets, and asteroids.*

SEE ALSO **asteroid, planet, star**

cell

❶ A cell is a fundamental unit of living organisms.

• *All cells are discrete units of protoplasm surrounded by a cell membrane.*

SEE ALSO **cell membrane, protoplasm**

❷ A cell is a system in which two electrodes are in contact with an electrolyte. The electrodes are normally metal or carbon (graphite).

• *Cells produce direct current as a result of the potential difference between the two different metals and the electrolyte.*

SEE ALSO **direct current, electrode, electrolyte**

➤ **cell size** The majority of cells in the human body are between 0.005 mm and 0.02 mm in diameter. Such cells can be seen clearly with the use of a microscope which magnifies 400 X. However, not all cells are so small.

• *An ostrich egg is a single cell and can be 20 cm long.*

Plant cell	Animal cell
Cell walls made of cellulose	Cell walls absent
Nucleus at the edge of the cell	Nucleus anywhere but often at the centre
Chloroplasts present in many cells	Chloroplasts never present
Thin lining of cytoplasm against wall	Cytoplasm throughout the cell
Often one large central vacuole	Small vacuoles throughout the cytoplasm

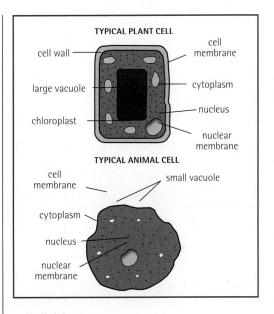

TYPICAL PLANT CELL

cell wall — cell membrane — large vacuole — cytoplasm — chloroplast — nucleus — nuclear membrane

TYPICAL ANIMAL CELL

cell membrane — small vacuole — cytoplasm — nucleus — nuclear membrane

cell division

There are three types of cell division: binary fission (in simple single-celled organisms), mitosis (in most types of cell) and meiosis (in sex cells only).

SEE ALSO **binary fission, cell, meiosis, mitosis**

cell membrane

The cell membrane forms the outer boundary of a cell. It is through the cell membrane that exchanges between the cell and its surroundings take place.

• *The cell membrane is semi-permeable, which means that it is selective about which substances it allows through.*

cell sap

is the solution of dissolved minerals and sugars that fills the large vacuoles of plants.

SEE ALSO **vacuole**

cell size *see* cell

cellular respiration

is an exothermic chemical process (one that releases energy) which occurs when simple products are made from the breaking down of food molecules. It occurs in all living cells all the time.

• *Cellular respiration also supplies essential adenosine triphosphate (ATP) molecules to living cells.*

SEE ALSO **adenosine triphosphate, cell, exothermic reaction**

cellulose
is a polysaccharide which acts as the main structural material of plants, found in their cell walls.
• *Cellulose consists of very long, unbranched chains of glucose monomers.*
SEE ALSO **cell wall, glucose, monomer, polysaccharide**

cell wall
The cell wall is a rigid outer wall of plant cells, made of cellulose. Because plant cells are rigid, they can build on top of one another. This support allows some plants, like trees, to grow very tall.
SEE ALSO **cellulose**

Celsius scale (*also* centigrade scale)
The Celsius scale is a common temperature scale based on the lower fixed point of ice at 0°C and the upper fixed point of steam at 100°C. The graduations on the Celsius scale are identical to those on the absolute scale of temperature.
• *The Celsius scale was named after a Swedish astronomer, Anders Celsius (1701-44).*
SEE ALSO **absolute scale**

central nervous system (*also* CNS)
The central nervous system is that part of the nervous system which coordinates and controls all of the neural activity in an organism. In vertebrates it consists of the brain and the spinal cord.
• *The central nervous system processes information from the sense organs and produces a response.*
SEE ALSO **brain, nervous system, spinal column**

centre of curvature (*also* C)
is the geometric centre of a circle of which the lens surface is a part. Since a lens has two surfaces, there are two centres of curvature.
• *Notation C is always given to the centre of curvature on the side of the incident light ray (the other is C').*
SEE ALSO **lens**

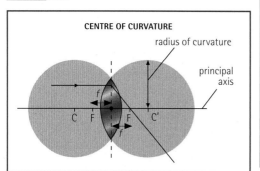

CENTRE OF CURVATURE

radius of curvature

principal axis

centre of gravity (*also* centre of mass)
The centre of gravity is a point on an object through which its total weight (or mass) appears to act.
• *Objects will balance if supported at their centre of gravity.*
SEE ALSO **equilibrium**

centrifuge
A centrifuge is an apparatus for the separation of substances by rotating them in a tube in a horizontal circle at high speed. It can be used to separate fine insoluble particles in a liquid suspension, or denser liquids from less dense ones. The denser particles are flung to the bottom of the test tube. The lighter particles can be decanted off.
SEE ALSO **suspension**

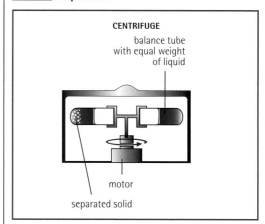

CENTRIFUGE

balance tube with equal weight of liquid

motor

separated solid

centripetal force
is the force directed toward the centre that causes a body to move in a uniform circular path. This force depends on several factors. A larger centripetal force is needed for a ball to follow a circular path if:

– the mass of the ball is increased
– the speed of the ball is increased
– the radius of the circle is decreased.

These relationships are shown by the following equation:

$$\text{centripetal force} = \frac{\text{mass} \times (\text{velocity})^2}{\text{radius of circle}}$$

This inward **centripetal force** has no effect on the speed of the ball, as it acts at right angles to the direction of motion.
SEE ALSO **circular motion**

centromere

A centromere is the section in the middle of the chromosome where the chromatids join and where there are no genes.

SEE ALSO **chromatid, chromosome, gene**

ceramic

describes a material made by heating clay, or other silicate compound, to high temperatures (called firing). The result is a very hard but often brittle material, which is an excellent electrical insulator.

• *Ceramic materials are commonly used in the home for ornaments and crockery.*

SEE ALSO **clay, insulator, silicate**

cereal

A cereal is a type of grass plant whose seeds give us food.

• *Cereal plants include oats, wheat, maize, barley, and rice.*

cerebellum *see* brain

cerebral hemisphere *see* brain

cerebrospinal fluid (*also* CSF)

is a fluid similar to lymph which fills the cavities in the brain and spinal cord, nourishing and protecting the tissues.

SEE ALSO **brain, lymph, spinal cord**

cerebrum *see* brain

cervix

The cervix is the neck of the uterus at the inner end of the vagina.

SEE ALSO **uterus, vagina**

CFC (*also* chlorofluorocarbon)

CFCs are inert chemicals used as refrigerants or as solvents in aerosols. These CFCs float upwards into the upper atmosphere and react with solar radiation to release chlorine atoms which break down the protective ozone layer. 'Ozone holes' were first noticed over the South Pole in 1987. Increased amounts of ultraviolet radiation can kill tiny plants (phytoplankton) in the sea which are the main producers in many food chains. It can also cause skin cancer and eye cataracts in humans.

• *Alternatives to CFCs are used in 'ozone-friendly' products.*

SEE ALSO **ozone layer**

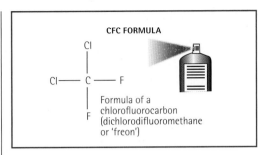

CFC FORMULA

Cl

Cl — C — F

F

Formula of a chlorofluorocarbon (dichlorodifluoromethane or 'freon')

change in momentum *see* momentum

change of state

A change of state occurs when a solid changes into a liquid or a liquid changes into a gas. It occurs also if the reverse happens, that is when liquids become solids or gases become liquids.

• *There is a change of state when water (liquid) becomes ice (solid) or water vapour (gas).*

SEE ALSO **condensation, evaporation, freezing**

charcoal

is a porous form of carbon made when organic material is heated with very little air. All forms of charcoal are porous, and are good at absorbing gases and purifying liquids (e.g. in sugar refining). Activated charcoal has been activated for absorption by heating in a vacuum.

• *Uses of charcoal include as a smokeless fuel for barbecues, for drawing by artists, and for absorbing odours in shoe linings, gas masks, etc.*

SEE ALSO **carbon**

animal charcoal

is made by heating bones and dissolving out the mineral salts with acid.

• *Animal charcoal is used in sugar refining as a filtering agent and adsorbent.*

wood charcoal

is formed by heating wood in the absence of air.

• *Wood charcoal is used as a fuel because it gives of less smoke (fewer pollutants) than coal or wood and burns at a higher temperature providing greater heat.*

a
b
c
d
e
f
g
h
i
j
k
l
m
n
o
p
q
r
s
t
u
v
w
x
y
z

charge *see* **electric charge**

Charles' law

states that the volume of a fixed mass of gas at constant pressure is directly proportional to its temperature (in kelvins):

$$V/T = constant$$

For an ideal gas the increase in volume for each degree rise in temperature is the fraction $\frac{1}{273}$ as long as the pressure of the gas remains unchanged.
• *Charles' law was named after the French scientist J.A.C. Charles (1746–1823).*
SEE ALSO **Boyle's law, ideal gas, pressure law**

Charles' law of pressure *see* **pressure law chart**

A chart is a graphical representation of data.
• *A pie* **chart** *shows the data as sections of a circle. A scattergram* **chart** *shows data with two variables.*

cheesemaking

is the conversion of milk into cheese by a controlled process using natural bacteria. Milk naturally contains bacteria (lactobacillus) which perform anaerobic respiration when provided with a source of sugar. Milk also contains the sugar lactose, which is converted by these bacteria into lactic acid and energy. The presence of the acid makes the milk turn sour, as the proteins in the milk coagulate and form clumps called curds in a watery liquid called whey. An enzyme called rennin may be added, to speed up this process. The curds are then separated and pressed to make cheese.
SEE ALSO **anaerobic respiration, bacteria**

chemical analysis (*also* qualitative analysis)

involves identifying pure chemical compounds or mixtures of chemical compounds. Various tests are carried out on an unknown chemical compound to identify the presence of different cations (positive ions) and anions (negative ions).
• *Chemical analysis is important for checking purity of food, drink, medicines, etc.*
SEE ALSO **anion, cation, compound**

chemical bond

A chemical bond is a strong force of attraction between atoms inside a molecule or crystal.
• *A* **chemical bond** *may be an ionic bond or a covalent bond.*
SEE ALSO **covalent bond, ionic bond**

chemical change

A chemical change occurs in a chemical reaction and produces a new chemical substance. This substance often looks quite different from the starting substances. For example, when hydrogen burns in oxygen, water is formed. This water is a colourless liquid and has none of the properties of its constituent elements, which are both gases. Always during a chemical change there is chemical energy taken in or given out. When hydrogen burns, heat energy is given out (as chemical bonds are made), as well as light energy (blue flame) and sometimes sound energy (a pop or bang). Most chemical changes are difficult to reverse. Although water can be electrolysed back into hydrogen and oxygen, it is difficult to do.
• *Many everyday changes like cooking, rusting, and the decay of food involve* **chemical changes.**
SEE ALSO **chemical energy, chemical reaction, decomposition**

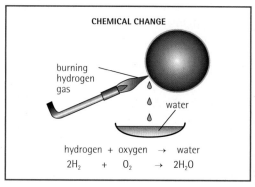

CHEMICAL CHANGE

burning hydrogen gas

water

hydrogen + oxygen → water
$2H_2$ + O_2 → $2H_2O$

chemical compound *see* **compound**

chemical digestion *see* **digestion**

chemical energy

is the energy which is released or absorbed when chemical bonds are rearranged. If stronger bonds are formed, then energy is released. Some chemical reactions produce electrical energy or light energy, but nearly all reactions involve heat changes. In many chemical reactions heat is produced, and this causes a temperature rise in the surroundings. Such chemical reactions are described as exothermic. Sometimes, the opposite happens and heat energy is taken in from the surroundings. This causes a temperature drop. Such chemical reactions are described as endothermic.
SEE ALSO **chemical bond, endothermic reaction, exothermic reaction**

➤ **calculation of energy change** is done by totalling the energy given out, by all the bonds formed, and then subtracting all the energy needed for breaking the various bonds in the reaction.

$$\text{energy change} = \frac{\text{sum of bonds}}{\text{formed}} - \frac{\text{sum of bonds}}{\text{broken}}$$

SEE ALSO **bond energy**

CALCULATIONS FROM CHEMICAL EQUATIONS

2 Mg(s)	$+$	$O_2(g)$	$\rightarrow$	2MgO(s)
2×24	$+$	2×16		$2 \times (24 + 16)$
48	$+$	32		80
48	$:$	32	$\rightarrow$	80
3	$:$	2	$\rightarrow$	5
reactants mass ratio				products mass ratio
eg 24g	$+$	16g	$\rightarrow$	40g
96g	$+$	64g	$\rightarrow$	160g
3g	$+$	2g	$\rightarrow$	5g

---

chemical equation

A chemical equation is a way of summarizing a chemical reaction. Although it can be written in words, an equation is often written using chemical symbols and chemical formulae. When you write chemical equations, to start with, it is advisable to follow these steps:

1. Write down the equations in words, using either the information given or your own chemical knowledge.

$$\text{sulfuric acid} + \text{sodium hydroxide} \rightarrow \text{sodium sulfate} + \text{water}$$

2. Then write down the correct chemical formula of every reactant on the left-hand side, and every product on the right-hand side.

$$H_2SO_4 + NaOH \rightarrow Na_2SO_4 + H_2O$$

3. Balance the equation. This involves making sure that the number of atoms of each element is the same on both sides of the equation, so that all atoms are accounted for and none are lost or gained. Do this by changing the proportions of reactants and products, making sure that you do not change any chemical formula.

$$H_2SO_4 + 2NaOH \rightarrow Na_2SO_4 + 2H_2O$$

4. Finally put state symbols in the equation for every reactant and product. Solid is (s), liquid is (l), gas is (g), and aqueous is (aq). Aqueous means dissolved in water.

$$H_2SO_4(aq) + 2NaOH(aq) \rightarrow Na_2SO_4(aq) + 2H_2O(l)$$

SEE ALSO **chemical reaction, ionic equation**

WORD BUILD

calculations from chemical equations

Chemical equations can be used to calculate the amounts of reactants being used and products being formed. Consider the burning of magnesium. From the equation and the relative atomic masses of the atoms involved (Mg = 24, O = 16), we find that 48 g of magnesium requires 32 g of oxygen and forms 80 g of magnesium oxide. The sum of the masses of the reactants must equal the sum of the masses of the product(s). Reaction between these atoms in this chemical equation is always in the same proportion by mass, which is 3 : 2 (for reactants) : 5 (for products).

SEE ALSO **mole, relative atomic mass**

---

chemical equilibrium

is a stage reached in a reversible chemical reaction when the forward and backward reactions take place at the same rate. This means that the overall concentrations of reactants and products remain the same.

• *A chemical equilibrium can only occur in an isolated system and is a dynamic equilibrium.*

SEE ALSO **dynamic equilibrium, isolated system, Le Chatelier's principle**

chemical feedstock

describes fractions of petroleum which are used in the production of various organic chemicals.

• *Naphtha is the chief chemical feedstock, as it provides hundreds of very useful chemicals for paints, cosmetics, drugs, detergents, fuel additives, glues, pesticides, etc.*

SEE ALSO **fraction, fractional distillation, petroleum**

chemical formula

A chemical formula is a way of showing the proportions of elements present in a chemical compound using symbols for the atoms present. Subscripts are used to show the number of atoms present. This can be worked out from the valency or combining power of each atom. **»**

a
b
c
d
e
f
g
h
i
j
k
l
m
n
o
p
q
r
s
t
u
v
w
x
y
z

• *The total number of atoms present in the chemical formula is called its atomicity.*

SEE ALSO **compound atomicity**

Chemical compound	Chemical formula	Atomicity
oxygen gas	O_2	2
carbon monoxide	CO	2
hydrogen chloride	HCl	2
water	H_2O	3
carbon dioxide	CO_2	3
ethanol (alcohol)	C_2H_5OH	9

Chemical compound	Atoms present	Atoms present
oxygen gas	2 oxygen atoms	
carbon monoxide	1 carbon atom, 1 oxygen atom	
hydrogen chloride	1 hydrogen atom, 1 chlorine atom	
water	2 hydrogen atoms, 1 oxygen atom	
carbon dioxide	1 carbon atom, 2 oxygen atoms	
ethanol (alcohol)	2 carbon atoms, 6 hydrogen atoms, 1 oxygen atom	

Compound	Valencies	Formula
copper(I) oxide	Cu^1O^2	Cu_2O
copper(II) oxide	Cu^2O^2	CuO
sodium nitrate	$Na^1NO_3^1$	$NaNO_3$
sodium sulfate	$Na^1SO_4^1$	Na_2SO_4
magnesium nitrate	$Mg^2NO_3^1$	$Mg(NO_3)_2$
ammonium nitrate	$NH_4^1NO_3^1$	NH_4NO_3
ammonium sulfate	$NH_4^1SO_4^2$	$(NH_4)_2SO_4$

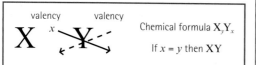

valency   valency

$$X \; {}^x \searrow \!\!\! Y \, {}_-$$

Chemical formula X_yY_x

If $x = y$ then XY

displayed formula

A displayed formula is a formula which shows the covalent bonding between the atoms present.

SEE ALSO **covalent bond**

empirical formula

An empirical formula is a chemical formula that shows the simplest ratio between the atoms in a molecule.

molecular formula

A molecular formula is a formula which simply gives the type and number of atoms present.

structural formula

A structural formula is a formula which shows the order in which the atoms are arranged.

Name	Empirical formula	Molecular formula
ethane	CH_3	C_2H_6
ethene	CH_2	C_2H_4
ethanol	C_2H_6O	C_2H_6O
ethanoic acid	CH_2O	$C_2H_4O_2$

Name	Structural formula	Displayed formula
ethane	$CH_3\,CH_3$	
ethene	$CH_2=CH_2$	
ethanol	$CH_3\,CH_2\,OH$	
ethanoic acid	CH_2COOH	

chemical potential energy

is the energy stored in systems such as fuel and oxygen, food and oxygen, and chemicals in batteries. This chemical energy is released during chemical reactions such as the burning of fuels or the respiration process.

SEE ALSO **chemical energy, potential energy**

chemical properties of halogens *see* **halogen**

chemical properties of the alkali metal *see* **alkali metal**

chemical properties of the alkaline–earth metals *see* **alkaline–earth metal**

chemical property

A chemical property is the way a material reacts with other materials resulting in a chemical reaction and chemical change.

• *How metals react with acids is a **chemical property**.*

SEE ALSO alkali metal, alkaline–earth metal, halogen, physical property

chemical reaction

A chemical reaction is a change by which chemical elements or compounds rearrange their atoms to produce new chemical elements or compounds. The total number of atoms in the reaction remains the same, so there is no change in the amount of matter.

• *All **chemical reactions** involve energy changes.*

SEE ALSO chemical energy, rate of reaction, reactivity series

Type of reaction	Meaning and example
Synthesis	Involves building up complicated molecules from simple ones.
	Photosynthesis involves synthesizing sugar molecules from simple molecules like carbon dioxide and water.
Decomposition	Involves breaking down compounds into simpler molecules or sometimes elements.
	Thermal decomposition of limestone to form lime and carbon dioxide.
Combustion	Involves chemical reaction of a substance with oxygen.
	Burning of fuels like methane gas produces carbon dioxide and steam.
Displacement	Involves a more reactive element displacing a less reactive element.
	Reactive metals will always displace a less reactive metal from its oxide or a solution of its salt.

Type of reaction	Meaning and example
Redox	Involves elements in the reaction gaining and losing electrons.
	Rusting is a redox reaction as iron loses electrons and oxygen gains the to form iron(III) oxide, which is rust.
Neutralization	Involves reactions between acids and bases.
	Acids will neutralize bases to form a salt and water.
Polymerization	Involves the joining together of large numbers of molecules to form a giant molecule.
	Formation of plastics and artificial fibres.
Exothermic	A reaction which involves giving out heat energy because chemical bonds have been made.
	Respiration is an exothermic reaction, as energy is released from foodstuffs.
Endothermic	A reaction which involves taking in heat energy because chemical bonds have been made.
	Dissolving is an endothermic reaction, as bonds are broken to spread the particles throughout the solution.

➤ **testing for gases** given off in chemical reactions can be used to identify the chemical compounds present. The table summarizes the tests for the common gases given off in chemical reactions. The table summarizes the tests for the common gases given off in chemical reactions.

Gas	Test	Observation
carbon dioxide	bubble gas through limewater	limewater turns cloudy white
hydrogen	hold a lighted splint in the gas	gas ignites with a pop
oxygen	hold a glowing splint in the gas	splint relights
chlorine	hold damp blue litmus paper in the gas	litmus paper turns red then bleaches white

a
b
c
d
e
f
g
h
i
j
k
l
m
n
o
p
q
r
s
t
u
v
w
x
y
z

»

• *Testing for gases like carbon dioxide indicates the presence of a carbonate compound.*

SEE ALSO **carbon dioxide, compound, hydrogen gas, chlorine, oxygen**

chemical species

are atoms, molecules, or ions which are subjected to identification or to a particular chemical process.

• *A balloon of pure helium (He) contains atoms of the same chemical species, whereas a balloon of hydrogen gas (H_2) contains molecules of the same chemical species.*

SEE ALSO **atom, ion, molecule**

chemical symbol

The chemical symbol represents one atom of a particular element. The first letter is always a capital letter and, if there is a second, it is a small letter.

• *Some chemical symbols are derived from the Latin name of the element e.g. iron Fe from ferrum.*

SEE ALSO **element**

chemical weathering see weathering

chemiluminescence

is the emission of light resulting from a chemical reaction.

• *Chemiluminescence occurs when phosphorus is exposed to air due to the chemical reaction of oxidation of phosphorus to form phosphorus oxide.*

SEE ALSO **chemical reaction, oxidation, phosphorus**

chemistry

is the scientific study of substances (chemicals) and the way in which they react with one another. The study includes both physical properties and chemical properties of materials and substances.

• *Chemistry is very important in the manufacture of drugs, detergents/cleaners, fuels, plastics, extraction of metals, etc.*

inorganic chemistry

is the branch of chemistry concerned with all elements and their compounds except the element carbon (but includes carbonates and oxides of carbon).

organic chemistry

is the branch of chemistry concerned with the compounds of carbon (except carbonates and oxides of carbon). 'Organic' relates to living 'organisms', and all organic compounds have been associated with living material.

chicken pox see childhood illness

childbirth see birth

childhood illness

A childhood illness is a disease which is most commonly suffered by children. They are less often suffered by adults.

• *Childhood illness is treated with drugs and medicines.*

SEE ALSO **inoculation, vaccine**

WORD BUILD

chicken pox

is a highly contagious viral disease that results in a skin rash which forms small itchy blisters. It usually starts on the chest, back and face. The same virus when caught by an adult results in a painful disease called shingles.

measles

is a viral disease showing symptoms of fever and red skin. Most young children (9-15 months) are vaccinated against measles by means of the MMR (measles, mumps, rubella) vaccine as it is a serious illness and can be fatal. Measles spreads by inhalation of droplets from sneezes and coughs.

mumps

is a viral infection affecting one of the salivary glands. It cause painful swelling in the side of the face under the ears (parotid glands). As with measles, prevention is by means of the MMR vaccine.

whooping cough

is a bacterial infection causing running nose, cough and fever. It can last several months and can be prevented by vaccination.

china clay see kaolin

chitin

is a tough substance that makes up the exoskeleton of insects. Chitin is a polysaccharide which is very similar to cellulose.

• *Chitin is also found in the exoskeleton of crabs.*

SEE ALSO **cellulose, exoskeleton, polysaccharide**

chlorination

is a method of purifying water by bubbling small amounts of chlorine gas through, to kill bacteria. Other sterilizing agents include ozone and ultraviolet radiation. The chlorination plant is the final stage of purification at the waterworks.

SEE ALSO **potable water**

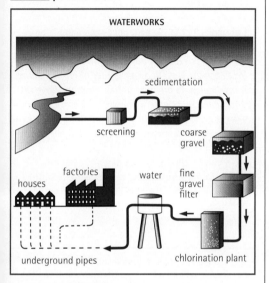

WATERWORKS

sedimentation

screening

coarse gravel

factories

water

fine gravel filter

houses

underground pipes

chlorination plant

chlorine *see* **halogen**

chlorofluorocarbon *see* **CFC**

chlorophyll

is the green pigment in the chloroplasts of plant cells and is the light-absorbing molecule needed for photosynthesis, which is an endothermic chemical process.

• *Chlorophyll absorbs the red and blue ends of the visible light spectrum and reflects green light.*

SEE ALSO **chloroplast, photosynthesis**

chloroplast

A chloroplast is a tiny structure in the cytoplasm of plant cells which contains a green pigment called chlorophyll.

• *Chloroplasts absorb energy from sunlight and so are important for photosynthesis.*

SEE ALSO **chlorophyll, cytoplasm, photosynthesis**

Chondrichthyes *see* fish

cholesterol

is produced by the liver and is a constituent of blood plasma and the fatty proteins (lipoproteins) that form the cell membrane.

• *Excess cholesterol in the blood can deposit lipids (fat) on the inner walls of the arteries and eventually obstruct blood flow (atherosclerosis).*

SEE ALSO **liver**

chordate (*also* Chordata)

Chordates are animals which at some stage during their development have a flexible skeletal rod or notocord running along the length of the body.

• *The most familiar chordates have a vertebral column or backbone and are called vertebrates.*

SEE ALSO **vertebrate animal**

choroid

The choroid is the black layer behind the retina which absorbs all the light after it has passed through the retina.

SEE ALSO **retina**

chromatic aberration

is the production of an optical image which has coloured fringes because of dispersion at the edges of the lens.

• *Chromatic aberration can be corrected by using an achromatic lens.*

SEE ALSO **achromatic lens, dispersion**

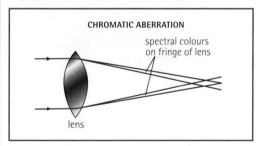

CHROMATIC ABERRATION

spectral colours on fringe of lens

lens

chromatid

A chromatid is one of the two 'arms' of a chromosome which has replicated before cell division.

SEE ALSO **chromosome**

chromatography

is a method of separating a mixture by carrying it in solution (or in a gas stream) across an absorbent material. The moving solution or gas is called the mobile phase and the absorbent material is called the stationary phase. Chromatography can be used to separate mixtures of gases, liquids, or

»

dissolved solids. It is a simple technique but it is very sensitive.
• *Chromatography is commonly used for identifying molecules for medical and biochemical analysis.*
SEE ALSO **mixture, solute, solution**

chromatogram

A chromatogram is the result obtained by chromatographic separation.

➤ **analysing chromatograms** involves the mobile phase moving over the stationary phase, carrying the components of the mixture with it. Each component will have a different attraction for the mobile and stationary phase. A substance which has a strong attraction for the stationary phase will not travel as far as a substance which has a strong attraction for the mobile phase.

paper chromatography

is a method of separating dissolved substances, such as dyes and pigments, by spreading them over absorbent paper (e.g. filter paper) with a suitable solvent. Solutes which are more soluble in the water trapped within the paper fibres travel less far in the solvent.

thin-layer chromatography

uses an absorbent solid as the stationary phase instead of absorbent paper. It is used to analyse liquid mixtures by passing them over a plate covered with a thin layer of the absorbent solid. After a given time the plate is dried and the location of the spots recorded.

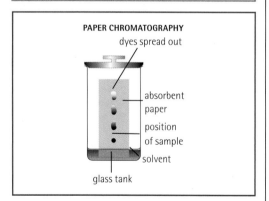

PAPER CHROMATOGRAPHY
dyes spread out
absorbent paper
position of sample
solvent
glass tank

chromium plating

is electroplating a thin layer of chromium metal onto steel to give it a shiny protective coating.
• *Chromium plating is used on bicycle handlebars, car bumpers, taps, cutlery etc.*
SEE ALSO **electroplating**

chromosome

A chromosome is a long coil of DNA which is made up of genes in a linear sequence which are found in the nucleus of plant and animal cells. They are arranged in pairs of homologous chromosomes.
• *Every species has its own number of chromosomes per cell, called its diploid number. Humans have 46 (22 matched pairs and one pair of sex chromosomes).*
SEE ALSO **centromere, chromatid, diploid, DNA, gene**

homologous chromosomes

are a pair of chromosomes having the same structural features. Each member of the pair of chromosomes has the same number and pattern of genes, but may have different alleles.
SEE ALSO **allele**

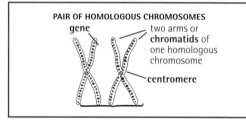

PAIR OF HOMOLOGOUS CHROMOSOMES
gene
two arms or **chromatids** of one homologous chromosome
centromere

chrysalis *see* **pupa**

chyle

is a milky fluid that forms from the absorption of fats into the lacteals of the small intestine.
SEE ALSO **lacteal, small intestine**

chyme

is the semi-digested food that passes from the stomach into the small intestine.
SEE ALSO **small intestine, stomach**

circuit *see* **electrical circuit**

circuit breaker

Circuit breakers are a popular alternative to fuses and automatically switch off if a large surge of current passes.
• *Circuit breakers can easily be 'flicked' back on, which is much easier than replacing the fuse wire in a fuse box, especially if the lights have gone out!*
SEE ALSO **fuse**

circular motion

is motion of an object in a circle. If the speed of the object remains the same, then it is uniform circular motion. However, the velocity does change, as the direction of the velocity is continually changing (though not its magnitude). This means the object is constantly accelerating towards the centre, so there is a force acting towards the centre. This is called the centripetal force.

SEE ALSO **centripetal force**

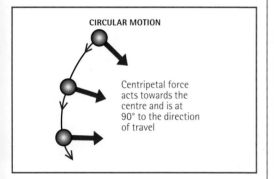

CIRCULAR MOTION

Centripetal force acts towards the centre and is at 90° to the direction of travel

circulatory system

The circulatory system consists of the heart, blood, blood vessels, lymphatic vessels, and lymph which together serve to transport materials throughout the body.

SEE ALSO **double circulation**

classification see animal kingdom, binomial classification, biological classification, plant kingdom

clay

is a fine-grained sedimentary deposit which has silicate chains interspersed with aluminium ions (aluminosilicate).

• *Most clays are brown in colour due to the presence of iron.*

SEE ALSO **silicate**

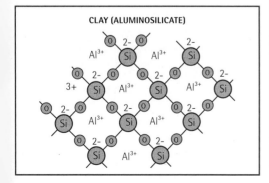

CLAY (ALUMINOSILICATE)

clay soil see soil

climatic factor see abiotic factor

clinical thermometer

A clinical thermometer is a liquid-in-glass thermometer used to measure body temperature. It has a narrow temperature range (35 - 43°C) and a very thin capillary tube to make it very sensitive and precise. The tube has a constriction so that the temperature reading can be taken after the thermometer has been removed from the patient's mouth.

SEE ALSO **liquid–in–glass thermometer**

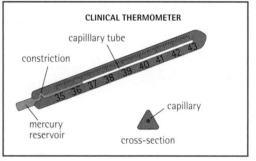

CLINICAL THERMOMETER

capilllary tube
constriction
capillary
mercury reservoir
cross-section

clinostat

A clinostat is a turntable device which rotates seedlings so that the effects of a stimulus are cancelled out.

• *A clinostat is used to study tropisms. It is most often used to study the growth of plant organs when the influence of gravity has been removed.*

SEE ALSO **tropism**

clitoris

The clitoris is the most sensitive part of the female reproductive organs.

• *The clitoris is made of erectile tissue which is rich in blood vessels and nerve endings.*

SEE ALSO **female reproductive organ system**

clone

A clone is a genetically identical descendant produced by vegetative reproduction from an original plant seedling. The new bulbs (called bulbils) which grow off the side of an old daffodil bulb are clones. The layered stolon of a strawberry plant is a clone of its parent.

• *As clones are genetically identical to their parent plant, any disease which affects the parent will also affect the clone.*

SEE ALSO **reproduction**

closed system

A closed system is one in which no material can escape, though energy can enter or leave the system. The temperature may not remain constant, so that no chemical equilibrium can be established.
SEE ALSO **chemical equilibrium, isolated system, open system**

close packing

is the packing of particles such as atoms or ions so as to occupy the minimum amount of space.

• *There are two main types,* **cubic close packing** *and* **hexagonal close packing,** *which are the structures adopted by most metals.*

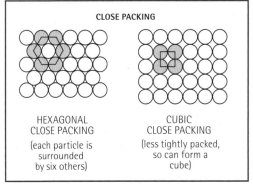

CLOSE PACKING

HEXAGONAL
CLOSE PACKING
(each particle is surrounded by six others)

CUBIC
CLOSE PACKING
(less tightly packed, so can form a cube)

cloud

A cloud is an aerosol type of colloid, consisting of billions of minute water droplets suspended in the atmosphere. These water droplets fall as rain when the cloud becomes too heavy.

• *Cloud forms as a result of water vapour in the air cooling and condensing to water droplets.*
SEE ALSO **colloid**

cloud chamber *see* radiation

cnidarian (*also* coelenterate, Cnidaria)

Cnidarians are aquatic invertebrates which have a body made up of two layers of cells, with only one body opening which acts as both mouth and anus. This opening is usually surrounded with tentacles.

• *Cnidarians include hydra, jellyfish, corals, and sea anemones.*
SEE ALSO **invertebrate animal**

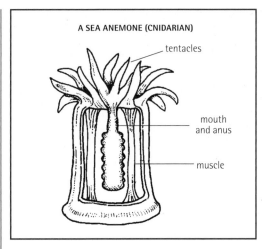

A SEA ANEMONE (CNIDARIAN)

tentacles

mouth and anus

muscle

CNS *see* central nervous system

CO *see* carbon monoxide

CO_2 *see* carbon dioxide

coagulation

is the process by which colloidal particles come together to form large masses, which can then be precipitated out.
SEE ALSO **colloid, precipitate**

coal

is a black, hard mineral consisting mainly of carbon.

• *Coal is a fossil fuel and is a source of various organic chemicals.*
SEE ALSO **fossil fuel**

coccus *see* bacteria

cochlea *see* inner ear

cocoon

A cocoon is a type of pupa (chrysalis) made up of fine threads that are spun by the caterpillar.

• *The silk moth caterpillar spins* **cocoons** *whose thread can be spun to make silk clothes.*
SEE ALSO **caterpillar, pupa**

co–dominance

is a situation in a heterozygous pair where both alleles are equally dominant. They are therefore both expressed in the phenotype. For example, the human blood group AB is a result of equally dominant alleles A and B.
SEE ALSO **allele, heterozygous, incomplete dominance, phenotype**

coelenterate *see* cnidarian

coil

A coil is a number of turns of insulated wire carrying a current. It is made by wrapping the wire around a shaped piece of material called the former.

• *Both flat coils and solenoids are used in electric generators and motors.*

SEE ALSO **solenoid**

coitus *see* **copulation**

coke

is the residue left behind after the destructive distillation of coal. Coke is used in blast furnaces and other chemical processes requiring a source of carbon. It is also important in domestic heating as a relatively smokeless fuel.

• *Coke is a greyish, brittle, porous solid containing about 85% carbon.*

SEE ALSO **blast furnace, coal**

cold-blooded animal (*also* **ectotherm, poikilotherm**)

Cold-blooded animals include all invertebrates, fish, amphibians and reptiles, whose body temperature is dependent upon their environment.

• *Cold-blooded animals become sluggish in cold weather, as the low temperature slows down their metabolic rate.*

SEE ALSO **warm-blooded animal**

collagen

is a fibrous protein found in connective tissue.

• *Collagen accounts for over 30% of the total body protein in mammals and is found in skin, ligament, tendon, cartilage, and bone.*

SEE ALSO **connective tissue, fibrous protein**

collision theory

explains rates of reaction in terms of the motion of particles in the reactants. Factors affecting particles in motion are listed in the table below.

SEE ALSO **rate of reaction**

temperature	At a higher temperature, reactant particles are moving faster, with greater average kinetic energy. A greater proportion of them therefore collide with enough energy to be converted from reactants to products. Rates of reaction, which are slow at room temperature, often double with a 10 degree rise in temperature.
concentration	At a higher concentration, there is a greater chance of reactant particles colliding with each other with enough energy to be converted into products. Rate of reaction therefore doubles if concentration is doubled.
pressure (in gases)	Increasing pressure decreases the volume of a certain mass of gas. This means that there are more particles in a certain volume (increase in concentration). Therefore there is a greater likelihood of collision and a faster rate of reaction at higher pressures.
surface area	Smaller particles, e.g. in powders, have a much greater surface area than lumps or crystals. With a greater surface area, more collisions can take place. Rate of reaction therefore doubles if the surface area of the reactant particles doubles.

colloid

A colloid is a substance consisting of very small particles (about 10^{-4} to 10^{-6} mm across) suspended and dispersed in a medium such as air or water.

• *Colloids are intermediate between solutions and suspensions. They have larger particles than solute molecules in solutions, but smaller particles than in suspensions.*

SEE ALSO **solute, solution, suspension**

➤ **colloidal** describes something relating to a colloid

WORD BUILD
continuous phase
is the phase in a colloid throughout which the colloidal particles are dispersed.
disperse phase
is the phase in a colloid of the colloidal particles themselves.

Type of colloid	Continuous phase	Disperse phase	Examples
Aerosol	air	liquid	fog, mist, cloud, paint sprays
Aerosol	air	solid	smoke, dust
Foam	water	gas	whipped cream, fizzy drinks, froth
Gel	water	solid	jelly, gelatin, agar, rubber
Emulsion	water	liquid	milk, salad cream, paint, mayonnaise
Sol	water	solid	paint, milk of magnesia

a
b
c
d
e
f
g
h
i
j
k
l
m
n
o
p
q
r
s
t
u
v
w
x
y
z

colon see large intestine

colony

A colony is a large group of animals living together.
• *Ants and penguins live in **colonies**.*

colour

is the visual sensation that is produced when light
of certain wavelengths reaches the retina of the eye.
The human eye can detect all the spectral colours,
each having its own characteristic wavelength of
light. Many more colours are possible when mixtures
of wavelengths reach the retina.

• *The **colour** of an object seen by the eye depends
on the wavelengths of the light that the object
reflects or transmits (other wavelengths being
absorbed).*
SEE ALSO **retina, wavelength**

complementary colours

Complementary colours with respect to light
are any two colours which on additive mixing
produce white light.
• *For example, yellow and blue are
complementary colours: yellow (a secondary
colour) contains two primary colours (green and
red), and blue is the missing third primary colour.*
SEE ALSO **additive mixing**

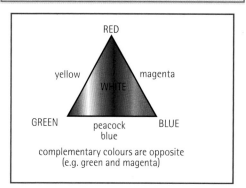

complementary colours are opposite
(e.g. green and magenta)

primary colours

Primary colours with respect to light are any of a
set of three coloured lights (red, blue, and green)
which can be mixed together to give white light.
They are called primary because they cannot be
made by combining other coloured lights.
• *By adding various **primary colour** lights in the
correct proportions it is possible to produce any
spectral colour.*

secondary colours

Secondary colours with respect to light are
colours that can be obtained by additive mixing
of two primary colours. For example:
  – yellow is the secondary colour formed by
    adding red and green light
  – magenta is the secondary colour formed by
    adding blue and red light
  – cyan (or peacock blue) is the secondary
    colour formed by adding green and blue
    light.
SEE ALSO **additive mixing**

spectral colours or visible light spectrum

The seven spectral colours in order of increasing
frequency are red, orange, yellow, green, blue,
indigo and violet.
• *Remember the **spectral colours** by the
mnemonic 'ROY G BIV'.*

Spectral colour	Wavelength (nm)
red	620–740
orange	590–620
yellow	570–590
green	500–570
blue	440–500
indigo	370–440
violet	300–370

colour blindness

is a genetic disease affecting colour vision and
results from a malfunction of certain cone cells in
the retina of the eye.
SEE ALSO **cones, genetic disease, retina**

colour filter

A colour filter absorbs all the light falling on it
except for the colour of the filter itself, which it
allows to pass through. For example, a yellow filter
will transmit red and green light, and a blue screen
will appear black through it. A yellow filter and
magenta filter together will transmit red light only.

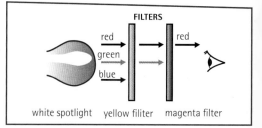

white spotlight   yellow filiter   magenta filter

combustion (*also* burning)

FIRE TRIANGLE

is a chemical reaction in which a substance (the fuel) reacts rapidly with oxygen and produces heat and light. All combustion reactions are exothermic.

• *Combustion can happen spontaneously, but usually the fuel needs heating in the presence of air (oxygen).*

SEE ALSO **exothermic reaction**

comet

A comet is a small lump of ice and rock orbiting the Sun in a noncircular orbit and in a different plane from that of the planets. As a comet nears the inner part of our solar system, the Sun heats it up to produce a tail of gas. As the comet moves in space, its tail streams away from the Sun. Comets travel faster when closer to the Sun, as the pull of gravity speeds them up.

• *Halley's comet can be seen from Earth every 76 years as it passes close to Earth (last time in 1986).*

commensalism

is a feeding relationship between two organisms where one benefits but the other is not harmed.

• *An example of commensalism is a sea anemone living on the shell of a hermit crab and eating bits of food that the crab drops.*

SEE ALSO **mutualism, parasitism**

common cold

The common cold is an illness caused by a virus. Patients may have a runny nose, cough, sneezing, and have a raised temperature. To get better, people need to rest, keep warm, and drink plenty of water.

• *Colds are spread by droplets of infection from one person to another.*

SEE ALSO **virus**

common salt *see* sodium chloride

communicable disease

A communicable disease is a disease caused by a pathogen (organism that causes disease) like bacteria, viruses, protists and fungi. Many skin infections, like HPV (viral infection) and athlete's foot (fungal infection) are spread by direct contact with the infected person or contact with the surface carrying the organism. Sexual diseases like syphilis, gonorrhoea and AIDS are passed from one sexual partner to another during sexual intercourse.

• *Communicable diseases are mainly spread by air-borne droplets or contaminated food and water.*

SEE ALSO **AIDS, bacteria, fungus**

communication

is the sending of information from one place to another.

communication satellite

Communication satellites are small, unmanned spacecraft in orbit above the Earth which are used for radio, television, and telephone transmissions.

• *Communication satellites use microwave transmission, as this is of higher energy (frequency) than normal radio waves.*

WORD BUILD

geostationary satellite

Geostationary satellites are communication satellites that orbit anticlockwise high above the equator at a speed to match the rate of rotation of the Earth on its axis. They therefore make one complete orbit every 24 hours and stay in the same positions above the Earth. They are used for television transmission.

polar satellite

Polar satellites are communication satellites that orbit over the North and South Poles. The size of their orbit is much less than that of a geostationary satellite. During the orbit they pass over all parts of the Earth's surface every few days. Such satellites are therefore useful for surveillance or for weather forecasting.

TYPES OF SATELLITE

polar satellite

geostationary satellite

community

A community is the total collection of living organisms (both plants and animals) living within a defined area or habitat.

• *Communities are often named after one of their dominant species or a major physical characteristic of the area.*

SEE ALSO **habitat**

commutator

A commutator is a device used in a d.c. electric motor to reverse the current direction every half turn.

• *It is made of a split metal ring so that the current will enter and leave the **commutator** through two carbon brushes.*

SEE ALSO **electric motor**

compact bone *see* bone

compass

A compass has a needle that always points to magnetic north. This is because the needle is a magnet which is attracted by the magnetic poles of the Earth.

SEE ALSO **Earth's magnetic field**

complementary colours *see* colour

composite material

A composite material is made from two or more materials, each with different properties, bound together in a resin or binder. The properties of a composite material are different from those of the materials it contains.

• *Composite materials are very common and include most clothing materials.*

compost

is a mixture which is used to grow plants as it is rich in soil nutrients and humus. It consists of organic matter like soil, peat, or coconut fibre.

• *Compost can be made by rotting down garden clippings and manure from animals.*

SEE ALSO **fertilizer, humus**

compound (*also* chemical compound)

A compound is a substance that consists of two or more different elements chemically bonded together in fixed proportions, as represented by the compound's chemical formula. The formation of a compound involves a chemical change. For example, water (H_2O) is a compound which has two hydrogen atoms and one oxygen atom chemically bonded together.

• *Some **chemical compounds** consist of molecules, while others consist of large structures held together by covalent bonds or ionic bonds.*

SEE ALSO **chemical change, chemical formula, covalent bond, mixture**

	Compound
1.	Constituent elements cannot be separated by physical means.
2.	Energy is often given out as chemical bonds are being made.
3.	Composition cannot vary.
4.	Physical properties are individual and not a result of its elements.
5.	Chemical properties are quite different from those of its elements.

compound microscope *see* microscope

compression *see* sound wave

compression forces *see* force

concave lens *see* lens

concentrate

To concentrate a solution is to make it 'stronger' by increasing the mass of solute dissolved in a particular volume of solvent. This can also be achieved by evaporating some of the solvent.

• *Concentrate is the opposite of dilute.*

SEE ALSO **molar solution, solute, solvent**

conception

is fertilization of the human egg and the implantation in the uterus of the resulting zygote.

• *Conception normally occurs in the oviduct, connecting the ovary to the uterus.*

SEE ALSO **fertilization, ovary, uterus, zygote**

concrete

is a very hard composite material that consists of cement, sand, and gravel (small stones). When water is added to this mixture a chemical reaction takes place which strongly binds the ingredients together.

SEE ALSO **composite material**

condensation

is the change of state from gas (or vapour) to a liquid.

• *Condensation is normally caused by cooling.*

condensation polymerization *see* polymerization

condom *see* contraception

conduction (*also* thermal conduction)

is the way in which heat energy is transferred through solids (and to a much lesser extent in liquids and gases). If the solid is a conductor, then heat energy is transferred quickly by movement of free

electrons. In insulators the heat energy is transferred slowly by the vibration of atoms.
SEE ALSO **conductor, heat transfer, insulator**

conductor
❶ A conductor is a substance which has a high thermal conductivity. Metals are good conductors because they have lots of free electrons. When a metal is heated, these electrons gain kinetic energy and move more quickly in all directions.
SEE ALSO **insulator, thermal conductivity**

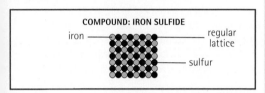

COMPOUND: IRON SULFIDE
iron — regular lattice
sulfur

❷ A conductor is a material through which electrons can flow. Metals are the best conductors, as their outermost electrons are loosely held and can move more freely between atoms. Carbon, water, and earth are also conductors.
• *Conductors can become charged by static electricity, but only if they are held in insulated handles.*

cones
are light-sensitive cells in the retina which are sensitive to bright light and give colour vision.
SEE ALSO **eye, retina, rods**

conifer
Conifers are cone-bearing plants which produce seeds, but without flowers or fruits. Most conifers are evergreen shrubs or trees like pines or firs. They can live in very dry places and their leaves are reduced to 'needles' or scales to prevent excessive water loss. Unlike bryophytes or ferns, they do not need water for fertilization. Conifers have male and female cones (their sex organs) and are usually wind-pollinated. The seeds are not protected by a fruit or carpel.
• *The wood of conifers is softwood, which is widely used as timber in the building industry.*

conjunctiva
The conjunctiva is a thin, transparent, self-repairing membrane at the front of the eye.
SEE ALSO **eye**

connecting neurone *see* neurone

connective tissue
is strong, tough tissue that holds organs or other tissues together.

• *Bone is a very hard connective tissue; cartilage is a less hard one, but is still tough.*
SEE ALSO **bone, cartilage, ligament**

conservation
is the protection of the environment from the effects of pollution and human activity, and the sensible use of the Earth's natural resources. A rapidly increasing human population has led to increased demands for food, fuel, wood, minerals, and other natural resources (see graph of population explosion). This must be balanced out by alternative food sources and renewable energy sources.
• *Conservation has become increasingly important due to the rapid increase in human population (see graph).*
SEE ALSO **energy conservation, environment, natural resource**

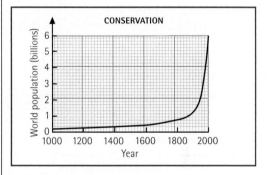

CONSERVATION

conservation of mass
conservation of mass
is the principle that during chemical reactions atoms are rearranged but not created or destroyed.
SEE ALSO **chemical reaction, mass**

conservative plate boundary *see* plate boundary

constant temperature
occurs when a body is absorbing radiation at the same rate as it is emitting radiation.
• *Constant temperature is important when measuring the exact volume of a gas.*
SEE ALSO **radiation, temperature**

constellation
A constellation is a group of stars in the sky which form a fixed pattern in relation to each other, as viewed from the Earth.
• *The stars in a constellation may not actually be close together in space.*
SEE ALSO **star**

constipation
is being unable to empty the bowels (large intestine) of faeces easily or regularly.
• *Constipation can be avoided by a diet of high-fibre foods.*
SEE ALSO **faeces, roughage**

constructive plate boundary *see* plate boundary

consumer
Consumers are organisms that feed on others below them in a food chain. All consumers feed by heterotrophic nutrition:

– Primary consumers feed on producers (plants)
– Secondary consumers feed on primary consumers
– Tertiary consumers feed on secondary consumers.

SEE ALSO **food chain, nutrition, producer**

contact force *see* force

contact process
This is the process for the manufacture of sulfuric acid by the catalytic oxidation of sulfur dioxide to sulfur trioxide.

$$\text{sulfur dioxide} + \text{oxygen} \rightarrow \text{sulfur trioxide}$$
$$2SO_2 \quad + \quad O_2 \quad \rightarrow \quad 2SO_3$$

SEE ALSO **sulfuric acid**

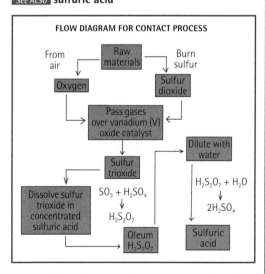

FLOW DIAGRAM FOR CONTACT PROCESS

➤ **conditions for the contact process** reflect the fact that the reaction between sulfur dioxide and oxygen is exothermic, but if the temperature is too low, the rate of the reaction is too slow. A moderate temperature of is 450°C is used together with a

vanadium (V) oxide catalyst. The pressure is 2-3 atmospheres and the sulfur trioxide produced (98% conversion) is dissolved in concentrated sulfuric acid to form oleum, which is then diluted to form sulfuric acid. The reaction of dissolving sulfur trioxide directly in water is too violent.
SEE ALSO **exothermic reaction, oleum**

continental crust
The continental crust rests above the oceanic crust and forms the continents. Its main rock component is granite and it is rich in the elements silicon and aluminium (called 'sial' or low-density rocks).
• *Much of the continental crust is very old and dates back almost to the formation of the Earth.*
SEE ALSO **Earth's structure, oceanic crust**

continental drift
is the slow movement of the continents across the surface of the Earth due to the motion of the underlying tectonic plates. This movement is caused by convection currents in the semiliquid mantle, and occurs at a rate of about 1–2 cm per year. Its existence was first seriously suggested by Alfred Wegener (1880–1930), a German scientist, who observed not only that the eastern coast of South America and the western coast of Africa fitted together, but also that there were similar geological features and matching fossils on both continents. It was later found that there are symmetrical patterns of magnetic stripes on either side of the Mid-Atlantic Ridge between the two continents, where rock has formed along a constructive plate boundary.
SEE ALSO **convection, plate boundary, plate tectonics**

continuous phase *see* colloid

continuous variation *see* variation

contraception (*also* birth control)
is the avoidance of fertilization during sexual intercourse.
• *Contraception is important in limiting the increase in human population.*

Method	How it works / For and against
Condom (barrier method)	Two types of condom: male worn over erect penis and female worn inside the vagina. Both prevent semen from entering the uterus.
	Reliable if used correctly.

Method	How it works / For and against
Diaphragm or cap (barrier method)	A rubber cap that fits over the cervix and prevents semen entering the uterus. Reliable if fitted correctly and used with sperm-klling cream around its edges (spermicide)
Spermicide	Jelly or cream which contains chemicals that kill sperm. Unreliable on their own and should be used in conjunction with condom, diaphragm, etc.
Intra-uterine device (IUD) or Inra-uterine system (IUS)	Coil or T-shaped device inserted into the uterus (womb) by a doctor, which prevents a fertilized egg from implanting in the uterus. Reliable with most women but an IUD can cause heavy periods and an IUS can disrupt or reduce periods.
Pill or oral contraceptive	Contains hormones (oestrogen, progesterone) found in pregnant women that prevent ovulation.. Very reliable, but some women experience unpleasant side effects such as nausea, change in breasts, or increased chance of blood clots.
Contraceptive implant	A small flexible rod inserted under the skin in the upper arm by a doctor or nurse. It releases hormone into the blook stream that prevent the release of an egg each month. Very reliable (can last for 3 years) but women may experience similar side effects as the oral contraceptive pill.
Vaginal ring	Small plastic ring that the woman places in her vagina. It releases hormones that are absorbed into the blood and prevent pregnancy. Very reliable with 1 ring providing contraception for 1 month. It is then replaced with a new ring.

Method	How it works / For and against
Rhythm method	Limits intercourse to the 'safe period', the days in the menstrual cycle when fertilization cannot take place. Recently, online trackers or apps have been introduced for this purpose. Unreliable, as periods are not always regular and sperm can remain active some time after intercourse.
Sterilization (vasectomy in men and ligation in women)	Permanent surgery to cut and tie sperm ducts or the fallopian tubes. Extremely reliable, but normally irreversible. However, recently vasectomy reversal has become available.

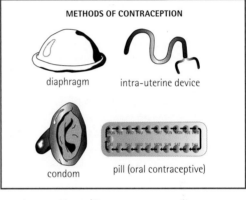

METHODS OF CONTRACEPTION

diaphragm   intra-uterine device

condom   pill (oral contraceptive)

contraceptive pill

A contraceptive pill contains female sex hormones (oestrogens) which, when constantly present in the blood, inhibit the production of FSH and stop eggs being released from the ovaries.

SEE ALSO **fertility treatment, ovary, sex hormone**

contract

To contract is to become smaller normally because of a lowering of surrounding temperature. Gases contract more than liquids, which contract more than solids. This is because the particles in gases are spaced far apart and as the temperature is lowered these particles lose energy and move much closer together.

• *Liquid mercury* **contracts** *when it gets cooler and this is used in mercury thermometers to record temperature drop.*

SEE ALSO **thermometric liquid**

a
b
c
d
e
f
g
h
i
j
k
l
m
n
o
p
q
r
s
t
u
v
w
x
y
z

contrast

A contrast is a difference clearly seen between one object or one part of an object and another.

• *Contrast is best achieved by difference in colour or shading or shape between contrasting objects.*

controlled variable

A controlled variable is a variable that you keep constant so as to ensure a fair experiment, such as the use of the same equipment each time you repeat an experiment.

SEE ALSO **dependent variable, independent variable, scientific variable**

convection

is the way in which heat energy is transferred through liquids and gases by movement of the particles in the liquid or gas. If a fluid (liquid or gas) is heated, it expands and becomes less dense. Cooler, more dense fluid then sinks, forcing the less dense material upwards against gravity. This circulating movement of a heated fluid is called a convection current.

• *Natural convection produces ocean currents and creates onshore and offshore winds at the coast during the summer (see diagram).*

SEE ALSO **heat transfer**

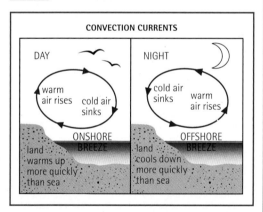

CONVECTION CURRENTS

conventional current direction

is from the positive terminal of a battery to the negative terminal and is shown as an arrow on the circuit diagram. This convention was decided before it was realized that current was a flow of negatively charged electrons from the negative terminal of the battery to the positive terminal.

SEE ALSO **battery**

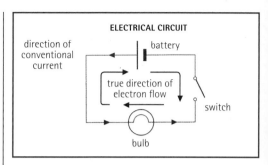

ELECTRICAL CIRCUIT

converging lens *see* lens

convex lens *see* lens

cooling curve

A cooling curve is a graph showing changes in temperature with time for a substance being cooled.

• *The shape of a cooling curve is the same as a heating curve, but in the opposite direction.*

SEE ALSO **heating curve**

coordination number

is the number of nearest neighbours of an atom or ion in a structure.

• *For the sodium chloride lattice, the coordination number of each ion is 6.*

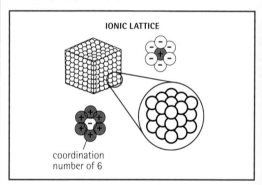

IONIC LATTICE

coordination number of 6

copulation (*also* sexual intercourse, coitus, mating)

is the process by which sperm from a male are inserted into the body of a female. In mammals the erect penis is inserted into the vagina. Movement of the pelvis stimulates nerve endings in the penis which cause a reflex action called ejaculation. This ejects about 5 cm^3 of semen containing around 300 million sperm into the top end of the vagina.

coral
A coral is a tiny invertebrate animal that lives in tropical seas. Corals live in colonies fixed to the sea bottom as coral reefs formed from the skeletons of these creatures.
• *Coral reefs are home to many different sea creatures.*
SEE ALSO **invertebrate animal**

core
The core is the material in the centre of a coil or solenoid which increases the strength of the field.
• *A core is normally a rod made of a ferromagnetic material such as soft iron (pure iron).*
SEE ALSO **coil, magnetic material, solenoid**

cork
is a light tough substance made from the bark of a south European oak tree.
• *Cork floats on water as it has a density of $0.7g$ cm^{-3}, which is less than that of water $(1.0g$ $cm^{-3})$.*
SEE ALSO **density**

corm *see* stem

cornea
The cornea is the transparent layer at the front of the eye. It is a continuation of the sclerotic, and acts like a lens, bending the light as it passes through.
• *The cornea has no direct blood supply, as a network of capillaries would interfere with the focusing of the light.*
SEE ALSO **eye, sclerotic**

cornified layer
The cornified layer is the tough, outermost layer of skin, consisting of dead cells. It is waterproof and protects the soft malpighian layer underneath.
• *On those parts of the body that get the most wear, like the soles of the feet, the cornified layer grows very thick.*
SEE ALSO **malpighian layer, skin**

corolla
is the collective name for all the petals of a flower.
SEE ALSO **flower, petal**

corrosion
is a chemical reaction between a metal and the gases in the air. Typically the metal reacts with oxygen to form an oxide layer on its surface (oxidation). Often this weakens the metal (as with iron), but sometimes this oxide coating forms a protective coat against further corrosion (as with aluminium).
SEE ALSO **chemical reaction, oxidation**

➤ **prevention of corrosion** has to stop the oxidation of the metal, so it must either prevent oxygen from reaching the metal, or prevent the metal from losing electrons. Coating metals (machine parts, tools, etc.) with grease or oil prevents air (oxygen) from reaching the metal. Painting metal objects or coating metal objects with plastic (garden chairs, dish racks, etc.) has the same effect and so helps to prevent corrosion.

cortex *see* kidney

cosmic rays (*also* cosmic radiation)
Cosmic rays are high-energy particles that fall on the Earth from space. Most of them are charged particles that have come from the Sun.
• *More cosmic rays bombard the Earth from the west, due to the deflection of the particles in the Earth's magnetic field.*

cotyledon *see* seed

coulomb (*also* C)
A coulomb is the quantity of electric charge transported by an electric current of 1 amp flowing for 1 second.

electric charge (C) = current (A) x time (s)

• *The amount of coulombs is an indication of the number of electrons flowing through an electrical circuit.*
SEE ALSO **electric charge, electric current**

coulomb force *see* electrostatic force

couple
A couple is two parallel turning forces which are equal and opposite but which do not act along the same line of action.
• *The resultant force of a couple is equal to the sum of the moments.*
SEE ALSO **moment, turning force**

covalent bond
A covalent bond is a chemical bond formed by the sharing between atoms of their outermost electrons.
• *All molecules contain covalent bonds. Electrons are shared so that the outermost shell of each atom has a stable inert gas configuration.*
SEE ALSO **chemical bond, ionic bond**

»

single covalent bond

A single covalent bond is the sharing between two atoms of two electrons (one from each atom).

double covalent bond

A double covalent bond is the sharing between two atoms of four electrons (two from each atom).

triple covalent bond

A triple covalent bond is the sharing between two atoms of six electrons (three from each atom).

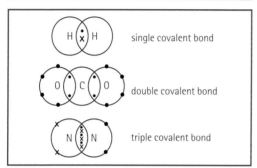

single covalent bond

double covalent bond

triple covalent bond

	Covalent compounds*
1.	are made of molecules
2.	have strong chemical bonds inside the molecule
3.	have weak attractive forces between molecules
5.	are often gases or volatile liquids
5.	have low melting and boiling points
6.	are often insoluble in water
7.	do not conduct electricity

*Macromolecules are exceptions

cps see hertz

crab

A crab is a decapod (ten-footed) crustacean as it has a single pair of claws and eight legs. Crabs live in either salt or fresh water and have a hard shell (exoskeleton).
• *Crabs belong to the largest phylum of invertebrates called arthropods.*
SEE ALSO **arthropod, crustacean**

cracking

is the chemical process of breaking down large molecules from heavy fractions into more useful smaller molecules. For example, the alkane hydrocarbons in the diesel oil fraction can be split

into more useful hydrocarbons for petrol. Cracking also produces unsaturated molecules like ethene which are useful in plastic manufacture.

large alkane → small alkane + alkene + alkene
$C_{16}H_{34}$ C_8h_{18} C_4H_8 $2C_2H_4$
(petrol)   (butene)   (ethene)

SEE ALSO **fraction, unsaturated molecule**

catalytic cracking (*also* cat cracking)

is the use of a catalyst together with heat to break up heavy fractions.
SEE ALSO **catalyst**

thermal cracking

is the use of heat alone to break up heavy fractions.

cranial reflex *see* reflex action

craniate *see* vertebrate animal

cranium (*also* brain case)

The cranium is the part of the skull that encloses and protects the brain, consisting of eight fused bones.
SEE ALSO **skull**

critical angle

The critical angle is the smallest angle of incidence at which total internal reflection occurs.
*In glass the **critical angle** is about 42 degrees, in water about 45 degrees.*
SEE ALSO **reflection of light, total internal reflection**

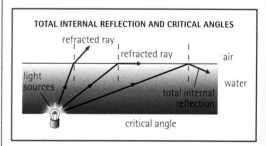

TOTAL INTERNAL REFLECTION AND CRITICAL ANGLES

refracted ray

refracted ray

air

light sources

water

total internal reflection

critical angle

critical mass

is the minimum mass of fissile material that will sustain a nuclear chain reaction. If the mass of the fissile material is too small ('subcritical mass'), too many of the neutrons produced by the first fission escape from the surface into the atmosphere, so a chain reaction does not occur.
SEE ALSO **fissile material, nuclear chain reaction**

critical pressure
is the pressure necessary to condense a gas at its critical temperature.
SEE ALSO **critical temperature**

critical temperature
is the temperature above which a gas cannot be liquefied, no matter how high the pressure.

cross–pollination *see* **pollination**

crude oil *see* **petroleum**

crustacean (*also* **Crustacea**)
Crustaceans are arthropods which have two pairs of antennae and more than four pairs of legs.
• *Examples of* **crustaceans** *include woodlice, shrimps, crabs, and lobsters.*
SEE ALSO **arthropod**

crystal (*also* **crystalline solid**)
Crystals are pure solids with a regular lattice structure giving a regular polyhedral shape.
• *All* **crystals** *of a particular substance have the same regular arrangement of molecules, ions, or atoms, and so have the same angles between their faces.*
SEE ALSO **lattice**

crystallization
is the process of forming crystals by heating a solution to evaporate some of the solvent. The hot, concentrated solution is then allowed to cool and crystals appear.
• *Crystallization will only work if a solute is more soluble in hot water than cold.*
SEE ALSO **crystal**

CSF *see* **cerebrospinal fluid**

current *see* **electric current**

cuspid *see* **tooth**

cuticle
❶ The cuticle is a protective layer of hard material which covers arthropods.
• *The* **cuticle** *is made of chitin, a light but strong material, and forms the exoskeleton.*
SEE ALSO **arthropod, exoskeleton**
❷ The cuticle is a waterproof waxy coating secreted by the epidermis and protecting a leaf.
SEE ALSO **epidermis, leaf**

cutting
A cutting is a small part of the root or stem which can be grown into a new plant.
• *Cuttings are used for vegetative reproduction.*
SEE ALSO **reproduction**

cyan *see* **secondary colour**

cycle
One cycle is one complete motion. For example, a cycle is one complete oscillation, or one complete orbit, or one complete rotation of a spinning object.
SEE ALSO **oscillation**

cycles per second *see* **hertz**

cyclone
A cyclone is a system of wind rotating around a calm central area.
SEE ALSO **depression**

cystic fibrosis
is a genetic disease causing an incorrect version of a protein to form in the cell's surface membrane, which results in excess mucus building up in areas such as the lungs.

$$\text{sulfuric acid} + \text{sodium hydroxide} \rightarrow \text{sodium sulfate} + \text{water}$$

• *Cystic fibrosis is caused by a recessive allele and is carried by about 1 in 20 people. If both parents are carriers, there is a 1 in 4 chance for each child that it will develop the disease.*
SEE ALSO **allele, cell membrane, genetic disease**

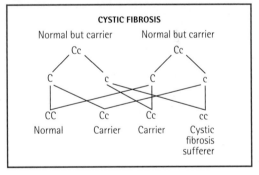

CYSTIC FIBROSIS

Normal but carrier   Normal but carrier
        Cc   Cc
   C   c   C   c

   CC   Cc   Cc   cc
 Normal   Carrier   Carrier   Cystic
                                 fibrosis
                                 sufferer

cytoplasm
is the protoplasm of a living cell which is found outside the nucleus. It is contained by a cell membrane.
• *In the* **cytoplasm** *all the chemical reactions take place which produce energy and maintain life. These take place in tiny bodies in the cytoplasm called organelles.*
SEE ALSO **cell, cell membrane, nucleus, organelle, protoplasm**

cytosine *see* **DNA**

Dd

Dalton's law
states that the total pressure exerted by a gaseous mixture is equal to the sum of the partial pressure of the gases. Atmospheric pressure is 1 atmosphere, and since air is approximately 80% nitrogen and 20% oxygen, the partial pressures of nitrogen and oxygen are approximately 0.8 and 0.2 atmospheres respectively.
SEE ALSO **partial pressure**

damping
is the decrease in the amplitude of an oscillating system due to energy being drained away, e.g. as waste heat in overcoming friction or other resistive forces.
• *An example of **damping** is the action of the shock absorbers on a car. These allow the oscillations of the car, after going over a bump, to die down as quickly as possible.*
SEE ALSO **amplitude, oscillation**

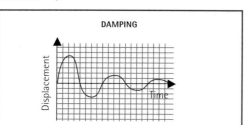

DAMPING

Darwinism
is a theory of evolution which states that present-day living creatures have developed by gradual changes over many generations as a result of natural selection.
• *Darwinism is named after the British naturalist Charles Darwin, who put forward his theory in a book called 'The Origin of Species' in 1859.*
SEE ALSO **evolution, natural selection**

data *singular* datum
Data is facts or information. Large amounts of data are normally produced and stored using a computer.
• *Data may be stored as numbers, symbols, graphics, or text.*

dB *see* decibel

d.c. *see* direct current

deafness
is an inability to hear, which can be partial or total, and either permanent or temporary. Too much wax in the ear can cause temporary deafness. A visit to your doctor to have your ears syringed will soon restore your hearing. Permanent deafness could be due to infection or damage to the eardrum. When this happens, the small bones in the middle ear do not vibrate correctly. Some people are deaf because the nerve cells in the cochlea of the inner ear are damaged and do not send any nerve impulses to the brain.
• *Deafness in old people is because the nerve cells in the cochlea wear out and are not replaced.*
SEE ALSO **hearing aid, inner ear**

deamination
is the removal of the amino group ($-NH_2$) from an amino acid. This group is converted to ammonia (NH_3) and then combined with carbon dioxide (CO_2) to form urea, which is then excreted.
SEE ALSO **amino acid, urea**

decantation
is the process of carefully pouring away the liquid above a precipitate or suspension once it has settled.
• *Decantation is used to separate immiscible liquids.*
SEE ALSO **immiscible, precipitate, suspension**

deceleration
is the rate of change of decreasing velocity (speed).
SEE ALSO **acceleration, velocity**

decibel (*also* dB)
A decibel is a commonly used unit of sound intensity or loudness. Each 10 dB increase represents a 10-fold increase in the energy (loudness) of the sound.
SEE ALSO **loudness**

Sound (pitch)	Frequency
upper limit of hearing	20,000 Hz
whistle	10,000 Hz
high note (treble)	1,000 Hz
low note (bass)	100 Hz
drum beat	20 Hz

deciduous tooth *see* tooth

deciduous tree
Deciduous trees are broad-leaved plants which shed their leaves at the end of the growing season to prevent dehydration.

• *Deciduous trees include all the woodland trees like ash, oak, and beech. The wood of these trees is hardwood, which is used for strong or decorative woodwork.*

decimal place (*also* dp)

The number of decimal places in a value is the number of digits after the decimal point.

SEE ALSO **rounding**

decomposer

Decomposers are saprophytes that fulfil a vital role in the ecosystem by returning organic matter to the soil as inorganic matter, which can then be taken into plants again as mineral salts.

• *Common decomposers are bacteria and fungi.*

SEE ALSO **ecosystem, natural cycle, saprophyte**

decomposition

is a chemical change by which a compound is broken down into simpler compounds or elements. Heat is normally required, and such chemical reactions are called thermal decomposition.

• *Calcium carbonate, when heated, undergoes thermal decomposition.*

$$\text{calcium carbonate} \rightarrow \text{calcium oxide} + \text{carbon dioxide}$$
$$CaCO_3 \quad \rightarrow \quad CaO \quad + \quad CO_2$$

SEE ALSO **thermal decomposition**

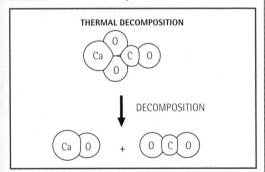

THERMAL DECOMPOSITION

DECOMPOSITION

Compound	Thermal decomposition			
Carbonate	metal carbonate	→	metal oxide	+ carbon dioxide
Nitrate	metal nitrate	→	metal oxide	+ nitrogen dioxide + oxygen
Hydroxide	metal hydroxide	→	metal oxide	+ steam

defecation

is expelling faeces through the anus.

SEE ALSO **faeces**

deforestation

is the destruction of forests by the excessive cutting down of trees for timber, paper, fuel, etc., or by the action of acid rain or soil erosion. When trees have been cut down, the soil is easily washed away, as there are no roots to hold it in place. Trees help to convert carbon dioxide from the atmosphere into oxygen by photosynthesis. Deforestation on a large scale (e.g. in the Amazon region of South America) creates an imbalance in this process.

• *Deforestation results in an increase in levels of carbon dioxide in the atmosphere, contributing to the greenhouse effect.*

SEE ALSO **acid rain, afforestation, greenhouse effect, reforestation**

deliquescence

is the spontaneous absorption by a substance of water from the atmosphere. Anhydrous salts are often deliquescent, and some absorb so much water that a concentrated solution of the salt is formed.

SEE ALSO **anhydrous**

demagnetization

is the removal of magnetism from a magnetic object by randomizing the alignment of the domains.

• *Demagnetization can be done by hammering the object repeatedly, by strong heating, or by placing it in a changing magnetic field such as that of a coil carrying alternating current.*

SEE ALSO **alternating current, domain, magnetic field, magnetization**

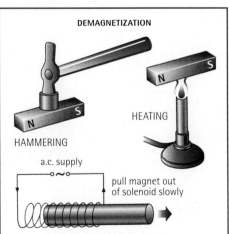

DEMAGNETIZATION

HEATING

HAMMERING

a.c. supply

pull magnet out of solenoid slowly

denaturing

Above 50°C the molecular shape of an enzyme is changed, and it becomes denatured and stops working.

SEE ALSO **enzyme**

dendrite see **dendron**

dendron (also **dendrite**)

A dendron is the part of the neurone that conducts electrical impulses towards the cell body of the nerve.
• Branching **dendrons** are called dendrites.

SEE ALSO **neurone**

density (also ρ)

The density of a material is its mass per unit volume. For an object of mass m and volume V, its density ρ is given as m/V. Its units are kg m^{-3} or g cm^{-3}. If one substance has a higher density than another, then the same mass of each substance will have a different volume, and the same volume of each substance will have a different mass.

$$\text{density} = \frac{\text{mass}}{\text{volume}}$$

• The heaviest solid is the element osmium, which has a **density** of 22.5 g cm^{-3} (more than twice as dense as lead). The lightest gas is hydrogen, with a density of 0.00009 gcm^3.

SEE ALSO **relative density**

Substance	Density kgm^3	Density gcm^3	Relative density
air	1.3	0.0013	0.0013
cork	250	0.25	0.25
wood (beech)	750	0.75	0.75
petrol	800	0.8	0.8
ice (at 0°C)	920	0.92	0.92
water	1,000	1	1
aluminium	2,700	2.7	2.7
stainless steel	7,800	7.8	7.8
copper	8,900	8.9	8.9
lead	11,400	11.4	11.4
gold	19,300	19.3	19.3

density bottle

A density bottle is a container which holds a precisely measured volume of liquid (at constant temperature). To measure the relative density of a liquid, completely fill a density bottle with the liquid

and measure its mass. Then fill the density bottle with water and find its mass. Divide the first mass by the second mass to find the relative density.

SEE ALSO **relative density**

dental caries see **tooth decay**

dentine see **tooth**

dependent variable

The dependent variable is the variable you measure (such as temperature, mass, volume, etc.).
• The **dependent variable** is usually plotted on the y-axis on a line graph.

SEE ALSO **controlled variable, independent variable, scientific variable**

depression (also **cyclone, low**)

A depression is a region of low atmospheric pressure caused when air flows in from below and rises to flow out at a higher level.
• As the air is rising upward, it cools. It therefore holds less water vapour, so **depressions** are associated with wet weather and rain.

SEE ALSO **atmospheric pressure**

dermis

The dermis is a thick layer of connective tissue underneath the epidermis of the skin. It contains elastic fibres. As a person ages, these fibres lose their elasticity and the skin becomes wrinkled.
• The **dermis** contains blood capillaries and nerve endings.

SEE ALSO **connective tissue, epidermis**

desalination

is the removal of common salt from sea water for irrigation or to provide drinking water (potable water). Normally it involves solar evaporation of sea water and collection of the pure water vapour that is produced.
• **Desalination** is commonly used in coastal countries with warm climates to provide drinking water.

SEE ALSO **evaporation, potable water**

destructive plate boundary see **plate boundary**

detecting radiation see **radiation**

detergent (also **soapless detergent, synthetic detergent**)

Detergents are substances added to water to improve its cleaning properties by helping it to dissolve grease. A detergent molecule is a large

molecule with a covalent 'tail' and an ionic 'head'. The covalent tail is a long hydrocarbon chain which dislikes water (hydrophobic) and attaches itself to grease. The ionic head is attracted to water (hydrophilic). Detergents do not form scum with hard water, as their calcium salts are water-soluble. They are manufactured from by-products of the refining of petroleum.
• *Detergents should be biodegradable and often contain enzymes to help break down stains like blood, sweat, etc.*
SEE ALSO **covalent bond, enzyme, ionic bond**

➤ **action of a detergent** Detergent molecules attach to grease so that the covalent hydrocarbon tail is buried in the grease or dirt and the ionic head is in the water. Agitation frees the grease or dirt from the fibres of the material and forms tiny suspended particles surrounded with detergent molecules.
• *Detergent molecules lower the surface tension of the water and help the water to thoroughly wet the material. They also help to emulsify fats and oils into solution.*

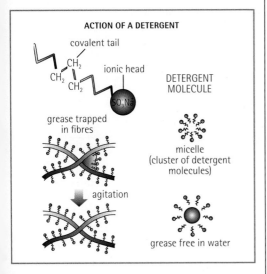

detritus
is organic material formed from dead and decomposing plants and animals.
• *Decomposers feed on detritus.*
SEE ALSO **decomposer**

deuterium (*also* ^2H)
is an isotope of hydrogen with a neutron as well as a proton in the nucleus of its atom.
• *Deuterium makes up roughly 0.015% of naturally occurring hydrogen.*
SEE ALSO **hydrogen, isotope**

dew
forms when water vapour condenses out of the air due to low temperature.
• *Dew droplets are often seen covering plants on cool mornings.*
SEE ALSO **condensation**

diabetes (*also* **diabetes mellitus**)
is a disease which results in high blood sugar. The hormone insulin moves sugar from the blood into your cells to be stored and used for energy.
• *With diabetes, your body does not make enough insulin or cannot effectively use the insulin it does make.*
SEE ALSO **hormone**

Type 1 diabetes
Here no insulin is made by the body as the immune system attacks and destroys the cells in the pancreas where the insulin is made. About 10% of people with diabetes have this type, which cannot be cured. It is controlled by sensible diet and daily injections of insulin.

Type 2 diabetes
The more common but less serious diabetes is characterized by the body losing its ability to respond to insulin. This is treated with tablets, not insulin injections. Being overweight or obese increases your risk of Type 2 diabetes.

dialysis
is the process of clearing waste substances such as urea and ammonia from the blood of people who have suffered kidney failure, using a 'kidney machine'.
• *Dialysis involves passing blood through a suitable membrane to remove waste substances.*
SEE ALSO **kidney transplant, urea**

diamond
is a natural transparent form of the element carbon, each diamond crystal being one single macromolecule. Inside such a molecule, each carbon atom is tetrahedrally joined by four single covalent bonds to four other carbon atoms.

»

• Because **diamond** is so stable, it is the hardest naturally occurring substance. It is therefore used for cutting and grinding tools.

SEE ALSO **carbon, covalent bond, macromolecule**

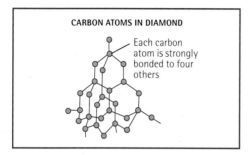

CARBON ATOMS IN DIAMOND

Each carbon atom is strongly bonded to four others

diaphragm (*also* **midriff**)
The diaphragm is a sheet of muscle situated below the lungs.

diaphragm *see* **contraception**

diaphragm cell
The diaphragm cell is used for the electrolysis of brine (concentrated sea water), which is a saturated solution of sodium chloride. The diaphragm cell has two electrodes separated by a porous membrane (diaphragm). Pure brine is pumped into the cell. Electrolysis causes the negative chloride ions Cl^- (aq) to be attracted to the anode, where chlorine gas is produced. This leaves a high concentration of sodium ions around the anode. Hydrogen ions H^+ (aq) are attracted to the cathode and form hydrogen gas. This leaves a high concentration of hydroxide ions OH^- (aq) around the cathode. The sodium ions Na^+ (aq) are drawn through the porous membrane, where they are attracted to the OH^- (aq) ions to form sodium hydroxide solution.

SEE ALSO **electrolysis**

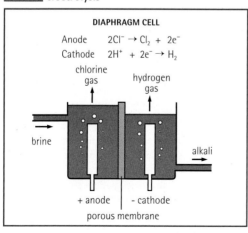

DIAPHRAGM CELL

Anode $2Cl^- \rightarrow Cl_2 + 2e^-$
Cathode $2H^+ + 2e^- \rightarrow H_2$

chlorine gas

hydrogen gas

brine

alkali

+ anode   - cathode

porous membrane

diarrhoea
is a condition of watery faeces caused by a bacterial infection in the intestines.

• *Diarrhoea* results in bowel movements which are very frequent and watery.

SEE ALSO **faeces, large intestine**

diastole *see* **heartbeat**

diatomic molecule
A diatomic molecule is formed from two atoms chemically bonded together.

• *Examples of **diatomic molecules** are oxygen gas O_2, carbon monoxide CO, and hydrogen chloride HCl.*

SEE ALSO **chemical bond, molecule, triatomic molecule**

dichotomous key
Dichotomous keys are the simplest type of key, made up of brief descriptions arranged in numbered pairs. You must begin at the first description and work your way through the key following the instructions. The key either names the organism, or gives you the next pair of descriptions to consult.

SEE ALSO **key, taxonomy**

1. (a) Hair present (b) Hair absent	MAMMALS Go to 2
2. (a) Feathers present (b) Feathers absent	BIRDS Go to 3
3. (a) Breathe using lungs (b) Breathe using gills	GO to 4 Go to 5
4. (a) Dry scaly skin (b) Moist scaleless skin	REPTILES AMPHIBIANS
5. (a) Fins with bony skeleton (b) Fins with cartilage skeleton	BONY FISHES CARTILAGE FISHES

dicotyledon (*also* **dicot**)
Dicotyledons are a class of angiosperm with two seed leaves (cotyledons). Dicotyledons generally have broad leaves, and their flower parts are in fours or fives or multiples of these.

• *There is a wide variety of **dicotyledons** which can be subdivided into herbaceous plants, deciduous trees, and shrubs.*

SEE ALSO **angiosperm, deciduous tree, herbaceous plant, monocotyledon**

diesel oil (*also* **gas oil**)
is the petroleum fraction with a boiling point range of 220–350°C. It is made up of a mixture

of hydrocarbons containing between 13 and 25 carbon atoms. Diesel oil is a fuel for diesel engines in lorries, ships, etc. It is called DERV (Diesel-Engine-Road Vehicles).

• *The diesel oil fraction can be 'cracked' to produce petrol and unsaturated molecules (ethene, propene etc.) which are useful for plastic manufacture.*
SEE ALSO **cracking, fraction, hydrocarbon, petroleum**

diffraction

is the spreading or bending of waves which occurs when a wave goes around an obstacle or through a gap. There is only a change in direction, not in velocity, frequency, or wavelength.
SEE ALSO **reflection, refraction, wave**

diffusion

is the spreading out of particles in a liquid (or solution) or gas, resulting in a net movement of the particles from an area of high concentration to an area of low concentration. Gases diffuse faster than liquids as their particles move for longer distances before collision. Diffusion is how substances (oxygen, carbon dioxide, waste materials) are moved in and out of living cells.

• *The rate of diffusion depends on temperature, the difference in concentration, and the surface area of the membrane the particles are diffusing through.*

digestion

Digestion is the breaking apart of ingested food into chemically simpler forms that can be easily absorbed and assimilated into the body.
SEE ALSO **sewage**

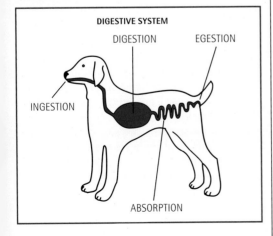

DIGESTIVE SYSTEM
DIGESTION
EGESTION
INGESTION
ABSORPTION

chemical digestion

is the chemical process of breaking large, insoluble food molecules into smaller, soluble molecules.
• *Enzymes are normally involved in chemical digestion.*
SEE ALSO **enzyme**

extracellular digestion

occurs in most animals, and takes place in the alimentary canal, outside the cells where respiration takes place.
SEE ALSO **alimentary canal**

intracellular digestion

occurs inside the cell in protozoans and other single cells (such as phagocytes).
SEE ALSO **phagocyte, protozoan**

mechanical digestion

is the physical process of breaking large pieces of food into small pieces using the teeth and the churning movements of the alimentary canal. Smaller pieces of food provide a greater surface area for chemical digestion.
SEE ALSO **mastication**

digestive tract *see* **alimentary canal**

digital reading

A digital reading is one produced by an electronic display of numerals. A digital reading gives a precise figure, but it may not be exactly accurate. For example, an electronic balance which reads to 0.1 g will read the mass of a certain object as either 3.1 g or 3.2 g. Its scale is not continuous and it cannot distinguish between masses of less than 0.1 g. If the balance reads 3.1 g, then the actual mass of the object may vary between 3.05 g and 3.14 g (to two decimal places).
SEE ALSO **analogue reading**

digital signal

Digital signals are signals which do not vary continuously, but normally consist of two voltage levels which can be represented as 0 (no voltage) and 1 (high voltage). They can be boosted to compensate for loss of energy due to attenuation without any loss in the quality of the signal. Also, they can be compressed ('squashed up') so that many more signals can be carried.

»

a b c d e f g h i j k l m n o p q r s t u v w x y z

• *Digital signals can transfer all types of information like numbers, letters or the individual pixel colours that make up images.*
SEE ALSO **analogue signal, attenuation**

dilute

To dilute a solution is to make it become less concentrated. When a solution is diluted more solvent (liquid) is added to lower the concentration of the solute (dissolved solid) that is present.
• *Dilute is the opposite of concentrate.*
SEE ALSO **molar solution, solute, solvent**

dinosaur

A dinosaur was a land reptile which became extinct around 65 million years ago. Most were herbivores, many with heavily armoured bodies (stegosaurus, triceratops, iguanodon, etc.). Some were carnivores (tyrannosaurus).
• *Birds are related to dinosaurs.*
SEE ALSO **extinction, reptile**

diode

A diode is an electronic device made from a semiconductor material such as silicon which can be used as a one-way switch. Diodes have very low resistance in one direction and very high resistance in the other.
• *Diodes can be used to change alternating current to direct current.*
SEE ALSO **alternating current, direct current, resistance, semiconductor**

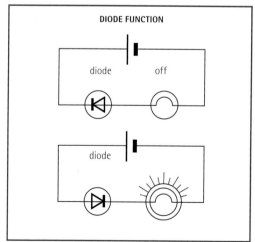

DIODE FUNCTION

diode   off

diode

diploid

describes a cell which has paired sets of homologous chromosomes in its nucleus. In each pair, one chromosome is from the female parent and the other from the male.
• *All cells in animals are diploid (except sex cells) and are formed by mitosis.*
SEE ALSO **chromosome, haploid, mitosis**

direct current (*also* d.c.)

is an electric current which is flowing in one direction only.
• *All battery-operated electrical devices use direct current.*
SEE ALSO **alternating current, electric current**

direct evaporation *see* evaporation

discontinuous variation *see* variation

disinfectant

A disinfectant is a chemical that kills or inhibits the growth of harmful microorganisms like bacteria. They are also, if undiluted, harmful to human tissue.
• *Disinfectants are used to clean surgical instruments, sick rooms and household drains.*
SEE ALSO **antibiotic, antiseptic**

dislocation

A dislocation is an imperfection or discontinuity in a crystal lattice. When molten substances solidify, crystals form, but when they meet, there is not a perfect fit, which results in a dislocation.
SEE ALSO **crystal, lattice**

disperse phase *see* colloid

dispersion

is the splitting up of visible light of mixed wavelengths by refraction into its component wavelengths, which give the different spectral colours. This occurs when visible light passes through a medium such as a glass prism. The shorter wavelengths (blue end of the spectrum) are refracted more than the longer wavelengths (red end of the spectrum), because of the different speeds at which different wavelengths pass through the medium.
SEE ALSO **colour, refraction, wavelength**

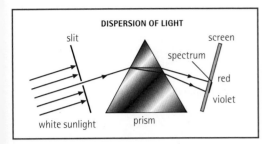

DISPERSION OF LIGHT

slit · screen · spectrum · red · violet · white sunlight · prism

displacement

is the distance and direction an object has moved from a fixed reference point.
• *Displacement is a vector quantity, as it has both size and direction. (Note: distance is a scalar quantity, as it has only size and no direction.)*
SEE ALSO **scalar quantity, vector quantity**

displacement can *see* eureka can

displacement reaction *see* reactivity series

displayed formula *see* chemical formula

distance ratio *see* velocity ratio

distance–time graph *see* graph

distillate

A distillate is the condensed liquid obtained by distillation.
SEE ALSO **distillation**

distillation (*also* simple distillation)

is the process of boiling a liquid and then condensing and collecting the vapour that is given off.
• *Distillation can be used to purify liquids or to separate miscible liquid mixtures.*
SEE ALSO **distillate, distilled water, fractional distillation**

distilled water

is water purified by distillation so that it is free from any dissolved salts or gases.
SEE ALSO **distillation**

diverging lens *see* lens

DNA

stands for deoxyribonucleic acid. DNA is a nucleic acid which contains the genetic information carried by every cell and directing all the activities of the cell. It is a polymer (large organic molecule) made up of two strands, twisted into a spiral staircase shape (double helix). Each nucleotide is made of a sugar molecule (deoxyribose), a base (adenine A, thymine T, guanine G, or cytosine C), and a phosphate. The sequence of nucleotides on one strand of the double helix determines the sequence on the other, as the bases in the nucleotides bind in pairs (A to T and G to C: these are called complementary base pairs).
SEE ALSO **nucleic acid, nucleotide, RNA**

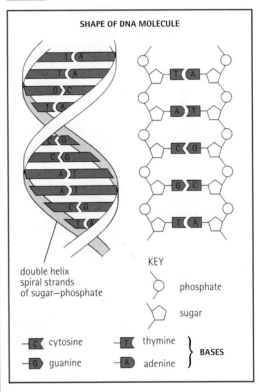

SHAPE OF DNA MOLECULE

double helix spiral strands of sugar–phosphate

KEY
○ phosphate
⬠ sugar

—C cytosine   —T thymine
—G guanine   —A adenine
} BASES

DNA fingerprinting *see* genetic fingerprinting

domain

Domains are regions in a magnet which, according to the domain theory of magnetism, are made up of many tiny molecular magnets called dipoles. Within a domain all the dipoles point in the same direction. A magnetic material becomes magnetized when the domains become aligned. When all the domains are aligned the magnet is 'magnetically saturated' (full strength).
SEE ALSO **magnetic material, magnetism**

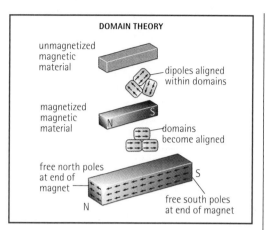

DOMAIN THEORY

unmagnetized magnetic material

dipoles aligned within domains

magnetized magnetic material

domains become aligned

free north poles at end of magnet

free south poles at end of magnet

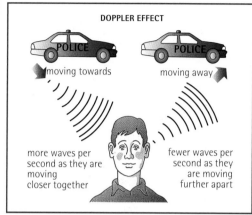

DOPPLER EFFECT

moving towards

moving away

more waves per second as they are moving closer together

fewer waves per second as they are moving further apart

dominant allele *see* allele

Doppler effect

The Doppler effect is the change in frequency of a sound caused by either the listener or the source moving relative to the other. As a police car moves towards you, the frequency of the sound increases (the sound becomes higher). As the car moves away from you, the frequency of the sound decreases (the sound becomes lower).

• *The Doppler effect is named after the Austrian physicist Christian Doppler (1803–53).*

SEE ALSO **frequency**

dosimeter *see* radiation

double circulation

is the type of circulatory system found in mammals, with a separate pulmonary circulation and systemic circulation.

SEE ALSO **circulatory system**

WORD BUILD
pulmonary circulation
is the circulation of blood to and from the lungs.
systemic circulation
is the circulation of blood to all parts of the body except the lungs.

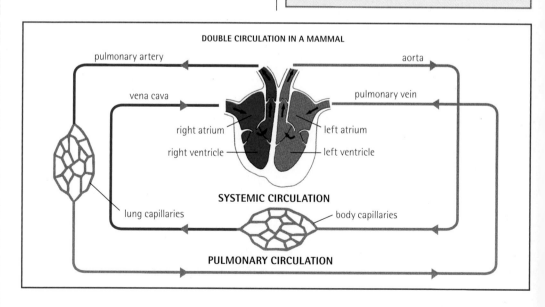

DOUBLE CIRCULATION IN A MAMMAL

pulmonary artery

aorta

vena cava

pulmonary vein

right atrium

left atrium

right ventricle

left ventricle

SYSTEMIC CIRCULATION

lung capillaries

body capillaries

PULMONARY CIRCULATION

double covalent bond *see* covalent bond

double decomposition (*also* ionic precipitation)

is a reaction producing insoluble salts by swapping the ionic partners of two soluble salts.

SEE ALSO **salt**

| silver nitrate | + | sodium chloride | → | silver nitrate | + | sodium nitrate |

$AgNO_{3\ error}$ + $NA_{error}\ Cl(aq)$ → $AgCl(s)$ + $NaNO_3\ (aq)$

double insulation

is produced by enclosing an electrical appliance in a plastic casing so that no metal parts are exposed. Such appliances do not need an earth wire, and so only require two-pin plugs and sockets.

SEE ALSO **electricity cable**

Down's syndrome

results when a person's cells contain three copies of chromosome 21 (instead of a homologous pair). The condition first occurs during meiosis in the woman's ovaries when one egg cell has two copies of chromosome 21, so that if it is fertilized it will have three copies.

SEE ALSO **chromosome, meiosis**

dp *see* decimal place

drone

A drone is an unmanned aerial device that is controlled by an operator on the ground. Small drones are invisible to pilots of aircraft so are a potential hazard.

• *Drones can carry cameras.*

drug

A drug is a chemical substance which affects the nervous system and changes some function of the body or mind. Drugs come in many different forms (e.g. tablets, pills, liquids, powders, or suspensions) but they all work by being absorbed into the bloodstream and carried to the brain. Here the central nervous system coordinates the drug's action at various sites around the body.

SEE ALSO **central nervous system**

➤ **testing for new drugs** is essential to identify dosage, efficacy, and possible toxicity and side effects. Preclinical testing is done in the laboratory using cell tissue and live animals. Clinical trials then use healthy volunteers and patients. Sometimes during clinical trials a placebo is used which is a harmless substance, given as if it were the medicine.

This is to confirm the drug itself is having the effect, not the 'mind of the patient'.

• *Testing for new drugs is a very thorough process and can take many years.*

SEE ALSO **tissue**

➤ **types of drug** There are four main groups of drugs which affect the body in different ways: analgesics, sedatives, stimulants, hallucinogens.

Type	Analgesic
Effect	A painkiller which numbs the part of the brain that senses pain (usually without causing unconsciousness).
Examples	aspirin, paracetamol, morphine, and heroin
Use and abuse	Powerful painkillers such as morphine and heroin are highly addictive.

Type	Sedative
Effect	A drug which slows down the activity of the brain and therefore has a calming effect and induces sleep.
Examples	Valium, Librium, and other tranquillizers (alcohol also has a sedative effect)
Use and abuse	Commonly used for treatment of high blood pressure and mental anxiety. Many sedatives after prolonged use are addictive.

Type	Stimulant
Effect	A drug which speeds up the mental activity of the brain to make a person more alert.
Examples	amphetamine ('speed'), caffeine, nicotine, ecstasy and cocaine
Use and abuse	Some stimulants are taken medically to relieve depression. Many stimulants are addictive (e.g. nicotine in cigarettes).

Type	Hallucinogen or deliriant
Effect	A drug which causes visual images that are sensed in the mind but which do not actually exist.
Examples	LSD, ecstasy (in high doses), and cannabis are hallucinogens; solvents of various aerosol products are deliriants
Use and abuse	There is widespread abuse of these drugs. Some are mixed with tobacco and smoked; others are taken in tablet form.

a
b
c
d
e
f
g
h
i
j
k
l
m
n
o
p
q
r
s
t
u
v
w
x
y
z

drug abuse

occurs because many stimulant drugs (e.g. amphetamines, caffeine, nicotine, ecstasy and cocaine) are addictive and are therefore overused, potentially harming the user. There is also abuse of hallucinogens (e.g. LSD, ecstasy, cannabis) which may be mixed with tobacco and smoked. Some volatile solvents found in aerosols, cleaning fluids, nail-varnish remover, paint thinner, etc. are hallucinogens. If these are regularly inhaled they may cause brain damage, kidney and liver failure. Solvent abuse (sometimes called 'glue sniffing') can kill.

• *Drug abuse is a serious social problem in many countries.*

SEE ALSO **alcohol abuse, alcoholism, drug**

dry cell

A dry cell is a voltaic cell which does not have any free-moving liquid electrolyte.

• *Dry cells are used in batteries to power many household electronic devices such as clocks, torches, cameras, calculators, smoke alarms etc.*

SEE ALSO **voltaic cell, alkaline cell**

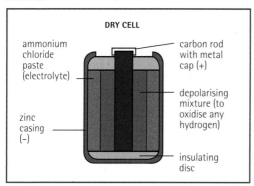

DRY CELL

ammonium chloride paste (electrolyte)

carbon rod with metal cap (+)

depolarising mixture (to oxidise any hydrogen)

zinc casing (−)

insulating disc

ductile *see* metal

ductless gland *see* endocrine gland

duodenum *see* small intestine

dwarf planet

A dwarf planet is an object which orbits a star but whose gravitational force is not strong enough to have attracted all the space debris near it.

• *Pluto is now regarded as a dwarf planet in our solar system.*

SEE ALSO **planet**

dynamic equilibrium

is a type of equilibrium where a balance is reached because movement in one direction is cancelled out by the same rate of movement in the other direction.

• *A person walking up a moving escalator at the same rate as the escalator is going down is an example of dynamic equilibrium. Overall the person stays in the same position.*

SEE ALSO **chemical equilibrium, equilibrium, phase equilibrium, static equilibrium**

dynamic frictional force *see* friction

dynamics

is the study of bodies in motion under the action of forces. The mass, inertia, and momentum of a body all affect the action of the force on that particular body.

• *Dynamics is a branch of physics.*

SEE ALSO **force, inertia, mass, momentum**

dynamo (*also* d.c. generator)

A dynamo is a generator which produces electrical energy in the form of direct current.

• *A dynamo is a machine which converts mechanical energy into electrical energy by rotating conducting coils in a magnetic field.*

SEE ALSO **direct current, generator, mechanical energy**

Ee

Eₐ *see* **activation energy**

ear

The ear is the sensory organ for hearing, and in vertebrates also for the maintenance of balance.

➤ **structure of the human ear** The human ear can be divided into the outer, middle, and inner ear. The outer and middle ear both contain air, but the inner ear is filled with liquid.

SEE ALSO **inner ear, middle ear, outer ear**

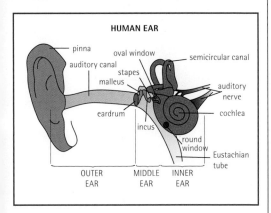

HUMAN EAR

pinna
oval window
auditory canal
semicircular canal
stapes
malleus
auditory nerve
eardrum
cochlea
incus
round window
Eustachian tube

OUTER EAR · MIDDLE EAR · INNER EAR

eardrum *see* **outer ear**

earth leakage

is a type of sensitive switch which cuts off the mains current if any electric current is detected along the earth wire.

earthquake

Earthquakes are sudden movements of the Earth's crust caused by the plates moving against one another. As the plates try to move relative to each other, strains build up. Eventually the tension is released, causing the ground to shake violently. The energy released travels through the Earth as a series of shock waves called seismic waves.

• *Earthquakes occur mainly along the boundaries of plates in the crust.*

SEE ALSO **Earth's structure, plate boundary, Richter scale**

WORD BUILD

epicentre
The epicentre is the point on the Earth's surface directly above the focus of an earthquake.

focus
The focus is a point inside the Earth's crust where an earthquake originates.

seismic wave
Seismic waves are the shock waves of an earthquake. There are three types: p-waves, s-waves, and l-waves.

p-waves
p-waves (or primary waves) are longitudinal waves which make rock particles vibrate backwards and forwards in the same direction as the motion. They travel quickly and are the first to be detected. They can travel through solids and liquids and can therefore pass through the Earth's core.

s-waves
s-waves (or secondary waves) are transverse waves which make rock particles vibrate at right angles to the direction of motion. Such waves cannot travel though liquids, and therefore cannot pass through the outer core. S-waves travel more slowly than p-waves but faster than l-waves.

l-waves
l-waves (or long waves) are the slowest-moving shock waves, and travel only through the Earth's crust. They make the ground move, and are responsible for most of the damage that an earthquake can cause.

shadow zone
The shadow zone is an area where p-waves are not recorded because they are refracted due to the increasing density of the core with depth.

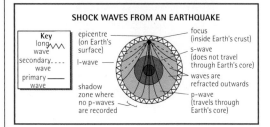

SHOCK WAVES FROM AN EARTHQUAKE

Key
long wave
secondary wave
primary wave

epicentre (on Earth's surface)
l-wave
shadow zone where no p-waves are recorded

focus (inside Earth's crust)
s-wave (does not travel through Earth's core)
waves are refracted outwards
p-wave (travels through Earth's core)

Earth's axis
The Earth's axis is an imaginary line through the centre of the Earth.
• *The tilt of the **Earth's axis** explains why places at different latitudes have different lengths of day and night.*
SEE ALSO **Earth's rotation**

Earth's crust *see* **Earth's structure**

Earth's magnetic field
The Earth's magnetic field is believed to be caused by the oscillating electric fields in the outer core of the Earth's structure. The Earth acts as though there were a giant bar magnet through its centre (see diagram). With no other magnets around, a compass needle (which acts as a freely suspended magnet) would point to magnetic north. This differs from true geographic north by the angle of declination.
SEE ALSO **angle of declination, Earth's structure, magnetic field**

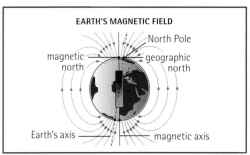

EARTH'S MAGNETIC FIELD

North Pole
magnetic north
geographic north
Earth's axis
magnetic axis

Earth's rotation
The Earth rotates in an anticlockwise direction on its axis and one complete revolution takes 24 hours.

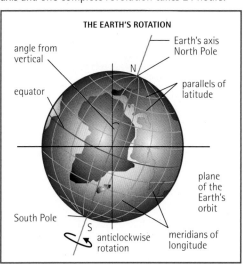

THE EARTH'S ROTATION

angle from vertical
Earth's axis North Pole
N
parallels of latitude
equator
plane of the Earth's orbit
South Pole
S
anticlockwise rotation
meridians of longitude

Earth's shape
The shape of the Earth is an oblate spheroid, which means that it is shaped like a ball but is slightly flattened at the poles. The gravitational force is slightly greater at the poles than at the equator, because of the shorter distance to the centre of the Earth.
SEE ALSO **gravitational force**

Earth's structure
The Earth's structure consists of distinct layers called the crust, mantle, outer core, and inner core.

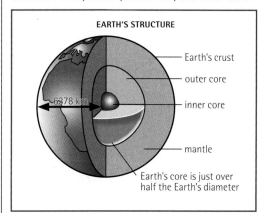

EARTH'S STRUCTURE

Earth's crust
outer core
6378 km
inner core
mantle
Earth's core is just over half the Earth's diameter

➤ **day and night** are caused by the rotation of the Earth on its axis: when a place on Earth faces the Sun it is day; when it faces away from the Sun it is night. The time taken for the Earth to make one complete revolution on its axis is 24 hours and is called a solar day.
SEE ALSO **Earth's axis, Earth's rotation**

WORD BUILD
crust
The Earth's crust is the outer 'skin' of the Earth, consisting of large plates of rock which are floating on the mantle. The **crust** is very thin in comparison with the overall diameter of the Earth. Its thickness varies between 5 km under the oceans to 70 km under the highest mountains. • *The density of the Earth's **crust** is 2 to 3 gcm³ and it includes continental crust and oceanic crust.* SEE ALSO **continental crust, oceanic crust**

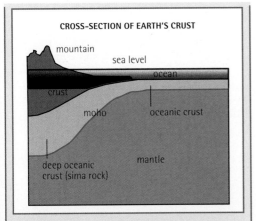

CROSS-SECTION OF EARTH'S CRUST

mountain

sea level

ocean

crust

moho

oceanic crust

deep oceanic
crust (sima rock)

mantle

mantle

The mantle is a thick layer of dense, semi-liquid rock which extends some 2,900 km below the Earth's crust. The density of this layer is 3.4 to 5.5 gcm^3 and the rock is rich in silicon and magnesium. Pressure and temperature increase deeper in the mantle, but even at the surface of the mantle some rocks are hot enough to be molten. Convection currents inside the mantle cause the plates of the Earth's crust to move.

SEE ALSO **plate tectonics**

moho (*also* Mohorovičić discontinuity)

The moho is the boundary between the Earth's crust and the mantle.

• *The moho was named after the Yugoslavian geophysicist Andrya Mohorovičić (1857–1936).*

inner core

The inner core is formed of solid rock at the centre of the Earth which is extremely dense and at very high temperature and pressure. The density of the inner core is 12 to 18 gm/cm^3.

outer core

The outer core is formed of dense liquid rock at very high temperatures, composed mainly of the dense magnetic elements nickel and iron. Its density is 10 to 12 gcm^3. The Earth's magnetic field arises from convection currents in the outer core, which generate electric currents and make the outer core act as an electromagnet.

earthworm

An earthworm is an invertebrate animal which lives in the soil. It is a hermaphrodite as each individual worm has both male and female reproductive organs.

• *Earthworms have no hard parts to support their body, which is kept in shape by the fluid inside them.*

SEE ALSO **annelid, hermaphrodite**

ecdysis (*also* moulting)

is the periodic loss of the cuticle in arthropods. Animals with exoskeletons can only grow by shedding their outer cuticle. The animal grows while the new cuticle is still soft. It is then hardened.

SEE ALSO **cuticle, exoskeleton**

echinoderm (*also* Echinodermata)

Echinoderms are marine invertebrates which have spiny skins and 'sucker feet'. These feet have water-filled canals which provide hydraulic power for movement, feeding, and respiration.

• *Echinoderms include starfish, sea urchins, sea cucumbers, and brittle stars.*

SEE ALSO **invertebrate animal**

echo

An echo is a reflection of a sound wave by a surface or an object so that a weaker version is detected after the original.

SEE ALSO **reflection**

echolocation

is a method of using the reflection of sound waves off an object to determine its exact position. If you measure the distance there and back to the object and the time taken for an echo to return, the speed of sound is the distance divided by the time.

• *Bats use echolocation when flying and hunting at night.*

SEE ALSO **echo, reflection**

eclipse

An eclipse is the total or partial blocking of sunlight when one celestial body (Earth or Moon) passes in between the Sun and the other celestial body.

lunar eclipse

A lunar eclipse occurs when the Earth moves into a position directly between the Sun and the Moon. As a result, an area of full shadow totally covers the Moon. Normally the Moon is out of line with the Earth, and the Sun's light falls on it to give a full moon.

»

LUNAR ECLIPSE (NOT TO SCALE)

SUN   Earth Moon

solar eclipse

A solar eclipse occurs when the Moon moves
into a position directly between the Sun and the
Earth. As a result, a circular shadow is cast on the
Earth. Such an eclipse appears as a total eclipse if
it is viewed from the umbra region, or as a partial
eclipse if viewed from the penumbra region.
• *Solar eclipses do not happen very often as,
although the Moon circles the Earth every
28 days, only rarely are all three celestial bodies
(Sun, Moon, and Earth) in a straight line.*
SEE ALSO **penumbra, umbra**

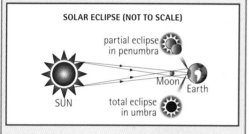

SOLAR ECLIPSE (NOT TO SCALE)

partial eclipse
in penumbra

Moon
Earth

SUN   total eclipse
in umbra

ecology

is the study of the interaction between different
living organisms, and between them and their
environment.
SEE ALSO **environment, organism**

ecosystem

An ecosystem is a biological community and the
physical environment that is associated with it.
Fxamples of natural ecosystems are woodland,
meadows, hedgerows, sand dunes, seashore,
marshland, pond, river, sea, etc.
• *A greenhouse is a managed ecosystem, in which
the temperature, humidity, and light can be
regulated and pests controlled.*
SEE ALSO **biosphere, community**

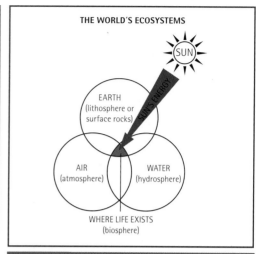

THE WORLD'S ECOSYSTEMS

SUN

SUN'S ENERGY

EARTH
(lithosphere or
surface rocks)

AIR
(atmosphere)

WATER
(hydrosphere)

WHERE LIFE EXISTS
(biosphere)

WORD BUILD

studying ecosystems

involves identifying living organisms within the
ecosystem and estimating the abundance of
each species. Identifying living organisms can be
helped by using biological keys. Estimating the
abundance of a species can be done by taking
samples using a quadrat or a transect. All samples
must be random, and the larger your sample, the
more reliable your estimate of abundance.
SEE ALSO **quadrat, transect**

studying ecosystems: mark, release, and recapture

is a method used to estimate the population
of organisms which move around. First capture,
let's say, 20 woodlice and mark each with a
small spot of waterproof paint. Release these
woodlice. After about 24 hours, capture another
20 woodlice. See how many have the spot of
paint. If 2 out of 20 do, then we can assume
that $\frac{2}{20}$ or $\frac{1}{10}$ of the population have been
recaptured, so 20 woodlice is about a $\frac{1}{10}$ of the
total population. The total population is around
200 woodlice.

ectotherm *see* cold-blooded animal

eczema

is a skin condition that causes the skin to become
dry, sore, and itchy.
• *Eczema can be caused by an allergy to pets or
to certain foods.*
SEE ALSO **allergy**

edaphic factor *see* abiotic factor

eddy current

Eddy currents are currents induced in a piece of metal when the magnetic field around it changes. Eddy currents are a nuisance, as they produce heat and waste energy.

• *In transformers the soft-iron core is laminated (layered into thin, varnished sheets) to reduce eddy currents.*

SEE ALSO **magnetic field, transformer**

effector

An effector is an organ such as a muscle or gland which can produce a response to a particular situation.

• *Information is transmitted to effectors by motor neurones.*

SEE ALSO **neurone**

efferent neurone *see* neurone

efficiency

is the ratio of usable energy output to energy input, expressed as a percentage. It can also be defined as work or power output divided by work or power input, expressed as a percentage.

• *Efficiency is a measure of how good a machine is at doing its job. Most machines lose useful energy through frictional forces, producing heat and sound.*

Device	Energy input	Energy output	Efficiency
petrol engine	100J	25J	25%
diesel engine	100J	35J	35%
human	100J	15J	15%
power station	100J	30J	30%
tungsten filament bulb	60J	3J (light)	5%
energy-efficient bulb	15J	5J (light)	33%
electric	100J	80J	80%

efflorescence

is a process by which some hydrated salts lose their water of crystallization. Washing soda (hydrated sodium carbonate $Na_2CO_3.10H_2O$), if left exposed to the air, is efflorescent and forms a white, powdery deposit of anhydrous sodium carbonate Na_2CO_3.

SEE ALSO **anhydrous, water of crystallization**

➤ **efflorescent** describes a hydrated salt that loses its water of crystallization and forms a powdery deposit.

effluent

is waste material discharged from factories and other industrial sites, which may contain heavy metals such as mercury, lead, and cadmium, and solvents or detergents.

• *Strict laws ensure that before effluent is discharged into natural water, it is treated to neutralize any harmful chemicals.*

SEE ALSO **water pollution**

egestion

is the removal of food such as plant fibre which cannot be digested or absorbed. It takes place through the anus. The material forms a semi-solid mass called faeces.

• *Egestion must not be confused with excretion.*

SEE ALSO **excretion, faeces**

egg *see* ovum

elasticity

is the property of a material of stretching when a force is applied to it and it cannot move. When the deforming force is removed, the material returns to its original shape provided that its elastic limit has not been reached.

• *Rubber, nylon, and coiled springs have elasticity.*

SEE ALSO **elastic limit, Hooke's law**

elastic limit

The elastic limit is the point beyond which a material loses elasticity and stops obeying Hooke's law. After this point, permanent deformation occurs.

SEE ALSO **elasticity, Hooke's law**

elastic potential energy (*also* E_e)

is the stored energy an object has as a result of stretching or compressing. For a spring, the energy can be calculated by the equation:

$$E_e \text{ (J)} = 0.5 \times \text{spring constant (N/m)} \times \text{(extension)}^2 \text{ (m)}$$

• *Elastic potential energy can be stored in objects like stretched elastic bands or squashed springs.*

SEE ALSO **energy store**

electrical circuit (*also* circuit)

An electrical circuit is a continuous, conducting path along which electric current can flow. This circuit may include a variety of electrical components such as lamps, resistors, and ammeters. These components may convert the electrical energy carried by the current into other forms of energy such as heat or light. Current is not 'used up' by the electrical components, but electrical energy is transferred.

SEE ALSO **electric current, household circuit**

»

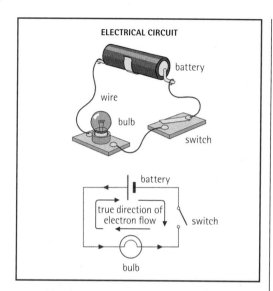

ELECTRICAL CIRCUIT

battery

wire

bulb

switch

battery

true direction of electron flow

switch

bulb

parallel circuit

A parallel circuit is formed when the components are arranged so that there is more than one path for the current to take. The current splits up and passes through each branch at the same time. The size of the current in each branch depends on the resistance of the branch. The total current is equal to the sum of all the currents in the branches. The potential difference, p.d., (voltage) is the same across each parallel component.

• *If a component in a parallel circuit breaks, then current can still pass through another branch.*

series circuit

A series circuit is formed when the components are arranged so that there is a single path for the current to take. The current passes through each component, one after another. The potential difference (voltage) across the battery is equal to the sum of all the p.d.'s across the components.

• *A disadvantage of series circuits is that if one component stops working, then no current will flow through the circuit.*

electrical circuit symbols

are used to represent electrical components. Common circuit symbols for various electrical components and devices are shown in the table.
SEE ALSO **electrical circuit**

electrical condenser *see* capacitor

electrical conductivity

is the ability of a substance to allow the passage of an electric current.

• *Good conductors have a high electrical conductivity. Insulators have a low conductivity.*
SEE ALSO **conductor, insulator, thermal conductivity**

electrical energy

is a form of energy which is carried by electric currents, and can be changed into other forms such as heat and light using various electrical appliances. The amount of electrical energy depends on how many electrons are flowing per second (current) and how much energy each is carrying (voltage). One joule of electrical energy is used when a current of 1 amp flows for 1 second (1 coulomb of charge) under a potential difference of 1 volt.

energy (J) = potential difference (V) × current (A) × time (s)

• *This electrical energy may be converted into heat or light.*
SEE ALSO **electric current, joule**

electrical power

is the rate at which electrical energy is converted into other forms, e.g.

$$\text{power (W)} = \frac{\frac{\text{electrical energy used (J)}}{\text{time (s)}}}{\text{time (s)}} = \frac{\text{Voltage}}{\text{(V)}} \times \frac{\text{(current)}}{\text{(A)}} = (\text{current})^2 \times \frac{\text{resistance}}{(\Omega')}$$

• *Electrical power is measured in watts or kilowatts (1 kW = 1,000 W) or megawatts (1 MW = 1,000,000 W).*
SEE ALSO **electrical energy, watt**

electrical relay *see* relay

electrical resistance *see* resistance

electric bell

An electric bell is a device which uses an electromagnet to operate a hammer striking a bell. It uses direct current which, when the switch closes, activates the electromagnet, which then pulls the hammer on to the bell. This breaks the circuit, which switches the electromagnet off, so that the hammer returns. The process repeats itself, with the hammer repeatedly striking the bell, until the bell push is released.
SEE ALSO **electromagnet**

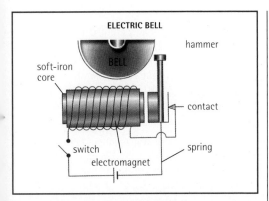

ELECTRIC BELL

hammer

soft-iron core

BELL

contact

switch

spring

electromagnet

electric charge (*also* **charge, Q**)

is the overall excess or deficiency of electrons on an object. If there is an excess of electrons, the object has an overall negative charge. If there is a deficiency of electrons, the object has an overall positive charge.

SEE ALSO **electron**

negative charge

results when electrons are gained by being 'rubbed off' on to a material. If a polythene rod is rubbed with a woollen cloth, some of the electrons on the cloth are rubbed on to the rod, and the rod becomes negatively charged.

positive charge

results when electrons are 'rubbed off' from the outermost shells of atoms. Normally atoms have equal numbers of protons (positive +) and electrons (negative -), so the overall net charge of a material is zero. If a Perspex (acetate) rod is rubbed with a woollen cloth, some of the electrons on the rod are rubbed off on to the cloth, and the rod becomes positively charged.

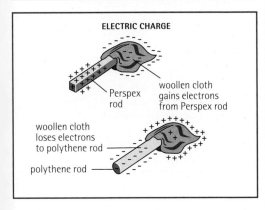

ELECTRIC CHARGE

Perspex rod

woollen cloth gains electrons from Perspex rod

woollen cloth loses electrons to polythene rod

polythene rod

electric current (*also* **current, I**)

An electric current is a flow of electric charge through a conductor. Current in an electrical circuit is measured in amperes.

• *If the conductor is a metal wire in an electrical circuit, then the electric charge is a flow of electrons. The size of the* **electric current** *is the rate of flow of electrons.*

SEE ALSO **alternating current, ampere, direct current, electric charge, electron**

electric field

An electric field is a region within which a particle bearing an electric charge experiences a force. The force is represented by 'electric field lines' which never cross each other. The intensity of the electric field is shown by the closeness of the lines. The direction of an electric field line shows the path that would be taken by a positive charge which was free to move in the field.

SEE ALSO **electric charge, electric potential**

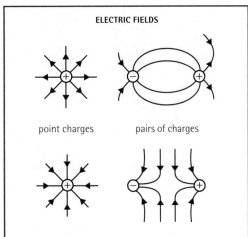

ELECTRIC FIELDS

point charges

pairs of charges

electricity

is the flow of charged particles. The charged particles may be electrons or ions.

• *Electricity flows around an electrical circuit as an electric current.*

SEE ALSO **electrical circuit, electric current**

electricity cable (*also* **power cable**)

Electricity cables usually have three insulated wires inside: live (brown wire), neutral (blue wire), and earth (yellow/green wire). The live and neutral wires carry the current and the earth wire is a safety device. If there is a fault (for example, if

»

a
b
c
d
e
f
g
h
i
j
k
l
m
n
o
p
q
r
s
t
u
v
w
x
y
z

the insulation around the live wire is worn) then the metal body of an appliance could become live and give a dangerous shock to anyone touching it. The earth wire 'earths' this current and blows the fuse.

SEE ALSO **fuse**

electric motor

An electric motor is a device which uses the motor effect to change electrical energy into mechanical energy. A simple direct current, d.c., motor consists of a flat coil of current-carrying wire placed in a magnetic field. One side of the coil experiences an upward force, and the other side a downward force, so the coil rotates to produce mechanical motion.

SEE ALSO **electrical energy, mechanical energy, motor effect**

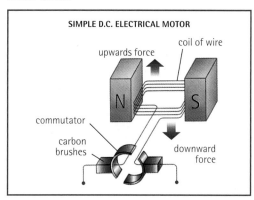

SIMPLE D.C. ELECTRICAL MOTOR

electric potential (also **electric potential energy**)

is the energy associated with a charge at a particular point within an electric field. It is calculated by considering the work which must be done to move a small positive charge from 'earth' to that particular point. For convenience, earth potential is given a value of zero.

$$\text{electric potential (V)} = \frac{\text{work done (J)}}{\text{charge moved (C)}}$$
$$\text{or } V = \frac{W}{Q}$$

• The **electric potential** needed to do 1 joule of work on a charge of 1 coulomb is the equivalent to 1 volt.

SEE ALSO **electric field, potential difference, volt**

electrode

An electrode is a piece of metal or carbon (graphite) placed in an electrolyte which allows electric current to enter and leave during electrolysis.

SEE ALSO **anode, cathode, electrolysis, electrolyte**

electrolysis

is the process by which an electric current flowing through a liquid containing ions causes the liquid to undergo chemical decomposition.

• During **electrolysis**, the electric current is carried not by electrons but by the movement of the ions.

SEE ALSO **electrolyte ion, ionic theory of electrolysis**

electrolyte

Electrolytes are liquids which conduct electricity. All ionic compounds when molten or in aqueous solution are electrolytes, as their ions are free to move. (Liquid metals, in which the conduction is by free electrons, are not regarded as electrolytes.)

SEE ALSO **ionic bond**

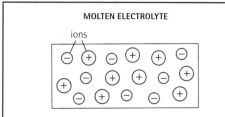

MOLTEN ELECTROLYTE

non-electrolyte

Non-electrolytes are liquids which do not conduct electricity. Such liquids contain covalent molecules which cannot carry electric current.

SEE ALSO **covalent bond**

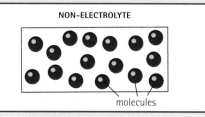

NON-ELECTROLYTE

strong electrolyte

Strong electrolytes are liquids with a high concentration of ions.

• Strong acids and alkalis are **strong electrolytes**, as their aqueous solutions are fully ionized.

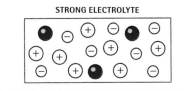

STRONG ELECTROLYTE

weak electrolyte

Weak electrolytes are liquids with a low concentration of ions.
• *Weak acids and alkalis are* **weak electrolytes**, *as their aqueous solutions are only partially ionized.*

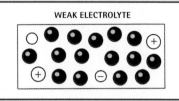

WEAK ELECTROLYTE

electrolytic reduction

is the use of a cathode during electrolysis to donate electrons and cause reduction.

SEE ALSO **cathode, electrolysis, reduction**

electrolytic refining *see* electrorefining

electromagnet

An electromagnet is a solenoid with a core of ferromagnetic material such as soft iron. This forms a temporary magnet which can be switched on and off simply by switching the current on and off.
• *Electromagnets have many uses as switches and in turning electrical energy into mechanical energy.*

SEE ALSO **core, electromagnetism, solenoid**

electromagnetic force

is the force (F) acting on a current-carrying conductor placed at right angles to a magnetic field. The size of this force depends on three variables:

– magnetic flux density (B)
– size of current (I)
– length of conductor (L)

$$\text{Force (F)} = \frac{\text{magnetic flux density (B)}}{} \times \text{current (I)} \times \frac{\text{length of conductor (L)}}{}$$

An increase in any of these three variables causes an increase in the magnitude (size) of the force.
• *Electromagnetic forces are used in many types of electric switches.*

SEE ALSO **conductor, electric current, force, magnetic flux density**

electromagnetic induction

is the creation of an electromotive force (emf) in a conductor which is moving in a magnetic field, or is placed in a changing magnetic field. Current only flows when the wire is cutting through magnetic field lines. If the wire is stationary, or moves parallel to the magnetic field lines, there is no induced emf.

SEE ALSO **electromotive force, magnetic field**

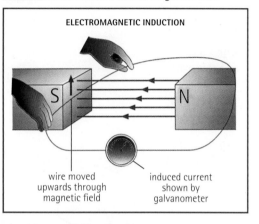

ELECTROMAGNETIC INDUCTION

wire moved upwards through magnetic field

induced current shown by galvanometer

electromagnetic spectrum

The electromagnetic spectrum is the range of frequencies over which electromagnetic waves are propagated. Although the spectrum is continuous it can be split into seven overlapping regions (see table).

SEE ALSO **electromagnetic wave**

➤ **interaction of waves with matter** The waves at each end of the electromagnetic spectrum tend to pass through materials. Waves nearer the middle of the spectrum tend to be absorbed. When the waves are absorbed by metals, they produce heat, and also create a tiny alternating current with the same frequency as the radiation.

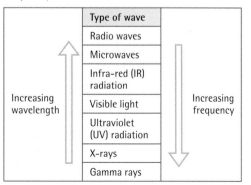

	Type of wave	
	Radio waves	
	Microwaves	
	Infra-red (IR) radiation	
Increasing wavelength	Visible light	Increasing frequency
	Ultraviolet (UV) radiation	
	X-rays	
	Gamma rays	

electromagnetic wave

Electromagnetic waves are transverse waves produced by oscillating electric and magnetic fields at right angles to one another. They do not require a medium in which to propagate and can travel through a vacuum. As waves, they undergo reflection, refraction, and diffraction. For example, radio waves of long and medium wavelengths can be reflected off the ionosphere. This allows signals to travel great distances without being blocked by the curvature of the Earth. They can also be bent by diffraction, e.g. when travelling over a hill.

SEE ALSO **diffraction, reflection, refraction, transverse wave**

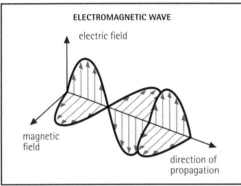

ELECTROMAGNETIC WAVE

electric field

magnetic field

direction of propagation

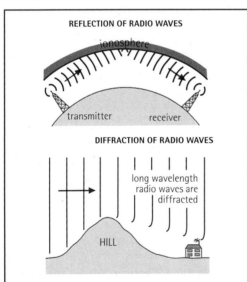

REFLECTION OF RADIO WAVES

ionosphere

transmitter   receiver

DIFFRACTION OF RADIO WAVES

long wavelength radio waves are diffracted

HILL

electromagnetism

is the combination of an electric field and a magnetic field and their interaction to produce a force. When an electric current flows in an insulated, straight wire, it produces a circular magnetic field around the wire. This field can be plotted using a small compass. The direction of the field depends upon the direction of the current in the wire.

• *Electromagnetism is important in electric motors, in generators, and in making powerful electromagnets.*

SEE ALSO **electric field, electric motor, electromagnet, generator, magnetic field**

electromotive force (*also* emf)

is equivalent to the potential difference across the terminals of a battery when it is not supplying a current. Like all electrical components, batteries have a resistance. This is called 'internal resistance'. This causes a drop in p.d. when the circuit is complete and current flows. Electromotive force can be regarded as the 'total p.d.' including the p.d. lost across the internal resistance of the battery.

• *Electromotive force is measured in volts.*

SEE ALSO **battery, potential difference, resistance, volt**

electron

An electron is a negatively charged, subatomic particle which is found orbiting the nucleus of atoms. Its charge is equal, but opposite, to that of a proton. However, its mass is only $\frac{1}{1840}$ th that of a proton or neutron. The chemical properties of the atom are determined by these orbiting electrons, in particular the outermost ones.

SEE ALSO **neutron, proton, subatomic particle**

electron acceptor *see* oxidizing agent

electron donor *see* reducing agent

electronics

is a branch of physics and technology concerned with the study and use of small electric currents passed through semiconductors and gases at low pressure. Many electronic components are used as switches in circuits because their ability to conduct electricity can be affected by factors like current direction (as with a diode), temperature (as with a thermistor), and light (as with a light-dependent resistor).

SEE ALSO **diode, light–dependent resistor, thermistor**

electronic structure (*also* electronic configuration)

is how the electrons are arranged in the various electron shells around the nucleus of an atom.

SEE ALSO **electron shell**

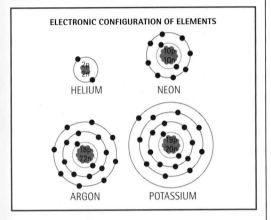

ELECTRONIC CONFIGURATION OF ELEMENTS

HELIUM   NEON

ARGON   POTASSIUM

electronic switch

Electronic switches are transistors and other electronic components which can be activated under different conditions. A potential divider is used to vary the voltage across the base and the emitter of the transistor. Resistors R_1 and R_2 (see diagram) form the potential divider, as they divide the voltage from the battery. When $R_2 \gg R_1$ there will be a high voltage between the base and the emitter, and a low voltage and small current going to the base. The transistor will switch on.

SEE ALSO **potential divider, transistor**

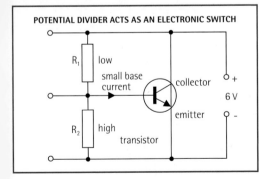

POTENTIAL DIVIDER ACTS AS AN ELECTRONIC SWITCH

heat-sensitive switch

A heat-sensitive switch is an electronic switch which responds to changes in temperature. The thermistor has a high resistance at low temperature and therefore has a high voltage across it. This means that there is a low voltage across the bottom resistor R, so there is no current from the base to the emitter and the transistor and bulb are switched off. When the temperature rises, the thermistor's resistance falls and the situation is reversed. The potential difference across resistor R becomes large enough for current to flow from the base to the emitter, so the transistor switches on and the warning bulb lights up.

SEE ALSO **thermistor**

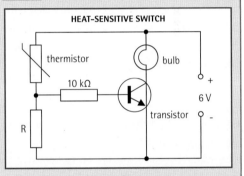

HEAT-SENSITIVE SWITCH

light-sensitive switch

A light-sensitive switch is an electronic switch which responds to changes in light intensity. The light-dependent resistor (LDR) has a high resistance in the dark and therefore has a high voltage across it. In the dark, the potential difference becomes large enough for current to flow from the base to the emitter, and the transistor switches on, so the bulb lights up. In the light, the transistor and lamp are switched off, as the potential difference between the base and the emitter is very low.

SEE ALSO **light-dependent resistor**

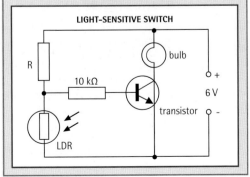

LIGHT-SENSITIVE SWITCH

electronic system

Electronic systems typically consist of input sensors which feed information into a processor, which is then connected to an output device controlled by the processor.

electron micrograph *see* microscope

electron microscope *see* microscope

electron shell

An electron shell is a group of electrons that share the same 'orbit' around the nucleus of an atom. These electrons are moving rapidly and at relatively great distances from the tiny nucleus. Each electron has its own specific orbit.

• *The first electron shell can hold up to two electrons, the second shell up to eight electrons.*

SEE ALSO atom, electronic configuration, energy level, nucleus

electrophoresis

is a technique for the analysis and separation of colloids.

• *Electrophoresis is extensively used when studying proteins, enzymes, carbohydrates, etc.*

SEE ALSO carbohydrate, colloid, enzyme, protein

electroplating

is the coating of a metal object with a thin layer of another metal by electrolysis. The object to be plated becomes the cathode, and the plating metal becomes the anode. The electrolyte is an aqueous solution of a salt of the plating metal.

SEE ALSO anode, cathode, electrolysis

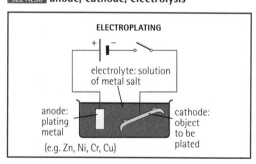

ELECTROPLATING

electrolyte: solution of metal salt

anode: plating metal (e.g. Zn, Ni, Cr, Cu)

cathode: object to be plated

electrorefining (*also* electrolytic refining)

is a method of purifying metals such as copper by electrolysis. The impure copper is made the anode. Copper ions dissolve and travel from the anode to the cathode where pure copper builds up. Impurities do not dissolve, and fall to the bottom as 'anode sludge'.

• *The sludge from electrorefining may contain valuable impurities (silver, gold) which are extracted by further electrolysis.*

SEE ALSO anode, cathode, electrolysis

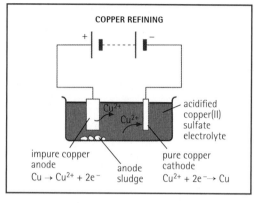

COPPER REFINING

acidified copper(II) sulfate electrolyte

impure copper anode
$Cu \rightarrow Cu^{2+} + 2e^-$

anode sludge

pure copper cathode
$Cu^{2+} + 2e^- \rightarrow Cu$

electroscope

An electroscope is an instrument for detecting small amounts of electric charge.

• *In the gold leaf electroscope the insulated metal rod becomes charged so the gold leaf is repelled away from the rod. The greater the charge, the more the gold leaf rises.*

SEE ALSO electric charge

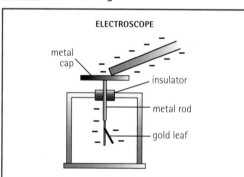

ELECTROSCOPE

metal cap

insulator

metal rod

gold leaf

electrostatic force (*also* coulomb force)

is the force of attraction or repulsion between charged particles or materials.

• *If the charged particles or materials have an opposite charge there is an attractive electrostatic force. If they have a similar charge then there is a repulsive electrostatic force.*

SEE ALSO non-contact force

➤ **law of electrostatics** The law of electrostatics states that like charges (two positive charges or two negative charges) repel one another, and unlike charges (positive and negative charges) attract each other. The closer the charges, the greater the force between them.

electrostatic smoke precipitator

An electrostatic smoke or dust precipitator is used in chimneys or extractor ducts to remove fine particles of soot or dust. It does this by passing the smoke between charged plates, which induces a charge on the tiny particles and attracts them onto the plates. Periodically the electricity is switched off, and the dust falls off the plates and is collected.

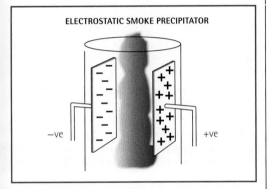

ELECTROSTATIC SMOKE PRECIPITATOR

element

An element is a substance that cannot be broken down into two or more simpler substances by chemical means. Atoms of one particular element have the same number of protons.
• *There are 92 naturally occurring* **elements,** *and each is given a chemical symbol.*
SEE ALSO **atom, chemical symbol**

embryo

An embryo is the organism formed by mitosis in the zygote so that it is a ball of cells. It takes several hours for the embryo to reach the uterus, and by this time the ball has 16 or 32 cells.
SEE ALSO **mitosis, uterus, zygote**

emf *see* electromotive force

emission of radiation *see* radiation

empirical formula *see* chemical formula

emulsion *see* colloid

endocrine gland (*also* ductless gland)

Endocrine glands are glands in an animal that secrete hormones directly into the bloodstream. These hormones dissolve in the plasma and then act at a distant site in the body.
SEE ALSO **adrenal gland, hormone, thyroid gland**

endoplasmic reticulum *see* organelle

endoskeleton

An endoskeleton is a skeleton that lies entirely inside the body of an animal.
• *The bony skeletons of vertebrate mammals (like the human skeleton) are* **endoskeletons.**
SEE ALSO **exoskeleton**

endotherm *see* warm-blooded animal

endothermic reaction

An endothermic reaction is a chemical reaction during which heat energy is taken in from the surroundings.
• *All* **endothermic reactions** *are accompanied by a temperature fall in the surroundings.*
SEE ALSO **chemical reaction, exothermic reaction, reaction profile**

Endothermic reactions			
Thermal decomposition	calcium carbonate ($CaCO_3$)	$\rightarrow$ calcium oxide (CaO)	+ carbon dioxide (CO_2)
Dissolving	ammonium nitrate	$\rightarrow$ water +	ammonium nitrate solution
Photosynthesis	carbon dioxide ($6CO_2$) +	water ($6H_2O$) $\rightarrow$	glucose ($C_6H_{12}O_6$) + oxygen ($6O_2$)

energy

is the capacity of a system to do work. The word is used in everyday life to describe the ability to do something useful. When work is done on or by an object, then the object gains or loses energy respectively. Energy exists in various forms and is only useful when converted from one form to another.
• *All forms of* **energy** *are measured in joules.*
SEE ALSO **chemical energy, kinetic energy store, mechanical energy, potential energy, work**

➤ **forms of energy** There are many different manifestations of energy. Some important forms are electricity, heat energy, sound, electromagnetic waves, and nuclear energy.
SEE ALSO **electrical energy, electromagnetic wave, heat energy, nuclear energy, sound**

energy conservation

is the process of not wasting energy resources. It is important to burn fuels efficiently, so they last longer, reducing the loss of energy as waste heat.
• *Energy conservation can also be achieved by using energy-efficient light bulbs, insulated buildings, and economical car engines.*

energy conversion *see* energy transfer

energy level

is the particular energy associated with an electron shell that surrounds the nucleus in a particular atom. The further from the nucleus, the higher the energy of the electron shell.
SEE ALSO **electron shell, nucleus**

energy level diagram *see* reaction profile

energy source

non-renewable energy source

A non-renewable energy source is one that cannot be replaced once it has been used up. Fossil fuels are non-renewable energy sources (also called 'non-replenishable' or 'finite' energy sources). It has been estimated that most of the Earth's resources of natural gas and oil will be used up within the next hundred years. Coal may last about 300 years.
SEE ALSO **fossil fuel**

renewable energy source (*also* replenishable energy source)

A renewable energy source is one that can be renewed (e.g. wood, which can be replaced by planting more trees). Wind, wave, biofuel, and biogas are renewable energy sources and all depend on the Sun's energy. Tidal and hydroelectric energy depend on the force of gravity.
SEE ALSO **biofuel, biogas, geothermal energy, hydroelectricity, solar energy, tidal energy, wave energy, wind power**

Renewable energy source	Advantages
Hydroelectric	1 pollution-free 2 immediate response to demand 3 no fuel required
Wind	1 pollution-free 2 no fuel required
Geothermal	1 pollution-free 2 no fuel required

Renewable energy source	Disadvantages
Hydroelectric	1 big impact on environment 2 initial costs high 3 limited to mountainous areas
Wind	1 unsightly as need large number of turbines 2 noisy
Geothermal	1 costs of drilling 2 limited to few places

energy store

An energy store is a form of energy that is stored so that it can be released at a later time.
• *Energy stores include these forms of energy: gravitational potential energy, chemical potential energy, elastic potential energy, kinetic energy, and thermal energy.*
SEE ALSO **chemical potential energy, elastic potential energy, gravitational potential energy store, kinetic energy store, thermal energy**

energy transfer (*also* **energy conversion**)

occurs when one energy form is changed into another energy form. Energy can be transferred by heat, waves (sound and light), electricity, or a force (leading to work being done). The original source of energy is often the Sun. The Sun's energy can be stored as chemical potential energy in fossil fuels and food. This can be released by burning or respiration to provide kinetic energy and heat energy, which can then be converted into electrical energy, sound energy, etc.
SEE ALSO **chemical potential energy**

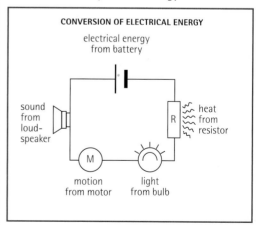

CONVERSION OF ELECTRICAL ENERGY

law of conservation of energy

This law states that energy cannot be created or destroyed but can be converted from one form to another. In any energy transfer the total number of joules of energy at the beginning and the end is the same, but the quality of energy is reduced because some of it is converted to waste heat (random thermal energy).

SEE ALSO **thermal energy**

E number

An E number is a code for permitted chemicals that can be used as food additives within the European Union and European Free Trade Association.

• *E numbers used in a particular food are commonly listed on the food label.*

environment

The environment consists of all the conditions in which a living organism exists.

• *Soil, climate, and other living organisms all count as part of the environment.*

environmental variation *see* variation

enzyme

An enzyme is a protein which alters the rate of a particular biochemical reaction. Enzymes are often called 'biological catalysts'. Enzymes are produced in living cells and work mostly in the cytoplasm. They work best at the normal temperature of the living cell, and within a narrow range of pH, which may be different for each enzyme.

• *Certain enzymes help in the chemical breakdown of food and are called digestive enzymes.*

SEE ALSO **active site, cell, cytoplasm, denaturing, protein, substrate**

Type of enzyme	Carbohydrase e.g. amylase
Where it is made	salivary glands pancreas intestine
Where it works	mouth small intestine
Which reaction it speeds up	breaks down starch into sugars

Type of enzyme	Protease e.g. pepsin, trypsin
Where it is made	stomach pancreas intestine wall
Where it works	stomach small intestine
Which reaction it speeds up	breaks down proteins to amino acids

Type of enzyme	Lipase
Where it is made	pancreas small intestine
Where it works	small intestine
Which reaction it speeds up	breaks down fat to fatty acids and glycerol

immobilized enzyme

Immobilized enzymes are insoluble enzymes which can be reused in industrial processes. An enzyme which does not dissolve but still allows the substrate to react with it can then be used again, which reduces waste. Such enzymes are called 'immobilized enzymes', as they are fixed in insoluble substances on permanent supports. The substrate flows over them and the enzyme catalyzes the reaction.

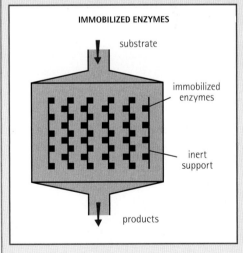

IMMOBILIZED ENZYMES

substrate

immobilized enzymes

inert support

products

epicentre *see* earthquake

epidermis

❶ The epidermis is the outer, protective layer of the skin. It consists of a living layer of epithelial tissue (the Malpighian layer) and a hard layer of dead cells (the cornified layer).

SEE ALSO **cornified layer, Malpighian layer, skin**

❷ The epidermis is the layer of cells covering the top and bottom of a leaf.

SEE ALSO **cuticle, leaf, mesophyll layer**

epiglottis

The epiglottis is a valve-like flap of cartilage which closes off the trachea or windpipe and prevents food from going into the lungs when you swallow.

SEE ALSO **cartilage, trachea**

epithelium (*also* epithelial tissue)

Epithelium is tissue which lines cavities or tubes in the body such as the intestines, bladder, and lungs.

• *Some epithelial tissue is permeable, and some is glandular, containing goblet cells which secrete mucus.*

SEE ALSO **mucous membrane, tissue**

equations of motion (*also* kinematic equations)

Equations of motion are equations used to solve problems involving moving objects.

$v = u + at$

$s = \frac{1}{2}(v + u)t$

$s = ut + 1\,at^2$

$v^2 = u^2 + 2as$

s = distance (m)

v = final velocity (m s^{-1})

u = initial velocity (m s^{-1})

a = acceleration (m s^{-2})

t = time (s)

$$\text{speed} = \frac{\text{distance travelled}}{\text{time taken}}$$

$$\text{acceleration} = \frac{\text{change in speed}}{\text{time taken}}$$

equator

The equator is an imaginary line around the Earth that is exactly halfway between the North and South Poles.

• *The equator divides the Earth into the northern and southern hemispheres.*

SEE ALSO **latitude**

equilibrium

occurs when the overall clockwise moments acting on an object are equal to the overall anticlockwise moments.

SEE ALSO **chemical equilibrium, dynamic equilibrium, isolated system, phase equilibrium, static equilibrium**

neutral equilibrium

is the state of an object which, when moved a small distance from its equilibrium position, remains in the new position. This happens when the centre of gravity remains at the same height (as with a ball).

SEE ALSO **centre of gravity**

stable equilibrium (*also* stability)

is the state of an object which will return to its original position when tilted. This happens if the centre of gravity is raised when the object is moved. Stability of objects is increased by having a low centre of gravity and a wide base.

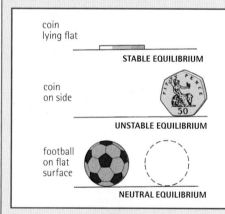

coin lying flat — **STABLE EQUILIBRIUM**

coin on side — **UNSTABLE EQUILIBRIUM**

football on flat surface — **NEUTRAL EQUILIBRIUM**

unstable equilibrium

is the state of an object which will not return to its original position when tilted. For such objects, the slightest movement causes the centre of gravity to move to a lower position.

equinox
An equinox is the time of year when both day and night are of equal lengths (12 hours each). Equinoxes occur when the Sun appears to cross over the equator. This occurs twice a year. In the northern hemisphere the spring or vernal equinox is about March 21st and the autumn equinox about September 22nd. The dates are reversed for the southern hemisphere.
SEE ALSO **day and night, solstice**

erosion
is the removal of the weathered parts of rock.
• *Erosion always involves movement, and rock particles can be carried away by rain, wind, rivers, and streams, or the movement of glaciers.*
SEE ALSO **weathering**

error of parallax *see* parallax error

erythrocyte *see* red blood cell

escape speed *see* escape velocity

escape velocity (*also* escape speed)
is the minimum speed a satellite must travel to escape the Earth's gravitational pull. For example, a rocket must travel at speeds of greater than 11.2 km s^{-1} to escape into space. This velocity is such that it gives a greater kinetic energy to the rocket than the potential energy resulting from the gravitational pull of the Earth.
SEE ALSO **kinetic energy store, potential energy, satellite**

ester
Esters are organic compounds formed by the reaction of a carboxylic acid and alcohol. For example, if ethanoic acid is warmed with ethanol, in the presence of a few drops of concentrated sulfuric acid (hydrogen ions are the catalyst), then the ester ethyl ethanoate is formed.
• *Esters are volatile, fragrant substances used in perfumes and as flavourings in the food industry.*
SEE ALSO **alcohol, carboxylic acid**

ethanoic acid (*also* acetic acid)
is a carboxylic acid formed by the oxidation of ethanol. It is a weak organic acid and it is used for flavourings and as a preservative.
• *Vinegar contains 5% ethanoic acid.*
SEE ALSO **carboxylic acid**

ethanol
Ethanol (CH_3CH_2OH) is the commonest alcohol, and is a colourless, water-soluble liquid (boiling point 78°C). It is formed in beers, wines, and spirits by the process of fermentation, which is also one method of large-scale production, if sugar is plentiful. However, it is sometimes more economical to produce ethanol from ethene gas obtained by cracking petroleum fractions. The reaction involves passing ethene and steam over a catalyst of phosphoric(V) acid at 300°C and 60 atmospheres pressure.

$$C_2H_4 \quad + \quad H_2O \quad \rightarrow \quad C_2H_5OH$$
$$\text{ethene} \quad + \quad \text{water (steam)} \quad \rightarrow \quad \text{ethanol}$$

The most important chemical properties of ethanol are combustion and oxidation.

➤ **combustion of ethanol** Like all alcohols, ethanol burns in a plentiful supply of air to form carbon dioxide and steam. The reaction gives out lots of heat energy and is exothermic. Ethanol is sometimes used as a fuel in cars or rockets.

➤ **oxidation of ethanol** If left exposed in the air, ethanol turns 'sour'. This is the common fate of wines and beers which are opened but not drunk. The reason is that the ethanol has been oxidized to ethanoic acid (vinegar).

$$C_2H_5OH \quad + \quad 3O_2 \quad \rightarrow \quad 2CO_2 \quad + \quad 3H_2O$$
$$\text{ethanol} + \text{oxygen} \rightarrow \text{carbon dioxide} + \text{water (steam)}$$

$$C_2H_5OH \quad + \quad O_2 \quad \rightarrow \quad CH_3COOH \quad + \quad H_2O$$
$$\text{ethanol} + \text{oxygen} \rightarrow \text{ethanoic acid} + \text{water}$$

SEE ALSO **fermentation**

eukaryote
A eukaryote is an organism like a plant or an animal whose cells have a cell membrane, cytoplasm, and genetic material enclosed in a nucleus.
• *Eukaryotes include all organisms except bacteria.*
SEE ALSO **cell membrane, cytoplasm, nucleus**

eureka can (*also* displacement can)
A eureka can is used to find the volume of an irregularly shaped object. The object is completely submerged in the eureka can, which is first filled with water. The volume of the water displaced is equal to the volume of the object. If its mass is known, its density can be calculated.
SEE ALSO **density, density bottle**

»

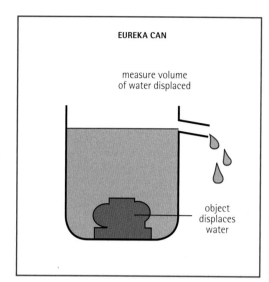

EUREKA CAN

measure volume
of water displaced

object
displaces
water

Eustachian tube
The Eustachian tube connects the middle ear to the
back of the throat. It helps to equalize the pressure
on both sides of the eardrum, allowing it to vibrate.
Unequal pressure causes the ears to 'pop'.
SEE ALSO **middle ear**

eutrophication (*also* **unintentional enrichment**)
is an overgrowth of aquatic plants like algae caused
by the presence of dissolved fertilizers or untreated
sewage, which are rich in nitrates and phosphates.
These plants use up the oxygen in water, causing the
death of fish and other aquatic life.
SEE ALSO **leaching, water pollution**

evaporation
is the process of a liquid changing into a vapour at
temperatures below its boiling point. It only occurs
on the surface of a liquid when a particle has by
chance sufficient energy to escape.
• *After* evaporation *the remaining particles in
the liquid have a lower temperature (lower kinetic
energy).*
SEE ALSO **boiling point, kinetic energy store**

direct evaporation
is used to separate a dissolved solid from a
solution by heating. The solvent evaporates and
the solute is left behind.
SEE ALSO **solute, solvent**

steam evaporation
is slow evaporation by heating the solution
using a water bath. It is useful if the solvent is
flammable and also prevents loss of solute due to
spitting.
SEE ALSO **solute, solvent**

evergreen
describes trees and shrubs that do not lose
their leaves in winter. Holly, pine trees, and ivy
are evergreen plants. The leaves of evergreens
are often reduced in size or adapted to reduce
excessive water loss. Examples include the
leathery, waxy leaves of the holly or the thin
needles of pine trees.
• *Evergreen plants are common in tropical
countries where there is little difference between
the seasons.*

evolution
is the gradual changing of a species of living
organism over a long period of time.
SEE ALSO **Darwinism, natural selection**

➤ **evidence for evolution** comes from fossils,
and from homologous and vestigial structures.
Comparison of fossil records show the gradual
change over millions of years. Fossils can be
accurately dated by radioactive carbon dating.
However, there are many missing links, as most
organisms decay almost completely and leave no
fossil remains. Very occasionally an organism is
found completely preserved (e.g. a mammoth in
a glacier, or an insect in the fossilized resin called
amber).
SEE ALSO **carbon dating, fossil, homologous
structure, vestigial structure**

excretion
is the removal of waste products formed as a result
of biochemical reactions inside a living organism.
Excretion is important in maintaining a constant
internal environment in the organism (homeostasis).
In mammals, the important excretory organs are the
lungs (which excrete carbon dioxide), skin (which
excretes sweat), and kidneys.
SEE ALSO **homeostasis, kidney, lung, skin**

➤ **excrete** A living organism excretes when it
removes waste products from inside it.

➤ **excretory** describes a process or organ that
relates to excretion

exhalation *see* expiration

exocrine gland

Exocrine glands are glands which secrete substances through a duct (tube) directly to the organ or body surface where it is needed.

• *Digestive glands such as the pancreas, gastric glands, and salivary glands are exocrine glands.*

SEE ALSO **pancreas**

exoskeleton

An exoskeleton is a skeleton found on the outside of the animal. Examples are the bony plates of tortoises, the shells of molluscs, the hard shell of crustaceans, and the hard cuticle of arthropods.

SEE ALSO **endoskeleton**

exosphere *see* atmosphere

exothermic reaction

An exothermic reaction is a chemical reaction during which heat energy is transferred to the surroundings.

• *All exothermic reactions are accompanied by a temperature rise in the surroundings.*

SEE ALSO **chemical reaction, endothermic reaction, reaction profile**

Exothermic reactions		
Combustion	carbon (C) + oxygen (O_2) →	carbon dioxide (CO_2)
Respiration	glucose ($C_6H_{12}O_6$) + oxygen ($6O_2$) →	carbon dioxide ($6CO_2$) + water ($6H_2O$)
Neutralization	sodium hydroxide (NaOH)) + hydrochloric acid (HCl) →	sodium chloride (NaCl) + water ($6H_2O$)

expand

To expand is to become larger normally because of an increase in surrounding temperature. Gases expand more than liquids which expand more than solids. This is because the particles in gases are free to move and as the temperature is increased they gain energy and move much further apart.

• *Liquid mercury is a good conductor of heat and expands when it gets warmer. It is used in mercury thermometers to record temperature rise.*

SEE ALSO **thermometric liquid**

expansion of the universe *see* universe

experiment

An experiment involves testing an idea (hypothesis) by changing one variable at a time and controlling other variables that might affect the results.

SEE ALSO **scientific variable**

expiration (*also* exhalation)

is the movement of air out of the lungs by the diaphragm relaxing upwards and the intercostal muscles relaxing so that the ribcage moves inwards.

SEE ALSO **diaphragm, intercostal muscle**

extensor muscle *see* muscle

external ear *see* outer ear

external fertilization *see* fertilization

external respiration *see* gaseous exchange

extinction

is the complete and irreversible disappearance of all living members of a species or group of organisms from the Earth. Examples are the dinosaurs, mammoths, and the dodo of Mauritius. Evidence about extinct species comes only from their fossil remains.

• *Extinction of species can be caused by destruction of habitat (e.g. deforestation), by hunting (e.g. overfishing), or by disease.*

extracellular digestion *see* digestion

extraction of alkali metals *see* alkali metal

extraction of metals

The method used to extract a metal depends upon its position in the reactivity series. The extraction of a metal from its ore involves the metal ion gaining electrons and is therefore reduction. Metals which are high in the series form stable compounds, and must be extracted by electrolytic reduction. Middle-order metals can be extracted by heating strongly with a reducing agent (smelting). Metals low in the reactivity series form unstable compounds, and can be extracted just by heating the ore.

SEE ALSO **aluminium extraction, blast furnace, electrolytic reduction, metal, ore, reactivity series, reducing agent, reduction, smelting**

»

Metal	Main ore	Main constituent
potassium	carnallite	$KMgCl_3$
sodium	rock salt	$NaCl$
calcium	chalk	$CaCO_3$
magnesium	dolomite	$CaMg(CO_3)_2$
aluminium	bauxite	Al_2O_3
zinc	zinc blende	ZnS
iron	haematite	Fe_2O_3
tin	tinstone	SnO_2
lead	galena	PbS
copper	copper pyrites	$CuFeS_2$
mercury	cinnabar	HgS

Metal	Extraction method
potassium sodium calcium magnesium aluminium	electrolyte extraction in which the metal is deposited at the cathode
zinc iron tin lead	extraction by heating with coke (carbon) in a furnace
copper mercury	roasting by heating the ore

extremophile

An extremophile is a microorganism that lives in extreme conditions (e.g. extreme heat, cold, pressure, or pH) that are harmful to most forms of life.

• *Extremophiles live in environments like deserts, ice caps, deep sea vents, and underground inside hot, molten rock.*

SEE ALSO **microorganism** .

extrinsic muscle

Extrinsic muscles are the muscles attached to the outside of the eyeball which allow the eye to move and rotate so that it can follow and focus on objects.

SEE ALSO **eye**

extrusive rock see rock

eye

The eye is the organ of sight, which focuses and detects light and passes nerve impulses to the brain via the optic nerve.

SEE ALSO **aqueous humour, blind spot, choroid, cones, conjunctiva, cornea, extrinsic muscle, fovea, iris, lens, orbit, pupil, retina, rods, sclerotic, vitreous humour**

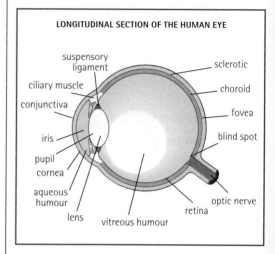

LONGITUDINAL SECTION OF THE HUMAN EYE

suspensory ligament — ciliary muscle — conjunctiva — iris — pupil — cornea — aqueous humour — lens — vitreous humour — sclerotic — choroid — fovea — blind spot — optic nerve — retina

eye socket see orbit

eye-tooth see tooth

Ff

F *see* **focal point, force**

f *see* **focal length, frequency**

F_1 (first filial generation)
is the first generation of offspring in a genetic cross (in humans, the children).

F_2 (second filial generation)
is the second generation of offspring in a genetic cross (in humans, the grandchildren).

factor
A factor is something that affects the results in an experiment.
• *Factors which affect how well a plant grows are how much light and water it has and the surrounding temperature.*
SEE ALSO **scientific variable**

faeces
is undigested food that is eliminated through the anus.
SEE ALSO **defecation, egestion**

Fahrenheit scale
The Fahrenheit scale is a temperature scale in which the temperature of boiling water is taken as 212°F and the temperature of melting ice as 32°F. Average body temperature in adults is 98.6°F. To convert to the Celsius scale the formula is

$$C = \frac{5(F-32)}{9}$$

• *The Fahrenheit scale was named after the German physicist Gabriel Fahrenheit (1686–1736). It is rarely used in scientific work.*
SEE ALSO **Celsius scale**

fair test
A fair test is one in which only one variable is changed each time measurements are made.
SEE ALSO **scientific method, scientific variable**

Fallopian tube *see* **oviduct**

fall-out
is radioactive particles that fall to Earth from the atmosphere. Increased levels of radioactive fall-out result from a nuclear explosion. An accident in 1986 at the nuclear reactor at Chernobyl in the Ukraine resulted in fall-out over large populated areas. The most hazardous radioactive isotopes in fall-out are strontium-90 and iodine-131. Both can be taken in by grazing animals (sheep, cows) and then passed on to humans in milk, milk products, and meat. Strontium-90 accumulates in the bones and iodine-131 in the thyroid gland.
SEE ALSO **radioactivity, radioisotope**

faraday
A faraday is a quantity of electric charge equivalent to the Avogadro constant (6.02×10^{23}) of electrons.
• *A faraday can be defined as a mole of electrons and is equal to about 96,500 coulombs.*
SEE ALSO **Avogadro's number, coulomb, electric charge, mole**

Faraday's law of induction
states that the size of an induced electromotive force (emf) in a conductor is directly proportional to the rate at which the magnetic field changes. This induced emf can be increased by:
    − increasing the speed of the wire's movement
    − increasing the length of the wire in the magnetic field
    − increasing the strength of the magnetic field.
SEE ALSO **electromagnetic induction, electromotive force, magnetic field**

Faraday's laws of electrolysis
are two laws named after the British scientist Michael Faraday (1791–1867).
First law: The amount of chemical change during electrolysis is directly proportional to the quantity of electrical charge passed.
Second law: The amount of chemical change during electrolysis is inversely proportional to the charge on an ion.
SEE ALSO **electrolysis**

fat
❶ Fats are naturally occurring esters of a fatty acid and glycerol. They are solids at body temperature and are widely used by plants and animals as a means of storing food which can be used as a fuel.
SEE ALSO **carboxylic acid, ester**
❷ Fats and oils are a group of organic compounds made up of carbon, hydrogen, and a small amount of oxygen, and are an important fuel source, having twice the energy value of carbohydrates. Fats are solids and oils are liquids at room temperature.
• *Foods rich in fats include butter, lard, margarine, olive oil, etc.*
SEE ALSO **carbohydrate**   »

Food	Energy per 100 g
lard (fat)	3,700 kJ
sugar (carbohydrate)	1,600 kJ
bread (carbohydrate)	100 kJ
fish fingers (protein)	750 kJ
lettuce	35 kJ

➤ **hydrolysis of fats** (*also* **saponification**) is the chemical reaction of a fat with water to break it down into a fatty acid and glycerol.
• *Hydrolysis of fats is important in digestion of food, and in the manufacture of detergents.*
SEE ALSO **digestion, hydrolysis**

fatty acid *see* **carboxylic acid**

fauna
is a general term to describe all the animal life present in a particular region or time.
• *Fauna was first used to categorize animals in 1745 by the Swedish scientist Carl Linnaeus.*
SEE ALSO **biological classification, flora, kingdom**

feeding *see* **ingestion, nutrition**

feeding level *see* **trophic level**

female reproductive organ system
(*also* **genital organs, genitalia**)
The female reproductive organ system comprises three main organs: ovaries, uterus, and vagina.
SEE ALSO **ovary, uterus, vagina**

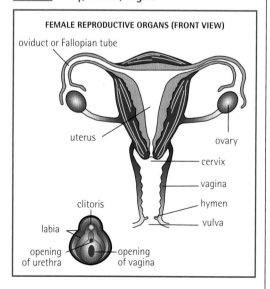

FEMALE REPRODUCTIVE ORGANS (FRONT VIEW)

oviduct or Fallopian tube
uterus
ovary
cervix
vagina
hymen
vulva
clitoris
labia
opening of urethra
opening of vagina

femur *see* **human skeleton**

fermentation
is the conversion of sugars into ethanol and carbon dioxide gas by the action of microorganisms such as yeast, in the absence of air. Fermentation is a type of anaerobic respiration, carried out by enzymes (zymase) in the yeast which work best at temperatures of around 25–30°C.
• *Fermentation is the basis of baking, winemaking, and brewing beer.*
SEE ALSO **anaerobic respiration, enzyme, ethanol, yeast**

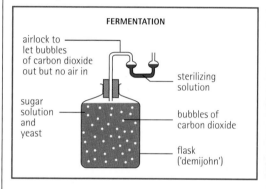

FERMENTATION

airlock to let bubbles of carbon dioxide out but no air in
sterilizing solution
sugar solution and yeast
bubbles of carbon dioxide
flask ('demijohn')

fern
Ferns are perennial, flowerless plants with large leaves called fronds. These fronds grow either from a short stem or a rhizome (underground stem) and gradually uncurl as they become more mature. Like bryophytes, ferns need water for fertilization, but they can live in slightly drier places.
• *Ferns reproduce by means of spores released from capsules on the underside of their fronds.*
SEE ALSO **bryophyte, spore**

ferromagnetic material *see* **magnetic material**

fertility treatment
A hormone called FSH (follicle stimulating hormone) can be taken by women which helps to stimulate egg production in the ovaries.
• *Fertility treatment can sometimes lead to multiple births (twins, etc.).*
SEE ALSO **hormone**

fertilization
❶ In animals, fertilization is the fusion of the nuclei of the male and female gametes during sexual reproduction to form a single cell called the zygote. Fertilization normally takes place in the

oviduct of the female. The sperm (male gamete) reaches the ovum (female gamete) by swimming (using its tail) from the vagina through the uterus and meets the egg travelling along the oviduct. Usually only one sperm enters the egg. Only the head, containing the nucleus, goes in, leaving the tail outside. When the successful sperm has entered the egg, the egg membrane becomes hard so no other sperm can enter. The unsuccessful sperm will all die.

SEE ALSO **gamete, oviduct, ovum, sperm, zygote**

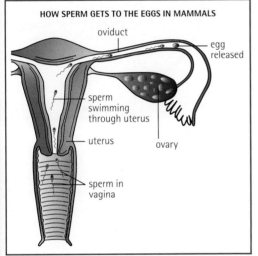

HOW SPERM GETS TO THE EGGS IN MAMMALS

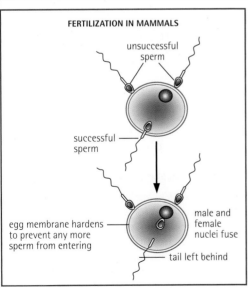

FERTILIZATION IN MAMMALS

external fertilization

is fertilization which occurs outside the body of the female. It occurs in most aquatic animals.

internal fertilization

is fertilization which occurs inside the body of the female, into which sperm are introduced. It occurs in most terrestrial animals, including humans.

❷ In plants, fertilization is the fusion of the male nucleus (from the pollen) with the female nucleus (in the ovule). This happens after pollination. The pollen, if it lands on the right type of stigma, grows a pollen tube down through the style towards the ovary. It does this by secreting enzymes to digest a path through the style. The male nucleus travels down the pollen tube. In the ovary, each ovule is protected by a double layer of cells (integuments). At one end there is a small hole (micropyle). The male nucleus passes through this hole and fuses with the female nucleus in the ovule. Fertilized ovules become seeds.

SEE ALSO **ovule, pollen, seed, stigma, style**

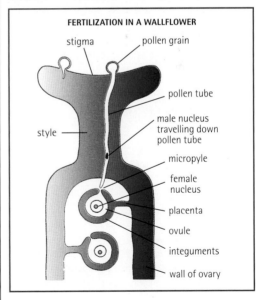

FERTILIZATION IN A WALLFLOWER

fertilizer

A fertilizer is any substance that is added to the soil to increase the fertility of the soil. **»**

natural fertilizer

Natural fertilizers are of natural organic origin and consist of animal or plant remains. Natural animal fertilizers are called manure and are rich in trace elements. Natural plant fertilizers are called compost.

SEE ALSO **trace element**

synthetic fertilizer

Synthetic fertilizers are artificially manufactured fertilizers and are normally inorganic. The most important are nitrogenous fertilizers, which are normally made by converting ammonia into compounds such as ammonium nitrate NH_4NO_3 or ammonium sulfate $(NH_4)_2SO_4$. These are solids, for ease of handling, and are water-soluble so they seep into the soil to be absorbed by the roots of the plant. The proportion of nitrogen present in a particular fertilizer is usually marked on the bag.

SEE ALSO **ammonia, NPK values**

Fertilizer	ammonium sulfate
Formula	$(NH_4)_2SO_4$
Mr	132
Proportion of nitrogen	28/132 = 21.2%

Fertilizer	ammonium nitrate
Formula	NH_4NO_3
Mr	80
Proportion of nitrogen	28/80 = 35%

Fertilizer	urea
Formula	NH_2CONH_2
Mr	60
Proportion of nitrogen	28/60 = 46.6%

fetus (*also* **foetus**)

A fetus is the embryo of a mammal (especially a human) when it has reached a stage of development so that it has recognizable features of the adult form.

• *In humans the embryo is called a* **fetus** *from the eighth week until birth.*

SEE ALSO **birth, embryo**

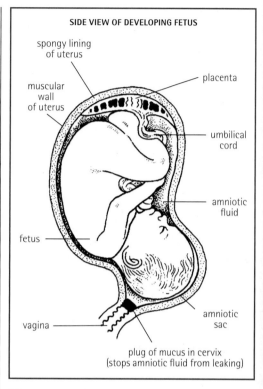

SIDE VIEW OF DEVELOPING FETUS

spongy lining of uterus

muscular wall of uterus

placenta

umbilical cord

amniotic fluid

fetus

amniotic sac

vagina

plug of mucus in cervix (stops amniotic fluid from leaking)

fibre *see* **roughage**

fibreglass

is a composite material which consists of fine glass fibres embedded in a resin. It is used to make small boats, surfboards, etc.

• *Fibreglass is much lighter than glass, easier to shape, and much less fragile.*

SEE ALSO **composite material**

fibrous protein *see* **protein**

fibula *see* **human skeleton**

filament (*also* **plant filament**)

A filament is the stalk of a flower's stamen which supports the anther.

SEE ALSO **anther, stamen**

filter

❶ A filter is a device for separating insoluble particles from a liquid. The simplest laboratory filter for liquids is a funnel in which a cone of paper (filter paper) is placed. The insoluble solid collects as the residue inside the filter paper and the clear liquid (filtrate) passes through.

SEE ALSO **filtrate, filtration, residue**

❷ *see* **colour filter**

filtrate

is the clear liquid that passes through the filter during filtration.

SEE ALSO **filtration, residue**

filtration

is a method of separating solid particles from a liquid by passing the mixture through a porous material such as filter paper or glass wool.

SEE ALSO **Bowman's capsule, sewage**

fish (also Pisces)

Fishes are vertebrates which are aquatic and cold-blooded, and have skin covered with scales. Most fishes have gills for breathing and fins for movement.

• *Fishes can be divided into two main subclasses: bony fishes and cartilaginous fishes.*

SEE ALSO **vertebrate animal**

bony fish (also Osteichthyes)

Bony fishes are marine and freshwater fishes with a bony skeleton and a swim bladder which allows them to suspend themselves in water at any depth by letting air in or out of the bladder. Most bony fishes have a flap of skin (operculum) covering their gill slits.

• *Examples of bony fishes include perch, cod, and salmon.*

cartilaginous fish (also Chondrichthyes)

Cartilaginous fishes are marine fishes which have a skeleton made of soft bone called cartilage. Unlike bony fishes, they do not have a swim bladder, and therefore avoid sinking only by constant swimming. They are mainly carnivores.

• *Examples of cartilaginous fishes include sharks, rays, and skates.*

SEE ALSO **cartilage**

fissile material

is material whose nuclei will undergo nuclear fission, either spontaneously or by induction through neutron bombardment.

• *The elements uranium-235 and plutonium-239 are fissile materials.*

SEE ALSO **nuclear fission**

fission bomb (also atomic bomb, A-bomb)

A fission bomb is one in which two or more subcritical masses of fissile material are brought together to make a mass in excess of the critical mass. This results in an uncontrolled nuclear chain reaction, releasing huge amounts of energy.

SEE ALSO **critical mass fissile material, nuclear chain reaction**

fission reactor

A fission reactor is a common type of nuclear reactor in which heat is produced by nuclear fission. This heat produces steam, which drives a turbine in a nuclear power station to generate electricity.

SEE ALSO **nuclear fission**

fixed points

The fixed points are the temperatures which are used as standards for a particular temperature scale. For example, on the Celsius scale the lower fixed point (temperature of pure ice melting) is 0°C and the upper fixed point (temperature of steam at atmospheric pressure) is 100°C.

SEE ALSO **Celsius scale, fundamental interval**

flaccid

describes the state of plant cells which are limp through the lack of turgor.

• *Flaccid plant tissue is due to the cytoplasm within the cells shrinking, due to lack of water, and contracting away from the cell wall.*

SEE ALSO **cytoplasm turgor**

flame emission spectrometry (also flame photometry)

is an instrumental analysis to identify samples of metal ions from the light emitted when the sample is heated in a flame. The energy provided excites electrons in the metal ions into higher energy electron shells. When the electrons fall back to lower energy levels they emit light of a specific wavelength. This explains flame tests which are used to identify metal ions.

• *Flame emission spectrometry is used to detect metal ions in very low concentration (1.0×10^{-9} g).*

SEE ALSO **electron, electron shell, flame test, instrumental analysis, ion, wavelength**

flame photometry see flame emission spectrometry

flame test

A flame test is carried out to identify certain metal cations. The test involves dipping a nichrome wire into concentrated hydrochloric acid and then dipping the wire into the compound to be tested. The wire is then held in a hot Bunsen flame. The colour of the Bunsen flame is used to identify the metal ion present.

SEE ALSO **cation**   »

Metal cation	Flame test colour
lithium Li$^+$	red
sodium Na$^+$	yellow
potassium K$^+$	lilac
calcium Ca^{2+}	orange-red
copper Cu^{2+}	green-blue

flammable (*also* **inflammable**)

describes material that burns very easily. Oxygen gas is essential for burning to take place but is not a flammable gas as it does not catch alight and burn itself.
• *Hydrogen is a highly **flammable** gas and burns with a popping sound.*

Fleming's left-hand rule (*also* **motor rule**)

gives the direction of the motor effect. The thumb and first two fingers of the left hand are held at right angles to each other. The thumb shows the direction of motion. The first finger points to the direction of the magnetic field and the second finger shows the direction of the current.
SEE ALSO **motor effect**

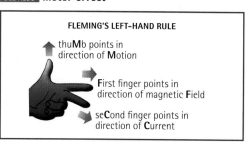

FLEMING'S LEFT-HAND RULE

thu**M**b points in direction of **M**otion

First finger points in direction of magnetic **F**ield

se**C**ond finger points in direction of **C**urrent

flexor muscle *see* **muscle**

floating

is being suspended in a fluid. An object will only float if its density is the same or less than the density of the surrounding fluid. If an object has a higher density than the surrounding fluid, it sinks.
SEE ALSO **density, principle of flotation**

flora

is a general term to describe all the plant life present in a particular region or time.
• *Flora does not include fungi.*
SEE ALSO **biological classification, fauna, kingdom**

floral formula

A floral formula shows the various numbers of the main parts of the flower for a particular species. The main parts are the calyx (K), corolla (C), androecium (A), and gynaecium (G).
• *The **floral formula** $K_5 C_5 A_{10} G_{10}$ means 5 sepals (calyx), 5 petals (corolla), 10 stamens (androecium), and 10 carpels (gynaecium).*
SEE ALSO **androecium, calyx, corolla, gynaecium**

flotation *see* **principle of flotation**

flower

A flower is the organ of sexual reproduction in flowering plants (angiosperms). Most flowers have both the male stamens and female carpels inside the same flower.
• *Many **flowers** attract insects which help with pollination.*
SEE ALSO **angiosperm, carpel, pollination, stamen**

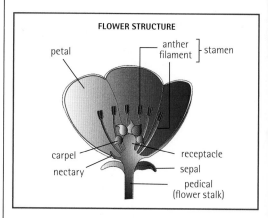

FLOWER STRUCTURE

petal

anther
filament } stamen

carpel

nectary

receptacle

sepal

pedical (flower stalk)

flowering plant *see* **angiosperm**

flowers of sulfur *see* **sulfur**

flow of water analogy

The flow of water analogy is a way of thinking about electricity. If you regard the amount of water flowing through a pipe as 'current' and the pressure of the water as 'voltage', then 'resistance' is any restriction to the flow of water. Narrow pipes will have high resistance and create high pressure (high voltage). Wide pipes will have low resistance which will allow lots of water to flow (large current).
SEE ALSO **electric current, resistance, voltage**

fluid

A fluid is a state of matter that can flow, like gases or liquids.

SEE ALSO state of matter

fluoridation

is the addition to drinking water of small amounts of fluoride salts, usually sodium fluoride NaF or calcium fluoride CaF_2. These fluoride salts combine with the enamel (calcium phosphate) on the teeth to form a more protective coating (calcium fluorophosphate).

• *Fluoridation helps prevent tooth decay.*

fluorine see halogen

FM see frequency modulation

foam see colloid

focal length (*also* °f)

is the distance between the optical centre and the focal point of a lens.

SEE ALSO focal point, lens, optical centre

focal point (*also* principal focus, F)

The focal point is a point through which all rays travelling parallel to the principal axis pass after refraction through a lens.

• *A lens has a focal point on both its sides.*

SEE ALSO lens, principal axis

focus see earthquake

foetus see fetus

fog

is an aerosol type of colloid, consisting of tiny water droplets or ice crystals suspended in the air near the Earth's surface. The moisture in the fog is often generated locally, perhaps from a nearby body of water such as a lake, marsh, or ocean.

• *Fog can be considered as a type of low-lying cloud.*

SEE ALSO cloud, colloid

foil

describes a very thin, flexible sheet of metal. Silver, gold, and aluminium are suitable foil materials as they are malleable metals.

• *Aluminium foil is often used to protect food.*

SEE ALSO metal

food see nutrition

food chain

A food chain is a feeding relationship between organisms in an ecosystem. Producers (usually green plants) begin a food chain, as they are the only organisms that can make their own food. Biomass is then transferred through the food chain to consumers (primary to secondary to tertiary) which are usually animals.

SEE ALSO biomass, consumer, producer, trophic level

food production

is the production of food for humans and animals. The efficiency of food production can be improved by reducing the number of stages in particular food chains, so that less energy is lost. Normally in a food chain around 90% of biomass is lost between feeding (trophic) levels. This can be reduced by limiting the activity of animals, e.g. raising hens in battery cages. Alternative new sources of food like mycoprotein can be made from microorganisms. Such food is high in protein and can be grown quickly and cheaply. It is often used as animal feed.

SEE ALSO biomass, food chain

food web

A food web is a network of interrelated food chains representing the complex feeding relationships of organisms in an ecosystem.

• *All food webs contain producers, consumers, and decomposers.*

SEE ALSO consumer, decomposer, food chain, producer

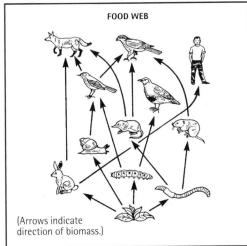

FOOD WEB

(Arrows indicate direction of biomass.)

force (*also* contact force, F)

A force is a pushing or pulling action which can change the shape of an object, or make a stationary

»

object move, or a moving object change its speed or direction. Forces have direction (vector quantity), so they are represented by arrowed lines. The length of the arrow indicates the size of the force and the direction of the arrow its direction. If equal and opposite forces act on an object, the result may be that the object becomes stretched or squashed.

• *The sizes of forces are measured in units called newtons.*

SEE ALSO balanced forces, centripetal force, electric field, electromagnetic force, electromotive force, friction, gravitational force, intermolecular force, intramolecular force, magnetic field, newton, turning force, vector quantity

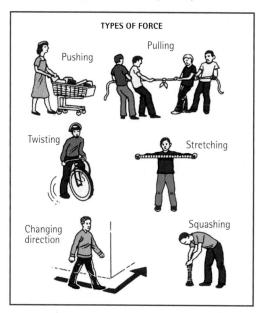

TYPES OF FORCE

Pushing

Pulling

Twisting

Stretching

Changing direction

Squashing

➤ **force and acceleration** are directly proportional and are related by the equation:

$$force = mass \times acceleration$$

When you double the force acting on an object, you will double its acceleration (as long as its mass remains constant).

SEE ALSO acceleration

➤ **measurement of force** is usually carried out using a spring balance or newton balance. Such balances contain a helical spring, the extension of which is directly proportional to the force applied, provided that the spring is not overstretched.

SEE ALSO Hooke's law

compression forces

are equal and opposite forces which, when applied to an object, result in a decrease in its length.

tension forces

are equal and opposite forces which, when applied to an object, result in an increase in its length.

force ratio *see* **mechanical advantage**

formic acid *see* **methanoic acid**

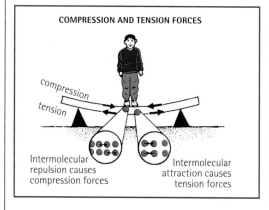

COMPRESSION AND TENSION FORCES

compression

tension

Intermolecular repulsion causes compression forces

Intermolecular attraction causes tension forces

forms of energy *see* **energy**

formula mass *see* **molar mass**

formulation

A formulation is made by mixing chemical compounds in carefully measured quantities to ensure the product has the required properties.

• *Formulations are important in the manufacture of medicines, alloys, fertilizers, paint, and foods.*

SEE ALSO compound

forward reaction

The forward reaction is the direction from original reactants to products in a reversible chemical reaction.

• *The forward reaction goes from left to right in the chemical equation.*

SEE ALSO backward reaction, reversible reaction

fossil

Fossils are remains of dead animals and plants that have been preserved in sedimentary rocks. The organic matter of living material usually rots away, but the hard parts like animal bones or the cellulose and lignin of plant tissue survive for longer. These can slowly absorb minerals from circulating water to replace the decayed organic material, and so the remains are slowly turned into stone (petrification). The oldest fossils are often found buried in the deepest layers of sedimentary rock. More recent fossils are found in upper layers. However, during movements of the Earth's crust, older rocks and their fossils may be pushed upwards.

SEE ALSO rock

fossil fuel

Fossil fuels are formed from the remains of ancient buried organisms. Examples are coal, petroleum, and natural gas. All fossil fuels have a high percentage of carbon or hydrogen which, during combustion, combine with oxygen to form carbon dioxide and water.

• *When we burn fossil fuels, we are using the Sun's energy that has been stored as chemical energy underground for millions of years.*

SEE ALSO coal, natural gas, petroleum

fovea

The fovea is the most sensitive part of the retina of the eye where the receptor cells (all cones) are packed most closely together.

SEE ALSO eye, retina

fracking (*also* hydraulic fracturing)

is the process of injecting fluid at high pressure into underground rock or shale so as to force open existing fissures to release petroleum and natural gas.

• *An advantage of fracking over traditional oil production is that it is easier to capture greenhouse gas emissions (like methane).*

SEE ALSO natural gas, petroleum

fraction

fraction is a mixture of liquids of similar boiling point. Light fractions have lower boiling points and condense higher up the fractionating column than heavy fractions. 90% of petroleum is used as a fuel and 10% as a chemical feedstock (similar to our food which is 90% fuel, 10% material for growth). Most fuels and feedstocks are the light fractions.

SEE ALSO chemical feedstock, fractional distillation

Light fractions	Heavy fractions
contain small hydrocarbon chains	contain long hydrocarbon chains
are volatile	are not volatile
are quite flammable	are less flammable
are pale-coloured liquids or gases	are darker liquids

fractional distillation (*also* fractionation)

is a method of separating mixtures of liquids by distillation. These liquids must be miscible and have different boiling points. Separation is achieved by using a long, vertical fractionating column attached to the distillation flask. Consider separating a mixture of water (boiling point 100°C) and ethanol (boiling point 78°C). When the temperature at the top of the fractionating column reaches 78°C, molecules of ethanol can remain as vapour and pass over into the Liebig condenser. Water molecules, with a higher boiling point, condense and fall back into the flask. This continues until most of the ethanol has boiled off. Then the temperature rises to 100°C and the water vapour passes into the condenser.

• *Fractional distillation is important in the separation of the components of air and petroleum.*

SEE ALSO distillation, fraction, fractionating column, Liebig condenser, petroleum

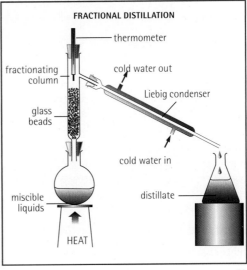

FRACTIONAL DISTILLATION

thermometer

fractionating column

cold water out

Liebig condenser

glass beads

cold water in

miscible liquids

distillate

HEAT

»

FRACTIONAL DISTILLATION
IN FRACTIONATING COLUMN

LIGHTEST
FRACTION — refinery gases

20°C

100°C — gasoline

bubble cap — 200°C — kerosine

rising vapour

300°C — diesel

400°C furnace — oil

400°C — lubricating oil

petroleum

bitumen

residue

➤ **fractional distillation of petroleum** The petroleum is heated at the bottom of the column to around 400°C. It vaporizes and is split into fractions which travel up the column and become cooler. When a fraction reaches a tray at a temperature just below its boiling point, it condenses onto the tray and is drawn off along pipes (see diagram).

fractionating column
A fractionating column is a long vertical tube packed with glass beads or some other unreactive substance. This provides a large surface area for condensation and re-evaporation.

fractionation see **fractional distillation**

fraternal twins see **non–identical twins**

free fall
describes the motion of an object caused due to the gravitational force acting on the object. In a gravitational field, free fall takes place at a constant acceleration.
• *Free fall on Earth occurs at a constant acceleration of 9.8 ms^{-2}.*
SEE ALSO **gravitational force**

freezing
is the solidification which occurs when a liquid is cooled. The forces between the particles become stronger until they just vibrate about fixed positions and the material becomes a solid.

freezing point
is the temperature at which all of a liquid changes into a solid.
• *The freezing point of a pure substance is the same temperature as its melting point. Impurities lower (depress) freezing points.*
SEE ALSO **boiling point, melting point**

frequency (also f)
❶ The frequency of a wave is the number of oscillations per second. It is related to wavelength by the equation $c = f \times \lambda$, where c is the velocity of light, f is the frequency of the wave, and λ is the wavelength. As c is a constant, it follows that high-frequency waves have short wavelength and low-frequency waves have long wavelength. High-frequency waves also have greater energy and are therefore more penetrating.
SEE ALSO **oscillation, wavelength**
❷ The frequency of a motion is the number of complete cycles of the motion in one second. The SI unit of frequency is hertz (Hz), which is equal to one cycle per second (c.p.s.). Frequency is also the reciprocal of the period of the motion.
SEE ALSO **period, periodic motion**

frequency modulation (also FM)
is a form of radio transmission in which the sound being broadcast is conveyed by variations in the frequency of the radio carrier wave.
• *Frequency modulation is used on shorter wavebands.*
SEE ALSO **amplitude modulation, carrier wave, frequency**

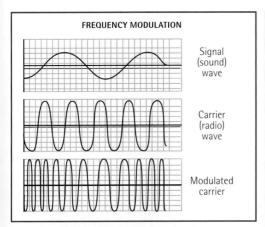

FREQUENCY MODULATION

Signal (sound) wave

Carrier (radio) wave

Modulated carrier

friction (*also* frictional force)

is the force which acts to oppose the motion between two surfaces as they move over each other. It is because of friction that most people think forces are needed to keep something moving (contrary to Newton's first law). Friction helps to give grip and traction between surfaces such as tyres on the road, brakes, etc. Sometimes friction has unwanted effects such as the generation of heat or the wearing of surfaces.

Friction can be reduced by:
- streamlining, which reduces air or water resistance.
- lubrication between surfaces with oil or grease.
- minimizing surface contact by using ball bearings.

SEE ALSO **Newton's first law**

dynamic frictional force (*also* kinetic frictional force)

is the value of the frictional force when one surface is sliding over another.
• *The dynamic frictional force is less than the static frictional force.*

static frictional force (*also* limiting frictional force)

is the maximum value of the frictional force between two surfaces which can prevent one surface from sliding over another.

frictional electricity *see* **static electricity**

frictional force *see* **friction**

frog

A frog is an amphibian which is a vertebrate animal that lays its eggs in water. The eggs hatch to form tadpoles which have gills so that they can live in water. These tadpoles undergo metamorphosis and turn into adult frogs.
• *Adult frogs live on land as they have lungs.*
SEE ALSO **amphibian, metamorphosis**

frost

is water vapour in the air that has cooled and condensed to liquid and then frozen. It happens when the air temperature is below 0°C.
• *Ground frost occurs when the ground is colder than the air.*
SEE ALSO **condensation, freezing**

fruit

True fruit develops from the ovary wall after fertilization. The ovary wall forms a protective layer (pericarp) around the seed. Examples are the stone of a plum, the hard shell of a nut, and the pod of a bean. In a 'false fruit', the receptacle of the old flower swells up to form a fleshy outer core, as in apples, pears, or strawberries. These false fruits help in seed dispersal, as they are attractive to eat.
SEE ALSO **ovary, receptacle, seed dispersal**

fuel

A fuel is a substance which releases useful heat or energy during combination with oxygen. Until the 18th century, wood, animal products, and vegetable oil were the main fuels. Since then these have been replaced by fossil fuels.
SEE ALSO **energy, fossil fuel**

fuel cell

A fuel cell is a special cell in which the chemical energy of the fuel is converted directly into electrical energy. There is no intermediate stage such as the turbine in a conventional generator.
• *Fuel cells are more efficient than conventional generators, and produce much less pollution.*
SEE ALSO **cell, generator**

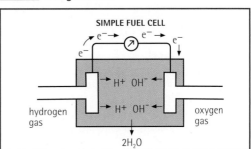

SIMPLE FUEL CELL

e^- e^- e^-

e^-

H^+ OH^-

H^+ OH^-

hydrogen gas   oxygen gas

$2H_2O$

a
b
c
d
e
f
g
h
i
j
k
l
m
n
o
p
q
r
s
t
u
v
w
x
y
z

fuel gas *see* **refinery gas**

fullerene

Fullerenes form a third allotrope of carbon (in addition to diamond and graphite) consisting of spherical clusters of carbon atoms, which were discovered in 1985. The most symmetrical is buckminsterfullerene, which is composed of 60 carbon atoms bonded together. It is named after the American architect Buckminster Fuller (1895–1983), because it looks like the symmetrical 'geodesic' domes which he designed. It can be made by electrically evaporating graphite electrodes in helium gas at low pressure.

• *Fullerenes have important uses as lubricants, catalysts, semiconductors, and superconductors. They can even be used for 'drug delivery' to a specific site in the human body in a highly controlled manner.*

SEE ALSO **allotrope, graphene, nanotube**

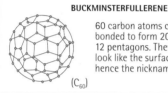

BUCKMINSTERFULLERENE

60 carbon atoms covalently bonded to form 20 hexagons and 12 pentagons. They fit together to look like the surface of a football, hence the nickname **buckyballs**.

(C_{60})

fuming sulfuric acid *see* **oleum**

functional group

A functional group is an atom or group of atoms that give an organic molecule its typical chemical properties.

• *Only alkanes do not have a functional group.*

SEE ALSO **alkane, homologous series**

alkene	$\overset{}{>}C=C\overset{}{<}$
alkyne	$-C\equiv C-$
alcohol	$-\overset{\mid}{\underset{\mid}{C}}-O-H$
carboxylic acid	$-C\overset{\displaystyle O}{\underset{O-H}{\parallel}}$

fundamental interval

The fundamental interval is the distance on a thermometer between the lower and upper fixed points.

• *On the Celsius scale the **fundamental interval** is divided into 100 degrees.*

SEE ALSO **Celsius scale, fixed points**

fungus *plural* fungi

A fungus is a plant-like organism but does not contain chlorophyll and is therefore incapable of photosynthesis. It is a saprophyte or parasite and feeds on organic material such as bread, faeces, dead plants, or animals. Mushrooms, toadstools, and yeasts are all fungi.

• *The protein derived from **fungi** is called mycoprotein and this is a valuable source of protein for vegetarians.*

SEE ALSO **parasite, saprophyte**

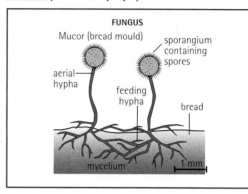

FUNGUS

Mucor (bread mould)

sporangium containing spores

aerial hypha

feeding hypha

bread

mycelium   1 mm

fuse

A fuse is a short, thin piece of wire which overheats and melts to break the electrical circuit if more than a certain value of current flows through.

• *Fuses, like switches, are always placed on the live wire. All three-pin plugs are fused.*

SEE ALSO **circuit breaker**

fuse rating

Fuse ratings specify the maximum amount of current that can pass before the fuse overheats and melts (e.g. 3A, 5A, 13A, or 30A). A suitable fuse must be used for each electrical appliance.

SEE ALSO **fuse**

Electrical appliance	Power (watts)	Fuse rating
cooker	8,000	30A
immersion heater	3,000	13A
kettle	2,400	1A
iron	800	5A
colour TV	120	3A
table lamp	60	3A

fusion

is the change in state from a solid to liquid of a substance which is a solid at room temperature and pressure.

fusion bomb (*also* hydrogen bomb, H-bomb)

A fusion bomb is one in which a mixture of deuterium and tritium (isotopes of hydrogen) are fused together. The energy released by this uncontrolled nuclear fusion is about thirty times greater than a conventional fission bomb of the same size.

SEE ALSO **deuterium, nuclear fusion, tritium**

Gg

galaxy

A galaxy is a giant collection of gas, dust, and stars held together by gravitational attraction between its components. Galaxies are not spread evenly throughout the universe, but are grouped in clusters.

• *There are over a billion galaxies in the universe.*

SEE ALSO **Milky Way**

SPIRAL GALAXY

Sun   galactic centre

gall bladder

The gall bladder is a small storage organ for the bile which is produced by the liver.

SEE ALSO **bile**

galvanic cell *see* voltaic cell

galvanizing

is a method of protecting a metal (e.g. iron or steel) from corrosion by covering it with a thin layer of zinc through dipping or electroplating. Corrugated roofing sheets or sheets for dustbins made of mild steel are often galvanized by dipping them in molten zinc. The galvanized iron remains protected even if the surface is scratched because of sacrificial protection.

SEE ALSO **electroplating, sacrificial protection**

gamete (*also* sex cell)

A gamete is a specialized sex cell formed by meiosis which contains only half the number of chromosomes (haploid). In animals the gametes are the sperm (male) and ovum (female).

• *Gametes combine during fertilization to form the zygote, which develops into the new offspring.*

SEE ALSO **fertilization, haploid, meiosis, ovum, sperm, zygote**

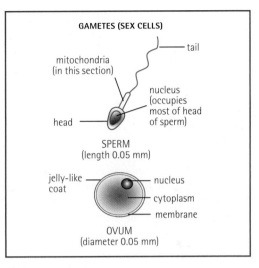

GAMETES (SEX CELLS)

tail

mitochondria (in this section)

nucleus (occupies most of head of sperm)

head

SPERM (length 0.05 mm)

jelly-like coat

nucleus

cytoplasm

membrane

OVUM (diameter 0.05 mm)

gamma emission

is caused by a rearrangement of particles inside the nucleus of the atom, resulting in a loss of energy as gamma rays.

• *Gamma emission causes no change in atomic number or mass number.*

SEE ALSO **atomic number, mass number**

gamma ray (*also* γ)

A gamma ray is an electromagnetic wave of very short wavelength and high frequency. They are often emitted at the same time as an alpha or beta particle. Gamma rays have no charge or mass and have the least ionizing effect of nuclear radiations, but they are the most penetrating, and potentially the most hazardous.

SEE ALSO **alpha particle, beta particle, electromagnetic wave**

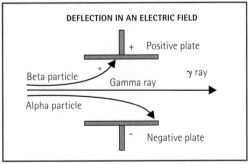

DEFLECTION IN AN ELECTRIC FIELD

+   Positive plate

Beta particle

γ ray

Gamma ray

Alpha particle

−   Negative plate

gas
A gas is the physical state of matter in which the particles are far apart and moving randomly.
• *A gas is a basic state of matter (along with solid and liquid) with both melting point and boiling point below room temperature.*
SEE ALSO **boiling point, state of matter**

gaseous exchange (*also* external respiration)
involves the passing of oxygen and carbon dioxide in and out of an organism. Gaseous exchange often takes place in a respiratory organ with a large surface area, e.g. lungs (adult amphibians, reptiles, birds, and mammals), gills (larval amphibians, fish and other aquatic animals), trachea and spiracles (insects) or stomata (plants).
SEE ALSO **lung, stoma**

gas oil *see* diesel oil

gasoline (*also* petrol, naphtha)
is the petroleum fraction with a boiling point range of 40 – 180°C. It is made up of a mixture of hydrocarbons containing between five and ten carbons. Petrol is a mixture of the hydrocarbons heptane C_7H_{16} and octane C_8H_{18} and is an important motor fuel. Naphtha, another mixture of hydrocarbons in this fraction, is the main chemical feedstock for making a wide range of chemicals, including drugs, paint, and plastics.
SEE ALSO **chemical feedstock**

gastric juice
is an acidic mixture of digestive enzymes (e.g. pepsin) secreted into the stomach to begin the first stage of digestion.
SEE ALSO **enzyme, stomach**

gastrointestinal tract *see* alimentary canal

gastropod
A gastropod is an invertebrate animal that moves around on a single fleshy foot. Gastropods are molluscs and include slugs and snails.
• *Gastropod means 'stomach foot'.*
SEE ALSO **mollusc**

Gay-Lussac's law
states that when gases react chemically, their volumes are in a simple ratio to one another and to the volume of the products, providing the volumes are measured at the same temperature and pressure. The law was first stated in 1808 by the French chemist Joseph Gay-Lussac (1778–1850) and led to Avogadro's law.
SEE ALSO **Avogadro's law**

EXAMPLE OF GAY-LUSSAC'S LAW

N_2	+	$3H_2$	→	$2NH_3$
1 vol.		3 vol.	→	2 vol.
25 cm³		75 cm³		50 cm³

gear
A gear is a simple machine in which toothed wheels engage to transmit motion between rotating shafts. If there are twice as many teeth on the output shaft, the input shaft will rotate twice as many times and therefore has a velocity ratio of 2.
SEE ALSO **machine, velocity ratio**

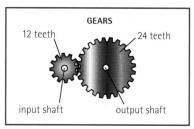
GEARS
12 teeth   24 teeth
input shaft   output shaft

Geiger counter *see* radiation

gel *see* colloid

gender
is an indication of the sexuality (male or female) of an animal. Some animals like worms are hermaphrodite and have no gender as they have both male and female reproductive organs.
SEE ALSO **sexual reproduction**

gene
A gene is the unit of hereditary information, composed of a section of DNA which acts as a chemical instruction for protein synthesis. Each gene determines the synthesis of a particular protein. Each gene occupies a specific position on a chromosome, called its locus.
• *Genes can undergo mutation.*
SEE ALSO **chromosome, mutation**

gene pool
A gene pool consists of all the genes and their alleles present in a population of a plant or animal species. No individual in the species can have all the genes. For example, although there are different genes for every hair colour in the UK population, each individual will only have a few of them.
SEE ALSO **allele, gene**

genera see genus

generator
A generator is a device which produces electrical
energy from mechanical energy. A flat coil
of conducting wire is rotated in a magnetic
field. This induces an emf in the wire and a
current flows.
SEE ALSO **electromotive force**

gene therapy
is an application of genetic engineering for treating
genetic diseases by the insertion of favourable genes
into carriers (called vectors), such as a bacterial
plasmid or a virus. Such vectors infect the human
cells and reproduce the healthy gene, without
causing illness.
• *Gene therapy is used to treat cystic fibrosis.*
SEE ALSO **genetic disease, genetic engineering,
plasmid, cystic fibrosis**

genetically modified food (*also* GM food)
is food (meat, fruit, cereals, etc.) which has been
produced from plants or animals which have
had certain genes modified for economic or
scientific reasons.
• *Genetically modified food is an application of
genetic engineering.*
SEE ALSO **genetic engineering**

genetic code
The genetic code is a set of rules by which a
sequence of three nucleotides on a DNA (or RNA)
molecule is translated to a specific amino acid
sequence in proteins.
SEE ALSO **DNA, nucleotide, RNA**

genetic disease (*also* inherited disease)
A genetic disease is caused by faulty alleles,
often recessive, which can be passed on to future
generations.
• *Common genetic diseases are Down's syndrome,
cystic fibrosis, and sickle cell anaemia.*
SEE ALSO **allele, gene therapy**

genetic engineering
is a technique of altering an organism's genotype
by inserting genes from another organism into
its DNA.
• *Genetic engineering can be used to make
microorganisms produce useful proteins such as
human insulin.*
SEE ALSO **DNA, plasmid**

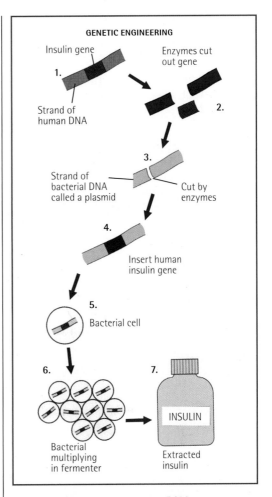

GENETIC ENGINEERING

1. Insulin gene / Strand of human DNA
Enzymes cut out gene
2.
3. Strand of bacterial DNA called a plasmid — Cut by enzymes
4. Insert human insulin gene
5. Bacterial cell
6. Bacterial multiplying in fermenter
7. INSULIN — Extracted insulin

genetic fingerprinting (*also* DNA fingerprinting)
is a technique in which an individual's DNA is
analysed. This can reveal a sequence of the bases in
DNA which is claimed to be specific to the individual
concerned. Sufficient DNA can be obtained from
very small samples of body tissue such as hair, blood,
or semen.
• *Genetic fingerprinting is useful in forensic
science, paternity disputes, and veterinary science.*
SEE ALSO **DNA**

genetics
is the branch of biology which is concerned with the
study of hereditary information transferred from
one generation to the next.
• *Genetics studies the chemical nature of genes
and the way they replicate and transmit.*
SEE ALSO **gene**

genetic variation *see* **variation**

genitalia *see* **female reproductive organ system, male reproductive organ system**

genital organs *see* **female reproductive organ system, male reproductive organ system**

genome
The genome is the entire genetic material of an organism. The Human Genome Project used computers to identify the order of the bases in each DNA strand (DNA sequencing) of all 46 chromosomes in every living cell in the human body.
• *Genome knowledge can help with the understanding and treatment of inherited disorders and other types of disease.*
SEE ALSO **chromosome, DNA**

genotype
An organism's genotype is the genetic information about that particular organism as specified by its alleles.
SEE ALSO **allele**

genus *plural* **genera**
A genus is a group of closely related species. Some genera contain only one species.
• *All genera are grouped in families.*

geology
is the study of the origin, structure, and composition of rocks.
SEE ALSO **rock**

geostationary satellite *see* **communication satellite**

geothermal energy
is heat energy from hot rock deep in the Earth's crust.
• *Geothermal energy can be used to heat water in homes, or to make steam for driving turbines to generate electricity.*

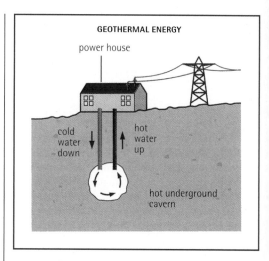

GEOTHERMAL ENERGY
power house
cold water down
hot water up
hot underground cavern

geotropism *see* **gravitropism**

germ
A germ is a microorganism that can infect us and cause disease.
• *Germs are normally either a type of bacteria, fungus, or virus.*
SEE ALSO **microorganism**

germicide *see* **antiseptic**

germination
is the initial stages of growth of a seed to form a seedling. In order to germinate, seeds require warmth, moisture, and oxygen. During germination, the plumule (young shoot) and radicle (young root) emerge through the seed coat.
• *A seed will often remain 'dormant' until conditions are suitable for germination.*

gestation *see* **pregnancy**

giant structure *see* **macromolecule**

gill
A gill is an organ that allows animals to breathe and live underwater. Fish absorb dissolved oxygen in the water as the water flows through the mouth, over the gills and out through the gill slits.
• *A gill flap covers the gill and protects the blood vessels inside.*
SEE ALSO **fish**

glass
is a transparent or translucent material consisting mainly of calcium and sodium silicates, and is a non-crystalline solid in which the atoms are arranged randomly. Glass is sometimes referred to as a

'supercooled liquid' because it has no well-defined melting point.

• *Glass is made by heating together sand (silicon doxide), limestone (calcium carbonate), and soda (sodium carbonate) at 1,500°C.*

SEE ALSO **sand, silicate**

limestone	+	sand	→	calcium silicate	+	carbon dioxide
$CaCO_3$	+	SiO_2	→	$CaSiO_3$	+	CO_2
soda	+	sand	→	sodium silicate	+	carbon dioxide
Na_2CO_3	+	SiO_2	→	Na_2SiO_3	+	CO_2

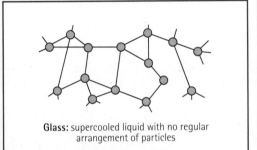

Glass: supercooled liquid with no regular arrangement of particles

gliding joint *see* **joint**

global dimming

is caused by particulate matter in the Earth's atmosphere absorbing the Sun's radiation.

• *Global dimming may help to reduce global warming.*

SEE ALSO **global warming, particulate matter**

global warming

is the Earth warming up as it is absorbing more radiation than it is emitting. This is because of the greenhouse gases in the air absorbing infrared radiation reflected from the Earth's surface as it is warmed up by the Sun. Global warming results in changes in weather patterns, causing drought, storms, and heavy rain (as warmer air can hold more moisture).

• *Global warming melts the polar ice caps to bring about severe flooding of low-lying coastal areas and islands.*

SEE ALSO **greenhouse effect, greenhouse gas**

globular protein *see* **protein**

glomerulus *see* **Bowman's capsule**

glove box

A glove box is a closed cupboard that has gloves fixed into holes in the wall of the cupboard. Glove boxes for highly radioactive material may be shielded by concrete and special glass so that an operator can safely handle highly radioactive material and toxic chemicals.

glucagon *see* **hormone**

glucose

($C_6H_{12}O_6$) is a simple sugar, which is the main monomer unit in most polysaccharides, and provides the fuel for respiration in cells.

SEE ALSO **monomer, polysaccharide**

glycogen (*also* **animal starch**)

is a polysaccharide found in vertebrate animals and is the main energy store in the liver and muscles.

• *Glycogen is converted by the enzyme amylase into glucose, which is used in respiration to release energy.*

SEE ALSO **glucose, polysaccharide**

GM food *see* **genetically modified food**

Golgi complex *see* **organelle**

gonad

Gonads are reproductive organs of an animal. These normally occur in pairs: two testes in the male and two ovaries in the female.

• *Gonads also act as endocrine glands, which secrete many important sex hormones.*

SEE ALSO **endocrine gland, ovary, sex hormone, testis**

gonorrhoea

is the disease caused by a bacterium (*Neisseria gonorrhoeae*) transmitted during sexual intercourse. An infected person may become sterile (unable to produce children). A woman infected with gonorrhoea may pass the disease to her baby at birth. The bacteria in the vagina may enter the baby's eyes and cause blindness.

SEE ALSO **endocrine gland, ovary, sex hormone, testis**

GPE *see* **gravitational potential energy store**

gram molecular volume *see* **molar volume**

granulocyte *see* **phagocyte**

graph

A graph is a diagram to show how information or data is related.

• *Graphs can be used to show trends and can be used to predict future change.*

SEE ALSO scientific variable

bar graph

A bar graph shows the data in bars which may be vertical or horizontal.

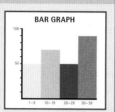

line graph

A line graph shows the data as a line joining a series of points. The vertical axis (y-axis) normally plots the dependent variable you are measuring (distance, velocity, volume, mass, etc.). The horizontal axis (x-axis) normally plots the independent variable you are measuring (time, etc.).

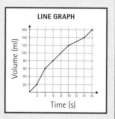

distance–time graph

A distance–time graph is one showing the change in distance with time. The speed at a particular time is equal to the gradient (slope) of the graph at that point.

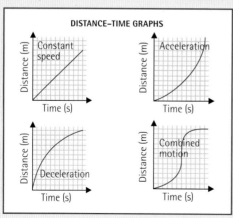

velocity–time graph

A velocity–time graph is one showing the change of velocity with time. The acceleration at a particular time is equal to the gradient (slope) of the graph at that point. The area underneath a velocity–time graph is numerically equal to the total distance travelled.

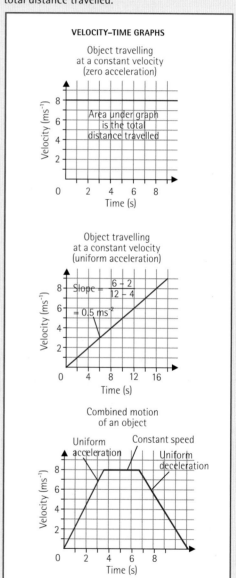

graphene
is an allotrope of carbon that resembles a single
layer of graphite made up of flat hexagonal carbon
rings. It is almost transparent and is a 2-dimensional
material. However it is extremely strong and also
(like graphite) is a good conductor of electricity.
• *Graphene may be used in the future in making
faster, more powerful computer chips.*
SEE ALSO **allotrope, graphite**

graphite (*also* **black lead, plumbago**)
is a natural black form of the element carbon which
exists as a macromolecule with a layered structure
of flat hexagons. The bonds inside each hexagon are
strong covalent bonds. The bonds between the layers
are weak van der Waals forces, which makes graphite
soft and flaky and suitable for use as a lubricant or
in pencil leads. Graphite is also a good conductor
of electricity and heat, as each carbon atom has
only used three of its four outermost electrons in
covalent bonding to three other carbon atoms. The
spare electron can become delocalized along the flat
hexagons, which therefore conduct electricity.
• *Graphite, when aligned along its hexagons, can
form very strong and light carbon fibres.*
SEE ALSO **conductor, covalent bond, carbon fibre,
macromolecule, van der Waals forces**

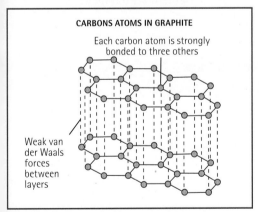

CARBONS ATOMS IN GRAPHITE

Each carbon atom is strongly
bonded to three others

Weak van
der Waals
forces
between
layers

gravitational force (*also* **gravitation,
gravity**)
is the force of attraction that objects have on one
another because of their masses. Like magnetic or
electric forces, it is a force that acts at a distance
according to the inverse square law. Normally the
gravitational force between two objects is very
weak. However, if one of the objects is massive, such
as a planet, the force becomes noticeable. On the
surface of the Earth the gravitational force acting on
a mass of 1 kilogram is approximately 9.8 N. The size
of this force becomes smaller as the object moves
further away from the surface of the Earth. Outside
the Earth's gravitational field an object becomes
'weightless'. (Its mass, however, remains the same.)
• *Gravity is the force of attraction which holds
comets, moons, satellites and space stations in orbit.*
SEE ALSO **acceleration of gravity, circular motion,
inverse square law, Newton's law of gravitation**

gravitational potential energy store
(*also* E_p)
is the stored energy an object has because of its
position above the Earth. The further away from the
Earth, the greater the gravitational potential energy
store. The relationship can be expressed by the
following equation:

$$E_p(J) = mass\ (kg) \times gravitational\ force\ (N/kg) \times height\ (m)$$

An object of 1 kg mass which is 1 metre away from
the Earth's surface has a gravitational potential
energy of 9.8 J (assuming g = 9.8 N/kg). When the
object falls to Earth it loses this potential energy,
which is changed to kinetic energy.
SEE ALSO **energy store, kinetic energy store**

gravitropism (*also* **geotropism**)
is the growth response of a plant to the pull of
gravity. The root of a plant is positively gravitropic
as it grows towards the pull of gravity. The stem is
negatively gravitropic as it grows away from the pull
of gravity.

gravity *see* **gravitational force**

gray (*also* **Gy**)
A gray is the SI unit for measuring absorbed dose of
radiation, equivalent to the absorption of 1 J/kg of
ionizing radiation.
SEE ALSO **radioactive contamination**

green–belt area
Green-belt areas are areas around towns and
cities where housing or industrial development is
restricted. Such areas prevent 'urban sprawl' or
'ribbon development' along roads.
• *To protect **green–belt areas** around towns and
cities priority should be given to the development of
derelict sites within towns or cities.*

greenhouse effect
The greenhouse effect is the trapping of heat
energy in the atmosphere because of the effects
of greenhouse gases. The infra-red radiation (heat
energy) emitted from the Earth's surface, as it is

»

warmed by the Sun, has a lower frequency than that emitted directly from the Sun. It is absorbed and re-emitted by the greenhouse gases in the atmosphere.
• *The greenhouse effect results in global warming.*
SEE ALSO **global warming, greenhouse gas**

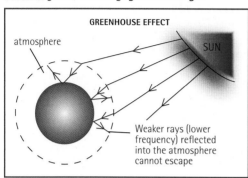

GREENHOUSE EFFECT

atmosphere

SUN

Weaker rays (lower frequency) reflected into the atmosphere cannot escape

greenhouse gas
Greenhouse gases are gases in the atmosphere which absorb infra-red radiation, causing an increase in air temperature. The most important is carbon dioxide, which is increased by burning fossil fuels and by deforestation, which reduces the amount of carbon dioxide removed by photosynthesis.
• *Methane is a greenhouse gas, a by-product of rice-farming, cattle rearing, and landfill sites.*
SEE ALSO **carbon dioxide, photosynthesis**

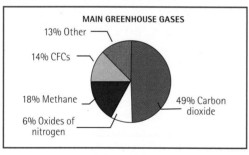

MAIN GREENHOUSE GASES

13% Other
14% CFCs
18% Methane
6% Oxides of nitrogen
49% Carbon dioxide

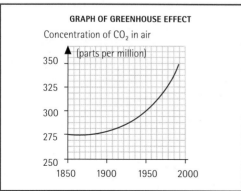

GRAPH OF GREENHOUSE EFFECT

Concentration of CO_2 in air (parts per million)

gristle see cartilage

group
A group is a vertical column of elements in the periodic table. Groups are numbered using roman numerals. Elements within a particular group have similar chemical properties because they have the same number of valence electrons (electrons in the outermost shell). Within groups of metallic elements, the reactivity of the metal increases as we go down the group. Within groups of non-metallic elements, the reactivity of the non-metal decreases as we go down the group. Group IV contains carbon (the element of life) and silicon (the element of rocks).
SEE ALSO **element, periodic table, valence electron**

Group number	Common name
I	Alkali metals
II	Alkaline-earth metals
VII	Halogens
VIII	Noble gases

group 0 element see noble gas

group I element see alkali metal

group II element see alkaline-earth metal

group VII element see halogen

grub
A grub is another word for the larva of an insect, especially the larva of beetles.
SEE ALSO **larva**

gullet see oesophagus

guanine see DNA

gum disease
results if plaque is not removed and the bacteria present infect the gums. The gums swell, and when you brush your teeth, they may bleed. If the bacteria are allowed to spread, they could infect the root. The tooth becomes loose and may have to be extracted.
• *Gum disease can be prevented by regular brushing of the teeth (two or three times a day), especially just after meals. Regular visits to the dentist allow treatment of any early signs of tooth decay or gum disease.*
SEE ALSO **plaque, tooth decay**

Gy see gray

gynaecium
is the collective term for all the female parts (carpels) of a flower.
SEE ALSO **carpel, ovary, stigma, style**

Hh

H *see* **hydrogen**

H⁺ *see* **hydrogen ion**

H₂ *see* **hydrogen molecule**

Haber process
The Haber process is the process for the manufacture of ammonia gas from direct combination of nitrogen and hydrogen gases in the ratio of 1:3 (see equation). It is immensely important, as the ammonia gas is used to manufacture fertilizers.

$$\text{nitrogen} + \text{hydrogen} \rightleftharpoons \text{ammonia}$$
$$N_2 + 3H_2 \rightleftharpoons 2NH_3$$

• *The Haber process is named after the German chemist Fritz Haber (1886–1934).*
SEE ALSO **ammonia, fertilizer**

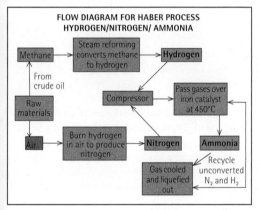

FLOW DIAGRAM FOR HABER PROCESS
HYDROGEN/NITROGEN/ AMMONIA

➤ **conditions for the Haber process** Conditions for the process reflect the fact that the reaction between hydrogen and nitrogen gases is reversible and exothermic. A high yield of ammonia is favoured by low temperature. However, if the temperature is too low, the rate of the chemical reaction is too slow. A moderate temperature of 450°C is therefore used, with a catalyst of iron and promoters of aluminium and potassium oxides. The higher the pressure, the greater the yield of ammonia. In practice, pressures of around 250 atmospheres are used. Higher pressures pose technical problems and unacceptable expense.
SEE ALSO **catalyst, exothermic reaction, reversible reaction**

habitat
A habitat is the physical environment where an organism or a community of organisms lives. Habitats are named after their major physical characteristic e.g. river, woodland, grassland, desert, mountain, etc.
• *A habitat might be just one field or a large area of grassland.*
SEE ALSO **community, ecosystem**

WORD BUILD

alien
describes an animal or plant that is living out of its usual habitat. For example, a zebra would be an alien to a forest environment.

indigenous
describes an animal or plant that is living in its usual habitat. For example, a zebra would be indigenous to a grassland environment.

macro–habitat
A macro-habitat is a large habitat and may have the same name as the ecosystem (woodland, grassland, etc.) but excludes the living organisms within the ecosystem.

micro–habitat
A micro-habitat is a very small habitat. It might be a rotting tree or log or a single rock pool.

haemoglobin
is the blood pigment in red blood cells which transports oxygen.
• *When haemoglobin combines with oxygen to form oxyhaemoglobin it becomes bright red in colour.*
SEE ALSO **red blood cell**

haemophilia
is a genetic disease in which a blood clotting substance (factor VIII) is missing or faulty, causing a person's blood to clot very slowly. This is because there are too few platelets, or because the platelets are unable to release thromboplastin. Haemophilia is caused by a recessive allele carried on the X-chromosome. It therefore affects males, but females can be carriers of the disease. The diagram shows the filial offspring (F1) of a normal male (XY) and female carrier (XhX) of haemophilia.
SEE ALSO **allele, blood clotting, genetic disease, platelet, sex chromosome**

»

HAEMOPHILIA		
	Normal male	
Gametes	X	Y
Female carrier X^h	XX^h	X^hY
X	XX	XY

Offspring (F_1):
Normal male   XY
Normal female   XX
Carrier female XX^h
Haemophiliac male X^hY

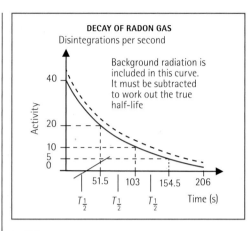

hair follicle
A hair follicle is a long, narrow tube in the epidermis which contains a hair.
• *The hair grows as new cells are added at its base from cells lining the hair follicle.*
SEE ALSO **epidermis**

half equation
A half equation is a model for the change that happens to one reactant in a chemical reaction. For example, consider the chemical reaction of magnesium with oxygen to form magnesium oxide.

$$2Mg(s) + O_2(g) \rightarrow 2MgO(s)$$

The half equation for the magnesium reactant shows it changing to form magnesium ions in the magnesium oxide product.

$$2Mg \rightarrow 2Mg^{2+} + 4e-$$

The half equation for the oxygen reactant shows it changing to form oxide ions in the magnesium oxide product.

$$O_2 + 4e- \rightarrow 2O^{2-}$$

• *Half equations are useful to see if a reactant has been oxidized (losing electrons) or reduced (gaining electrons).*
SEE ALSO **chemical equation, chemical reaction, oxidation, product, reactant, reduction**

half-life (*also* $T_{\frac{1}{2}}$)
The half-life is the time taken for half the atoms in a radioactive sample to undergo radioactive decay. Half-life is therefore the time for the radiation emitted to be halved in intensity.
• *Half-life values vary enormously. For example, radon gas has a half-life of 51.5 seconds, whereas carbon-14 has a half-life of 5,600 years.*
SEE ALSO **radioactive decay**

halide
Halides are the salts formed when halogens react with metals. If chlorine gas is passed over heated iron wool, the iron wool glows brightly and forms a brown smoke of iron(III) chloride.

iron   +   chlorine $\rightarrow$ iron (III) chloride
2Fe   + $3Cl_2$ $\rightarrow$ $2FeCl_3$

SEE ALSO **halogen, hydrogen halide**

➤ **testing for halides** Metal halide salts are ionic substances and therefore usually dissolve in water. However, the silver halides are insoluble and this can be used as a test for the halides.
The test involves dissolving the halide salt in dilute nitric acid and then adding silver nitrate solution. If a precipitate forms a halide ion must be present. You use nitric acid to dissolve the halide to remove any carbonate ions, as these would also form a precipitate with the silver ions, so must be removed.

Halide	Addition of silver nitrate solution
chloride	white precipitate of silver chloride AgCl
bromide	cream precipitate of silver bromide AgBr
iodine	yellow precipitate of silver iodide AgI

hallucinogen *see* **drug**

halogen (*also* **group VII element**)
Halogens are the elements in Group VII of the periodic table, which have seven valence electrons in their outermost shell. The ions and compounds of halogens are called halides.
• *The name* **halogen** *is derived from Greek and means 'salt-maker'.*
SEE ALSO **halide, periodic table, valence electron**

➤ **physical properties of halogens** The halogens are all diatomic molecules (F_2, Cl_2, Br_2, and I_2), which have poisonous vapours or gases. As we go down the group, the molecules become larger and heavier, and the melting and boiling point increases. Fluorine and chlorine are gases, bromine is a liquid, and iodine is a solid (at room temperature and pressure).

SEE ALSO **diatomic molecule**

➤ **chemical properties of halogens** The halogens are reactive non-metals whose reactivity decreases as we go down the group. This is because, as the atoms become larger, it makes it more difficult for the nucleus to attract electrons. Because the halogens have seven valence electrons, they react with metals to form the negatively charged halide ions F^-, Cl^-, Br^-, and I^-. As they are good at accepting electrons, they act as oxidizing agents.

Element	Diatomic molecule	Interatomic distance
Fluorine	F_2	0.14 nm
Chlorine	Cl_2	0.19 nm
Bromine	Br_2	0.23 nm
Iodine	I_2	0.27 nm

Element	Melting point (°C)	Boiling point (°C)
Fluorine	−220	−188
Chlorine	−101	−35
Bromine	−7	59
Iodine	114	184

Element	Solubility in water	Appearance
Fluorine	very soluble	pale yellow-green gas
Chlorine	quite soluble	pale green-yellow gas
Bromine	slightly soluble	dark red fuming liquid giving off brown vapour
Iodine	almost insoluble	silvery-black solid (gives off purple vapour on heating)

➤ **bleaching action** Halogens in aqueous solutions are bleaching agents. Chlorine dissolves in water to form chlorine water. This is a mixture of two acids, namely hydrochloric acid and chloric(I) acid.

chlorine + water → hydrochloric acid + chloric(I) acid
$$Cl_2 + H_2O \rightarrow HCl + HClO$$

Chloric(I) acid is a bleach, as it is an oxidizing agent. When the dye is oxidized, it becomes colourless.

➤ **displacement reactions** Any halogen above another in the group is more reactive and a more powerful oxidizing agent. It will therefore displace any halogen below it from a solution of its salt. For example, chlorine displaces both bromide and iodide ions, as it oxidizes these ions to the element.

chlorine + potassium bromide → potassium chloride + bromine
$$Cl_2 + 2KBr \rightarrow 2KCl + Br_2$$

bromine + potassium iodide → potassium bromide + iodine
$$Br_2 + 2KI \rightarrow 2KBr + I_2$$

➤ **affinity for hydrogen in halogens** Chlorine has a strong attraction for hydrogen and it will remove hydrogen from many compounds, especially hydrocarbons, to form hydrogen chloride gas. Hydrogen will even burn in chlorine gas. This is used in the industrial preparation of hydrochloric acid, as hydrogen chloride gas readily dissolves in water to produce this acid.

SEE ALSO **non-metal, oxidizing agent**

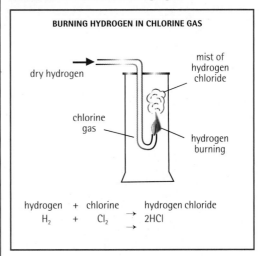

BURNING HYDROGEN IN CHLORINE GAS

dry hydrogen

mist of hydrogen chloride

chlorine gas

hydrogen burning

hydrogen + chlorine → hydrogen chloride
$$H_2 + Cl_2 \rightarrow 2HCl$$

a
b
c
d
e
f
g
h
i
j
k
l
m
n
o
p
q
r
s
t
u
v
w
x
y
z

»

	Uses of halogens
1.	Fluorine is added as fluoride salts to drinking water to reduce dental decay.
2.	Chlorine in solution is used as a bleach and for sterilizing water.
3.	Bromine is used as bromide salts on black-and-white photographic film.
4.	Iodine in solution in alcohol is used as an antiseptic (tincture of iodine). When dissolved in KI solution, it is used as a test for starch (turns from brown to black).

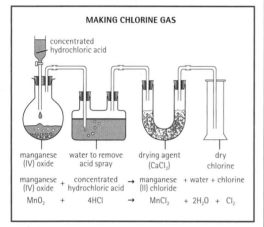

MAKING CHLORINE GAS

concentrated hydrochloric acid

| manganese (IV) oxide | water to remove acid spray | drying agent ($CaCl_2$) | dry chlorine |

$$\text{manganese (IV) oxide} + \text{concentrated hydrochloric acid} \rightarrow \text{manganese (II) chloride} + \text{water} + \text{chlorine}$$

$$MnO_2 + 4HCl \rightarrow MnCl_2 + 2H_2O + Cl_2$$

handling radioactive sources
see **radioactive source**

haploid
describes a cell which has a single set of unpaired chromosomes in its nucleus.
• *Gamete or sex cells are* **haploid** *and are formed by meiosis.*
SEE ALSO gamete, meiosis

hard magnetic material see **magnetic material**

hard water
is water that is difficult to lather with soap because of dissolved calcium and magnesium ions in the water. These ions react with soap to form a scum, and also fur up kettles and hot-water pipes.
SEE ALSO soft water

Advantages of hard water	Disadvantages of hard water
pleasant taste	needs more soap
good for teeth and bones	leaves messy scum
evidence that it helps prevent heart disease	leaves fur, scale in pipes and kettles

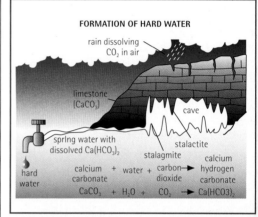

FORMATION OF HARD WATER

rain dissolving CO_2 in air

limestone ($CaCO_3$)

cave

spring water with dissolved $Ca(HCO_3)_2$

stalactite

stalagmite

hard water

$$\text{calcium carbonate} + \text{water} + \text{carbon dioxide} \rightarrow \text{calcium hydrogen carbonate}$$

$$CaCO_3 + H_2O + CO_2 \rightarrow Ca(HCO3)_2$$

WORD BUILD

permanent hardness
is hardness which cannot be removed by heating. It is caused by dissolved calcium or magnesium sulphate ($CaSO_4$ or $MgSO_4$).

temporary hardness
is hardness which can be removed on heating. It is due to dissolved calcium (or magnesium) hydrogen carbonate, which, on heating, decomposes to calcium (or magnesium) carbonate. This is deposited as a scale or fur on the heating element.

$$\text{calcium hydrogen carbonate} \xrightarrow{\text{heat}} \text{calcium carbonate} + \text{water} + \text{carbon dioxide}$$

$$Ca(HCO_3)_2(aq) \rightarrow CaCO_3(s) + H_2O(l) + CO_2(g)$$

harmonic (*also* overtone)
Harmonics are frequencies of a wave which are multiples of the fundamental frequency.
• *When a stretched spring vibrates, the simplest vibration is the 'fundamental' or first* **harmonic**.
SEE ALSO frequency

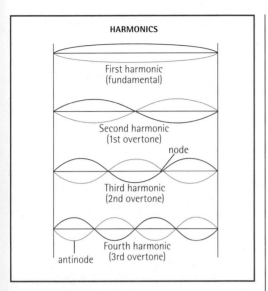

HARMONICS

First harmonic
(fundamental)

Second harmonic
(1st overtone)

node

Third harmonic
(2nd overtone)

antinode

Fourth harmonic
(3rd overtone)

hazard symbol
A hazard symbol is an international symbol used on chemicals which are potentially harmful.
• *Hazard symbols appear on the labels of chemical bottles and alert us to the presence and type of potential hazards.*
SEE ALSO flammable, oxidizing agent, toxin

H–bomb *see* fusion bomb

HDPE *see* high–density polyethene

headphone
A headphone is an electrical device which changes electrical signals into sound energy. The receiver of the headphone contains an electric coil which uses the motor effect to cause vibration to produce the sound.
• *Headphones often have a receiver held over the ears by a band fitting over the head.*
SEE ALSO loudspeaker, motor effect, sound wave

hearing
is the sense by which we detect sounds.

hearing aid
Hearing aids are used by people with hearing difficulties. They are placed close to the ear and contain a small electrical amplifier. This makes the sound louder, so that it can be picked up by fewer sensory cells.

heart
The heart is a muscular organ which pumps blood around the body through the blood vessels. The heart's pumping action is driven by cardiac muscle in its walls.
SEE ALSO aorta, atrium, bicuspid valve, inferior vena cava, pulmonary artery, pulmonary vein, superior vena cava, tricuspid valve, ventricle

a
b
c
d
e
f
g
h
i
j
k
l
m
n
o
p
q
r
s
t
u
v
w
x
y
z

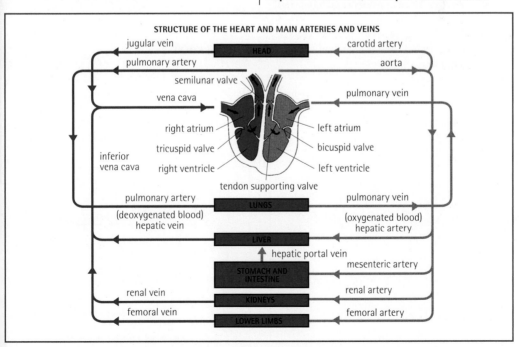

STRUCTURE OF THE HEART AND MAIN ARTERIES AND VEINS

jugular vein
HEAD
carotid artery

pulmonary artery
aorta

semilunar valve

vena cava
pulmonary vein

right atrium
left atrium

tricuspid valve
bicuspid valve

inferior vena cava
right ventricle
left ventricle

tendon supporting valve

pulmonary artery
LUNGS
pulmonary vein

(deoxygenated blood)
hepatic vein
(oxygenated blood)
hepatic artery

LIVER

hepatic portal vein

STOMACH AND INTESTINE
mesenteric artery

renal vein
KIDNEYS
renal artery

femoral vein
LOWER LIMBS
femoral artery

heartbeat

A heartbeat is the alternate contraction and relaxation of the heart muscles.

WORD BUILD

diastole

is the phase of a heartbeat when the heart muscles relax so that the ventricles can fill with blood.

systole

is the phase of the heartbeat when the heart muscles contract and the ventricles force blood into the arteries.

pulse rate

is the number of heartbeats per minute (usually around 70).

heat

is the process of energy transfer from one body to another as a result of temperature difference.
• *Heat always flows from a hotter body to a cooler body.*
SEE ALSO heat energy

➤ **prevention of heat loss** in the home and workplace helps to conserve energy:
  – **loft insulation** fibreglass or vermiculite between ceiling joists reduces conduction and radiation through the roof
  – **double glazing** two panes of glass with partial vacuum between reduces conduction and radiation through windows
  – **a cavity wall insulation** filling the gap between cavity walls with plastic foam reduces convection and radiation through walls
  – **carpet or felt on floors** reduces conduction and convection through floors.

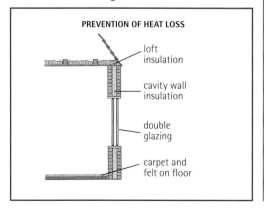

PREVENTION OF HEAT LOSS

loft insulation
cavity wall insulation
double glazing
carpet and felt on floor

heat capacity (*also* thermal capacity, C)

is the heat energy absorbed or released by an object when its temperature changes by 1K. The heat capacity of an object depends upon its mass and the type of material the object is made of.
• *The SI unit of* **heat capacity** *is joule per kelvin (JK^{-1}).*
SEE ALSO specific heat capacity

heat energy

is the energy that flows from one place to another as a result of a difference in temperature. Energy will always naturally flow from a place of high energy to a place of low energy, and therefore from high temperature to low temperature (except in a heat pump).
SEE ALSO heat pump, thermal energy

➤ **calculations of heat energy** Knowing the mass and specific heat capacity of a substance, you can calculate the amount of energy required to produce a particular temperature rise in that substance. The relationship is given by the following formula.

$$Q = m \times c \times \Delta T$$

heat energy (J)	mass (kg)	specific heat capacity (J kg^{-1} K$_{-1}$)	change in temperature (K)

heat exchanger

A heat exchanger is a device for removing heat from two fluids (liquids or gases) without allowing the fluids to contact one another.

heating curve

A heating curve is a graph showing changes in temperature with time for a substance being heated. The flat sections on the graph indicate the melting and boiling points. Here the temperature remains the same over a period of time, as the heat energy is being used to change the structure of the substance.
SEE ALSO cooling curve

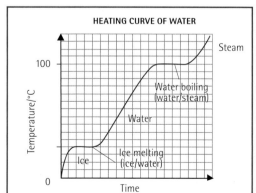

HEATING CURVE OF WATER

Steam
100
Water boiling (water/steam)
Water
Temperature/°C
Ice melting (ice/water)
Ice
0
Time

heat pump
A heat pump is a device for transferring heat from a region of low temperature to a region of high temperature by doing work, using an energy supply such as an electric motor.
• *A refrigerator is a heat pump which transfers heat energy from the colder inside to the warmer outside.*
SEE ALSO heat energy, work

heat-sensitive switch *see* electronic switch

heat stroke
is a failure of the body's temperature regulation in high surrounding temperatures. The sweat glands fail to produce sweat and the person must be moved to cool surroundings.
SEE ALSO sweat gland

heat transfer
occurs whenever there is a temperature difference, as heat energy is transferred from a hotter to a colder place. This heat transfer continues until both places are at the same temperature and have the same thermal energy. There are three possible ways heat energy can be transferred: conduction, convection, and radiation.
SEE ALSO conduction, convection, heat energy, radiation, temperature, thermal energy

heliotropism *see* phototropism

helium *see* noble gas

herbaceous plant
Herbaceous plants are plants which die back above ground level during the winter but have organs for survival beneath the soil. These organs are called 'perennating organs'. They include bulbs, corms, rhizomes, and tubers (see stem).
SEE ALSO dicotyledon, stem

herbivore
Herbivores are animals like cattle, deer, rabbits, and sheep which feed on plants. These animals have grinding teeth (molars) and an alimentary canal that can digest cellulose.
• *All herbivores are primary consumers.*
SEE ALSO consumer

heredity
is the process that makes living things develop in a similar way to their parents or ancestors. The unit of hereditary information is the gene which is transferred from one generation to the next.

• *Heredity accounts for why children often resemble their parents in appearance, for example in hair colour, eye colour, etc.*
SEE ALSO chromosome, gene

hermaphrodite
refers to an organism which contains both male and female reproductive organs.
• *The term hermaphrodite is applied to animals such as worms which contain both male and female organs.*
SEE ALSO bisexual

hertz (*also* Hz, cycles per second, cps)
is the SI unit of frequency.
• *10 hertz (Hz) means 10 oscillations per second, producing 10 complete waves per second or 10 complete cycles per second (cps).*
SEE ALSO frequency

Hertzsprung–Russell diagram
Hertzsprung-Russell diagrams are graphs which plot the brightness of the stars against their colour. Blue stars are very hot and at the beginning of their life. A red star is cooler and generally older. Our Sun is a yellow star in the middle part of its life (main sequence).
SEE ALSO stellar evolution

Hess's law
states that in a particular chemical reaction the overall energy change is the same no matter which route is taken in going from reactants to products.
• *Hess's law was named after the Russian chemist Germain Henri Hess (1802–50).*
SEE ALSO chemical reaction, intermediate, product, reactant

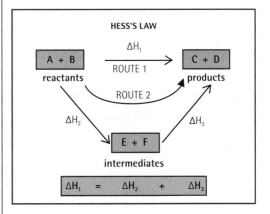

heterogeneous mixture *see* mixture

heterotrophic nutrition *see* nutrition

heterozygous
describes an organism that possesses two different alleles of a particular gene in a given pair of chromosomes. Two organisms which are heterozygous for a particular character will produce equal numbers of offspring which are homozygous or heterozygous with respect to that particular character. The overall phenotype for such a cross is always in a ratio of 3:1. (see diagram)

SEE ALSO **allele, homozygous, variation**

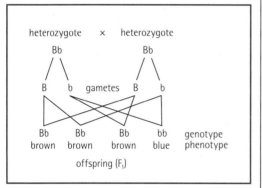

heterozygote × heterozygote
Bb   Bb

B   b   gametes   B   b

Bb   Bb   Bb   bb   genotype
brown   brown   brown   blue   phenotype

offspring (F₁)

hibernation
Hibernation is when an animal hides from the world and goes into a deep sleep. During hibernation various body changes occur such as lowering of body temperature and pulse rate. This helps the animal to live on their reserves of body fat. Bears, bats, hedgehogs, and butterflies hibernate in winter.
• *Hibernation normally takes place in winter when food is scarce.*

➤ **hibernate** Animals hibernate when they go into hibernation.

high blood pressure
may be associated with various circulatory diseases.

WORD BUILD

thrombosis (*also* embolism)
is the formation of a small solid lump of blood (blood clot) inside a blood vessel which restricts (or stops) the flow of blood.

stroke (*also* apoplexy)
is caused by a cerebral thrombosis (blood clot on the brain). After a stroke, a certain area of the brain may stop working. This may result in muscles being paralysed and memory being affected.

arteriosclerosis
is hardening of the arteries with age as the muscular walls become less elastic, which reduces blood flow.

atheroma
is the build up of a fatty substance called cholesterol inside the artery walls. Such a blockage increases blood pressure and may cause:
- heart attack (or coronary), which occurs when a coronary artery is blocked by thrombosis or atheroma
- angina pectoris, which is caused by partial blockage of one or both of the coronary arteries by atheroma, resulting in severe pains in the chest.

high-density polyethene (*also* HDPE)
is formed when ethene gas is bubbled into a hydrocarbon solvent with special catalysts at 100°C and atmospheric pressure. HDPE has few branching chains, so the polymer chains can pack close together. It is a hard plastic with a density around 0.96 g cm^{-3}.
• *The uses of high-density polyethene include making trays, bottle crates, etc.*

SEE ALSO **low-density polyethene**

hinge joint *see* joint

hip girdle *see* pelvic girdle

HIV
stands for 'human immunodeficiency virus' and is the virus which causes AIDS. This virus is found in body fluids such as semen, vaginal fluid, and blood. HIV can be spread:
- when an infected person has sexual intercourse with another person
- when a person uses contaminated needles from syringes when abusing drugs, from ear-piercing, or from tattooing

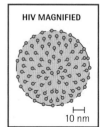

HIV MAGNIFIED

10 nm

– during blood transfusions if blood is passed from an infected donor
– during pregnancy or childbirth from the mother to the baby.

SEE ALSO **AIDS**

HIV positive
indicates having antibodies against the HI-Virus (antigen) and thereby being infected with the HI-Virus.

Hoffmann voltameter
A Hoffmann voltameter is a type of electrolytic cell which is used to collect and measure volumes of gases liberated during electrolysis. Electrolysis of acidified water produces twice as much hydrogen as oxygen. This indicates a ratio of 2:1 in the chemical composition of water (H_2O).

SEE ALSO **electrolysis**

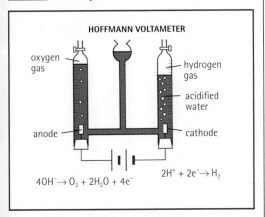

HOFFMANN VOLTAMETER

oxygen gas

hydrogen gas

acidified water

anode

cathode

$4OH^- \rightarrow O_2 + 2H_2O + 4e^-$ $2H^+ + 2e^- \rightarrow H_2$

holophytic nutrition *see* **nutrition**

holozoic nutrition *see* **nutrition**

homeostasis
is the maintenance of a constant internal environment of an organism. Examples of homeostasis include keeping body temperature constant (in warm-blooded animals), keeping composition of body fluids constant, and maintaining a constant metabolic rate. The detection of any deviation from normal is achieved by the passing of information to organs such as the lungs, skin, kidneys, and liver. The correction of these deviations is achieved by negative feedback.

SEE ALSO **metabolic rate, negative feedback**

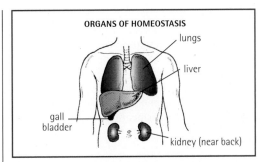

ORGANS OF HOMEOSTASIS

lungs

liver

gall bladder

kidney (near back)

homogeneous mixture *see* **mixture**

homoiotherm *see* **warm–blooded animal**

homologous chromosome *see* **chromosome**

homologous series
A homologous series is a series of related organic compounds with the same functional group. Members of such a series can be represented by a general formula. Each member of the series differs from the next by an additional $-CH_2-$ group.
For example with the alcohol homologous series the functional group is $-OH$ and the general formula is $C_nH_2n + 1OH$ with members like methanol (CH_3OH), ethanol (C_2H_5OH) etc.
• *Members of a* **homologous series** *have similar chemical properties. Their physical properties gradually change as the molecule gets larger.*

SEE ALSO **functional group alcohol, alkane, alkene, alkyne**

homologous structure
Homologous structures are structures in different organisms which have fundamental similarities although they may have developed quite different functions.
• *An example of a* **homologous structure** *is the forelimb of a vertebrate animal as they all have a similar bone structure.*

SEE ALSO **vestigial structure**

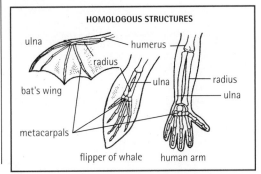

HOMOLOGOUS STRUCTURES

ulna

humerus

radius

ulna

radius

bat's wing

ulna

metacarpals

flipper of whale   human arm

Homo sapiens

is the species of animal called a human being. The species developed from primates (apes) and appeared about 100 000 years age as Neanderthal man.

• *Homo sapiens is the Latin for 'wise man' and is the binomial classification of Carl Linnaeus (1758).*

SEE ALSO **binomial classification**

homozygous

describes an organism that possesses identical alleles of a particular gene in a given pair of chromosomes. Two organisms that are homozygous for a particular character will produce offspring which are also homozygous and identical to the parent with respect to that particular character. Two organisms that are dominant and recessive homozygous will produce offspring which are all heterozygous (see diagram).

SEE ALSO **allele, heterozygous, variation**

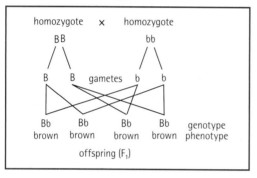

honey

is a sweet, sticky, yellowish substance made by bees from the nectar they collect from flowers.

• *Bees store honey in a honeycomb and feed it to their growing larvae.*

SEE ALSO **nectary**

Hooke's law

states that the extension of an elastic material is directly proportional to the force that is stretching it. It can be expressed by the following relationship:

$$\text{force (N)} = \text{spring constant (N/m)} \times \text{extension (m)}$$

This relationship is only true up to the 'elastic limit' of the material so that when the force is removed the spring returns to its original length.

• *Hooke's law was named after the English scientist Robert Hooke (1635–1703).*

SEE ALSO **elasticity, elastic limit**

hormone

A hormone is a substance produced within the body of an animal or plant, or made synthetically, and carried by the blood or sap to an organ which it stimulates.

SEE ALSO **sex hormone**

Hormone	Endocrine gland	When secreted
Insulin	islet of Langerhans in pancreas	when blood glucose level rises above normal
Glucagon	islet of Langerhans in pancreas	when blood glucose level drops below normal
Adrenalin	adrenal gland (above kidneys)	small amounts all the time - large amounts when frightened
Thyroxine	thyroid gland (in neck)	throughout life
Testosterone (androgen)	testes	in larger quantities from puberty onwards
Oestrogen	ovaries	in larger quantities from puberty onwards particularly when follicle is developing in ovary
Progesterone	corpus luteum (in ovaries)	after ovulation through pregnancy
Anti-Diuretic Hormone (ADH)	pituitary gland (base of brain)	when quantity of water in blood gets low
Thyroid-Stimulating Hormone (TSH)	pituitary gland	throughout life
Growth hormone	pituitary gland	throughout life but especially when young
Gonadotrophic hormones — FSH (Follicle-Stimulating Hormone) — LH (Luteinising Hormone	pituitary gland	from puberty onwards

Hormone	Function
Insulin	stimulates the liver to remove glucose by converting it into glycogen
Glucagon	stimulates the liver to break down glycogen and release glucose back into the blood
Adrenalin	prepares the body for "fight or flight"
Thyroxine	controls metabolic rate, especially respiration in the mitochondria of cells
Testosterone (androgen)	controls development of male sex organs and secondary sex characteristics - greater amounts in males gives aggression and a competitive urge
Oestrogen	controls development of female sex organs and secondary sex characteristics - causes lining of uterus to become thick and spongy
Progesterone	maintains the lining of the uterus (lack can cause a miscarriage)
Anti-Diuretic Hormone (ADH)	allows kidneys to reabsorb water
Thyroid-Stimulating Hormone (TSH)	causes thyroid gland to secrete thyroxine
Growth hormone	stimulates growth (lack causes dwarfism; excess causes giantism)
Gonadotrophic hormones	stimulate changes during menstrual cycle
— FSH (Follicle-Stimulating Hormone)	causes an egg to develop in one of the ovaries and stimulates ovaries to produce oestrogen
— LH (Luteinising Hormone)	stimulates the release of an egg at day 14 during the menstrual cycle

animal hormone

Animal hormones are special chemical 'messengers' secreted in small quantities directly into the bloodstream by an endocrine gland. They travel all over the body, but normally a hormone has a specific effect on one particular organ (target organ) or tissue (target cell).
• *Animal hormones typically have long-lasting effects, and control things which need constant adjustment or control over long periods.*
SEE ALSO **endocrine gland**

plant hormone

Plant hormones are specific chemicals produced by the cells of plants which, at very low concentration, can affect growth and development. Such hormones have various uses for both gardeners and farmers:
– as weedkillers: growth hormones, such as auxins, can make weeds grow so fast that they exhaust themselves and die
– to produce seedless fruit: growth hormones applied to unpollinated flowers cause the fruits to grow without seeds (e.g. seedless grapes)
– as rooting compounds: cut stems can be dipped in rooting hormones, such as gibberellins, to encourage growth.

antagonistic hormones

are hormones that produce opposite effects.
• *Insulin and glucagon are antagonistic hormones.*

hormone replacement therapy (*also* HRT)

is used by women after the menopause to replace female sex hormones which would normally be produced during ovulation.
• *Hormone replacement therapy has been shown to carry some risks, like increase incidence of cancer or heart disease.*
SEE ALSO **menopause**

host

A host is the organism on which a parasite lives.
• *The host provides nourishment and shelter for the parasite.*
SEE ALSO **parasite, parasitism**

hot-air balloon

A hot-air balloon has a gas heater to warm the air inside the balloon's bag. This makes the air inside the bag less dense. As the hot air is less dense than the surrounding cooler air an upthrust force is created that makes the balloon rise.
SEE ALSO **density, upthrust**

household circuit

Household circuits can be classified into three main types: cooker circuit, ring main, and lighting circuits. Each of these circuits has a different fuse rating (e.g. cooker 30A, ring main 15A, lighting 5A). Appliances are arranged in these circuits in parallel, so that if an appliance breaks or is switched off, other appliances in the circuit can still work.
SEE ALSO **electrical circuit, fuse rating**

a
b
c
d
e
f
g
h
i
j
k
l
m
n
o
p
q
r
s
t
u
v
w
x
y
z

»

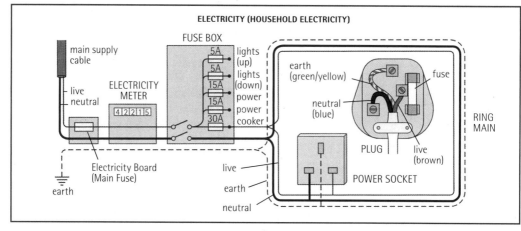

HRT *see* **hormone replacement therapy**

human hearing range

The human ear can detect sounds with frequencies between 20 and 20,000 Hz (hertz). The ability to hear sounds in the upper part of the frequency range decreases with age.

SEE ALSO **audible sound, hearing**

human immunodeficiency virus *see* HIV

human senses

The human senses include the five distinct senses of hearing, sight, smell, touch, and taste. Each human sense has a specific sensory organ. The sense organs are connected to the central nervous system which processes all the information gathered by the sense organs and then produces an appropriate response in the human body.

• *Human senses are essential to detect our environment.*

SEE ALSO **ear, eye, nose, sense organ, skin, taste bud, tongue**

Human sense	Sensory organ
sight	eye
hearing	ear
touch	skin
taste	tongue
smell	nose

human skeleton

The human skeleton is an endoskeleton consisting of 206 bones, the largest being the femur (thigh bone) and the smallest being the stapes in the middle ear. Its main functions are support and protection of the body, movement, and the making of blood cells in the marrow of the long bones.

– The axial skeleton is the main longitudinal section of the skeleton, i.e. skull, vertebral column, and rib cage.
– The appendicular skeleton is the term for those parts of the skeleton that are attached to the axial skeleton, i.e. pectoral girdle, pelvic girdle, arms and legs.

SEE ALSO **endoskeleton**

humus

is the dark brown organic component of the soil. It is formed by the action of decomposers (e.g. bacteria, fungi, earthworms) on dead plants, animal remains, and excrement. Humus lightens the texture of the soil and also provides important nutrients for healthy plant growth. Acidic humus (called mor) is found in coniferous forest, and is formed mainly by fungi. Alkaline humus (called mull) is found in deciduous forest and grassland, and supports an abundance of bacteria and small animals such as earthworms.

SEE ALSO **decomposer, soil**

hurricane

A hurricane is a storm with a huge mass of spinning rain and wind.

• *The violent wind of a **hurricane** has the highest rating (above 73 mph or force 12) on the Beaufort scale for wind speed.*

HUMAN SKELETON

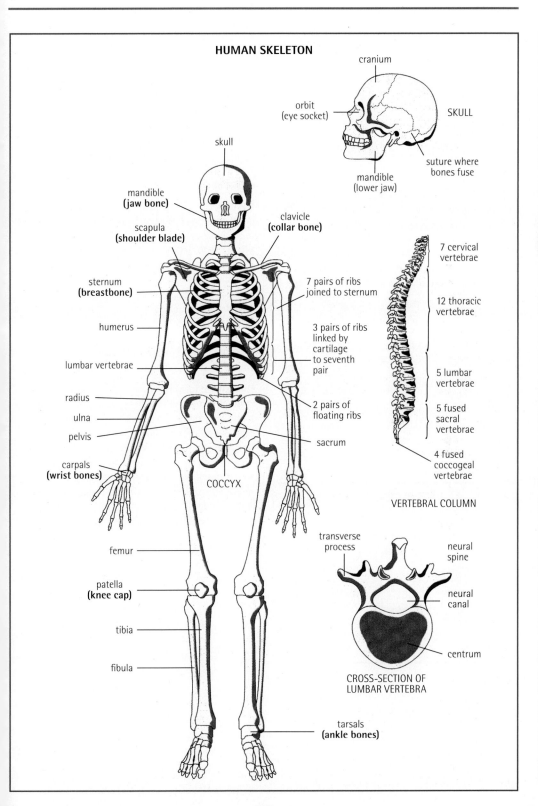

cranium

orbit
(eye socket)

SKULL

mandible
(lower jaw)

suture where
bones fuse

skull

mandible
(jaw bone)

scapula
(shoulder blade)

clavicle
(collar bone)

sternum
(breastbone)

7 pairs of ribs
joined to sternum

humerus

3 pairs of ribs
linked by
cartilage
to seventh
pair

lumbar vertebrae

radius

2 pairs of
floating ribs

ulna

pelvis

sacrum

carpals
(wrist bones)

COCCYX

7 cervical
vertebrae

12 thoracic
vertebrae

5 lumbar
vertebrae

5 fused
sacral
vertebrae

4 fused
coccogeal
vertebrae

VERTEBRAL COLUMN

femur

patella
(knee cap)

tibia

fibula

transverse
process

neural
spine

neural
canal

centrum

CROSS-SECTION OF
LUMBAR VERTEBRA

tarsals
(ankle bones)

a
b
c
d
e
f
g
h
i
j
k
l
m
n
o
p
q
r
s
t
u
v
w
x
y
z

139

hybrid

A hybrid is the offspring of plants or animals produced from the cross of two closely related species. For example, the hybrid of a female horse (mare) and a male donkey is a mule.

• *Hybrids between different animals are usually sterile (cannot reproduce themselves).*

hydraulic fracturing *see* fracking

hydraulic machine

Hydraulic machines are machines which use liquids under pressure instead of levers or cogs. They work on the principles that a liquid is virtually incompressible, and that if pressure is applied to the trapped liquid then the pressure is transmitted to all parts of that liquid. The diagram shows a cross-section of a hydraulic jack. If we push down on the smaller piston with a force of 50N, it acts over an area of 0.01 m².

$$\text{pressure} = \frac{\text{force}}{\text{area}} = \frac{50}{0.01} = 5{,}000 \text{ Pa}$$

This pressure is transmitted through the liquid, so underneath the larger piston (at the same height) there is exactly the same pressure.

$$\frac{\text{Upward force on}}{\text{large slave piston}} = \frac{\text{pressure}}{\times \text{ area}} = \frac{5{,}000}{\times 0.1} = 500 \text{ N}$$

Therefore, assuming no heat loss from friction, an effort of 50 N pushing down can lift a load of 500 N. Overall, the amount of work done by both pistons is the same. The smaller piston moves 10 times further than the larger piston as its force is 10 times smaller.

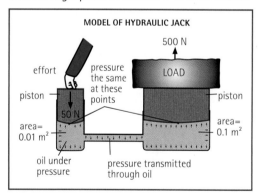

MODEL OF HYDRAULIC JACK

hydrocarbon

Hydrocarbons are organic compounds that contain only carbon and hydrogen atoms. There are three main classes, alkanes, alkenes and alkynes. All hydrocarbons have covalent molecules.

• *Hydrocarbons are found naturally in petroleum and natural gas.*

SEE ALSO **alkane, alkene, covalent bond, alkynes**

hydroelectricity

is electricity produced by trapping rainwater at a high level and then allowing it to flow through electrical turbines at a lower level. Dams are often built to trap the water high up in the valleys. This water is then released and flows downhill through turbines which drive electrical generators.

• *The energy change during the production of hydroelectricity is from gravitational potential energy to kinetic energy, and then to electrical energy.*

SEE ALSO **energy source**

hydrogel

is a macromolecular cross-linked polymer resulting in a colloidal gel in which water is the disperse phase. Hydrogel is a smart material as it can change its structure in response to salt concentration, pH, and temperature. Hydrogels are highly absorbent and can hold lots of water.

• *Hydrogel is used as a primary dressing for wounds as it can release water for rehydration of the wound if necessary.*

SEE ALSO **colloid, macromolecule, phase, polymer, smart plastic**

hydrogen (*also* H)

is the first and lightest element in the periodic table. It has the simplest atom with a proton number of one. Hydrogen is the most abundant element in the universe and is the main constituent of stars. It is present in water (H_2O) and in all organic compounds.

• *Hydrogen has three isotopes (hydrogen-1, deuterium, and tritium), and its overall relative atomic mass is 1.008.*

SEE ALSO **deuterium, hydrogen–1, tritium**

Uses of hydrogen	
1.	making ammonia by the Haber process: – making methanol CH_3OH by reaction with carbon monoxide under pressure over heated catalysts. carbon monoxide + hydrogen → methanol CO + 2H2 → CH_3OH
2.	hydrogenation of oils (addition of hydrogen across unsaturated double bonds) to make saturated fats (e.g. in margarine).
3.	as a fuel for spacecraft, though there is a risk of explosion and it is hard to liquefy for storage.
4.	if steam is passed over heated carbon, a mixture of carbon monoxide and hydrogen gases are formed. This is a useful fuel called 'water gas.

SEE ALSO **Haber process, methanol**

hydrogen–1 (*also* ^1H)

is the common isotope of hydrogen.

SEE ALSO **isotope**

hydrogen bomb *see* fusion bomb

hydrogen bonding

is the strong force of attraction between certain molecules that contain hydrogen, such as water molecules.

• *Hydrogen bonding is an intermolecular force which results when a hydrogen atom is between two electronegative atoms such as oxygen atoms.*

SEE ALSO **intermolecular force**

hydrogen gas

is a colourless, odourless gaseous element made up of hydrogen molecules. It is the lightest of all gases (density is 0.0899 g dm^{-3}) and it is difficult to liquefy (b.p. −253°C, m.p. −259°C).

• *Hydrogen gas is a good reducing agent and is flammable in air.*

SEE ALSO **reducing agent**

➤ **testing for hydrogen** When a lighted splint is held at the mouth of a test tube containing hydrogen gas, the gas burns explosively, making a 'popping' sound. Hydrogen burns in air (or oxygen) with a blue flame to form steam.

$$hydrogen + oxygen \rightarrow water$$
$$2H_2 + O_2 \rightarrow 2H_2O$$

➤ **hydrogen preparation** There are three simple ways of making hydrogen gas in the laboratory:
1. Reaction of reactive metal and water: Sodium and potassium metals react violently with water so it is best to use calcium metal:

$$calcium + water \rightarrow calcium\ hydroxide + hydrogen$$
$$Ca + 2H_2O \rightarrow Ca(OH)_2 + H_2$$

Hydrogen gas is insoluble in water and can be collected using an inverted funnel and test tube full of water.
2. Reaction of metal with acids: Suitable metals are iron, zinc, and magnesium. Calcium, sodium, and potassium are much too violent and copper has no reaction with acids.

$$zinc + sulfuric\ acid \rightarrow zinc\ sulfate + hydrogen$$
$$Zn + H_2SO_4 \rightarrow ZnSO_4 + H_2$$

The hydrogen gas can be dried by bubbling through concentrate sulfuric acid and collected by 'upward delivery and downward displacement of air' in an inverted container.

3. Electrolysis of acidified water: The hydrogen gas collects at the anode during electrolysis.

$$hydrogen\ ions + electrons \rightarrow hydrogen\ gas$$
$$^2H + 2e \rightarrow H_4$$

SEE ALSO **electrolysis, steam reforming**

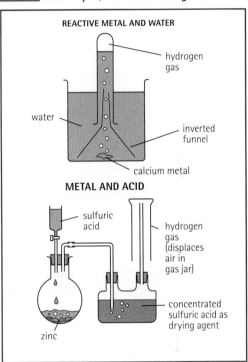

REACTIVE METAL AND WATER

hydrogen gas
water
inverted funnel
calcium metal

METAL AND ACID

sulfuric acid
hydrogen gas (displaces air in gas jar)
concentrated sulfuric acid as drying agent
zinc

hydrogen halide

Hydrogen halides are colourless gases which are very soluble in water and dissolve to form the corresponding acid.

SEE ALSO **halide**

Hydrogen halide	Acid formed
hydrogen chloride HCl(g)	hydrochloric acid HCl(aq)
hydrogen bromide HBr(g)	hydrobromic acid HBr(aq)
hydrogen iodide HI(g)	hydroiodic acid HI(aq)

hydrogen ion (*also* H^+)

A hydrogen ion is a hydrogen atom which has lost its electron and is therefore just a proton.

• *Hydrogen ions combine with water molecules to form the hydroxonium ion (H_3O^+). Excess*

hydroxonium ions (hydrated hydrogen ions) make a solution into an acid.
SEE ALSO **proton**

hydrogen molecule (*also* H_2)
The hydrogen molecule is the simplest and smallest molecule. It is a diatomic molecule made up of two hydrogen atoms bonded together by a single covalent bond.
SEE ALSO **covalent bond, diatomic molecule**

hydrogen preparation *see* hydrogen gas

hydrogen sulfide
is a colourless, poisonous gas, H_2S, which smells of 'bad eggs' and is used in 'stink bombs'.
• *Hydrogen sulfide is water soluble and forms a weak acid and salts called sulfides.*
SEE ALSO **sulfide**

hydrological cycle *see* water cycle

hydrolysis
is the chemical reaction of a compound with water which causes it to break down.
• *A polymer which undergoes hydrolysis breaks into smaller pieces, or right down into monomers.*
SEE ALSO **fat, monomer, polymer, protein, starch**

hydrolysis of fats *see* fat

hydrolysis of proteins *see* protein

hydrolysis of starch *see* starch

hydrometer
A hydrometer is an instrument for measuring the density or relative density of a liquid. It often consists of a calibrated hollow tube which is weighted at the bottom so that it floats in the liquid. The less dense the liquid, the greater the volume which must be displaced for the upthrust to equal the weight, and so the more the hydrometer is submerged.
SEE ALSO **density, relative density**

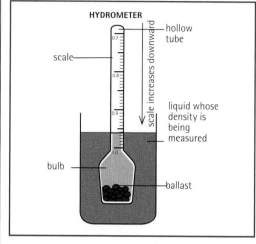

HYDROMETER — hollow tube — scale — scale increases downward — liquid whose density is being measured — bulb — ballast

hydroponics
involves growing certain crop plants in solutions containing correct proportions of essential minerals, rather than in the soil.
• *Hydroponics can guarantee to produce large amounts of crops in a specific area (e.g. greenhouses) and therefore has commercial potential.*
SEE ALSO **mineral, mineral salt**

hydrostatic skeleton
A hydrostatic skeleton is one in which support is provided by liquid under pressure in the body cavity. The skeletons of soft-bodied land animals like slugs, earthworms, and caterpillars are of this type.
SEE ALSO **skeleton**

hydrotropism
is the growth response of a plant towards water. Roots often grow sideways, as there is more water closer to the surface.

hypermetropia *see* long–sightedness

hypertonic
describes a solution with greater osmotic pressure than some other solution.
• *When comparing two solutions the hypertonic solution is always the more concentrated of the two.*
SEE ALSO **hypotonic, osmotic pressure**

hypha *plural* hyphae

A hypha is a microscopic hollow filament in a fungus. Together the hyphae make up a network called the mycelium.

SEE ALSO **fungus, mycelium**

hypothalamus *see* brain

hypothermia

is the gradual lowering of body temperature due to heat loss in cold weather. Normal body temperature is 37°C, but if this drops by 2°C, the person becomes drowsy due to a decrease in metabolic rate. If temperature drops further, the person becomes unconscious and may die.

• *Warm drinks, many layers of clothes, and lots of activity prevent* **hypothermia**.

SEE ALSO **metabolic rate**

hypothesis

A hypothesis is a suggestion or possible explanation put forward to account for certain observations and used as a basis for further experimentation to prove or disprove the hypothesis.

hypotonic

describes a solution with lower osmotic pressure than some other solution.

• *When comparing two solutions the* **hypotonic** *solution is always the more dilute of the two.*

SEE ALSO **hypertonic, osmotic pressure**

Hz *see* hertz

I *see* electric current

ideal gas

An ideal gas is a theoretical gas which obeys the various gas laws. Many real gases behave in approximately the same way when at low/medium pressures and temperatures. The assumptions about an ideal gas are as follows:

– The size of the molecules in the gas are so small that their total volume is negligible.
– The molecules are so far apart that the attractive forces between the molecules are negligible.
– The molecules move in straight lines and lose no energy when they collide (elastic collisions).
– The molecules can convert heat energy into kinetic energy (and vice versa).

SEE ALSO **Boyle's law, Charles' law, pressure law**

ideal gas equation

The ideal gas equation is the combined equation of the three gas laws, which states that for a fixed mass of ideal gas, pV/T = constant.

$$P_1 V_1 / T_1 = P_2 V_2 / T_2$$

P_1 = initial pressure
V_1 = initial volume
T_1 = initial temperature
P_2 = final pressure
V_2 = final volume
T_2 = final temperature

SEE ALSO **Boyle's law, Charles' law, ideal gas, pressure law**

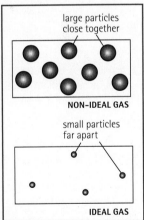

large particles close together

NON–IDEAL GAS

small particles far apart

IDEAL GAS

identical twins

Identical twins can develop when one egg is fertilized by one sperm, and then splits into two.

• *Identical twins always share the same placenta and have the same genes (same sex and appearance).*

SEE ALSO **gene, non–identical twins, placenta**

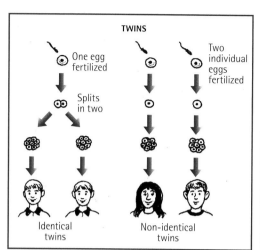

TWINS

One egg fertilized

Splits in two

Two individual eggs fertilized

Identical twins

Non-identical twins

igneous rock *see* **rock**

ileum *see* **small intestine**

image

An image is a point from which rays of light entering the eye appear to have originated.

> ### inverted image
>
> An inverted image is one that is upside down. The image of a pinhole camera is inverted, and so are the images on the retina at the back of the eye.
> *SEE ALSO* **retina**
>
> ### real image
>
> A real image is one that can be focused on a screen, as rays of light actually pass through the image. The image of a pinhole camera is real.
>
> ### virtual image
>
> A virtual image is one which cannot be focused onto a screen because rays of light do not actually pass through the image. Images formed by a plane mirror are virtual, as only imaginary rays (dotted lines) can be traced back to the image.

imago

The imago is the sexually mature adult form of an arthropod.
• *The appearance of the* **imago** *is often very different form the larval or pupal stages of the arthropod.*
SEE ALSO **arthropod, larva, pupa**

immiscible

describes two or more liquids that will not mix together (e.g. oil and water). When shaken together, such liquids separate into layers.
SEE ALSO **miscible**

immobilized enzyme *see* **enzyme**

immunity

is protection of an organism against infection.

> ### active immunity
>
> is the production of antibodies by the body in response to the presence of antigens.
> • *Vaccines are used to stimulate* **active immunity.**
> *SEE ALSO* **antibody, vaccine**
>
> ### natural immunity
>
> is passed on from mother to offspring via the placenta or breast milk, or develops as a result of infection.
>
> ### passive immunity
>
> is produced by ready-made antibodies injected into the body to assist in the fighting of disease (e.g. an anti-tetanus jab). It must be 'boosted' periodically.

immunization

is the production of immunity by artificial means.
• *Immunization is achieved most commonly through vaccination.*
SEE ALSO **vaccine**

impermeable

describes a material like metal, plastic, ceramic, or glass which will not allow liquids or gases to pass through.
• *Water cannot pass through an* **impermeable** *material.*
SEE ALSO **permeable**

inbreeding (*also* **selective breeding**)

is the modification of a species by choosing parents (animal or plant) with desirable characteristics. Such breeding programmes may be used for beef cattle to get the best beef (taste, texture, appearance, etc.).
• *The disadvantage of* **inbreeding** *is that there is a reduction in the gene pool, as the same genes are being chosen each time. It is for this reason that mongrel dogs (random cross-breeds) are often healthier than those chosen by inbreeding.*

incident ray *see* **reflection of light**

incisor *see* **tooth**

incomplete dominance

is a situation in a heterozygous pair where neither allele is dominant. As a result, the phenotype is an 'average' of both alleles. For example, the snapdragon plant with alleles for both red and white flowers produces pink flowers.

SEE ALSO **allele, co-dominance, heterozygous, phenotype**

incubation

is the process of maintaining the fertilized eggs of birds, some reptiles, and egg-laying mammals at the best temperature for the development of the embryo inside the egg.

• *Incubation is not necessary for live-bearing animals.*

SEE ALSO **embryo**

independent variable

The independent variable is the variable that you deliberately change during the experiment (like time).

• *The independent variable is usually plotted on the x-axis on a line graph.*

SEE ALSO **controlled variable, dependent variable, scientific variable**

indicator

An acid base indicator changes colour, reversibly, according to whether a solution is acidic or alkaline.

• *Many plant extracts, such as red cabbage juice, act as indicators.*

SEE ALSO **acid, alkali, litmus, pH**

universal indicator

A universal indicator is a mixture of several indicators and turns a range of colours corresponding to different pH values.

pH value	Colour of universal indicator	Strength
0		
1	red	strong
2		acid
3		
4	pink	weak
5	orange	acid
6	yellow	
7	green	neutral
8	turquoise	
9	blue	weak
10	dark blue	alkali
11		
12	violet	strong
13		alkali
14		

indigenous *see* habitat

induction of charge

is caused by the attraction of opposite charges and the repulsion of like charges. It is for this reason that a comb, charged by pulling it through your hair, will pick up tiny pieces of paper. It is also why dust is attracted to objects with static charge, such as TV or computer screens. Charged particles will always attract small uncharged particles by induction.

SEE ALSO **electric charge, static electricity**

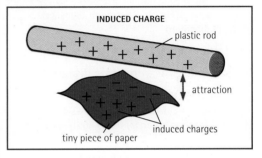

INDUCED CHARGE

plastic rod

attraction

induced charges

tiny piece of paper

inert gas *see* noble gas

inertia

is the tendency of an object to resist a change in speed (acceleration) caused by a force. It is directly related to its mass. Objects with large mass have a large inertia, and are more difficult to speed up or slow down than smaller objects of low mass and low inertia.

• *Inertia is often described as 'resistance to motion'.*

inference

An inference is a conclusion reached by reasoning and logic.

inferior vena cava

The inferior vena cava is a main vein which carries deoxygenated blood from the lower body to the heart.

SEE ALSO **superior vena cava, vein**

inflorescence

An inflorescence is a group of flowers on the same stalk.

influenza (*also* **flu**)

Influenza (or the flu) is an infection caused by a virus. It is important to rest and to drink lots of fluids when you have the flu. People with the flu can catch a secondary bacterial infection which can lead to the more serious illness of pneumonia.

• *Influenza is a common disease but it can be prevented with the 'flu' vaccine.*

SEE ALSO **pneumonia, virus**

infra-red radiation *see* radiation

infrasound

is sound below the threshold of the human hearing range, around 20 Hz (hertz).

• *Infrasound is used by whales for communication. Such waves have few uses, as they are distressing to humans.*

SEE ALSO **human hearing range, ultrasound**

ingestion (*also* feeding)

is the taking of food into an organism (usually through the mouth) for subsequent digestion.

SEE ALSO **digestion**

inhalation *see* inspiration

inherited disease *see* genetic disease

inhibitor (*also* negative catalyst)

An inhibitor is a substance which slows down a chemical reaction, often by reducing the power of the catalyst.

• *Inhibitors sometimes 'poison' the catalysts by destroying intermediate chemical species.*

SEE ALSO **catalyst**

inner core *see* Earth's structure

inner ear

The inner ear is a structure in vertebrates which is surrounded by bone of the skull and which contains the organs of hearing and balance.

SEE ALSO **ear, middle ear, outer ear, oval window, round window**

WORD BUILD

auditory nerve

The auditory nerve carries nervous impulses from the inner ear to the brain.

cochlea

The cochlea is a spiral tube of the inner ear which produces nervous impulses in response to sound waves. The vibrations of the oval window are transmitted through a fluid (perilymph) which fills the cochlea and causes the membrane of the cochlea to move up and down. Sensory hairs on the cochlea membrane produce nervous impulses which are sent to the brain along the auditory nerve. The brain interprets these impulses as sensations of sound.

SEE ALSO **oval window**

semicircular canal

The semicircular canals are the organs of balance in the inner ear. These three canals are at right angles to each other and are filled with fluid (endolymph). Each has a swelling at its base called an ampulla containing tiny sensory hair cells. Movement of the fluid, caused by motion of the head, stimulates the sensory hairs to produce nervous impulses. These travel to the brain along the auditory nerve. The brain then interprets these impulses and coordinates muscle movement to keep the body upright.

inoculation

is the introduction of a vaccine or serum into the body into the body to help fight disease.

SEE ALSO **serum, vaccine**

inorganic chemistry *see* chemistry

insect (*also* Insecta)

Insects are arthropods which have three parts to the body, three pairs of legs, and two pairs of wings (though one or both may be reduced in size). Over 70% of all animals are insects, including ants, beetles, butterflies, fleas, bees, etc. There are about 1 million species, and about 8000 new species are discovered each year. Their exoskeleton prevents loss of water from the body, so they can live in very dry places.

• *Many insects undergo metamorphosis.*

SEE ALSO **arthropod, exoskeleton, metamorphosis**

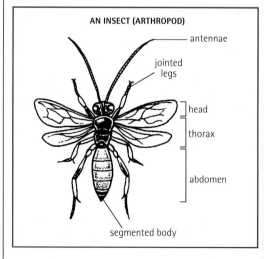

AN INSECT (ARTHROPOD)

antennae

jointed legs

head

thorax

abdomen

segmented body

insectivorous plant (*also* **carnivorous plant**)

Insectivorous plants are plants that supplement their supply of nitrates by trapping and digesting insects. The Venus flytrap has spiny, hinged leaves that are thigmotropic and snap shut on alighting insects.

• *The sundew is an insectivorous plant that has sticky hairs which curl around and trap an insect when it touches the hair.*

SEE ALSO **thigmotropism**

insemination

is the insertion of semen (sperm) into the uterus (womb) of a female.

• *In mammals insemination normally occurs during copulation (sexual intercourse).*

SEE ALSO **artificial insemination, copulation**

insoluble

describes a substance that will not dissolve in a liquid.

• *Insoluble substances can be removed by filtration.*

SEE ALSO **filtration, soluble**

inspiration (*also* **inhalation**)

is the movement of air into the lungs by the diaphragm being pulled down (flattened) and the rib cage being raised by contraction of the intercostal muscles.

SEE ALSO **diaphragm, intercostal muscle**

instinct

An instinct is a natural tendency to know how to do something without being taught. All animals have reactions which are based on instinct.

• *Baby turtles act on instinct when after birth on the beach they start to run towards the sea to escape predators.*

SEE ALSO **predator, prey**

instrumental analysis

is important to industries and involves analysing their production methods and checking any emissions during the manufacturing process.

• *Instrumental analysis is very important in the life-cycle assessment (LCA) for a manufactured product.*

SEE ALSO **life-cycle assessment**

insulator (*also* **poor conductor**)

❶ An insulator is a substance which has a low thermal conductivity. Non-metals, wood, plastic, and most liquids and gases are insulators. Materials with trapped air inside, such as expanded polystyrene, wool, fibreglass, etc., are good insulators. The particles in air are far apart, so little heat energy is transferred by collision of particles.

• *Insulators help to keep hot objects hot and cold objects cold.*

SEE ALSO **conductor, thermal conductivity**

❷ An insulator is a material which allows no electrons (or very few) to pass through. In such materials the electrons are tightly held in the atoms and cannot move. Rubber, glass, air, and plastics are insulators.

• *Insulators can become charged with static, as they do not allow the electrons to flow away.*

insulin *see* **hormone**

intercostal muscle

Intercostal muscles are muscles between the ribs.

interference

is the interaction of two or more waves of the same frequency emitted from coherent sources. If the waves are in phase, they may reinforce one another (constructive interference). If they are out of phase, they tend to cancel each other out (destructive interference).

SEE ALSO **frequency, wave**

intermediate

An intermediate is a short-lived chemical species sometimes formed in a chemical reaction and stabilized by the presence of a catalyst. This intermediate is still very unstable, and reacts to form products and the original catalyst. The physical appearance of the catalyst may change, but it does not change chemically.

SEE ALSO **catalyst, chemical reaction**

intermolecular force

Intermolecular forces are forces between molecules. They are much weaker than intramolecular forces.

SEE ALSO **intramolecular force**

internal energy *see* **thermal energy**

internal fertilization *see* **fertilization**

intervertebral disc

Intervertebral discs are discs of cartilage which separate the vertebrae in the vertebral column. They absorb shock and give flexibility.

• *If an intervertebral disc is displaced ('slipped disc'), it causes severe pain.*

SEE ALSO **cartilage, vertebra, vertebral column**

intracellular digestion *see* **digestion**

intramolecular force

Intramolecular forces are forces between atoms inside molecules.

• *Intramolecular forces are strong and typically measure around 1000 kJ mol⁻¹.*

SEE ALSO **intermolecular force**

intra-uterine device *see* contraception

intra-uterine system *see* contraception

intrusion

An intrusion is a mass of molten rock which forces its way in between layers of rock.

• *Metamorphic rocks are often formed around an intrusion by the heat and pressure.*

SEE ALSO **rock**

intrusive rock *see* rock

inverse square law

Waves emitted from a point source in a vacuum obey the inverse square law. If you double the distance from the source, the intensity of the wave becomes a quarter of its previous value.

SEE ALSO **electromagnetic wave**

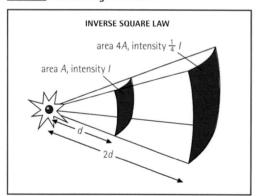

INVERSE SQUARE LAW

area 4A, intensity $\frac{1}{4}$ I

area A, intensity I

d

$2d$

invertebrate animal

Invertebrate animals are animals that do not have a vertebral column or spine.

SEE ALSO **annelid, arthropod, cnidarian, echinoderm, mollusc, platyhelminth**

inverted image *see* image

in vitro fertilization (*also* IVF)

is a process of fertilization where the egg is combined with the sperm outside the body. The following stages are involved:

– Giving the mother hormones (FSH and LH) to stimulate maturation of eggs

– Collecting the eggs from the mother and fertilizing with sperm from the father in the laboratory

– Fertilized eggs develop into embryos and one or two embryos are inserted into the mother's uterus (womb).

• *Although IVF gives a woman a chance to have a baby of her own, it can be emotionally and physically stressful. The success rate is not very high. It can lead to multiple births, which can be a risk to both the babies and the mother.*

SEE ALSO **conception, fertilization**

involuntary action

Involuntary actions are actions which are not controlled by conscious activity of the brain. Such actions are controlled by the hypothalamus through neurones of the autonomic nervous system, and the effectors are involuntary muscles.

• *Involuntary actions include gland secretion, heartbeat, peristalsis, accommodation of the eye, pupil contraction/dilation, etc.*

SEE ALSO **autonomic nervous system, brain, muscle**

involuntary muscle *see* muscle

ion

An ion is a charged particle formed when an atom (or group of atoms) gains or loses one or more electrons.

SEE ALSO **anion, cation, electron**

ion exchange resin

Ion exchange resins remove hardness in water by exchanging soft sodium ions in the resin for the calcium and magnesium ions present in the hard water.

SEE ALSO **hard water**

ionic bond

An ionic bond is a chemical bond formed by transfer of one or more electrons from the outer shell of a metal atom to the outer shell of a non-metal atom. The metal atom, as it loses electrons, becomes a positive ion. The non-metal atom, as it gains electrons, becomes a negative ion. The bonding is the electrostatic attraction between these oppositely charged ions. Enough electrons are transferred or gained to ensure that the outermost shell of the ion formed has a stable inert gas configuration.

SEE ALSO **chemical bond, ion**

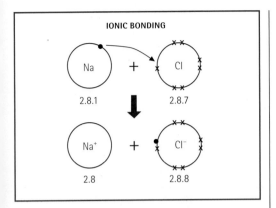

IONIC BONDING

2.8.1   2.8.7

2.8   2.8.8

	Ten important functions of the liver
1.	are made of charged particles (ions)
2.	have strong chemical bonds between ions
3.	form giant ionic lattices
4.	are crystalline solids
5.	have high melting and boiling points
6.	are usually water soluble
7.	conduct electricity when molten or aqueous

ionic crystal

Ionic crystals are crystals composed of ions regularly arranged in a giant lattice. Each ion is surrounded by oppositely charged ions. Ionic crystals have strong electrostatic forces between their ions (ionic bonds). They therefore usually have high melting and boiling points.

• *Because their ions are in fixed positions, ionic crystals do not conduct electricity.*

SEE ALSO **ionic bond, ionic lattice**

ionic equation

An ionic equation can be used for a chemical reaction involving the coming together of ions in solution. Consider the neutralization of sulfuric acid with sodium hydroxide. If all the ions are written out fully we have the following:

$$2H^+_{(aq)} + SO_4^{2-}_{(aq)} + 2Na^+_{(aq)} + 2OH^-_{(aq)} \rightarrow 2Na^+_{(aq)} + SO_4^{2-}_{(aq)} + 2H_2O_{(l)}$$

If we cancel out the ions that are common to both sides of the equation (called spectator ions) and then simplify the equation we obtain the ionic equation for the neutralization of an acid:

$$2H^+(aq) + 2OH^-(aq) \rightarrow 2H_2O(l) \text{ so } H^+(aq) + OH^-(aq) \rightarrow H_2O(l)$$

SEE ALSO **chemical equation**

ionic lattice

An ionic lattice is a giant structure of tightly packed ions. It is a regular arrangement and each ion is surrounded by oppositely charged ions.

• *Many crystalline substances have ionic lattices.*

SEE ALSO **ion, lattice, lattice energy**

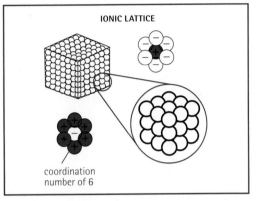

IONIC LATTICE

coordination number of 6

ionic precipitation *see* **double decomposition**

ionic theory of electrolysis

The ionic theory explains how electricity passes through an electrolyte. During electrolysis, cations travel to the cathode where they gain electrons to form atoms. Anions travel to the anode where they lose electrons to form atoms. This results in an overall movement of electrons from the cathode to the anode, which constitutes an electric current.

SEE ALSO **anion, anode, cathode, cation, electrolysis**

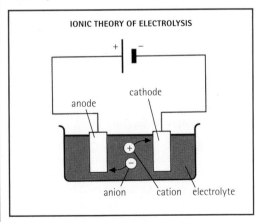

IONIC THEORY OF ELECTROLYSIS

anode

cathode

anion   cation   electrolyte

ionosphere *see* **atmosphere**

iris

The iris is the coloured part of the eye and controls the amount of light that reaches the retina. It has two types of muscle: circular muscles running around the pupil, which contract in bright light (form small pupil), and radial muscles running outwards from the edge of the pupil, which contract in dim light (form large pupil).

SEE ALSO **eye, pupil, retina**

iron see **reactivity series**

iron extraction see **blast furnace**

irradiation (*also* **sterilization**)

is the process of exposing something to radiation.
• *Irradiation is used to kill bacteria in food, sterilize hospital equipment, etc.*

irreversible reaction

An irreversible reaction is a chemical reaction which continues until one or all of the reactants is used up.
• *In an irreversible reaction the products do not react with each other and the reaction goes to completion.*

SEE ALSO **chemical reaction, reversible reaction**

irritability see **sensitivity**

islets of Langerhans

The islets of Langerhans are a group of specialized cells in the pancreas which secretes two hormones, insulin and glucagon, to control the level of glucose in the blood.

SEE ALSO **hormone**

isobar

An isobar is a line joining places with the same atmospheric pressure. Isobars are used on weather maps, which use the millibar (mb) as a unit of pressure.
• *In the UK, atmospheric pressure varies from isobars of 975 mb (low pressure) to isobars of 1,030 mb (high pressure).*

SEE ALSO **atmospheric pressure**

isolated system

An isolated system is one in which no material or energy can escape or enter. If the reaction is reversible, this allows a chemical equilibrium to be established, at a particular temperature.

SEE ALSO **chemical equilibrium, closed system, open system**

isomer

Isomers are substances that exhibit isomerism.
• *Isomers have different physical properties, but similar chemical properties.*

SEE ALSO **isomerism**

isomerism (*also* **structural isomerism**)

occurs when compounds with the same molecular formula have different structural formulae.
• *Butane and isobutane (methyl propane) are examples of isomerism.*

SEE ALSO **chemical formula**

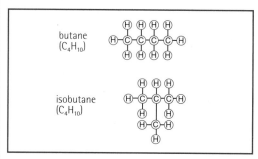

butane (C_4H_{10})

isobutane (C_4H_{10})

isotonic

describes two solutions that have the same osmotic pressure.
• *Isotonic drinks have the same osmotic pressure as blood, so are quickly absorbed.*

SEE ALSO **hypertonic, hypotonic, osmotic pressure**

isotope

Isotopes are atoms of the same element (same number of protons and electrons) with different numbers of neutrons, and so different mass numbers. Nearly all elements found in nature are mixtures of several isotopes.
For example the element chlorine exists as chlorine-35 (18 neutrons) and chlorine-37 (20 neutrons).
• *Isotopes of a particular element have similar chemical properties but slightly different physical properties (density, rate of diffusion, etc.).*

SEE ALSO **element, mass number, neutron**

isotopic abundance

is the percentage of a particular isotope which is found in the naturally occurring element.
• *The isotopic abundance of the element chlorine is 75% chlorine-35 and 25% chlorine-37.*

SEE ALSO **isotope, relative atomic mass**

IVF see **in vitro fertilization**

Jj

jet stream

The jet stream is a strong, narrow wind current that occurs in the atmosphere above the troposphere.

• *The jet stream flows towards the east at speeds of 60 km/hr (in summer) to 125 km/hr (in winter).*

SEE ALSO **atmosphere**

joint

A joint is the point of contact between two or more bones together with the tissue that surrounds it. Some joints between bones are immovable joints, e.g. the sutures of the skull. Most joints in the body are movable joints. The bones in such joints are held together by ligaments and lubricated by the fluid from the synovial membrane.

SEE ALSO **bone, ligament, synovial membrane**

ball-and-socket joint

Ball-and-socket joints are the most flexible of movable joints which allow bones to swivel and move in many directions. The round head of one bone fits into a cup-shaped socket of another bone (see diagram).

• *The hip joint and shoulder joint are examples of ball-and-socket joints.*

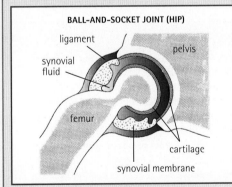

BALL-AND-SOCKET JOINT (HIP)

ligament
pelvis
synovial fluid
femur
cartilage
synovial membrane

gliding joint (*also* sliding joint, plane joint)

Gliding joints are movable joints which allow flat bones to glide over one another.

• *Gliding joints occur between the carpals in the hand and the tarsals in the foot.*

hinge joint

Hinge joints are movable joints which allow movement in a single plane only (like the hinge of a door).

• *Examples of hinge joints are the knuckle, knee, and elbow joints.*

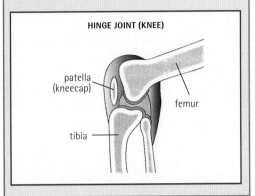

HINGE JOINT (KNEE)

patella (kneecap)
femur
tibia

joule (*also* J)

A joule of work is done by a force of 1 newton moving 1 metre in the direction of the force. The joule is the SI unit of both work and energy.

• *The joule is named after the British physicist James Joule (1818–89).*

SEE ALSO **energy, newton, work**

jugular vein

The jugular vein is one of two large veins in the throat and neck which carries deoxygenated blood from the head to the heart.

SEE ALSO **heart, superior vena cava**

joulemeter

A joulemeter is a meter which measures the amount of joules of energy a particular electrical device is using.

• *A joulemeter can be used to compare the amount of energy used by different electrical appliances in the home.*

SEE ALSO **electrical energy, joule**

Jupiter *see* **planet**

a
b
c
d
e
f
g
h
i
j
k
l
m
n
o
p
q
r
s
t
u
v
w
x
y
z

Kk

K *see* **kelvin**

kaolin (*also* china clay)
is a soft, white form of clay composed mainly of kaolinite (hydrated aluminium silicate).
• *Kaolin is widely used for making china and porcelain, and in some medicines.*
SEE ALSO **clay**

kelvin (*also* K)
is the unit of temperature on the absolute scale and is the SI unit of thermodynamic temperature.
• *The degree sign ° is not used with the kelvin. 1K represents the same temperature difference as 1°C.*
SEE ALSO **absolute scale**

Kelvin scale *see* absolute scale

kerosene (*also* paraffin oil)
is the petroleum fraction with a boiling point range of 160–250°C. It is made up of a mixture of hydrocarbons which have eleven or twelve carbon atoms. Kerosene is a fuel for jet aircraft and oil-fired domestic heating.
• *The kerosene fraction is also used for cracking to produce motor fuel.*
SEE ALSO **cracking, fraction**

key
A key in science is something which is used as a means of classifying or achieving a particular result.
SEE ALSO **dichotomous key**

kg *see* kilogram

kidney
The kidney is the main excretory organ in vertebrates. Kidneys remove unwanted substances from the blood and regulate the amount of water and salts in the body.
• *In humans a pair of kidneys are situated at the back of the body, just below the ribs.*
SEE ALSO **nephron, urinary system**

➤ **structure of the kidney** A longitudinal section through the kidney shows three main parts:
  – cortex (or renal cortex) is the outermost layer of tissue in the kidney
  – medulla (or renal medulla) is the central tissue of the kidney. The outer cortex and the inner medulla are made up of thousands of tiny tubules called nephrons
  – pelvis (or renal pelvis) is the cavity in the kidney that receives urine from the nephrons which then drains into the ureter.

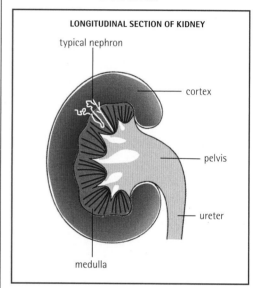

LONGITUDINAL SECTION OF KIDNEY

typical nephron

cortex

pelvis

ureter

medulla

kidney transplant
Kidney transplants are an alternative to dialysis and are one of the most successful of transplant operations. Best results occur if the donor has similar tissue and body chemistry (identical twins have very successful transplants). If the donor is unrelated, then the body may reject the new kidney as if it were a disease organism. This can be treated with drugs.
SEE ALSO **dialysis**

kidney tubule *see* nephron

kilogram (*also* kg)
A kilogram is the SI unit of mass.
• *One kilogram is equal to 1,000 g, and one metric tonne is equal to 1,000 kg.*
SEE ALSO **mass**

kilowatt (also kW)

A kilowatt is a unit of electrical power equal to 1,000 watts.

SEE ALSO **watt**

kilowatt–hour (also kWh)

A kilowatt-hour is the unit of electrical energy. It is the amount of electrical energy used by a 1-kilowatt device in 1 hour (1 kW = 3,600,000 J).

electrical energy (kWh) = power (kW) × time (h)

• *The kilowatt-hour is the commercial unit of electricity and is recorded by electricity meters.*

SEE ALSO **electrical energy, joule**

kinematic equations *see* equations of motion

kinetic energy store (also E_k)

is the energy possessed by an object or particle because it is moving. The greater the mass of the object and/or the greater its velocity, the greater its kinetic energy. The relationship can be expressed by the following equation:

$$E_k \text{ (J)} = 0.5 \times \text{mass (kg)} \times \text{(velocity)}^2 \text{ (m/s)}^2$$

SEE ALSO **energy, energy store**

kinetic frictional force *see* friction

kinetic theory

states that matter is made up of particles which move with a vigour proportional to their absolute temperature. In solids, particles vibrate about fixed positions; in liquids, they still vibrate but can move past each other; in gases, the particles are separate and able to move freely.

SEE ALSO **state of matter**

kinetic theory of gases

The kinetic theory of gases states that in the gaseous state, molecules of a gas are far apart and in random motion. They travel in straight lines until they collide with other molecules or with the walls of the containing vessel. There are various gas laws which describe the behaviour of these gases. However, these laws assume that the gas behaves as an ideal gas.

SEE ALSO **ideal gas**

KINETIC THEORY OF MATTER

solid
The particles in a solid are:
• very close together
• arranged in regular rows
• held together very tightly
• not moving from their position but vibrating

melting
freezing

liquid
The particles in a liquid are:
• touching but further apart
• not regularly arranged
• held together loosely
• moving by sliding past each other

boiling
condensing

gas
The particles in a gas are:
• very far apart
• randomly arranged
• free to move (diffuse)
• moving in all directions, occasionally colliding

---

kingdom

A kingdom is the highest rank in the classification of living organisms. Traditionally only two kingdoms, plants and animals, were recognized. In modern classification, five kingdoms are recognized, including Monera (bacteria), Protista, and Fungi, as well as plants and animals.

SEE ALSO **animal kingdom, biological classification, fungus, Monera, plant kingdom, protist**

krypton *see* noble gas

kwashiorkor

is a form of malnutrition in tropical countries caused by a lack of protein in the diet. It is most common in children between 9 months and 2 years, after they have stopped feeding on breast milk.

• *Kwashiorkor is often caused by poverty but sometimes because of a lack of knowledge about eating a balanced diet.*

SEE ALSO **balanced diet, protein**

kWh *see* kilowatt–hour

a
b
c
d
e
f
g
h
i
j
k
l
m
n
o
p
q
r
s
t
u
v
w
x
y
z

Ll

L *see* **Avogadro's number, latent heat**

labour

is the process by which the contractions of the strong muscles of the uterus push the baby out as a mother gives birth. As it passes into the cervix, the amnion bursts and the fluid escapes (breaking of the waters).

SEE ALSO **cervix, uterus**

lacteal

Lacteals are minute, blind-ended lymph vessels found inside each villus in the small intestine.
• *Digested fats are absorbed into the lacteals.*

SEE ALSO **lymph, small intestine, villus**

Lamarckism

is an early theory of evolution proposed by the French biologist Jean-Baptiste de Lamarck (1744–1829). The theory has been rejected and superseded by Darwinism. Lamarck thought that acquired characteristics during an individual's lifetime are passed on to its offspring. He explained the long neck and limbs of a giraffe as having evolved by the animal stretching its neck to reach the foliage of trees. It is now accepted that variation in the giraffe resulted in the natural selection of long necks and limbs which, when passed on to the offspring, improved its chances of survival.

SEE ALSO **acquired characteristic, Darwinism, natural selection, variation**

landfill

describes the disposal of solid waste material by burying it underground, often in previously excavated pits such as gravel or sand pits. Landfill waste can be reduced by recycling, reducing, and reusing materials (3Rs). Many tons of organic matter, such as food waste, grass cuttings, etc., are put into landfill and this decays anaerobically (in the absence of oxygen) to release methane gas (landfill gas). This gas is 25 times more potent than carbon dioxide as a greenhouse gas. However, methane gas can be collected in pipes and recycled into electricity and fuel.
• *Landfill can contaminate the surrounding environment, especially groundwater.*

SEE ALSO **greenhouse gas, land pollution**

land pollution

is a general term for pollution caused by the burying of household and commercial waste. Waste material such as plastic is often non-biodegradable and remains in the soil for a long time. Radioactive waste (nuclear waste) from nuclear reactors and laboratories takes thousands of years to become safe.

SEE ALSO **landfill, nuclear waste**

lanthanoid (*also* **rare-earth metal, lanthanide metal**)

Lanthanoids are a series of metallic elements of atomic numbers 57 to 71 inclusive.
• *The properties of lanthanoids are very similar to those of the metal aluminium.*

SEE ALSO **periodic table**

large intestine (*also* **bowel**)

The large intestine is the portion of the alimentary canal between the small intestine and the anus.
• *The large intestine consists of the caecum, colon, and rectum.*

SEE ALSO **alimentary canal, small intestine**

WORD BUILD

anus

The anus is the terminal opening of the alimentary canal, which is used for egestion.
• *The anus is surrounded by a muscular ring or sphincter.*

SEE ALSO **egestion**

appendix (*also* **vermiform appendix**)

The appendix is an outgrowth of the caecum, which in humans is a vestigial organ and has no function in digestion.
• *In herbivorous animals (such as rabbits, sheep, and cows) the appendix is highly developed and contains a large population of bacteria which are needed to break down the cellulose in grass.*

caecum

The caecum is a pouch in the large intestine between the small intestine and colon.

colon

The colon is the section of the large intestine between the caecum and the rectum. The main purpose of the colon is to absorb water and minerals from undigested food, leaving a semi-solid mass called faeces.

rectum

The rectum is the last section of the large intestine, between the colon and the anus. It holds the indigestible faeces prior to removal through the anus.

larva

A larva is the juvenile stage in the life cycle of many arthropods such as a nymph, caterpillar, grub, or maggot.

• *A larva hatches from the egg, and is usually unlike the adult and incapable of reproduction.*

SEE ALSO arthropod, pupa

larynx (*also* **voice box**)

The larynx is a region of the trachea containing the vocal cords, which vibrate to produce sound.

• *Muscles control the tension on the vocal cords of the larynx. High tension results in taught cords producing high pitched sounds.*

SEE ALSO pitch, trachea

laser

A laser is a device that generates an intense and highly concentrated beam of light or other electromagnetic radiation. The word laser comes from the initials of 'light amplification (by) stimulated emission (of) radiation'.

• *Lasers are used on optical discs (CD, DVD, or Blu-ray) to read or write data. They can also be used in delicate surgery on the eye.*

SEE ALSO electromagnetic wave

latent heat (*also* L)

is the quantity of heat energy absorbed or released when a substance changes state without changing its temperature. The heat energy is used to change the arrangement of particles in the various states. For example, when a solid melts to become a liquid, heat energy must be absorbed to move the particles apart. The same is true when a liquid boils to become a gas (or vapour), as heat energy must be absorbed to separate the particles.

SEE ALSO heat energy

➤ **specific latent heat of fusion (L_f)** is the quantity of heat energy absorbed when 1 kg of a substance changes from a solid to a liquid at its melting point.

• *For water the specific latent heat of fusion has a value of 334,000 J kg^{-1}.*

➤ **specific latent heat of vaporization (L_v)** is the quantity of heat energy absorbed when 1 kg of substance changes from a liquid to a gas (or vapour) at its boiling point.

• *For water the specific latent heat of vaporization has a value of 2,260,000 J/kg^{-1}.*

lateral inversion

is the apparent reversal (left to right, right to left) of the image formed in a plane mirror. The real reversal is from front to back, as the image is turned through itself to face the object.

SEE ALSO image

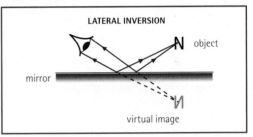

LATERAL INVERSION

object

mirror

virtual image

lateral line *see* sense organ

latitude

The latitude of a point on the Earth's surface is its distance from the equator, measured in degrees.

• *Points on the equator have a latitude of 0°. The North and South Poles have latitudes of 90°N and 90°S.*

SEE ALSO longitude, parallel of latitude

lattice

A lattice is a structure in which there is a regular arrangement of atoms, ions, or molecules.

SEE ALSO ionic lattice, metallic lattice

lattice energy

is the energy required for the complete separation of ions in one mole of an ionic substance.

• *Lattice energy is an indication of the strength of the ionic bond.*

SEE ALSO ionic bond

lava

is liquid rock that flows or erupts from a volcano. As a liquid it is very hot and extremely dangerous, as it will destroy buildings and set alight vegetation and trees.

• *Lava can travel a long distance from the volcano before it cools to become hard igneous rock.*

SEE ALSO rock

a b c d e f g h i j k l m n o p q r s t u v w x y z

law of conservation of energy *see* **energy transfer**

law of electrostatics *see* **electrostatic force**

law of magnetism *see* **magnetism**

laws of reflection *see* **reflection of light**

laws of refraction *see* **refraction of light**

LCA *see* **life-cycle assessment**

LDPE *see* **low-density polyethene**

LDR *see* **light-dependent resistor**

leaching

is the washing out of soluble materials by a liquid passing through a solid. It occurs when rainwater flows through the soil. Acid rain will leach away important minerals from the soil, and fertilizers are leached from the soil to cause eutrophication and nitrate pollution.

SEE ALSO **acid rain, eutrophication, nitrate pollution**

lead–acid accumulator *see* **car battery**

lead metal *see* **reactivity series**

lead pollution

is caused by motor vehicles which emit tiny lead particles in their exhaust fumes. Lead compounds are added to petrol so that it does not ignite too soon. Lead, when inhaled, can build up in the body, causing hyperactivity (especially in young children), liver and kidney damage, and a lowering of IQ.

• *Lead pollution is reduced by the use of unleaded petrol.*

SEE ALSO **acid rain, eutrophication, nitrate pollution**

leaf

A leaf is a structure of a plant, usually flat and green, which grows from the stem. Green leaves produce food for the plant and are the sites for the processes of transpiration and photosynthesis. Simple leaves consist of a single leaf blade (lamina). Compound leaves have a number of small leaf blades (leaflets) growing from the same leafstalk (petiole).

SEE ALSO **cuticle, epidermis, leaf vein, mesophyll layer, photosynthesis, stem, stoma, transpiration**

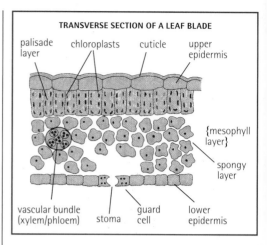

TRANSVERSE SECTION OF A LEAF BLADE

palisade layer — chloroplasts — cuticle — upper epidermis — {mesophyll layer} — spongy layer — vascular bundle (xylem/phloem) — stoma — guard cell — lower epidermis

leaf vein

A leaf vein is a long strip formed by vascular bundles in the leaf. They supply water and mineral salts and remove the food made in the leaf. Some plants like grasses have parallel veins but most have a main vein (midrib) with branching veins coming off it.

SEE ALSO **leaf, vascular bundle**

Le Chatelier's principle

states that if a change in temperature, pressure, or concentration occurs to a system in chemical equilibrium, then the system will tend to adjust itself so as to counteract the effect of that change so that a new chemical equilibrium is established. For example, in the Haber process, ammonia is created from nitrogen and hydrogen gases.

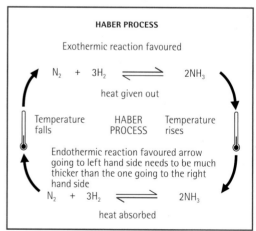

HABER PROCESS

Exothermic reaction favoured

$$N_2 + 3H_2 \rightleftharpoons 2NH_3$$

heat given out

Temperature falls   HABER PROCESS   Temperature rises

Endothermic reaction favoured arrow going to left hand side needs to be much thicker than the one going to the right hand side

$$N_2 + 3H_2 \rightleftharpoons 2NH_3$$

heat absorbed

Le Chatelier's Principle: temperature

• The forward reaction gives out heat and is exothermic. Therefore, according to Le Chatelier's principle, if the temperature is lowered, more ammonia is produced. This counteracts the effect of a decrease in temperature. The backward reaction takes in heat and is endothermic. Therefore, if the temperature increases, more nitrogen and hydrogen gases are produced. This counteracts the effect of a decrease in temperature. The backward reaction takes in heat and is endothermic. Therefore, if the temperature increases, more nitrogen and hydrogen gases are produced. This counteracts the effect of the increase in temperature. Low temperature favours ammonia production (but not too low or the rate will be too slow: optimum is 450°C).

Le Chatelier's Principle: concentration

• If we increase the concentration of the reactants, hydrogen and nitrogen, then – according to Le Chatelier's principle – the equilibrium will move to the right-hand side. This will produce more ammonia, and counteracts the effects of the increase in concentration of hydrogen and nitrogen. High concentration favours ammonia production.

Le Chatelier's Principle: pressure

• High pressure would favour the side of the equilibrium which has the lowest volume. This would counteract the effect of an increase in pressure. This is the ammonia side, as two volumes of ammonia are produced from four volumes (one volume of nitrogen and three volumes of hydrogen) of reactants. High pressure (normally around 250 atmospheres) favours ammonia production.
SEE ALSO **chemical equilibrium, endothermic reaction, exothermic reaction, Haber process**

LED *see* light–emitting diode

length

Length usually means the measurement along a line or a curve. The measurement of length depends upon the magnitude of the length. A metre rule can measure to the nearest division, which is 1 mm. The reading error is therefore to the nearest 0.5 mm, which for smaller lengths is unacceptable. For more accurate readings of smaller lengths, we use either a vernier caliper or a micrometer screw gauge.
SEE ALSO **micrometer screw gauge, vernier caliper**

lens

❶ The lens is the part of the eye that acts as a convex lens and bends the light as it passes through the eyeball so that the light is focused on the retina. It consists of layers of transparent material. The lens is held in place by suspensory ligaments attached to its outer rim. These are attached to a ring of muscle fibres around the lens called the ciliary muscles.
SEE ALSO **accomodation, eye, retina**

accommodation

is changing the thickness of the lens to focus on objects at various distances from the eye. When the ring of ciliary muscles contracts, the suspensory ligaments are loosened and the lens becomes fatter to focus on nearby objects. When the ciliary muscles are relaxed, the suspensory ligaments are tightened, which makes the lens thinner to focus on distant objects.

❷ A lens is a piece of glass which is used to focus or change the direction of a beam of light passing through it. Lenses are usually convex or concave in shape and have different uses.
• *Lenses are used in a variety of optical instruments such as cameras, projectors, and telescopes.*
SEE ALSO **centre of curvature, focal length, focal point, optical centre, principal axis**

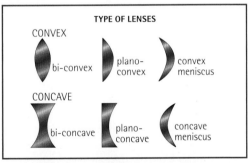

TYPE OF LENSES

CONVEX — bi-convex, plano-convex, convex meniscus

CONCAVE — bi-concave, plano-concave, concave meniscus

concave lens (*also* diverging lens)

A concave lens is one whose surface curves inwards.
• *When light is passed through such a lens, it is refracted outwards away from the principal axis. A concave lens is therefore described as a diverging lens.*
SEE ALSO **principal axis, refraction of light**

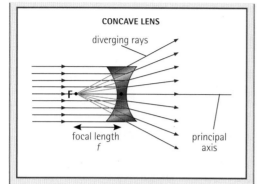

CONCAVE LENS

diverging rays

F

focal length
f

principal axis

convex lens (*also* **converging lens**)

A convex lens is one whose surface curves outwards.

• *When light is passed through such a lens, it is refracted towards the principal axis. A convex lens is therefore described as a converging lens.*

SEE ALSO **principal axis, refraction of light**

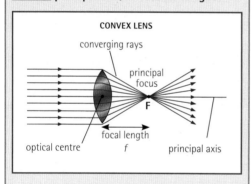

CONVEX LENS

converging rays

principal focus

F

focal length
f

optical centre

principal axis

leucocyte *see* **white blood cell**

lever

A lever is a simple machine consisting of a rigid bar supported or pivoted at a point along its length called the fulcrum. An effort applied at one point on the bar can move a load at another point. There are three orders of lever:

- first-order lever: the fulcrum (pivot) is between the load and the effort
- second-order lever: the fulcrum (pivot) is closer to the load than the effort
- third-order lever: the fulcrum (pivot) is closer to the effort than the load.

SEE ALSO **machine**

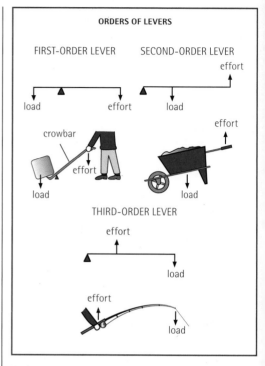

ORDERS OF LEVERS

FIRST-ORDER LEVER

load   effort

SECOND-ORDER LEVER

effort

load

crowbar

effort

load

effort

load

THIRD-ORDER LEVER

effort

load

effort

load

lichen

A lichen is a low, crusty plant which grows on rocks, walls, and tree trunks. It consists of two organisms: a fungus and a green alga. The fungus extracts minerals from the rock or soil and the alga photosynthesizes.

• *Lichen reproduce with spores.*

SEE ALSO **algae, fungus, photosynthesis, spore**

Liebig condenser

A Liebig condenser is a straight, glass tube surrounded by a glass jacket through which cold cooling water is circulated.

• *The Liebig condenser is named after the German chemist Justus von Liebig (1803–1873).*

SEE ALSO **distillation, fractional distillation**

life cycle

A life cycle shows the way in which a living thing changes as it grows.

• *The life cycle of a butterfly goes through the stages of egg to larva to pupa to adult butterfly.*

SEE ALSO **imago, larva, nymph, pupa**

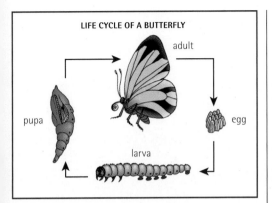

LIFE CYCLE OF A BUTTERFLY

adult

pupa

egg

larva

life-cycle assessment (also LCA)

is the 'cradle to grave' impact that a manufactured product has on society, including making, using, and disposing of the manufactured product. It assesses the overall impact on the environment of the following:

- obtaining and processing raw materials for the product
- making the product (and packaging if necessary) and distribution
- using (reusing/recycling) and maintaining the product
- disposing of the product at the end of its useful 'life'.

Life-cycle assessment is used by government agencies, business, and industry.

SEE ALSO **instrumental analysis**

life of a star see stellar evolution

lifestyle factor

Lifestyle factors include exercise, diet, alcohol, smoking, and drug abuse. These factors can have a direct effect on the incidence of a particular disease. Heavy smokers are more likely to develop lung cancer and heavy drinkers are more likely to develop serious liver diseases like cirrhosis of the liver. People who overeat and do little exercise are much more likely to develop type 2 diabetes.

• *Lifestyle factors such as regular sunbathing (exposure to ultraviolet radiation) can increase the risk factor of developing skin cancer.*

SEE ALSO **alcohol abuse, alcoholism, cancer, diabetes, drug abuse, smoking**

ligament

A ligament is a tough, elastic structure of connective tissue that connects bones together at movable joints.

SEE ALSO **connective tissue**

ligation see contraception

light

is the visible part of the electromagnetic spectrum and is a form of energy emitted by luminous objects like the Sun. Light energy travels as waves in straight lines away from its source (rectilinear propagation).

• *The human eye is sensitive to light, and our visual awareness of our surroundings depends upon light.*

SEE ALSO **electromagnetic spectrum, energy, wave**

➤ **speed of light** (also c) Light (together with all other electromagnetic waves) travels at the same speed in a vacuum, which is approximately 3×10^8 m s^{-1} or 300,000 km s^{-1}.

light-dependent resistor (also LDR)

A light-dependent resistor is a resistor made from a semiconductor (e.g. cadmium sulfides or selenium) whose resistance changes with light intensity. In the dark LDRs have very high resistance but in the light a low resistance.

LDR

• *LDRs can be used as light-dependent switches for opening automatic doors or in alarm systems.*

SEE ALSO **semiconductor**

light-emitting diode (also LED)

A light-emitting diode is a semiconducting diode that has a higher resistance than normal and produces light instead of heat. Like many electronic components, they work with very small currents.

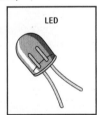

LED

• *LEDs are widely used for displaying letters and numbers in digital instruments in which a self-luminous display is needed, e.g. calculators, watches, TV, mobile phones etc.*

lightning

is the sudden flow of electricity from a thundercloud which has become charged by the rubbing together of air and water molecules. As the charge builds up in the cloud so does the voltage, until suddenly a giant spark of lightning results. The point action of a lightning conductor can conduct this flow of electricity safely down to earth.

SEE ALSO **electric charge, point action**

»

a
b
c
d
e
f
g
h
i
j
k
l
m
n
o
p
q
r
s
t
u
v
w
x
y
z

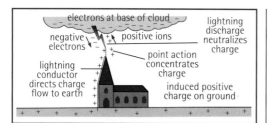

light-sensitive switch *see* electronic switch

light-year

A light-year is an astronomical unit of distance (not time) and is equal to the distance travelled by light in 1 year.

• *The nearest star, called Proxima Centauri, is 4.2 light-years from Earth. The nearest galaxy, called Andromeda, is about 1 million light-years away.*

SEE ALSO parsec

lime kiln

A lime kiln is a heating tower used to make lime by the thermal decomposition of limestone. The kiln is charged from the top with the limestone, and also with coke, which burns with the air to supply the heat to decompose the limestone. The carbon dioxide escapes from the top of the kiln and the lime falls, as a solid, to the bottom. Like many industrial processes, it is continuous.

$$limestone \rightarrow lime + carbon\ dioxide$$
$$CaCO_3 \rightarrow CaO + CO_2$$

Lime is often called quicklime because it is 'quick' to react with water. When it does, it has 'slaked' its thirst and forms slaked lime (calcium hydroxide).

$$lime + water \rightarrow slaked\ lime$$
$$CaO + H_2O \rightarrow Ca(OH)_2$$

SEE ALSO decomposition

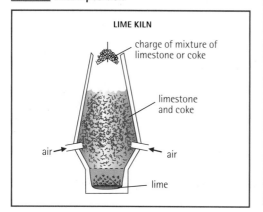

LIME KILN

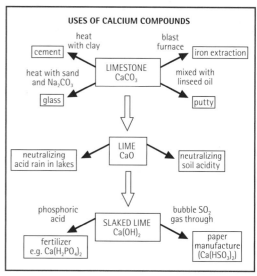

USES OF CALCIUM COMPOUNDS

liming

Liming soil with a mixture of chalk and lime can help to neutralize excess acidity (e.g. caused by acid rain), and can improve drainage in clay soils by causing small particles to clump together to form larger particles (flocculation).

SEE ALSO acid rain, soil

limiting factors *see* photosynthesis

limiting frictional force *see* friction

limiting reactant

In a chemical reaction, the limiting reactant is the reactant that is completely used up when other reactants still remain. If there are two reactants in a chemical reaction, it is common to use an excess of one to ensure all of the other reactant is used up.

• *The limiting reactant is always the reactant that gets used up first in a chemical reaction.*

SEE ALSO chemical reaction, reactant

line graph *see* graph

line of magnetic force *see* magnetic field line

lipase

A lipase is an enzyme in intestinal juice which breaks down fats (lipids) into fatty acids and glycerol.

SEE ALSO enzyme, fat

liquid

A liquid is the physical state of matter in which the particles are not regularly arranged and move by sliding past one another.

• *A liquid is a basic state of matter (along with solid and gas) with a melting point below room temperature but a boiling point above room temperature.*
SEE ALSO boiling point, melting point, state of matter

liquid–in–glass thermometer
The liquid-in-glass thermometer is a common laboratory thermometer which measures temperature by the expansion of a liquid in a very narrow glass capillary tube. A glass bulb at the bottom acts as a reservoir for the liquid.
SEE ALSO thermometer

lithosphere
The lithosphere is the solid crust of the Earth, contrasted with the hydrosphere (sea/oceans) and atmosphere (air).

litmus
is an indicator made from a lichen (a tiny plant) which turns red in acidic solutions and blue in alkaline solutions.
SEE ALSO indicator

liver
The liver is a large and important organ which acts as a 'chemical factory' and has a wide range of functions. It receives all the digested food dissolved in the blood from the intestines via the hepatic portal vein. It has two main homeostatic functions: regulation of glucose and regulation of amino acids and proteins.

WORD BUILD

regulation of blood glucose
The amount of glucose in the blood needs to be regulated. Glucose concentration in the blood is normally around $100\,mg/100\,cm^3$. If there is too much glucose in the blood, the liver removes excess by converting it into glycogen (animal starch), which it stores in its cells. When there is too little glucose, some of the glycogen is broken down to increase blood sugar levels
SEE ALSO islets of Langerhans

regulation of amino acids and proteins
The amount of amino acids and proteins in the blood needs to be regulated. Proteins are broken down in the intestines into amino acids, which are then absorbed into the blood and taken to the liver by the hepatic portal vein. Those amino acids that are needed by the body are released back into circulation. Those that are not needed undergo deamination to carbohydrate and ammonia. The carbohydrate is stored, but the ammonia is converted to urea and excreted via the kidneys.
SEE ALSO bile, deamination, glycogen, homeostasis, islets of Langerhans, urea

	Ten important functions of the liver
1.	Controls the amount of glucose in the blood using the hormones insulin and glycogen.
2.	Regulates the amount of amino acids and proteins by converting excess into urea and carbohydrates.
3.	Makes bile, which is stored in the gall bladder and helps in the digestion of fats.
4.	Stores carbohydrates like glucose as the polysaccharide glycogen (animal starch).
5.	Stores vitamins A and D (both fat-soluble).
6.	Makes cholesterol, which is needed to repair cell membranes.
7.	Produces fibrinogen, which is used by the blood platelets as a clotting substance.
8.	Produces heat as a result of the many metabolic reactions.
9.	Breaks down old red cells, storing the iron and excreting the remaining pigments in bile.
10.	Removes harmful substances such as alcohol.

living organism *see* **organism**

loamy soil *see* **soil**

local action
is the reaction of the negative plate with an acid electrolyte in a primary cell. Hydrogen gas is produced, which reduces the electromotive force or emf of the cell.
SEE ALSO electromotive force, polarization, primary cell

longitude
The longitude of a point on the Earth's surface is its distance around the Earth's circumference, measured in degrees east or west, and starting at the meridian which runs through Greenwich, near London.
• *Greenwich has a longitude of 0°.*
SEE ALSO latitude, meridian

longitudinal wave
A longitudinal wave is a progressive wave – one in which the oscillation or vibration is along the line of the direction in which the wave is travelling

»

(direction of energy movement). Mechanical waves such as sound are longitudinal waves. As the oscillating object moves forward, it squashes the particles in the medium together (compressions or high pressures). When the object moves backwards, the particles in the medium become widely spaced (rarefactions or low pressures).

SEE ALSO **progressive wave, sound**

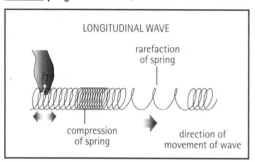

LONGITUDINAL WAVE

rarefaction of spring

compression of spring

direction of movement of wave

long-sightedness (*also* hypermetropia)

is a vision defect which makes people able to focus clearly only on distant objects.

• *The solution to* **long-sightedness** *is to wear glasses or contact lenses with convex (converging) lenses. These bend the rays inwards so that they focus on the retina and not behind it.*

SEE ALSO **lens, short-sightedness, transverse wave**

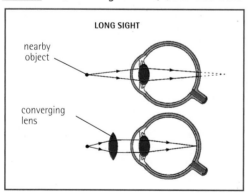

LONG SIGHT

nearby object

converging lens

loudness

is a property of a sound wave determined by its amplitude. The greater the amplitude, the louder the sound. The sensation of loudness in the ear is subjective and depends on the sensitivity of the ear to the particular frequencies.

• *Loudness is often measured in decibels.*

SEE ALSO **amplitude, decibel**

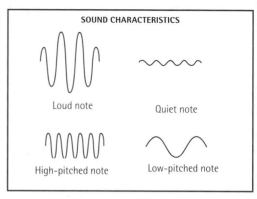

SOUND CHARACTERISTICS

Loud note

Quiet note

High-pitched note

Low-pitched note

Sound (loudness)	dB level
threshold of hearing	0 dB
bird singing	30 dB
normal conversation	60 dB
road drill	80 dB
loud thunderclap	110 dB
threshold of pain	130 dB

loudspeaker

A loudspeaker is a device which uses the motor effect to change electrical energy into sound energy. It consists of a coil of wire in a radial magnetic field. The coil is attached to a paper cone. The changing current in the coil makes the paper cone vibrate, producing sound.

SEE ALSO **magnetic field, motor effect**

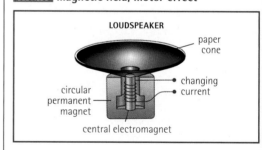

LOUDSPEAKER

paper cone

changing current

circular permanent magnet

central electromagnet

louse *plural* lice

A louse is a small insect that lives as a parasite on animals and plants. A louse is an insect as it has six legs and three different sections to its body.

• *Many* **lice** *are bloodsucking insects.*

SEE ALSO **parasite**

low *see* depression

low-density polyethene (*also* LDPE)

is formed when ethene gas with a trace of oxygen gas (as an initiator) is heated to 200°C and subjected to extremely high pressures of 1,500 atmospheres. LDPE has many branching chains, which cannot be packed together tightly. It is a soft plastic with a density around 0.92 g/cm^3.

• *The uses of* **low-density polyethene** *include making plastic bags, bin liners, cling film, and packaging.*

SEE ALSO **high-density polyethene, polythene**

lubricating oil

is the petroleum fraction with a boiling point range of 300–400°C. It is made up of a mixture of hydrocarbons containing 20 to 70 carbon atoms. It is used for lubricants, waxes, greases and polishes. However, most of the fraction is used for cracking.

SEE ALSO **cracking, fraction**

luminous object

Luminous objects are objects which emit visible light. Light is emitted by very hot objects such as the Sun, or the filament in a bulb, or the hot gases in a flame. The intensity of the light emitted by such an object or source is called its luminous intensity and is measured in candelas.

SEE ALSO **non-luminous object**

lunar eclipse *see* eclipse

lung

A lung is an organ for gaseous exchange in vertebrates. The lungs play a major role in controlling the levels of oxygen and carbon dioxide in the blood and body tissue.

SEE ALSO **gaseous exchange, respiration**

➤ **lung capacity** The capacity of an adult human lung is about 5 litres. In normal breathing only about 500 cm^3 of air is breathed in and out (tidal volume). However, there is no stagnant air, as inspired air mixes with all the air inside the lung. Both oxygen and carbon dioxide gases are soluble in the mucus of the lungs. Nitrogen gas is insoluble at normal atmospheric pressure, so the percentage of nitrogen in inhaled and exhaled air remains the same.

Gas	Approximate volume inhaled	Approximate volume exhaled
oxygen	21%	17%
nitrogen	78%	78%
carbon dioxide	0.03%	4%

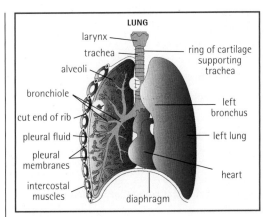

LUNG

larynx · trachea · alveoli · bronchiole · cut end of rib · pleural fluid · pleural membranes · intercostal muscles · ring of cartilage supporting trachea · left bronchus · left lung · heart · diaphragm

lymph

is a colourless fluid which contains the products from digestion of fats, and transports both types of white cell.

• *The* **lymph** *fluid eventually enters the blood system near the heart.*

SEE ALSO **lymphatic system, white blood cell**

lymphatic system

The lymphatic system is a network of lymph vessels and lymph nodes (sometimes called 'glands') which helps to circulate lymph throughout the body.

SEE ALSO **lymph**

lymphatic tissue (*also* lymphoid tissue)

is tissue which has large numbers of lymph vessels and lymph nodes, which produce antibodies and white blood cells. It is of different types:
  – adenoids are lymphatic tissue located at the back of the nose
  – tonsils are lymphatic tissue located in the throat
  – the spleen is lymphatic tissue in the abdomen. It also stores and removes red blood cells from the blood system.

SEE ALSO **antibody, white blood cell**

lymphocyte (*also* agranulocyte)

Lymphocytes are white blood cells made in the lymphatic tissue which produce antibodies to fight disease. They are found in the lymphatic system as well as in the blood.

• **Lymphocytes** *have a large nucleus and their cytoplasm has no granules, unlike the other white cell (phagocyte) which has a smaller nucleus and granulated cytoplasm.*

SEE ALSO **antibody, cytoplasm, lymphatic system, phagocyte, white blood cell**

lysosome *see* organelle

a b c d e f g h i j k l m n o p q r s t u v w x y z

Mm

M *see* **molar solution**

MA *see* **mechanical advantage**

machine
A machine is a device for doing work. In most machines a small force, the effort, is used to overcome a larger force, the load. Such machines are also called force multipliers.
SEE ALSO **mechanical advantage, velocity ratio, work**

Mach number
is the ratio of the speed of a moving object to the speed of sound in the same medium and under the same temperature and pressure.
• *Mach 1 is the speed of sound (330 ms^{-1} in air) and Mach 2 is twice the speed of sound.*
SEE ALSO **subsonic, supersonic**

macro-habitat *see* **habitat**

macromolecule (*also* giant structure)
Macromolecules are very large molecules, often containing many thousands of atoms.
• *Natural polymers (like proteins) and synthetic polymers (like plastics) are* **macromolecules,** *as are giant covalent molecules like diamond and graphite.*
SEE ALSO **natural polymer, polymer, synthetic polymer**

maggot
A maggot is the larval stage of a fly (order Diptera). There are many different types of maggot.
• *Maggots used by fishermen are often from houseflies, especially the large bluebottle fly.*
SEE ALSO **larva, life cycle**

magma
is hot, molten rock that originates from the Earth's mantle. Magma is extruded as lava on to the Earth's surface as a result of volcanic activity.
• *When* **magma** *cools and solidifies, it forms igneous rock.*
SEE ALSO **Earth's structure, rock**

magnesium (*also* Mg)
is a chemical element, a silvery white metal that burns with an intensely bright flame.
• *Magnesium is an essential trace element for plants.*
SEE ALSO **mineral salt, trace element**

➤ **uses of magnesium** Magnesium is the only alkaline-earth metal used on a commercial scale: beryllium is too rare, and calcium, strontium, and barium are too reactive to have many uses. Magnesium is combined with aluminium to make lightweight alloys. As magnesium burns with an intense white light, it is used as a light source in flares and in photography.
• *Flash bulbs contain* **magnesium** *ribbon or powder in an atmosphere of oxygen.*
SEE ALSO **alkaline-earth metal**

magnetic axis
The magnetic axis is a line joining the north and south poles of a magnet about which the magnetic field is symmetrical.
SEE ALSO **magnetic field**

magnetic field
A magnetic field is a field of force that exists around a magnet or a current-carrying conductor. Magnetic objects entering this field are affected by the magnet's forces of attraction and repulsion due to the interaction between their fields.
SEE ALSO **Earth's magnetic field**

magnetic field line (*also* magnetic flux line, line of magnetic force)
Magnetic field lines are lines which indicate the direction of the magnetic field around a magnet or between magnets. This is the direction a north pole would move in the magnetic field.

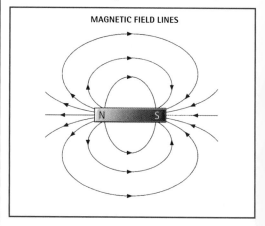

MAGNETIC FIELD LINES

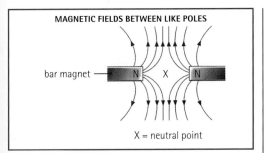

MAGNETIC FIELDS BETWEEN LIKE POLES

bar magnet — N   X   N

X = neutral point

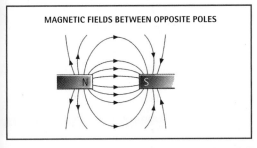

MAGNETIC FIELDS BETWEEN OPPOSITE POLES

N   S

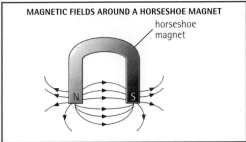

MAGNETIC FIELDS AROUND A HORSESHOE MAGNET

horseshoe magnet

N   S

magnetic flux density (*also* **B**)

is a measurement of the strength of a magnetic field at a particular point. It is shown by the closeness of the magnetic field lines to each other.
• *Magnetic flux density is always highest around the magnetic poles.*

magnetic flux line *see* **magnetic field line**

magnetic induction *see* **magnetization**

magnetic material (*also* **ferromagnetic material**)

is material which can be magnetized strongly, such as iron, cobalt, nickel, and their alloys.

hard magnetic material (*also* **permanent magnet**)

describes a ferromagnetic material such as steel, which retains its magnetism. Such materials are 'hard' to magnetize, but once magnetized they keep their magnetism.

soft magnetic material (*also* **temporary magnet**)

describes a ferromagnetic material such as pure iron (called 'soft iron') or wrought iron. Soft magnetic material is easy to magnetize but loses most of its magnetism when the external magnetic field is removed.

non-magnetic material

describes materials like silver, gold, copper, brass, aluminium, and non-metals, which apparently cannot be magnetized. However, all material has some magnetic property, and very strong magnets can influence non-magnetic material.

magnetic permeability *see* **permeability**

magnetic pole

The magnetic poles are regions near the ends of a magnet from which the magnetic forces appear to originate.
• *A bar magnet has two **magnetic poles**, the north pole and south pole.*

north pole (*also* **north–seeking pole, N pole**)

A north pole is the end of a magnet which, when suspended freely, points to the north (magnetic north).

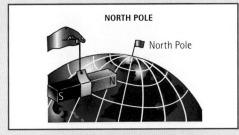

NORTH POLE

North Pole

south pole (*also* **south–seeking pole, S pole**)

A south pole is the end of a magnet which, when suspended freely, points to the south.

magnetic shielding

is surrounding an object with a material with a high permeability (e.g. soft iron), so that any magnetic field is effectively 'conducted' away from it.
• *Magnetic shielding is used in sensitive instruments like oscilloscopes.*
SEE ALSO **permeability**

magnetic stripe

Magnetic stripes are bands of rock of alternate magnetic polarity. About every half million years, the Earth's magnetic field reverses direction. New rocks take on the new polarity, forming symmetrical stripes on each side of a ridge.

• *Magnetic stripes were discovered in the 1960s and provide evidence for plate tectonics.*

SEE ALSO **Earth's magnetic field, plate tectonics**

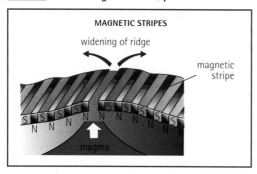

MAGNETIC STRIPES

widening of ridge

magnetic stripe

magma

magnetism

is a property of matter which produces a field of attractive and repulsive forces.

law of magnetism

The law of magnetism states that like poles of two magnets (two north poles or two south poles) repel one another, and unlike poles attract one another. To find out the polarity of a magnet, bring both its poles in turn near to the known pole of a suspended magnet. If there is repulsion, then the poles are similar in polarity. If there is attraction, then the poles are opposite in polarity.

SEE ALSO **magnetic pole**

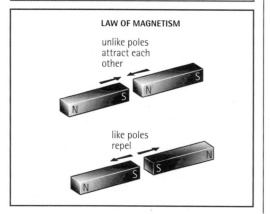

LAW OF MAGNETISM

unlike poles attract each other

like poles repel

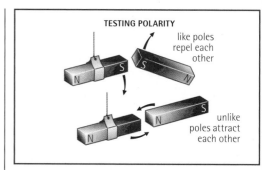

TESTING POLARITY

like poles repel each other

unlike poles attract each other

magnetization (*also* **magnetic induction**)

is inducing magnetism into magnetic material by aligning its domains. Material can be magnetized by the electrical method or the stroking method.

SEE ALSO **magnetic field**

electrical method

Place the piece of steel in a long coil made of several hundred turns of conducting wire. Pass a large direct current through the coil for a few seconds. The polarity of the magnet depends upon the direction of the current.

SEE ALSO **electromagnet**

stroking method

The piece of steel is repeatedly stroked with a permanent magnet. In 'single touch' stroking one pole of a magnet is used. In 'divided touch' stroking the piece of steel is stroked from the centre outwards with two permanent magnets simultaneously. These must have unlike poles (see diagram).

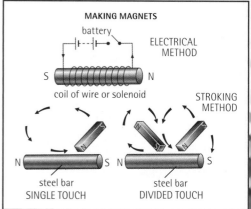

MAKING MAGNETS

battery

ELECTRICAL METHOD

coil of wire or solenoid

STROKING METHOD

steel bar
SINGLE TOUCH

steel bar
DIVIDED TOUCH

magnification

produced through lenses is the ratio of image height to object height.

• *Magnification is important when using a magnifying glass or a microscope.*

SEE ALSO lens, magnifying glass, microscope

magnification value *see* microscope

magnifying glass

A magnifying glass uses a convex lens to produce a magnified, upright, virtual image of a small object. To achieve this the object must be placed in front of the focal point of the lens.

SEE ALSO image, lens

mains electricity

is generated in power stations using large generators, usually powered by heat energy from burning fossil fuels or from nuclear fuels. This heat boils water to produce steam, which drives a turbine, which produces the rotary motion needed for the generator.

• *Mains electricity is transmitted around the country by the national grid system.*

SEE ALSO generator, national grid system

malaria

is a disease caused by the protist called Plasmodium. This is carried in the saliva of the female anopheles mosquito, which is therefore the vector of the disease. The mosquito sucks blood, and to stop the blood from clotting she injects some saliva. If her saliva contains plasmodium, the person can develop malaria.

SEE ALSO protist, vector

male reproductive organ system (*also* genital organs, *or* genitalia)

The male reproductive organ system comprises two main organs: penis and testes.

SEE ALSO penis, testis

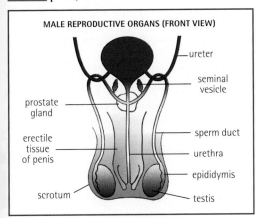

MALE REPRODUCTIVE ORGANS (FRONT VIEW)

- ureter
- seminal vesicle
- prostate gland
- sperm duct
- erectile tissue of penis
- urethra
- epididymis
- scrotum
- testis

malleable *see* metal

malleus *see* ossicle

malnutrition

is the state of poor health caused by a lack of sufficient food, lack of balanced diet, or a condition which prevents the body from absorbing or using nutrients properly.

• *Prolonged malnutrition can result in death when protein levels in the body are reduced to half their normal value.*

SEE ALSO balanced diet

Malpighian layer

The Malpighian layer is the uppermost living layer of the skin which produces new skin cells. These new cells gradually move towards the surface of the skin. As they move upwards, they die (average life about 4 weeks) and fill with a hard protein called keratin. This tough, dead layer of cells is the cornified layer on the surface of the skin.

SEE ALSO cornified layer, skin

mammal (*also* Mammalia)

Mammals are warm-blooded vertebrates whose skin is covered with hair and has sweat glands. They normally give birth to live young, which are nourished in a womb with a placenta. All female mammals have mammary glands to suckle their young. Other distinguishing characteristics are the presence of a diaphragm, ear ossicles (middle ear), and different types of teeth (incisors, canines, and molars).

• *Mammals evolved from carnivorous reptiles about 225 million years ago.*

SEE ALSO marsupial, monotreme, primate

mandible *see* human skeleton

manometer

A manometer is a U-shaped tube with a liquid inside, which is used for measuring fluid (gas or liquid) pressure. The pressure to be measured is fed into one side of the tube and the other is left open to the atmosphere. The difference in level of the liquid in the two limbs gives a measure of the unknown pressure.

SEE ALSO pressure in liquid   »

A
B
C
D
E
F
G
H
I
J
K
L
M
N
O
P
Q
R
S
T
U
V
W
X
Y
Z

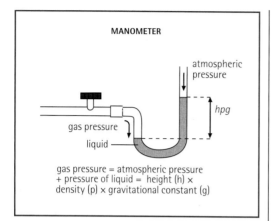

MANOMETER

atmospheric pressure

hpg

gas pressure

liquid

gas pressure = atmospheric pressure
+ pressure of liquid = height (h) ×
density (p) × gravitational constant (g)

mantle *see* **Earth's structure**

Mars *see* **planet**

marsupial
Marsupials are a subclass of mammals which raise their young in a pouch.
• *Examples of **marsupials** are possums, koalas, kangaroos, and wallabies.*
SEE ALSO **mammal**

mass
is the quantity of matter in an object (or body). Mass is also equivalent to inertia.
• *The unit of **mass** is the kilogram.*
SEE ALSO **inertia, kilogram**

➤ **measurement of mass** is achieved using a balance, which in a school laboratory may weigh to a milligram (0.001 g). Common school balances are the beam balance (scale pans hung from a centrally pivoted bar) and electronic balances. Most electronic balances have a 'tare' by which the mass of the empty container can be stored in the balance's memory and automatically deducted from the mass of the container plus its contents.

➤ **principle of conservation of mass** This principle states that, during any physical or chemical change, mass cannot be created or destroyed. There is always the same total mass before and after such changes (except nuclear reactions in which mass is converted into energy).

mass defect
is the difference in mass between the sum of individual masses of the protons and neutrons, and their total mass in the nucleus.

• *Mass defect is the mass equivalent (in a mass energy equation) if the energy involved is equal to the binding energy.*
SEE ALSO **binding energy, mass-energy equation**

mass-energy equation
shows the relationship $\Delta E = \Delta mc^2$, where ΔE = change in energy, Δm = change in mass and c is the speed of light (3×10^8 m s^{-1}).
• *From the **mass–energy equation** it can be seen that a very small change in mass results in a vast change in energy (multiplication factor of around 10^{17}).*

mass number (*also* nucleon number)
The mass number of an element is the total number of protons and neutrons found in the nucleus of an atom of the element.
• *The **mass number** of a particular element can vary, as the number of neutrons can change (isotopes).*
SEE ALSO **atomic number, isotope, neutron**

mass spectrometry
is an instrumental analysis using a mass spectrometer to analyze the mass composition of different parts of a molecule. The sample molecule is ionized by the machine to form a molecular ion. Such ions may break up to form fragments of the molecule.
• *Mass spectrometry is used in environmental science to detect toxic substances.*
SEE ALSO **instrumental analysis, molecule**

master gland *see* **brain**

mastication
is the process of chewing food and involves the movement of the jaws and teeth.
• *Mastication is part of mechanical digestion.*
SEE ALSO **digestion**

mating *see* **copulation**

matter
is the general word used by scientists to describe all the different types of materials that things are made of.
• *Matter is found everywhere except in a vacuum.*
SEE ALSO **mass**

maximum–and–minimum thermometer
A maximum-and-minimum thermometer is a special liquid-in-glass thermometer that records the maximum and minimum temperatures reached during

a certain period of time. A metal index is pushed up or down the tube by the liquid and stays at this maximum or minimum until reset using a magnet.
SEE ALSO **liquid-in-glass thermometer**

mean position
The mean position is the position about which an object will oscillate, and is the rest position of the object when the oscillation ceases. Passing through this position during an oscillation, the object has maximum kinetic energy as it has its greatest velocity. At the same time, the object has its minimum potential energy as it has zero displacement.
SEE ALSO **amplitude, oscillation**

measles *see* **childhood illness**

measurement of force *see* **force**

measurement of length *see* **length**

measurement of mass *see* **mass**

measurement of volume *see* **volume**

mechanical advantage (*also* **force ratio**)
The mechanical advantage for a simple machine is the ratio of the load (output force) to the effort (input force). A mechanical advantage greater than one means that the load is greater than the effort.

$$\text{mechanical advantage} = \frac{\text{load}}{\text{effort}}$$

SEE ALSO **machine**

mechanical digestion *see* **digestion**

mechanical energy
is the sum of the kinetic energy and the gravitational potential energy of an object.
SEE ALSO **gravitational potential energy store, kinetic energy store**

medicine
A medicine is a drug which helps to cure or minimize the effects of a disease. Such drugs may be:
  – analgesics (painkillers that numb part of brain)
  – sedatives (that slow down the activity of brain)
  – stimulants (that speed up mental activity)
  – hallucinogens (that cause visual images in the mind).
• *Medicines are normally prescribed by the doctor and should not be overused.*
SEE ALSO **drug**

medium
A medium is a substance through which a wave travels. A wave does not permanently disturb the medium through which it travels. A water wave travels across the surface, but the water particles do not travel with the wave. They vibrate up and down and remain in their original position.
SEE ALSO **wave**

medulla *see* **kidney**

medulla oblongata *see* **brain**

meiosis (*also* **reductive cell division**)
is division of a cell which results in each daughter cell receiving exactly half the number of chromosomes.
• *Meiosis takes place in the sex organs to produce gametes (sex cells) such as sperm, pollen, and eggs.*
SEE ALSO **gamete, mitosis, chromosome, chromatid**

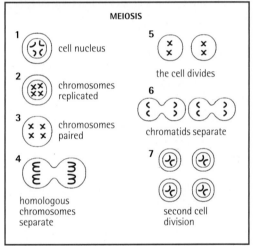

MEIOSIS

1 cell nucleus
2 chromosomes replicated
3 chromosomes paired
4 homologous chromosomes separate
5 the cell divides
6 chromatids separate
7 second cell division

melanin
is a brown pigment found in the cells of the epidermis. Melanin absorbs harmful ultraviolet rays from the Sun. It is responsible for tanning of skin exposed to sunlight.
SEE ALSO **epidermis**

melting
is the change in state from a solid to a liquid, usually caused by heating. On heating, the particles in a solid gain energy and move more. They remain in contact but with weaker forces of attraction, and so they are not held in fixed positions and the material becomes a liquid.
• *The reverse of the **melting** process is called freezing.*

melting point

is the temperature at which a solid completely changes into a liquid.

• *A pure substance has an exact **melting point**. Impurities cause lower melting points.*

SEE ALSO **boiling point, freezing point**

Mendel's laws

summarize the theory of inheritance. They were first stated by Gregor Mendel (1822-84), who lived in what is now the Czech Republic. The laws are:

- the law of segregation which states that each hereditary characteristic is controlled by two genes (alleles) which, during meiosis, separate and pass into gamete or sex cells
- the law of independent assortment which states that each member of a pair of genes (allele) can join with either of the two members of another pair when the cell divides to form a gamete or sex cells.

SEE ALSO **gamete, meiosis**

meninges *singular* meninx

Meninges are three protective membranes that cover the surface of the central nervous system in vertebrates:

- the dura mater is the tough outer meninx, which protects the delicate inner meninges
- the arachnoid membrane is the middle meninx, which carries cerebrospinal fluid and cushions the nervous tissue
- the pia mater is the innermost meninx, which secretes cerebrospinal fluid.

• *Inflammation of the **meninges** is called meningitis.*

SEE ALSO **central nervous system**

menopause

The menopause is the time in a woman's life (usually between the ages of 45 and 55) when ovulation and menstruation stop, and she ceases to be able to have children.

• *A common side effect of the **menopause** is 'hot flushes' (sudden feeling of heat in the face, neck, and chest).*

SEE ALSO **menstruation, ovulation**

menstrual cycle

The menstrual cycle is a roughly monthly cycle of female reproductive physiology during which ovulation and menstruation occur. The events of this cycle are controlled by hormones produced by the ovaries (oestrogen) and pituitary gland (gonadotrophic hormones). An area of tissue in the

ovary, the follicle, develops to produce an egg. When mature, the follicle bursts, releasing an egg from the ovary (ovulation), and changes into the corpus luteum, which secretes progesterone hormone, causing the lining of the uterus to become thick and rich in blood vessels. If the egg is fertilized, the developing embryo becomes implanted in this lining. If the egg is not fertilized, then menstruation occurs.

• *The **menstrual cycle** continues in a woman from puberty to the menopause.*

SEE ALSO **menopause, menstruation, ovulation**

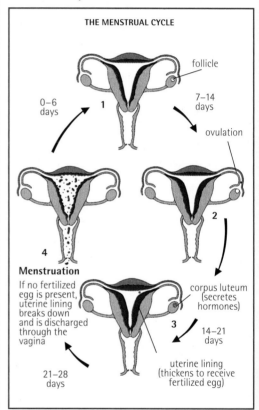

THE MENSTRUAL CYCLE

follicle

0–6 days   1   7–14 days

ovulation

4

Menstruation
If no fertilized egg is present, uterine lining breaks down and is discharged through the vagina

corpus luteum (secretes hormones)

2

3   14–21 days

21–28 days

uterine lining (thickens to receive fertilized egg)

menstruation

is the breakdown of the lining of the uterus and its gradual discharge through the vagina (called a period).

• *Menstruation* normally begins between 12 and 15 years of age and continues until the menopause.*

SEE ALSO **menopause**

Mercury *see* **planet**

mercury

is a silvery, dense, metallic element which is very chemically unreactive. It is a liquid at room temperature as it has a melting point of −39°C.

• *Mercury is often used in thermometers, as when it heats up its expansion is uniform and related to the temperature rise.*

SEE ALSO **element, thermometric liquid**

mercury barometer *see* barometer

meridian

The meridians of longitude are imaginary circles drawn around the earth passing through both poles.

SEE ALSO **longitude**

meristem

A meristem is a region of plant tissue which is actively dividing and producing living cells.

• *The most important **meristems** occur at the growing points at the top of the stem or shoot and at the tip of the root.*

SEE ALSO **tissue**

mesophyll

The mesophyll layer is the middle layer of a leaf, between the upper and lower epidermis.

SEE ALSO **epidermis, leaf**

palisade mesophyll

The palisade mesophyll is made up of regularly shaped cells which contain many chloroplasts.

SEE ALSO **chloroplast**

spongy mesophyll

The spongy mesophyll is made up of irregularly shaped cells with air spaces in between them, in which gases for photosynthesis can circulate by diffusion.

SEE ALSO **diffusion**

metabolic rate

is the rate at which an animal uses energy over a given time period.

• *Metabolic rate is affected by level of activity and temperature.*

metabolism (*also* metabolic activity)

is the sum of all the various biochemical reactions that occur in a living organism.

WORD BUILD

anabolism

is the phase of metabolism that is concerned with the building up of complicated molecules from simple ones, e.g. protein synthesis.

catabolism

is the phase of metabolism that is concerned with the breaking down of complicated molecules to simpler ones, e.g. respiration or digestion.

metal

Metals are a class of chemical elements which always form positive ions (cations) when they react to form compounds. They are often lustrous (shiny) solids which are good conductors of heat and electricity. They also form solid oxides that act as bases. In the periodic table, metallic elements are found on the left-hand side of the table. As we go down a group, the metallic character increases. As we go across a period, the metallic character decreases.

• *Caesium is the most reactive **metal** in the periodic table.*

SEE ALSO **base, extraction of metals, periodic table**

➤ **properties of metals** Typical metals (excluding Group I and Group II metals) have the physical properties listed in the table, which make them very useful.

Metallic property	Meaning
Density (high)	mass per unit volume
Durable	resistant to corrosion
Malleable	able to be made into sheets
Ductile	able to be made into wire
Sonorous	able to produce sound when struck
Electrical conductivity (high)	ability to conduct electricity
Thermal conductivity (high)	ability to conduct heat
Tensile strength (high)	strength of metal under stress

»

a b c d e f g h i j k l m n o p q r s t u v w x y z

Metallic property	Uses
Density (high)	lead fishing weights
Durable	zinc dustbins, aluminium windows
Malleable	cooper roofing, aluminium foil
Ductile	copper wire, iron cables
Sonorous	brass (copper alloy) musical instruments, bells
Electrical conductivity (high)	copper wire, aluminium cables
Thermal conductivity (high)	aluminium saucepans, copper kettles
Tensile strength (high)	steel (iron alloy) bridges

metal compound

A metal compound is a substance that consists of one or more metallic elements chemically bonded to another element.

SEE ALSO reactivity series

WORD BUILD

sodium chloride (*also* common salt, NaCl)

is a common crystalline salt used for seasoning and preserving food.

sodium hydroxide (*also* caustic soda, NaOH)

is a white, deliquescent (moisture-absorbing) solid which dissolves in water to form the important alkali aqueous sodium hydroxide. It is used in the manufacture of soaps, paper, and rayon.

sodium hydrogen carbonate (*also* bicarbonate of soda, NaHCO$_3$)

is a white solid used in baking. On heating, it gives off carbon dioxide gas, which makes the dough rise. In solution it is a weak acid, so it is also used as an antacid to relieve acid indigestion.

sodium carbonate (*also* soda, soda ash, Na2CO$_3$)

is a white powder which dissolves in water to form an alkaline solution. In crystalline form (with water of crystallization) it is called washing soda Na$_2$CO$_3$.10H$_2$O. It is used in the manufacture of glass and as a water softener.

potassium nitrate (*also* saltpetre, KNO$_3$)

is a colourless, water-soluble solid which is used in gunpowder, fertilizers, and as a preservative in meat.

potassium hydroxide (*also* caustic potash, KOH)

is a white, deliquescent (moisture-absorbing) solid which dissolves in water to form the alkali aqueous potassium hydroxide. It is used to make toilet soap.

magnesium hydroxide (*also* Mg(OH)$_2$)

is a white solid which is slightly soluble in water. This suspension (called 'milk of magnesia') is used for acid indigestion and as a laxative (treating constipation).

magnesium sulfate (*also* MgSO$_4$)

is a white, crystalline solid which is used in medicine as a laxative and in fire-proofing material. It occurs naturally as hydrated Epsom salts MgSO$_4$.7H$_2$O.

calcium oxide (*also* quicklime, lime, CaO)

is a white solid which is made in a lime kiln by heating calcium carbonate. It is used to treat acid soils and as a fluxing agent in blast furnaces.

calcium hydroxide (*also* slaked lime, Ca(OH)$_2$)

is a white powder which dissolves sparingly in water to form limewater Ca(OH)$_2$ (aq). It is a cheap alkali and is used to treat acid soils, and in the manufacture of whitewash, mortar, bleaching powder, and glass.

calcium carbonate (*also* CaCO$_3$)

is a white solid which is the main constituent of limestone, chalk, and marble.

calcium sulfate (*also* gypsum CaSO$_4$.2H$_2$O, plaster of Paris CaSO$_4$ $\frac{1}{2}$H$_2$O, anhydrite CaSO$_4$)

is a white solid or crystal used in ceramics, plaster, and blackboard chalk.

metallic bond

A metallic bond is a chemical bond of the type which holds together the atoms in a metal or alloy. The atoms are packed closely together in fixed positions in a lattice. This allows the outermost electrons in the atoms to become 'delocalized'. These electrons are able to move freely through the lattice. The result is positive metal ions in a 'sea of electrons'. The existence of free electrons accounts for the high electrical and thermal conductivity of metals.

SEE ALSO **chemical bond**

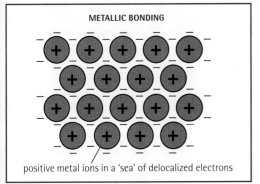

METALLIC BONDING

positive metal ions in a 'sea' of delocalized electrons

metallic lattice (*also* atomic lattice)

A metallic lattice has atoms of the metal closely packed together in layers surrounded by a sea of electrons. This close packing of atoms explains why many metals have a high density. There are also strong forces between these atoms, which is why most metals have high melting points. These forces, although they are strong, are not rigid. When a force is applied, the atoms can slip over one another. This allows the metal to be malleable (made into sheets) and ductile (drawn into a thin wire) without cracking or breaking.

• *The free electrons in a metallic lattice can readily conduct heat and electricity.*

SEE ALSO **close packing, lattice**

metalloid (*also* semimetal)

Metalloids are a class of elements intermediate in properties between metals and non-metals, such as boron and silicon.

• *Metalloids are often electrical semiconductors whose physical properties resemble metals but whose chemical properties resemble non-metals.*

SEE ALSO **metal, non–metal, semiconductor**

metamorphic rock *see* rock

metamorphosis

is the transformation that occurs in the life cycle of many arthropods from the egg through the larval and pupal stages to the adult form (imago).

• *Metamorphosis also occurs in amphibian vertebrates when they change from tadpoles into adults.*

SEE ALSO **arthropod, imago**

meteor (*also* shooting star)

A meteor is a particle from space which enters the Earth's atmosphere and becomes so hot from friction with air particles that it glows white. It appears as a streak of light in the sky.

• *Most meteors burn up before they reach the Earth's surface.*

meteorite

A meteorite is a rock formed when a large meteor does not burn up completely in the atmosphere and reaches the Earth's surface.

• *Most meteorites that land on Earth are 'micrometeorites', less than 1 mm in diameter.*

methane *see* alkane

methanoic acid (*also* formic acid)

is the simplest carboxylic acid, HCOOH, and occurs naturally in ants and stinging nettles.

• *Methanoic acid is formed by the oxidation of methanol.*

SEE ALSO **carboxylic acid, methanol**

methanol

(CH_3OH) is the simplest alcohol, and is a good solvent and fuel, but is also poisonous.

methylated spirits (*also* meths)

is a mixture of ethanol (90%) and methanol (9%) with small amounts of an emetic (to prevent it being drunk) and blue dye.

• *Methylated spirits is a common fuel and solvent.*

SEE ALSO **ethanol, methanol**

microbe *see* microorganism

microchip *see* silicon chip

microhabitat *see* habitat

micrometer screw gauge

A micrometer screw gauge is an instrument with a movable circular vernier for accurate measurement of lengths of up to about 30 mm to the nearest 0.01 mm.

a
b
c
d
e
f
g
h
i
j
k
l
m
n
o
p
q
r
s
t
u
v
w
x
y
z

• *A micrometer screw gauge can be used to measure accurately the thickness (diameter) of wires, etc.*

SEE ALSO **vernier caliper**

microorganism (*also* **microbe**)

Microorganisms are organisms which are too small to be seen without the aid of a microscope.

• *Bacteria, viruses, fungi, and protozoans are the main types of microorganisms.*

SEE ALSO **bacteria, fungus, protozoan, virus**

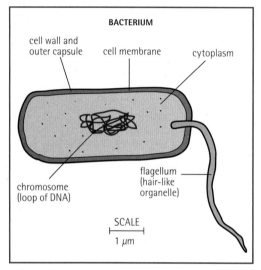

BACTERIUM

cell wall and outer capsule | cell membrane | cytoplasm
chromosome (loop of DNA) | flagellum (hair-like organelle)
SCALE
1 μm

microphone

A microphone is a device which converts sound waves into electrical signals which can then be amplified for transmission to a distant point. A carbon microphone has a movable diaphragm in contact with carbon granules. The movement of the diaphragm with the sound wave compresses/rarefies the carbon granules and varies their electrical resistance. This results in the variable electrical signal for a particular sound.

• *Microphones are transducers as they convert one energy form into another energy form (sound to electricity).*

SEE ALSO **sound wave, transducer**

micropropagation

is the taking of cuttings of the stem of a parent plant, each with a new bud. Each cutting is sterilized and placed in a special growing medium containing growth hormones. The stem grows roots, and the bud develops into a new plant which is a clone of the parent.

SEE ALSO **clone**

microscope

A microscope is an instrument which produces a magnified image of a small object which is often invisible to the naked eye.

compound microscope

A compound microscope uses two lenses (objective and eyepiece). The objective lens produces a real image, which is then magnified by the eyepiece lens to produce a final, much larger virtual image.

electron microscope

An electron microscope is a bulky machine which uses a beam of electrons to focus images instead of a beam of light.

• *A light microscope may magnify 1,500 times, but an electron microscope can magnify up to 1 million times.*

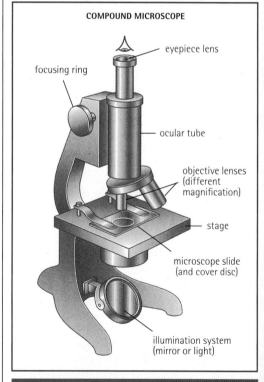

COMPOUND MICROSCOPE

eyepiece lens
focusing ring
ocular tube
objective lenses (different magnification)
stage
microscope slide (and cover disc)
illumination system (mirror or light)

WORD BUILD

electron micrograph

An electron micrograph is a photograph of the image produced by an electron microscope.

magnification value

The magnification value tells you how many times bigger a microscope or magnifying glass make the object. For a microscope, to find the total magnification you multiply the magnification of the objective and eyepiece lenses. For example, if the eyepiece is 10x, objective 40x, then the total magnification is 400x.

resolving power

is the ability of a microscope to separate two objects which are close together. It will depend not only on the quality of lenses but also the wavelength used. The shorter the wavelength, the higher the resolving power.

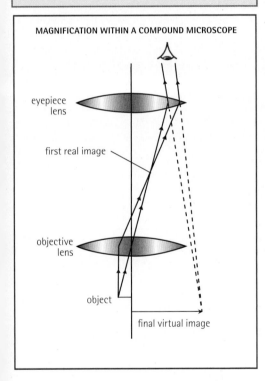

MAGNIFICATION WITHIN A COMPOUND MICROSCOPE

eyepiece lens

first real image

objective lens

object

final virtual image

microvillus *see* **villus**

microwave

A microwave is an electromagnetic wave with a slightly shorter wavelength than a radio wave. Like all electromagnetic waves, they produce a heating effect when they are absorbed. Food is very good at absorbing microwave frequencies, hence their use in microwave ovens for heating/cooking food.

• *Microwaves are commonly used for satellite TV, mobile phones (smartphones), and radar.*
SEE ALSO electromagnetic wave

middle ear

The middle ear is an air-filled cavity between the outer and inner ear.
• *The middle ear contains the ossicle bones, which amplify vibration of the eardrum.*
SEE ALSO ear, inner ear, ossicle, outer ear

midriff *see* **diaphragm**

milk tooth *see* **tooth**

Milky Way

The Milky Way is the galaxy to which our Sun belongs. It is a spiral galaxy with a central disc and curving spiral arms. The Sun is in one of these arms. The main part of the galaxy is visible from Earth as a faint band across the night sky (the 'Milky Way'). Our galaxy is thought to contain around 10^{11} 100 billion stars and to be around 100,000 light years across.
• *The Milky Way is part of a cluster of about 20 other galaxies.*
SEE ALSO galaxy

mineral

❶ A mineral is a naturally occurring, inorganic substance which has a particular chemical composition and usually a crystalline structure.
• *Mixtures of minerals together make up a rock.*
❷ Minerals are also natural, inorganic substances which are needed for building certain body tissues.
• *Plants depend on minerals in the soil, dissolved in the water and absorbed by the roots. Animals obtain minerals from plant or animal foods.*

Mineral	Needed for	Food source
Calcium	teeth, bones	cheese, milk, vegetables
Iron	making blood	red meat, eggs, bread
Sodium	muscle movement	common salt

mineral acid *see* **acid**

mineral oil *see* **petroleum**

mineral salt

Mineral salts are inorganic substances containing chemical elements essential to the health of a plant.

»

• *Mineral salts are also comprised of trace elements in animals, like iron for the haemoglobin of red blood cells.*

Element	Function in plant
Calcium	helps to hold cell walls together
Iron	part of enzyme which makes chlorophyll
Magnesium	part of chlorophyll molecule
Nitrogen	needed to make proteins
Phosphorus	essential for strong root system
Potassium	necessary for enzymes in photosynthesis

minor planet *see* asteroid

miscarriage
is spontaneous abortion caused by the rejection of the fetus by the mother's body. About 25% of pregnancies end in a miscarriage.
• *A miscarriage may result from poor implantation of the zygote, failure of the placenta to develop, or a deformed embryo.*
SEE ALSO **abortion**

miscible
describes two or more liquids which will diffuse together and form a single phase (e.g. alcohol and water). You can separate miscible liquids by fractional distillation.
• *You cannot distinguish by appearance the liquids present in a miscible mixture.*
SEE ALSO **immiscible, fractional distillation**

mitochondria *see* organelle

mitosis
is division of a cell to form two daughter cells, each with a nucleus containing the same number of chromosomes as the mother cell.
• *Mitosis is how most cells (except sex cells) divide.*
SEE ALSO **meiosis**

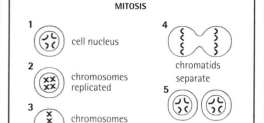

MITOSIS

1 — cell nucleus
2 — chromosomes replicated
3 — chromosomes line up
4 — chromatids separate
5 — the cell divides

mitral valve *see* bicuspid valve

mixture
A mixture is a combination of two or more substances that have not reacted chemically and can be separated using physical processes such as dissolving, crystallization, evaporation, etc. Examples of mixtures are air (mixture of gases), petroleum (mixture of liquids), and alloys (mixtures of metals).
• *Mixtures are not pure substances.*
SEE ALSO **air, alloy, compound, petroleum**

	Properties of mixture
1.	Component substances can be separated by physical means
2.	Generally little or no energy is given out or absorbed when formed
3.	Composition can vary
4.	Physical properties (colour, density) are intermediate between those of the substances in the mixture
5.	Chemical properties are the result of the substances in the mixture

heterogeneous mixture
A heterogeneous mixture is a mixture with a variable composition and therefore its properties vary from one part to another. Examples are suspensions such as chalk in water.
SEE ALSO **suspension**

HETEROGENEOUS MIXTURE

homogeneous mixture

A homogeneous mixture is a mixture which is the same throughout and therefore has similar properties throughout. Examples are solutions, which are homogeneous mixtures of solutes and solvents.

SEE ALSO **solution**

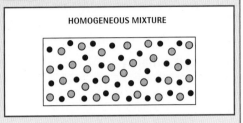

HOMOGENEOUS MIXTURE

mobile phase *see* **chromatography**

moho *see* **Earth's structure**

Mohorovičić discontinuity *see* **Earth's structure**

mol *see* **mole**

molar *see* **tooth**

molar mass (*also* formula mass)

is the mass of 1 mole of particles. For elements, molar mass is the mass of 1 mole of atoms and is equivalent to the relative atomic mass of the element in grams. For compounds, it is the mass of 1 mole of molecules and is equivalent to the relative molecular mass in grams.

molar solution (*also* molarity, M)

A molar solution contains 1 mole of solute in 1 dm^3 (1 litre) of solution. It is an indication of concentration of solution. Molar solutions have units of mol dm^{-3}. A 1 M solution contains 1 mole of solute in 1 dm^3 of solution (1 mol dm^{-3}). Dilute bench acids or alkalis are around 2 mol dm^{-3} and concentrated acids are around 10 mol dm^{-3}.

SEE ALSO **solution**

molar volume (*also* gram molecular volume, or molecular volume)

is the volume occupied by 1 mole of any gas at a particular temperature and pressure.

• *Normally molar volume is measured at room temperature and pressure (RTP) and occupies 24,000 cm³ (24 dm³ or 0.024 m³).*

mole (*also* mol)

The mole is the SI unit of 'amount of substance'. This 'amount of substance' is defined as that which contains Avogadro's number of particles (atom, ions, or molecules).

SEE ALSO **Avogadro's number**

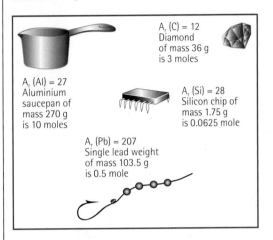

A_r (C) = 12
Diamond of mass 36 g is 3 moles

A_r (Al) = 27
Aluminium saucepan of mass 270 g is 10 moles

A_r (Si) = 28
Silicon chip of mass 1.75 g is 0.0625 mole

A_r (Pb) = 207
Single lead weight of mass 103.5 g is 0.5 mole

molecular formula *see* **chemical formula**

molecule

A molecule is the smallest part of a substance that can take part in a chemical reaction. A molecule is the fundamental unit of a volatile chemical compound, and consists of a group of atoms which are held together in fixed proportions by chemical bonds.

• *All molecules have a chemical formula and many molecules contain atoms of more than one element. These are molecules of chemical compounds.*

SEE ALSO **chemical formula, compound**

mollusc (*also* Mollusca)

Molluscs are invertebrates which normally have a muscular foot for movement and a soft-bodied hump or mantle, which is often protected by a shell. Members of the phylum include gastropods (snails, slugs), bivalves (mussels, oysters), and cephalopods (squids, octopuses).

• *Cephalopods are the most advanced group of molluscs, with excellent vision and a well-developed brain.*

SEE ALSO **invertebrate animal**

molten

describes the liquid state of a substance that is normally a solid at room temperature and pressure.

• *A molten substance has a melting point above room temperature.*

SEE ALSO **melting point**

moment

A moment of a force is a measure of the ability of a force to rotate an object about a pivot. The size of the moment is equal to the force multiplied by the perpendicular distance from the axis of the force to the pivot:

moment = force × perpendicular distance to pivot.

• *The SI unit of a moment is the newton metre (N m).*
SEE ALSO **turning force**

➤ **principle of moments** This principle states that when an object is in equilibrium (balanced), the sum of the clockwise moments (moments which tend to turn the object in a clockwise direction) is equal to the sum of the anticlockwise moments about the same point.
SEE ALSO **equilibrium**

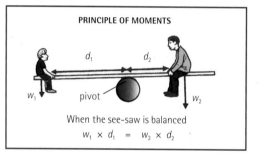

PRINCIPLE OF MOMENTS

When the see-saw is balanced
$$w_1 \times d_1 = w_2 \times d_2$$

momentum

The momentum of a moving object is its mass multiplied by its velocity.

momentum (Ns) = mass (kg) × velocity (m/s)

Stationary objects have zero momentum. Like velocity, momentum is a vector quantity, which means it has both magnitude and direction. An object travelling at constant velocity has no net force acting on it, but it does have momentum. Force is equal to the rate of change of momentum.

• *Momentum has the unit of newton second (N s).*
SEE ALSO **force, vector quantity**

➤ **change in momentum** occurs when objects collide. Reducing momentum change also reduces the force involved (Newton's second law) and explains the use of car seatbelts, airbags, crumple zones, and the wearing of safety helmets. The longer the duration of impact, the smaller the force for a given change in momentum.

• *Change in momentum is directly proportional to the force involved.*
SEE ALSO **force, Newton's second law**

Monera

is a kingdom which includes all bacteria, which are unicellular (single-celled) organisms having no nucleus or normal cell wall. The nuclear material consists of strands of DNA, but it is not enclosed in a distinct nuclear membrane. The oldest fossils belong to this kingdom, so it is probable that bacteria were the first living organisms on Earth.
SEE ALSO **bacteria**

monoclinic sulfur *see* sulfur

monoclonal antibody

A monoclonal antibody is a specific antibody that is produced from a single clone of cells. They are produced by stimulating lymphocytes, which acts as an antigen to make a particular antibody.

• *Monoclonal antibodies can be used to measure levels of hormones (for pregnancy tests) and in the treatment of cancer.*
SEE ALSO **antibody, antigen, cell**

monocotyledon (*also* monocot)

Monocotyledons are a class of angiosperm with only one seed leaf (cotyledon) within the seed. Monocotyledons generally have narrow leaves, and their flower parts (petals, sepals, carpels, etc.) are usually in threes or multiples of three.

• *Monocotyledons include crop plants (oats, wheat), grasses, tulips, daffodils, and lilies.*
SEE ALSO **angiosperm**

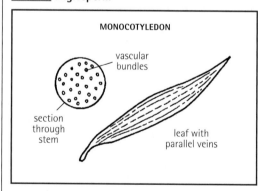

MONOCOTYLEDON

vascular bundles

section through stem

leaf with parallel veins

monoculture

is a form of agriculture in which one single crop is grown continuously over very large areas. This creates a conservation problem, as natural habitats such as hedges and trees are destroyed.

• *Often when developing monocultures large amounts of fertilizers and pesticides have to be used, which can cause pollution.*

monohybrid cross

A monohybrid cross is the inheritance of a single pair of alleles.

SEE ALSO **allele**

monomer

A monomer is a small molecule that joins with others to form a polymer.

• *Ethene is the* **monomer** *molecule in polyethene (polythene).*

SEE ALSO **polymer, polymerization**

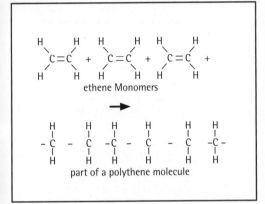

ethene Monomers

part of a polythene molecule

monotreme

Monotremes are a small subclass of mammals which lay eggs.

• *Examples of* **monotreme** *are the duck-billed platypus and the spiny anteater.*

SEE ALSO **mammal**

Moon

The Moon is the Earth's only natural satellite, orbiting at a mean distance of 384 400 km from Earth. It has a diameter of 3474 km and has no atmosphere or surface water. Its surface temperature varies between 80 K (–193 C night minimum) and 400 K (+127 C noon on the equator). The Moon takes slightly less than 28 days to orbit the Earth.

• *The* **Moon** *is held in orbit by the gravitational attraction of the Earth.*

➤ **phases of the Moon** The phases of the Moon are the eight different appearances of the Moon as it orbits the Earth in an anticlockwise direction. As the Earth is rotating on its axis, the Moon appears to move quite quickly across the night sky.

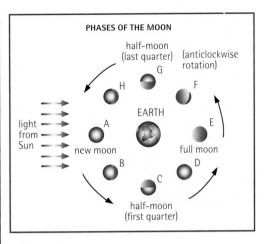

PHASES OF THE MOON

half-moon (last quarter) (anticlockwise rotation)

G

H

F

light from Sun

EARTH

A

E

new moon

full moon

B

D

C

half-moon (first quarter)

moss

is a primitive plant (bryophyte) with simple stems, leaves, and roots. It grows in damp areas such as bogs.

• *Mosses do not flower, and reproduce using spores.*

SEE ALSO **bryophyte**

motion

is change in an object's position. When a force acts on an object which is free to move, it may cause the object to move. The direction of movement is in the direction the force is acting, and a single force causes linear (rectilinear) motion.

SEE ALSO **circular motion, equations of motion, force**

motor effect

The motor effect is that when a wire carrying a current is brought into a magnetic field, there is repulsion between the magnetic field of the current and the field of the magnet, which causes a force on the wire. The size of this force can be increased by increasing the current and/or the strength of the magnetic field. The direction of this force is indicated by Fleming's left-hand rule.

SEE ALSO **electric current, Fleming's left-hand rule, force**

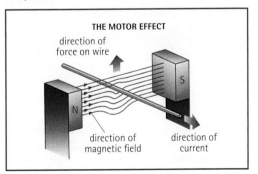

THE MOTOR EFFECT

direction of force on wire

S

N

direction of magnetic field

direction of current

motor neurone *see* **neurone**

motor rule *see* **Fleming's left-hand rule**

mould
is a fungus that feeds on organic matter like leaves, wood, or food.
• *Mould often forms on stale bread if left exposed to air, which contains the fungal spores.*
SEE ALSO **fungus, spore**

moulding plastics *see* **plastic**

moulting *see* **ecdysis**

mucous membrane
The mucous membrane has column-shaped cells called goblet cells, which secrete mucus to lubricate the respiratory tract and trap germs. Tiny hairs called cilia beat to move the mucus towards the mouth, where it is swallowed.
SEE ALSO **mucus**

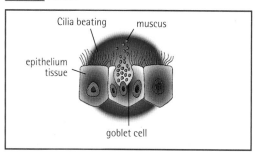

mucus
is a moist, sticky substance that is secreted by the mucous membrane and forms a protective covering inside hollow organs of the body like the nose, mouth, and throat. Mucus can lubricate the surface and helps to trap bacteria and dust particles.
• *When you sneeze, droplets of mucus shoot out of your nose.*
SEE ALSO **mucous membrane**

multicellular
describes living organisms made up of many cells.
• *Humans are multicellular beings made up of billions of cells (around 10^{14} cells).*
SEE ALSO **unicellular**

mumps *see* **childhood illness**

muscle
is special elastic tissue that contracts or relaxes to produce movement. This movement is stimulated by nervous impulses.

• *In humans there are about 600 muscles, which make up 40% of body weight.*
SEE ALSO **antagonistic pairs, intercostal muscle**

cardiac muscle
is a special type of involuntary muscle found in the heart.
• *Cardiac muscle can produce its own electrical impulses to provide constant rhythmical contractions without becoming tired.*

flexor muscle
Flexor muscles are muscles which flex (bend) a limb or part.
SEE ALSO **biceps**

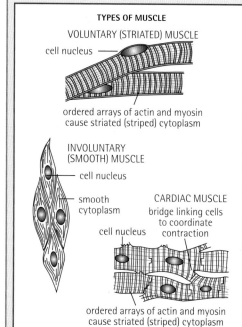

TYPES OF MUSCLE

VOLUNTARY (STRIATED) MUSCLE
cell nucleus
ordered arrays of actin and myosin cause striated (striped) cytoplasm

INVOLUNTARY (SMOOTH) MUSCLE
cell nucleus
smooth cytoplasm
cell nucleus

CARDIAC MUSCLE
bridge linking cells to coordinate contraction
ordered arrays of actin and myosin cause striated (striped) cytoplasm

extensor muscle
Extensor muscles are muscles which extend (straighten) a limb or part.
SEE ALSO **triceps**

involuntary muscle, (*also* **smooth muscle)**
Involuntary muscles are those whose action is not controlled by conscious activity, such as the movements of internal organs (e.g. stomach and intestines).

> ### voluntary muscle, (*also* striated muscle)
> Voluntary muscles are those whose action is controlled by conscious activity, such as the movement of the arms and legs.

> | WORD BUILD |
> |---|
>
> ### actin
> is a fibrous protein found in muscle fibres. Actin and Myosin interlock to form the main part of the contraction mechanism.
>
> ### myosin
> is a fibrous protein found in muscle fibres. Myosin and Actin interlock to form the main part of the contraction mechanism.

musical scale
A musical scale is a set of musical notes arranged in order of frequency or pitch.
• *A musical scale from a deep note (low frequency and low pitch) to a high note is called an ascending scale.*
SEE ALSO **frequency, pitch**

mutation
A mutation is a sudden random change in the genetic material of a cell, which may result from faulty DNA replication or faulty division of chromosomes. If a mutation occurs in a sex cell, then it may be passed on to the next generation. Most mutations are harmful, but some increase the 'fitness' of the organism to survive, e.g. when bacteria become resistant to antibiotics. Mutation is essential to evolution, because it is the ultimate source of genetic variation.
• *The likelihood of mutation is increased by radiation (ultraviolet rays, X-rays, and gamma rays) and by chemicals called mutagens, e.g. mustard gas, nitrosamines, and other carcinogens (cancer-causing chemicals).*
SEE ALSO **evolution, variation**

mutual induction
is the induction of an electromotive force, emf, in a coil of wire by changing the current in a nearby coil. The changing current (alternating current) in the first coil produces a changing magnetic field, which induces a current in the second coil.
• *Mutual induction occurs in transformers.*
SEE ALSO **electromagnetic induction, transformer**

mutualism (*also* symbiosis)
is a feeding relationship between two organisms from which both benefit.
• *An example of mutualism is lichen, which consists of two organisms, a fungus and a green alga. The fungus extracts minerals from the rock or soil, and the alga photosynthesizes.*
SEE ALSO **commensalism, parasitism**

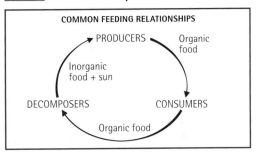

COMMON FEEDING RELATIONSHIPS

mycelium
is the mass of filaments which form the main part of a fungus.
• *The individual filaments of the mycelium are called hypha.*
SEE ALSO **fungus, hypha**

myelin sheath
A myelin sheath is a fatty insulating layer around the fibres of some nerve cells (sensory neurones and motor neurones).
SEE ALSO **neurone**

myopia *see* short–sightedness

myosin *see* muscle

myriapod (*also* Myriapoda)
Myriapods are arthropods with one pair of antennae and an elongated body made up of numerous segments.
• *Examples of myriapods are centipedes, which have one pair of legs per body segment, and millipedes, which have two pairs of legs per body segment.*
SEE ALSO **arthropod**

Nn

N *see* **newton, nitrogen**

nanocomposite

Nanocomposites are materials that have been mixed with nanoparticles to give the material specific properties, which it did not have before. For example, nanoparticles can be used in glass manufacture to produce a composite glass that is much better at absorbing ultraviolet radiation, which can be harmful and can cause skin cancer.

• *Nanocomposites are used a lot in the cosmetics industry for face creams, sun creams, deodorants, etc.*
SEE ALSO **composite material, nanoparticle**

nanoparticle

A nanoparticle is a particle between 1 nanometre (10^{-9} m) and 100 nanometres across. Nanoparticulate material has different properties from the same substance in bulk (grains, lumps, sheets, etc.).

• *Nanoparticles made of silver can be used to inhibit the growth of microorganisms.*

nanotube

A nanotube resembles a sheet of graphene rolled into a tube. Carbon nanotubes are extremely strong and have a breaking strain 100x greater than steel.

• *Nanotubes can be used to reinforce material like sports equipment (fishing rods, tennis rackets, golf clubs, etc.).*
SEE ALSO **carbon, graphene**

naphtha *see* gasoline

narcotic

describes a drug that causes sleep or drowsiness and relieves pain.

• *Narcotic drugs like morphine and other opiates can be dangerous and addictive so must only be prescribed by doctors.*
SEE ALSO **drug, medicine**

national grid system

The national grid is a network of overhead cables on pylons and underground cables, for transmitting electricity around the country. The grid supplies alternating current because it uses transformers which only work with alternating current. The electricity is transmitted at very high voltage (low current) so that less energy is wasted as heat.
SEE ALSO **alternating current, transformer**

natural cycle

Natural cycles are never-ending series of processes which maintain a balance in the environment of important substances that are essential for all plant and animal life. Atoms cannot be destroyed during biological and chemical processes on Earth, and are therefore constantly recycled.
SEE ALSO **carbon cycle, nitrogen cycle, water cycle**

natural fertilizer *see* fertilizer

natural frequency

is the frequency at which an object will vibrate if a vibration is started by a brief external force.

• *When you flick a wine glass with your finger from the outside, it will vibrate and then continue to vibrate at its **natural frequency**.*
SEE ALSO **resonance**

natural gas

is the gas that collects above underground deposits of oil. It is a mixture of hydrocarbons, mainly methane (about 85%).

• *Natural gas originates from the decomposition of organic matter and is widely used as a fuel.*
SEE ALSO **hydrocarbon**

natural immunity *see* immunity

natural polymer

are polymers produced by living organisms. They include natural rubber and natural foodstuffs.

• *All **natural polymers** are biodegradable, unlike most synthetic polymers.*
SEE ALSO **biodegradable, polymer**

natural radioactivity (*also* background radiation)

is the result of spontaneous disintegration of naturally occurring radioisotopes found in rocks and living material. It increases underground because of the surrounding rocks, and at high altitudes because of the effect of cosmic rays.

• *Local areas may have high **natural radioactivity** because the rocks below (e.g. igneous rocks such as granite) give off radon gas.*
SEE ALSO **radioisotope**

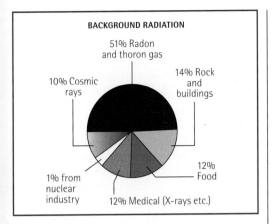

BACKGROUND RADIATION

51% Radon and thoron gas

14% Rock and buildings

10% Cosmic rays

12% Food

1% from nuclear industry

12% Medical (X-rays etc.)

natural resource

Natural resources can be categorized into two types: renewable and non-renewable resources.

SEE ALSO **energy source, non-renewable resource, renewable resource**

natural selection

The theory of natural selection states that the individual organism which is best adapted to its environment will survive to reproduce. This is the basic theory of Darwinism. It can be summarized as follows: overpopulation, variation, survival of the fittest, inheritance, adaptation.

SEE ALSO **Darwinism, variation**

WORD BUILD

overpopulation

Most organisms produce more young than will survive to adulthood

variation

Within any population of organisms there are slight variations. Some variations may better adapt the organism for survival.

survival of the fittest

Overpopulation causes competition in which only the fittest will survive.

inheritance

Organisms which have an advantageous characteristic are more likely to survive and reproduce. This advantageous variation will then be passed to its offspring, which will also stand a better chance of survival.

adaptation

Gradually over a period of time, each generation of a particular organism will become better adapted to its environment.

nature reserve

A nature reserve is where plants and animals are encouraged to live without interference from people. Nature reserves are increasingly important in preserving varieties of flora and fauna throughout the world.

• *A nature reserve is often called a nature conservation area.*

SEE ALSO **ecosystem, habitat**

neap tide *see* tide

nectary

A nectary is an area of cells at the base of the petals of a flower which can secrete a sweet, sugary liquid called 'nectar', which attracts insects for pollination.

SEE ALSO **pollination**

negative catalyst *see* inhibitor

negative charge *see* electric charge

negative feedback

❶ Negative feedback in biology is the process by which information about deviation from a norm passes to a controlling organ and produces a correction of the deviation. For example, if there is too much glucose in the blood, this is detected by the pancreas, which secretes a hormone called insulin. This hormone stimulates the liver cells to absorb glucose, which reduces the amount of glucose in the blood, so the pancreas stops secreting insulin.
❷ Negative feedback also occurs if the population of a species expands, so food becomes in short supply. The result is that the population then begins to fall.

SEE ALSO **homeostasis**

neon *see* noble gas

nephron (*also* kidney tubule)

A nephron is the filtering unit in the kidney. Through these nephrons, nitrogenous waste is filtered from the blood with the formation of urine. This involves the processes of filtration and reabsorption.

SEE ALSO **Bowman's capsule, kidney, urine** »

a
b
c
d
e
f
g
h
i
j
k
l
m
n
o
p
q
r
s
t
u
v
w
x
y
z

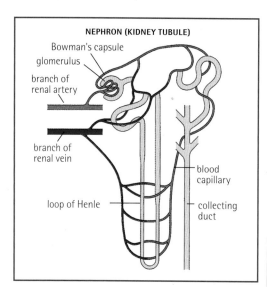

NEPHRON (KIDNEY TUBULE)

Bowman's capsule
glomerulus
branch of renal artery
branch of renal vein
loop of Henle
blood capillary
collecting duct

Neptune *see* planet

nerve cell *see* neurone

nerve fibre
A nerve fibre is a bundle of axons or dendrons of nerve cells (neurones).
SEE ALSO axon, dendron, neurone

nerve impulse
A nerve impulse is an electrical signal which moves along a nerve fibre. The surface of a nerve fibre is positively charged. Stimulating the surface mechanically (as in the ear), electrically or chemically causes the positive charge to be reversed (depolarization). Movement of this depolarization along the nerve fibre corresponds to the movement of the nervous (electrical) impulse.
SEE ALSO nerve fibre

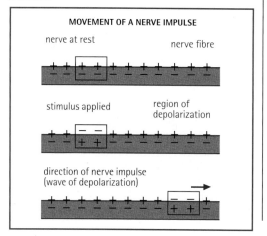

MOVEMENT OF A NERVE IMPULSE

nerve at rest
nerve fibre

stimulus applied
region of depolarization

direction of nerve impulse
(wave of depolarization)

nervous system
A nervous system is that part of an organism which allows it to detect its surroundings and to react accordingly.
SEE ALSO autonomic nervous system, central nervous system, peripheral nervous system

neurone (*also* nerve cell)
A neurone is an elongated, branched cell that is the basic unit of the nervous system. Neurones are specialized cells which can transmit electrical messages or nerve impulses around the body.
• *There are three main types of neurone: sensory neurone, motor neurone, and connecting neurone.*
SEE ALSO central nervous system, nerve impulse

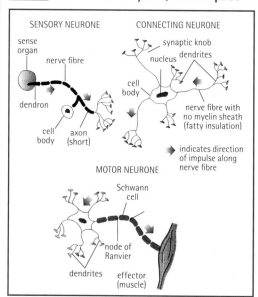

SENSORY NEURONE   CONNECTING NEURONE

sense organ
nerve fibre
synaptic knob
nucleus
dendrites
cell body
dendron
nerve fibre with no myelin sheath (fatty insulation)
cell body
axon (short)
indicates direction of impulse along nerve fibre

MOTOR NEURONE

Schwann cell
node of Ranvier
dendrites
effector (muscle)

connecting neurone (*also* relay neurone)
Connecting neurones pick up information from sensory neurones, and pass new nervous impulses to the motor neurones to initiate a response.
• *Connecting neurones are often found in the central nervous system.*

motor neurone (*also* efferent neurone)
Motor neurones transmit information as nervous impulses from the central nervous system to effectors.
• *Most motor neurones have branching dendrons (dendrites) and a long axon which is the nerve fibre.*
SEE ALSO axon, dendron

sensory neurone (also afferent neurone)

Sensory neurones transmit information as nervous impulses from receptors to the central nervous system.
• *Most sensory neurones have a long, single dendron and a short axon.*
SEE ALSO **axon, dendron**

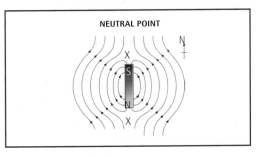

NEUTRAL POINT

neurotransmitter

A neurotransmitter is the chemical released by the axon end of one neurone to transmit (or inhibit) the transmission of a nerve impulse across a synapse to an adjacent neurone.
• *When neurotransmitter chemicals (like acetylcholine or noradrenalin) reach the dendron of the adjacent neurone, the nerve impulse is triggered.*
SEE ALSO **axon, dendron, nerve impulse**

neutral

describes a solution which has a pH of exactly 7 and is neither acidic nor alkaline. Neutral solutions have the same concentration of hydrogen and hydroxide ions.
• *Pure water, salt water, and various organic liquids are neutral solutions.*
SEE ALSO **pH**

neutral equilibrium *see* equilibrium

neutralization

is the chemical reaction of a base and an acid to produce a salt and water.
• *Everyday examples of neutralization include the use of indigestion tablets containing a base such as magnesium oxide to neutralize excess acid in the stomach, and the use of lime (calcium oxide base) to neutralize excess acid in the soil.*

$$\text{acid} + \text{base} \rightarrow \text{salt} + \text{water}$$
$$\text{HCl(aq)} + \text{NaOH(aq)} \rightarrow \text{NaCl(aq)} + \text{H}_2\text{O(l)}$$

SEE ALSO **acid, base, salt**

neutral point

A neutral point is a point at which the magnetic flux density of a magnetic field is zero (zero magnetism). Such points occur when equal but opposite magnetic fields cancel each other out, e.g. when two like poles of bar magnets face each other.
• *If a bar magnet is suspended with its north pole facing south, then it has two neutral points in line with its magnetic axis.*
SEE ALSO **magnetic axis, magnetic flux density**

neutron

A neutron is a neutrally charged subatomic particle which is found in the nucleus of atoms (except hydrogen).
• *A neutron has a mass roughly the same as that of a proton.*
SEE ALSO **nucleus, subatomic particle**

newton (also N)

The newton is the SI unit of force, defined as the force which gives a mass of 1 kilogram an acceleration of 1 ms^{-2}.
• *The newton was named after the British physicist Sir Isaac Newton (1642–1727).*
SEE ALSO **force**

Newton's law of gravitation

states that the gravitational force of attraction between two particles is given by the equation:

$$F = \frac{Gm_1m_2}{d^2}$$

where

F = gravitational force
G = gravitational constant
   m$_1$ and m$_2$ = mass of two particles
d = distance between the particles

SEE ALSO **gravitational force**

Newton's laws of motion

These are three laws relating to forces and motion, formulated by Sir Isaac Newton (1642–1727).

Newton's first law

states that an object will continue in a state of rest or uniform motion unless acted upon by an external force. This law implies that all changes in speed (acceleration) are caused by forces. The relationship between force and acceleration is:

$$\text{force} = \text{mass} \times \text{acceleration}$$

»

a
b
c
d
e
f
g
h
i
j
k
l
m
n
o
p
q
r
s
t
u
v
w
x
y
z

An object in free fall is accelerating by gravitational acceleration (g), and the force is gravitational force or weight.

weight = mass × gravitational acceleration

SEE ALSO **gravitational force, weight**

Newton's second law

states that the rate of change of momentum of an object is directly proportional to the force acting on the object. From this second law we can again deduce the relationship between force and acceleration. Normally the mass of an object is constant, so the force is directly proportional to the acceleration of the object, and acts in the same direction.

SEE ALSO **acceleration, force**

Newton's third law

states that forces always occur in equal and opposite pairs, called the action and reaction.

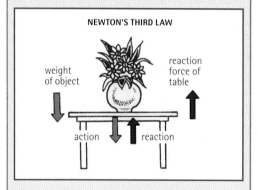

NEWTON'S THIRD LAW

weight of object

reaction force of table

action   reaction

nickel–cadmium cell see **alkaline cell**

nicotine

is a stimulant drug that increases blood pressure and makes your heart beat faster.
• *Nicotine is the drug that makes tobacco addictive.*
SEE ALSO **smoking**

night see Earth's axis

nitinol

is a metal alloy of nickel and titanium. It is a smart material used for making shape-memory wire. If this wire is accidentally squashed or stretched it changes back to its original shape.
• *Nitinol wire is used for eyeglass frames, dental braces, cell-phone aerials, etc.*
SEE ALSO **alloy, smart material**

nitrate (*also* nitrate (V) salt)

Nitrates are ionic compounds containing the nitrate ion NO_3: e.g. potassium nitrate KNO_3. Nitrates are the salts of nitric acid.
• *Ammonium nitrate is an important fertilizer. Sodium and potassium nitrates are used in explosives such as gunpowder.*

nitrate pollution

is the pollution of water by nitrates, caused mainly by the leaching of fertilizers from the soil. These dissolved nitrates can cause eutrophication of streams and rivers. They also cause health problems if they get into drinking water, as the body can convert them into nitrites, which can prevent the haemoglobin in the blood from absorbing oxygen. Babies are particularly vulnerable to this. The European Commission has set a maximum level of nitrates in drinking water of 10 mg/l or 10 ppm (parts per million).
SEE ALSO **eutrophication, leaching**

nitric(III) acid see **nitrous acid**

nitric acid (*also* nitric(V) acid)

is a colourless, extremely corrosive mineral acid, HNO_3. Industrially it is made by the Ostwald process.
• *The main large-scale uses of nitric acid are in making fertilizers, explosives, and dyes.*
SEE ALSO **acid, Ostwald process**

nitrogen (*also* N)

is the first element in group V of the periodic table and is a non-metal. Nitrogen is a colourless, odourless gas (N_2) which makes up 78% of the air. It takes part in the natural nitrogen cycle.

	Uses of nitrogen
1.	Nitrogen's main industrial use is in the manufacture of ammonia gas by the Haber process. Ammonia is very important in the manufacture of fertilizers such as ammonium nitrate.
2.	Nitrogen is a very unreactive gas and is used as an inert atmosphere to prevent explosions, and in food packaging, where it prevents the oxidation of natural oils and reduces bacterial decay.
3.	Liquid nitrogen is used as a refrigerant. Its low temperature of 196°C is ideal for rapidly freezing foods such as vegetables and meat.

SEE ALSO **ammonia, Haber process, nitrogen cycle**

➤ **oxides of nitrogen** Oxides of nitrogen $(NO)_x$ are compounds such as nitrogen monoxide NO and nitrogen dioxide NO_2 which are emitted from car exhausts, aircraft, and factories and cause pollution. They are acidic gases and contribute to acid rain.

nitrogen cycle
The nitrogen cycle is the constant circulation of nitrogen between the atmosphere, plants, animals, and the soil. Atmospheric nitrogen gas is inert and insoluble and cannot be used directly by plants. However, some of this gas undergoes nitrogen fixation by lightning or the action of nitrogen-fixing bacteria in the soil, which converts nitrogen into nitrates that dissolve in rain water. Nitrates in the soil are taken up by plants through their roots to make plant proteins. Animals feeding on the plants convert plant proteins into animal proteins. After death, the nitrogen-containing proteins of plants and animals are broken down by bacterial decay into ammonia, which can then be converted by other nitrifying bacteria back into nitrates. Some of the nitrogen in the nitrates is returned directly back into the atmosphere as nitrogen gas by denitrifying bacteria.
• *Artificial fertilizers that are added to the soil are also taken into the **nitrogen cycle**, but may also contribute to nitrate pollution.*
SEE ALSO **ammonia, nitrate, nitrate pollution**

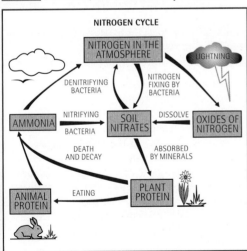

NITROGEN CYCLE

nitrogen fixation
is the chemical process by which atmospheric nitrogen gas is converted into nitrogen compounds and enters the nitrogen cycle. It is performed by bacteria in the soil, and in nodules on the root of leguminous plants (e.g. peas and beans) which contain symbiotic bacteria.
• *Nitrogen fixation also occurs when the electrical discharge of lightning combines the nitrogen and oxygen in the atmosphere.*
SEE ALSO **nitrogen, nitrogen cycle**

nitrous acid (*also* nitric (III) acid)
is a colourless, weak acid, HNO_2, which is easily decomposed.
• *Salts of **nitrous acid** are called nitrites.*

noble gas (*also* inert gas, rare gas, group VIII gas, group O gas)
Noble gases occupy around 1% of the atmosphere, of which most is argon. All are colourless, monatomic gases which are extremely inert because their atoms have full outermost electron shells.
• *The **noble gases** are argon, neon, helium, krypton, and xenon. All are chemical elements found in group VIII of the periodic table.*
SEE ALSO **air, electron shell, periodic table, element**

WORD BUILD
argon
is used to fill ordinary and long-life light bulbs. It prevents the filament inside the bulb from burning out. Argon is also used to provide an inert atmosphere in arc-welding metals.
helium
is very light and is used to inflate air ships and weather balloons. It is also used in the helium-neon laser and to dilute the oxygen in aqualungs for divers.
neon
is used in advertising signs because it glows red when electricity is discharged through it.
krypton and xenon
are used in lamps in lighthouses, stroboscopic lamps, and photographic flash units.

a
b
c
d
e
f
g
h
i
j
k
l
m
n
o
p
q
r
s
t
u
v
w
x
y
z

nocturnal

describes animals like owls, bats, and badgers that are active during night-time. Owls have big eyes to see at night. Many bats use echolocation to find their way in the dark.

SEE ALSO **echolocation**

node

A node is a point on a stationary (standing) wave where the amplitude is zero and there is no vibration.

SEE ALSO **antinode, stationary wave**

noise pollution

is caused by excessive unpleasant sounds, typically loud or high-pitched. Heavy urban traffic can produce noise levels of around 90 decibels. Large aircraft taking off produce around 120 decibels. Prolonged loud noise, such as over-amplified music or power tools, causes permanent hearing damage. There are many by-laws to minimize noise pollution. For example, car horns must not be used after dark, except in an emergency.

• *Noise pollution can be reduced by fitting silencers to engines, mufflers to machinery, and sound insulation in buildings (curtains, carpets, acoustic tiles, double glazing, etc.).*

nomenclature of salts *see* **salt**

non-biodegradable

describes any substance which cannot be broken down by natural processes of decay. Many plastics are non-biodegradable.

• *non-biodegradable material often ends up in landfill or in the sea and can have a detrimental effect on the environment and the living organisms within.*

SEE ALSO **biodegradable, landfill**

non-communicable disease

is in humans caused by the interaction of a number of factors, including lifestyle factors. They include many forms of cancer, some lung and liver diseases, cardiovascular diseases, and type 2 diabetes.

• *Non-communicable diseases can be life-threatening.*

SEE ALSO **cancer, cardiovascular disease, diabetes**

non-contact force

A non-contact force is a force acting on an object but not physically touching the object.

• *Non-contact forces include magnetic force, electrostatic force, and gravitational force.*

SEE ALSO **gravitational force, magnetic field**

non-electrolyte *see* **electrolyte**

non-identical twins (*also* **fraternal twins**)

Non-identical twins can develop if two or more completely separate eggs are released at the same time by the ovary and separately fertilized.

• *Each non-identical twin has its own placenta.*

SEE ALSO **identical twins, placenta**

non-luminous object

Non-luminous objects are objects which produce no light. Most objects are non-luminous and can be classified as either opaque, transparent, or translucent.

SEE ALSO **luminous object, opaque, translucent, transparent**

non-magnetic material *see* **magnetic material**

non-metal

Non-metals are elements which do not have the properties of a metal and always form negative ions (anions) when they react to form ionic compounds. Non-metallic elements are often gases (nitrogen, oxygen, fluorine, chlorine, and noble gases) or low melting point solids (phosphorus, sulfur, iodine). They are poor electrical and thermal conductors. Less than a quarter of the elements in the periodic table are non-metallic elements, and they are found on the right-hand side. As we go down a group, the non-metallic character decreases. As we go across a period, the non-metallic character increases.

• *In the periodic table the most reactive non-metal is the element fluorine.*

SEE ALSO **carbon, nitrogen, periodic table**

non-ohmic conductor

Non-ohmic conductors are conductors which do not obey Ohm's law and do not have a constant resistance. The higher the resistance of a conductor, the more difficult it is for the electrons to pass through. Electrical energy is therefore changed into heat energy: the temperature of the conductor rises and so does its resistance. Thin wires, such as filament bulbs, can glow white hot.

• *A graph of current against potential difference for non-ohmic conductors is a curve.*

SEE ALSO **conductor, Ohm's law**

»

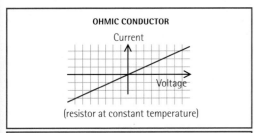

OHMIC CONDUCTOR

Current

Voltage

(resistor at constant temperature)

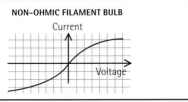

NON-OHMIC FILAMENT BULB

Current

Voltage

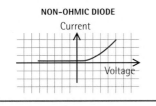

NON-OHMIC DIODE

Current

Voltage

NPK values

are numbers on a fertilizer bag which show the percentage by mass of the three important elements, nitrogen, phosphorus, and potassium, which are needed for healthy plant growth.

SEE ALSO **nitrogen, phosphorus**

Fertilizer	Why plants need it	Signs of deficiency
Nitrogen	To make proteins which are needed for healthy growth of stems and leaves	Undersized leaves and slow growth
Phosphorus	For good root growth and to make DNA	Stunted growth causing purple young leaves
Potassium	Helps enzymes in photosynthesis and respiration	Yellow leaves with dead spots

non-polar solvent *see* **solvent**

non-renewable energy source *see* **energy source**

non-renewable resource

Non-renewable resources include minerals and energy sources such as fossil fuels (coal, oil, and natural gas). Once such resources are used up, they cannot be replaced. Fossil fuels will last longer if more use is made of renewable energy sources, which also produce less pollution, or nuclear energy.

SEE ALSO **energy source, renewable resource**

normal line *see* **reflection of light**

northern lights *see* **aurora**

north pole *see* **magnetic pole**

north-seeking pole *see* **magnetic pole**

nose

The nose is the protuberance on the face that contains the olfactory organ (organ of smell).

• *The **nose** opens into a nasal cavity lined with a mucous membrane which helps trap dust, germs, etc.*

SEE ALSO **olfactory organ**

nuclear chain reaction

A nuclear chain reaction is one that is self-sustaining. Such reactions occur when a single neutron splits up one nucleus to produce (for example) three neutrons. These neutrons may split up three other nuclei, which then produce nine neutrons, and so on. A controlled chain reaction is allowed to occur in a fission reactor. An uncontrolled chain reaction occurs in a fission bomb.

SEE ALSO **fission bomb, fission reactor, nuclear fission**

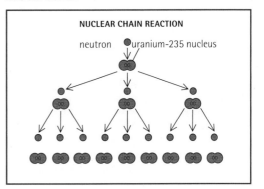

NUCLEAR CHAIN REACTION

neutron   uranium-235 nucleus

nuclear energy

is the energy released by nuclear fission or nuclear fusion. When small atoms are fused together, there is a small loss of mass, which is released as energy (nuclear fusion). Atoms heavier than iron have added mass and will release energy if they break down (nuclear fission).

SEE ALSO **nuclear fission, nuclear fusion**

nuclear equation

A nuclear equation shows the nuclides and radiation involved in a nuclear reaction.

SEE ALSO **nuclide, radionuclide**

nuclear fission

is the process by which a heavy, unstable nucleus is split up into two or more smaller nuclei called fission products. This releases vast amounts of energy and emits two or three neutrons called fission neutrons. Most fission is induced by firing high-energy neutrons at unstable nuclei (e.g. uranium-235 or plutonium-239). The neutrons released by induced fission will cause more fission, and so on. This is a nuclear chain reaction.

SEE ALSO **nuclear chain reaction, nuclear energy**

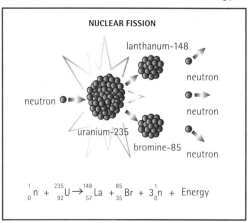

NUCLEAR FISSION

lanthanum-148

neutron

neutron

neutron

uranium-235

bromine-85

neutron

$$\,^{1}_{0}n\ +\ \,^{235}_{92}U \rightarrow \,^{148}_{57}La\ +\ \,^{85}_{35}Br\ +\ 3\,^{1}_{0}n\ +\ Energy$$

nuclear fusion

is the collision and joining together of two light nuclei to form a heavier, more stable nucleus. Nuclear fusion will only occur at extremely high temperatures (millions of degrees). It therefore only occurs naturally in the Sun (or other stars). Here hydrogen isotopes (deuterium, tritium) are fused together to form helium atoms with the release of vast amounts of energy. Such nuclear reactions requiring extremely high temperatures are called thermonuclear reactions.

SEE ALSO **isotope, nuclear energy**

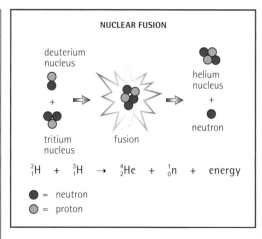

NUCLEAR FUSION

deuterium nucleus

helium nucleus

+

+

tritium nucleus

fusion

neutron

$$\,^{2}_{1}H\ +\ \,^{3}_{1}H\ \rightarrow\ \,^{4}_{2}He\ +\ \,^{1}_{0}n\ +\ energy$$

● = neutron
○ = proton

nuclear reaction

A nuclear reaction is any reaction in which there is a change in the nucleus of an atom.

SEE ALSO **nuclear chain reaction, nucleus**

nuclear waste (*also* **radioactive waste**)

is the waste from nuclear reactors, processing radioactive ores, reprocessing of nuclear fuel, and the manufacture of nuclear weapons. High-level radioactive waste (spent fuel rods, decommissioned reactor components, etc.) is extremely hazardous and can release radiation for thousands of years. It is vitrified in glass and then packed in stainless steel containers. These containers are then buried in thick concrete around 500m underground in suitable dense rock.

• *Low-level* **radioactive waste** *(contaminated clothing, paper, etc.) may be buried about 100m underground in stable geological formations.*

nuclei *see* **nucleus**

nucleic acid

Nucleic acids are complex organic acids found in a cell's nucleus and responsible for storing and transferring genetic information.

• *There are two types of* **nucleic acid:** *DNA (deoxyribonucleic acid) and RNA (ribonucleic acid).*

SEE ALSO **DNA, nucleotide, RNA**

nucleon

A nucleon is a general term to describe particles found in the nucleus of atoms.

• *Nucleons are either protons or neutrons.*

SEE ALSO **neutron, nucleus, proton**

nucleon number *see* **mass number**

nucleotide

Nucleotides are the basic units from which nucleic acids are formed.

SEE ALSO **DNA, nucleic acid, replication**

nucleus *plural* **nuclei**

❶ A nucleus is the very small central core of an atom, containing most of the atomic mass. It is made up of protons and neutrons (except in hydrogen) and has a positive charge. Surrounding the nucleus are 'orbiting' electrons. Any radioactive properties of an atom are associated with the nucleus.

• *If an atom was the size of a football pitch, then the **nucleus** (sitting on the centre spot) would be the size of a pea!*

SEE ALSO **neutron, proton**

❷ The nucleus is a cell's control centre and is contained within a nuclear membrane.

• *The **nucleus** controls all the chemical reactions of the cell and also contains the genetic material of the cell.*

SEE ALSO **cell**

nuclide

A nuclide is an atomic nucleus as defined by its atomic number and mass number.

SEE ALSO **atomic number, mass number, radionuclide**

nutrient

Nutrients are substances which are essential for healthy growth. Plants need carbon dioxide (from the air) and water (from the soil) for photosynthesis to make carbohydrates, and use minerals dissolved in the water to make other molecules such as proteins.

• *The **nutrients** for animals (and humans) are carbohydrates, proteins, and fats, and also vitamins and minerals (a balanced diet).*

SEE ALSO **balanced diet, carbohydrate, fat, mineral, protein**

nutrition (*also* **feeding**)

is the process by which living organisms obtain the substances they need to provide materials and fuel for growth, repair of tissues, etc.

• ***Nutrition** should not be confused with respiration, which is the chemical release of energy from food and oxygen.*

SEE ALSO **respiration**

autotrophic nutrition (*also* **holophytic nutrition**)

is a process by which organisms make their own food from inorganic material. All green plants feed this way by photosynthesis, making sugar and starch from carbon dioxide and water using the energy of sunlight.

SEE ALSO **photosynthesis**

heterotrophic nutrition (*also* **holozoic nutrition**)

is a type of nutrition in which all the energy is obtained from the tissue of other organisms (plant or animal). All animals feed this way as they are incapable of synthesizing food from inorganic material.

nylon (*also* **polyamide**)

is a synthetic polymer made by condensation polymerization of a diamine monomer and a dicarboxylic acid monomer.

SEE ALSO **polymerization, synthetic polymer**

nymph

A nymph is an immature form (larval stage) of an insect that does not change greatly as it grows. There is no pupal stage and the nymph develops directly into the adult insect.

• *Insects that have **nymphs** are dragonflies, mayflies, grasshoppers, earwigs and locusts.*

SEE ALSO **life cycle**

a
b
c
d
e
f
g
h
i
j
k
l
m
n
o
p
q
r
s
t
u
v
w
x
y
z

Oo

obesity
is the condition of being very overweight, often because of eating too much carbohydrate and fat. This can lead to heart disease, high blood pressure, etc. Many animal fats can cause high levels of cholesterol in the blood. Cholesterol deposits contribute to the blockage of arteries.
• *Obesity also raises your risk of developing type 2 diabetes.*
SEE ALSO **blood pressure, diabetes**

oceanic crust
The oceanic crust forms the bottom of the oceans and seas, and also lies deep below the less dense continental crust. It is continually being created and remelted, so the oldest oceanic crust is only 100 million years old.
• *The main rock component of the oceanic crust is basalt and it is rich in the elements silicon and magnesium (called 'sima' or high-density rocks).*
SEE ALSO **continental crust, Earth's structure**

octave
An octave is the interval between two musical notes such that the higher note has double the frequency of the lower note. Two notes an octave apart blend very well to the human ear.
• *Middle C has a frequency of 256 Hz, and the C above it has a frequency of 512 Hz (an octave above).*

oesophagus (*also* gullet)
The oesophagus is the section of the alimentary canal between the mouth and the stomach.
SEE ALSO **alimentary canal**

oestrogen *see* sex hormone

ohm (*also* Ω)
is the resistance of a conductor in which a current of one ampere flows when a potential difference of one volt is applied across its ends.
• *An ohm is the derived SI unit of electrical resistance.*
SEE ALSO **potential difference, resistance**

Ohm's law
states that the ratio of the potential difference across the ends of a metal conductor to the electric current flowing through the conductor is a constant. This constant is the resistance of the conductor. The law was discovered in 1827 by the German physicist Georg Ohm. Ohm's law is often expressed in an equation:

$$\text{voltage} = \text{current} \times \text{resistance}$$
$$V = I \times R$$

SEE ALSO **potential difference, resistance**

oil pollution
is caused by oil spillage into the sea, resulting in oil slicks which can devastate marine life and kill seabirds. Originally oil spillages were treated with detergents, but this just spread out (dispersed) the oil even more. Nowadays it is thought best to contain the slick and allow natural bacteria in the water to feed on the oil hydrocarbons and break them down. To encourage the oil-eating bacteria to multiply, special fertilizers are spread over the oil slick. For small spillages, chemicals are sprayed onto the oil which solidify it to a rubbery material which can be 'rolled up'.
SEE ALSO **detergent, hydrocarbon**

olefin hydrocarbon *see* alkene

oleum (*also* fuming sulfuric acid, pyrosulfuric acid, disulfuric acid)
is a colourless solid (m.p. 35°C) formed when sulfur trioxide dissolves in concentrated sulfuric acid.

$$\text{sulfur trioxide} + \text{sulfuric acid} \rightarrow \text{oleum}$$
$$SO_3 + H_2SO_4 \rightarrow H_2S_2O_7$$

SEE ALSO **contact process, sulfuric acid**

olfactory organ
The olfactory organ is the organ of smell situated in the roof of the nasal cavity. Extending from the roof are olfactory hairs containing the dendrites of sensory neurones. These act as chemoreceptors sensitive to volatile substances. Nervous impulses from the olfactory nerve are interpreted by the brain as sensations of smell. The human sense of smell is much more extensive than that of taste. Many flavours in food have as much to do with the sense of smell as with the sense of taste.
• *In most mammals the nose contains the olfactory organ.*
SEE ALSO **dendron, neurone, nose**

omnivore

Omnivores are animals which can eat both meat and plants.
- *Examples of **omnivores** are humans, monkeys, and pigs.*

SEE ALSO **carnivore, herbivore**

opaque

describes objects which absorb, scatter, or reflect light and do not allow any light to pass through.
- *You cannot see through **opaque** objects.*

SEE ALSO **translucent, transparent**

open system

An open system is one in which materials and energy can escape or enter. If the products from a reversible reaction escape (e.g. as gases) then this destroys the reversibility.
- *A chemical equilibrium cannot be established in an open system.*

SEE ALSO **chemical equilibrium, closed system, isolated system**

optical axis *see* **principal axis**

optical centre

The optical centre is the geometric centre of a lens.
- *Rays of light travelling through the **optical centre** pass through the lens in a straight line.*

SEE ALSO **focal length, lens, principal axis**

optical fibre

Optical fibres use total internal reflection to transmit light along very fine tubes of plastic or glass. Because the fibres are so fine, they can be bent without breaking and can carry light around corners. They are light, relatively cheap, and can carry light messages extremely fast over long distances with little loss in intensity or interference from electrical sources.
- *Optical fibres are used in medical viewing instruments and in telecommunications.*

SEE ALSO **total internal reflection**

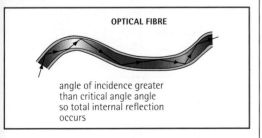

OPTICAL FIBRE

angle of incidence greater than critical angle angle so total internal reflection occurs

orbit

❶ (*also* **eye socket**)

The orbit is a deep cavity in the skull in which the eyeball is situated for protection.

SEE ALSO **eye**

❷ To orbit an object means to move around it in a circular motion. Satellites orbit (or are in orbit around) the Earth.
- *Planets **orbit** the Sun in a slightly elliptical orbit.*

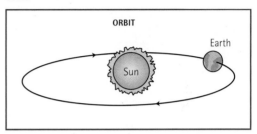

ORBIT

Earth

Sun

ore

An ore is a naturally occurring mineral from which a metal can be extracted on a commercial basis.
- *Most **ores** are oxides, carbonates, sulfides, sulfates, or chlorides.*

SEE ALSO **extraction of metals**

organ

An organ is a collection of different tissues which work together to perform some function in the organism.
- *Examples of **organs** are the skin, heart, lungs, brain, and kidneys.*

SEE ALSO **organ system**

organelle

Organelles are tiny bodies found in the cytoplasm of a cell. The following features are found in each cell:
- the endoplasmic reticulum is a network of membranes joined to the nuclear membrane. It has a large surface area and is involved in chemical reactions and fluid storage
- the ribosomes are tiny particles attached to the endoplasmic reticulum. They are involved in the synthesis of proteins
- the lysosomes are round sacs which contain powerful enzymes
- the mitochondria are the organelles in the cytoplasm where energy is produced from chemical reactions

»

— the Golgi complex collects and distributes the substances which are made in the cell.

SEE ALSO **cell, cytoplasm**

organic acid _see_ **acid**

organic chemistry _see_ **chemistry**

organism (_also_ **living organism**)

A living organism is an individual living system such as an animal, plant, or microorganism.

• _All **living organisms** are made up of cells and have the following life processes (remember by the mnemonic MRS GREN):_

- _Movement_
- _Reproduction_
- _Sensitivity_
- _Growth_
- _Respiration_
- _Excretion_
- _Nutrition_

organ system

An organ system is formed by a number of different organs which together carry out a particular bodily function. For example, the heart and blood vessels are organs which together make up the circulatory system.

• _Other **organ systems** include the urinary system, digestive system, reproductive system, and nervous system._

SEE ALSO **circulatory system, digestion, female reproductive organ system, urinary system**

orgasm

is the climax of sexual excitement in a male or female.

SEE ALSO **copulation, insemination**

orthorhombic sulfur _see_ **sulfur**

oscillation

An oscillation is periodic motion between two extremes about a mean position, like a weight on the end of a spring oscillating up and down. In oscillating systems there is a continuous change between kinetic energy and potential energy. The total sum of these energies remains constant (if there is no damping).

SEE ALSO **damping, periodic motion**

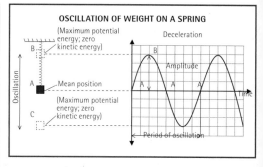

OSCILLATION OF WEIGHT ON A SPRING

osmoregulation

is the control of water content and the concentration of salts in an animal's body. This is controlled by an area at the base of the brain called the hypothalamus, which continually monitors the amount of water in the blood. If the water level is low, it sends a message to the pituitary gland which secretes the hormone ADH (antidiuretic hormone). This hormone makes you feel thirsty, so you drink more water. It also makes the kidneys reabsorb more water, so less is lost by excretion. The reverse also applies: if there is too much water in the blood, the pituitary gland stops secreting ADH.

SEE ALSO **brain, urinary system**

osmosis

is the movement of a solvent (usually water) from a dilute to a more concentrated solution by diffusion across a semipermeable membrane. The cytoplasm and cell sap inside the root of a plant are quite concentrated solutions and the water in the soil is a dilute solution. Water therefore diffuses into the root hair through the semipermeable cell membrane. A 'concentration gradient' allows the water to travel from cell to cell (dilute to more concentrated) until it reaches the xylem vessels in the centre of the root.

• _**Osmosis** accounts for the diffusion of water in and out of the living cells of plants and animals._

SEE ALSO **diffusion, semipermeable membrane, xylem**

osmotic pressure

is the pressure equal to that required to stop osmosis between a particular solution and pure water.

SEE ALSO **hypertonic, hypotonic, isotonic**

ossicle

The ossicles are a chain of three small bones in the middle ear which amplify the vibrations of the eardrum. They are:
- the *malleus* (or *hammer*) is the first ossicle, which vibrates as it touches the eardrum
- the *incus* (or *anvil*) is the second ossicle, which transmits the vibration from the malleus to the stapes
- the *stapes* (or *stirrup*) is the third ossicle, which causes the oval window to vibrate at the same frequency as the eardrum.

SEE ALSO **inner ear, middle ear, outer ear**

ossification

is the gradual replacement of cartilage by bone. In the skeleton of embryos and young animals and children, the percentage of cartilage is much greater.
• *Ossification occurs due to the build up of minerals inside the cartilage, changing it into bone.*

SEE ALSO **cartilage, bone**

Osteichthyes *see* fish

osteoporosis

is a condition caused by low levels of calcium in the bones. It makes the bones soft, weak, and fragile, and can be very painful.
• *Osteoporosis is especially common in older women.*

Ostwald process

The Ostwald process is the industrial synthesis of nitric acid by the catalytic oxidation of ammonia, and dissolving the resulting oxides of nitrogen in oxygenated water.

SEE ALSO **ammonia, nitric acid, nitrogen**

1. ammonia (4NH$_3$) + oxygen (5O$_2$) $\xrightarrow{\text{platinum catalyst}}$ nitrogen monoxide (4NO) + water (6H$_2$O)

2. nitrogen monoxide (2NO) $\rightarrow$ nitrogen dioxide (2NO$_2$) + oxygen (O$_2$)

3. nitrogen dioxide (2NO$_2$) + water (H$_2$O) $\rightarrow$ nitric acid (HNO$_3$) + nitrous acid (HNO$_2$)

outer core *see* Earth's structure

outer ear (*also* external ear)

The outer ear is the part of the ear external to the eardrum. It includes the ear flap (pinna) which is responsible for directing the sound along the auditory canal to the eardrum. The lining of the auditory canal contains special sebaceous glands which secrete wax.

WORD BUILD

eardrum (*also* tympanum, tympanic membrane)

The eardrum is a membrane at the end of the auditory canal which transmits sound vibrations from the outer ear to the ossicles of the middle ear.
SEE ALSO **middle ear, ossicle**

---

outer space

is the part of the universe that lies outside the Earth's atmosphere.
• *Between objects in outer space (planets and stars) there is very little matter, almost a vacuum.*

SEE ALSO **universe, vacuum**

outlier

An outlier is a piece of data that differs significantly from the other observations. Outliers should be ignored when working out a mean from a collection of data.
• *Outliers should be ignored when plotting graphs using data.*

ova *see* ovum

oval window (*also* fenestra ovalis)

The oval window is a membrane-covered opening between the middle and inner ear.
• *The oval window transmits vibrations to the cochlea.*

SEE ALSO **inner ear, middle ear, round window**

ovary *plural* ovaries

❶ The ovaries are the pair of female sex organs which are responsible for the production of ova (eggs) and oestrogen (female hormones).
• *The ovaries are oval in shape and attached to the back wall of the abdomen, below the kidneys.*

SEE ALSO **ovum, sex hormone**

❷ In a plant, the ovary is the main reproductive structure of the carpel which contains one or more ovules.

SEE ALSO **carpel, ovule**

overfishing

is a conservation problem caused by catching most of the fish in their feeding grounds, which does not leave enough fish to reproduce and replenish stocks. Even small fish which are thrown back often die. Some whale (blue whale) and herring stocks around Britain have suffered from overfishing. Countries fishing in international waters now have to abide by

»

their 'fish quotas'. Fish farms for salmon, trout, eels, etc., help to increase stocks by ensuring high levels of reproduction and quick growth.
SEE ALSO **conservation**

overtone *see* **harmonic**

oviduct (*also* **fallopian tube**)
The oviduct is a tube that connects the ovary to the uterus in the female reproductive organs.
• *Oviducts allow the passage of sperm to travel toward the eggs (released from the ovaries).*
SEE ALSO **female reproductive organ system, ovary, ovum**

ovulation
is the periodic release of an ovum (egg cell) from the ovaries to travel down the oviduct (or Fallopian tube) to the uterus, where it is available for fertilization.
• *Ovulation normally occurs on the 14th to 16th day of the approximately 28-day menstrual cycle.*
SEE ALSO **fertilization, menstrual cycle, ovary**

ovule
An ovule is the structure in female seed plants which contains the female sex cell (gamete).
• *The ovule is attached to part of the ovary wall, and after fertilization it develops into the seed.*
SEE ALSO **carpel, gamete**

ovum *plural* ova (*also* **egg**)
An ovum is the female gamete of animals. It is produced in the ovary. It is normally larger than the sperm and is not mobile.
• *An ovum is spherical, with a nucleus and cytoplasm. The cytoplasm acts as a 'food store' after fertilization.*
SEE ALSO **cytoplasm, fertilization, gamete**

oxidant *see* **oxidizing agent**

oxidation
is a chemical reaction involving the gain of oxygen (or the loss of hydrogen). Alternatively, oxidation can be regarded as a process which involves the loss of electrons by a substance. Many oxidation reactions are very useful, e.g. combustion to produce heat and light, and the process by which energy is released when foodstuffs and oxygen combine (respiration).

An oxidation reaction: burning of methane (CH_4)

$$CH_4 + 2O_2 \rightarrow CO_2 + 2H_2O$$

The carbon has gained oxygen and lost hydrogen.
SEE ALSO **electron, reduction, respiration**

oxide
An oxide is a compound of oxygen and one other element. They are described as binary compounds as they contain two different elements.
• *Oxides of metals are ionic compounds like magnesium oxide (MgO), a compound of magnesium and oxygen. Oxides of non-metals are covalent compounds like carbon dioxide (CO_2), a compound of carbon and oxygen.*
SEE ALSO **compound, ionic bond, covalent bond**

acidic oxide
Acidic oxides are oxides of non-metallic elements which react with water to form acids. Many non-metal oxides like sulfur dioxide and oxides of nitrogen are gases. If they are found in the atmosphere, they will dissolve in rainwater to form acid rain.
SEE ALSO **acid rain, nitrogen, non-metal**

basic oxide
Basic oxides are oxides of metallic elements that will react with acids to form a salt and water only.
• *A few basic oxides dissolve in water to form alkalis.*
SEE ALSO **alkali, metal, salt**

Acidic oxide	Acid formed in water
carbon dioxide	carbonic acid
sulfur dioxide	sulfurous acid
phosphorus(V) oxide	phosphorous acid
nitrogen dioxide	nitric/nitrous acids

Basic oxide	Alkali formed in water
potassium oxide	potassium hydroxide
sodium oxide	sodium hydroxide
calcium oxide	calcium hydroxide

oxides of nitrogen *see* **nitrogen**

oxidizing agent (*also* **oxidant electron acceptor**)
An oxidizing agent is a substance which helps oxidation to occur. It provides oxygen and/or accepts electrons.
• *Examples of strong oxidizing agents are potassium manganate (VII) $KMnO_4$ (acidified) and potassium dichromate $K_2Cr_2O_7$ (acidified).*
SEE ALSO **oxidation, reducing agent**

oxygen

is the most important gas in the air. Oxygen has many uses and is essential for combustion and respiration.

SEE ALSO **air, combustion, respiration**

	Five uses of oxygen
1.	Life support systems in hospitals use oxygen gas. Patients with breathing difficulties are also given oxygen gas.
2.	Oxyacetylene flames burn at very high temperatures (3300°C). Such flames are useful for welding and cutting metals.
3.	Steel manufacturing uses oxygen. The gas is 'blasted' into molten iron to remove any impurities. It does this by oxidizing the main impurities, sulfur and carbon, into their oxides which escape as gases.
4.	Liquid oxygen (LOX) is used with rocket fuels. Outside the Earth's atmosphere, no fuel can burn unless an oxygen supply is available. Any fuel will burn more fiercely in pure oxygen than in air.
5.	High-altitude workers (climbers, pilots) and underwater workers (divers) need oxygen. The higher up in the atmosphere you go, the lower the air pressure becomes. The air becomes thinner and so contains less oxygen in a given volume (e.g. a lungful of air).

➤ **oxygen debt** occurs when the body requires more oxygen than is available (e.g. during vigorous exercise). As a result, anaerobic respiration results in a build-up of lactic acid, especially in the muscles. Deep breathing after the vigorous exercise repays this debt and oxidizes the lactic acid eventually to carbon dioxide and water. A good measure of fitness is how quickly you can return to normal breathing (your 'recovery time').

SEE ALSO **anaerobic respiration**

ozone

is formed in the upper atmosphere (stratosphere) when ultraviolet radiation from the Sun breaks down oxygen molecules O_2 to form oxygen atoms which recombine as ozone O_3.

• *Ozone is also formed in the lower atmosphere by industrial activity, where it contributes to pollution.*

SEE ALSO **atmosphere, oxygen, ultraviolet radiation**

ozone layer (*also* ozonosphere)

The ozone layer is a region of the upper atmosphere at a height of between 20 and 40 km, containing a high concentration of ozone O_3. The layer is formed from oxygen by ultraviolet radiation from the Sun, and absorbs ultraviolet radiation which would otherwise reach the Earth's surface and cause harm to living organisms.

• *The ozone layer is at risk from pollutants like the inert chemicals (CFCs) which are used as refrigerants or as solvents in aerosol cans. Such chemicals can destroy the ozone layer and the protection it provides.*

$$\text{oxygen molecule } O_2 \xrightarrow[\text{light}]{\text{ultraviolet}} \text{oxygen atoms } 2O^{\bullet}$$

$$\text{oxygen molecule } O_2 + \text{oxygen atom } O^{\bullet} \longrightarrow \text{ozone molecule } O_3$$

$$\text{ozone molecule } O_3 \xrightarrow[\text{light}]{\text{ultraviolet}} \text{oxygen molecule } O_2 + \text{oxygen atom } O^{\bullet}$$

SEE ALSO **atmosphere, CFC, ozone**

Pp

P *see* **phosphorus**

p *see* **pressure of a gas**

Pa *see* **pascal**

pacemaker

A pacemaker is an electrical device that is placed on the heart to stimulate contractions. It is normally placed near the wall of the right atrium, near the opening for the vena cava.
• *A pacemaker is implanted surgically into the chest to produce and maintain the heartbeat.*
SEE ALSO **atrium, heart, inferior vena cava, superior vena cava**

palisade mesophyll *see* mesophyll layer

palps *see* sense organ

pancreas

The pancreas is a gland (in vertebrate animals) which secretes pancreatic juice into the duodenum.
• *The pancreas has specialized groups of cells called the islets of Langerhans which produce hormones.*
SEE ALSO **exocrine gland, hormone, islets of Langerhans, small intestine**

Pangaea

was a huge supercontinent which existed for over two hundred million years until the beginning of the Jurassic Period (age of the dinosaurs).
• *Pangaea split into two smaller supercontinents (Gondwanaland and Laurasia) which slowly divided into the present-day continents.*

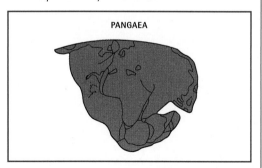

PANGAEA

paper chromatography *see* chromatography

paraffin hydrocarbon *see* alkane

paraffin oil *see* kerosene

parallax

is the apparent change in the position of an object when it is observed from two different viewpoints. A fixed object viewed through a mirror appears in different positions when viewed from different angles.
SEE ALSO **reflection of light**

parallax error (*also* error of parallax)

A parallax error is one which occurs when the eye is not placed directly opposite the scale from which a reading is being made.
SEE ALSO **accuracy, parallax**

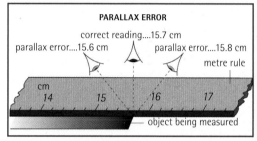

PARALLAX ERROR
correct reading....15.7 cm
parallax error....15.6 cm   parallax error....15.8 cm
metre rule
cm
14   15   16   17
object being measured

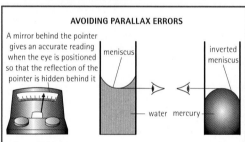

AVOIDING PARALLAX ERRORS
A mirror behind the pointer gives an accurate reading when the eye is positioned so that the reflection of the pointer is hidden behind it
meniscus
inverted meniscus
water mercury

parallel circuit *see* electrical circuit

parallel of latitude

The parallels of latitude are imaginary circles drawn around the Earth, parallel to the equator.
SEE ALSO **latitude**

paramecium *see* protozoa

parasite

A parasite is a living organism that feeds on another living organism (its host), e.g. tapeworm, flea, louse, mistletoe.
SEE ALSO **host, parasitism**

parasitism

is a feeding relationship in which one living organism (the parasite) feeds on another living organism (its host) and has a harmful effect on it.
SEE ALSO **host, parasite**

parent rock see bedrock

parsec
A parsec is an astronomical unit of distance equal to 3.26 light-years.
• *A parsec is equal to a distance of more than 30 trillion (thousand billion) kilometres.*
SEE ALSO **light-year**

parthenogenesis
is a method of asexual reproduction found in animals such as some insects (bees, aphids) where the development of a new organism is from an unfertilized egg.
• *The eggs formed by the female during parthenogenesis contain the full (diploid) number of chromosomes and are genetically identical.*
SEE ALSO **insect, reproduction**

partial pressure
is the pressure that each gas in a mixture of gases would exert if it alone filled the volume occupied by the mixture.
• *The partial pressure of the oxygen in the air (approximately 20% by volume) is approximately 0.2 atmosphere.*
SEE ALSO **Dalton's law, pressure of a gas**

particulate matter (also PM)
is very small particles (e.g. soot, smoke, ash, dust) produced in industrial processes and from incomplete combustion of fossil fuels. The smallest particulates (PM 2.5) are smaller than 2.5×10^{-6} m in diameter and when breathed in can settle in the lungs and cause bronchitis and other lung problems. Natural particulate matter like pollen can also irritate the throat and lungs and cause hay-fever.
• *Particulate matter contributes to global dimming.*
SEE ALSO **combustion, fossil fuel, global dimming**

parturition see birth

pascal (also Pa)
A pascal is the SI unit of pressure and is equivalent to a force of 1 newton acting over an area of 1 square metre:

$$1 Pa = 1 Nm^{-2}$$

• *The pascal was named after the French physicist Blaise Pascal (1623–62).*
SEE ALSO **pressure**

passive immunity see immunity

passive smoking
is breathing in cigarette smoke from someone else smoking. Children are susceptible to this if their parents smoke.
• *Passive smoking increases the risk of developing smoking-related diseases.*
SEE ALSO **smoking**

patella see human skeleton

pathogen
A pathogen is an organism which causes disease.
SEE ALSO **bacteria, fungus, protozoan, vector, virus**

Pathogen	Examples of diseases
bacteria	diphtheria, tuberculosis, pneumonia, typhoid, dysentery, food poisoning, cholera, whooping cough, yaws
viruses	common cold, measles, rubella (german measles), poliomyelitis, smallpox, influenza, mumps, chickenpox
protozoans	malaria, amoebic dysentery
fungi	athlete's foot, ringworm

p.d. see potential difference

peat
is a crumbly brown material made from vegetable matter that has partly decomposed by the action of water and become carbonized. When subjected to pressure and heat it may be converted into coal. It is found in boggy areas of land.
• *Peat is used to improve soil (helping gardening) and as a fuel.*
SEE ALSO **coal**

pectoral girdle (also shoulder girdle)
The pectoral girdle is the set of bones at the front end of a vertebrate's body which support the forelimbs. In humans it consists of two dorsal scapulae (shoulder blades) attached to the spine, and two ventral clavicles (collar bones) attached to the sternum (breastbone).
• *Attached to the pectoral girdle are the arms (forelimbs).*
SEE ALSO **human skeleton**

pelvic girdle (also hip girdle)
The pelvic girdle is the set of bones at the rear end of a vertebrate's body which supports the hindlimbs.
SEE ALSO **human skeleton**

pelvis

The human pelvis forms the pelvic girdle and is joined to the base of the spine.
- *The **pelvis** is made up of three fused bones (ilium, pubis, and ischium), and the legs are attached to it.*

SEE ALSO **pelvic girdle**

penicillin

Penicillins are a class of antibiotics (the commonest are penicillin G and penicillin V) produced from moulds of the genus *Penicillium*.
- ***Penicillins** kill bacteria by preventing the formation of the bacterial cell wall during the reproduction of the bacteria.*

SEE ALSO **antibiotic, bacteria**

penis

A penis is the male reproductive organ of mammals, through which sperm (male sex cells) are ejected into the female vagina during copulation. The sperm are produced in the testes and travel down sperm ducts and through the urethra. Part of the penis is made of erectile tissue, and it is rich in blood vessels and nerve tissue. When a male is sexually excited, it becomes erect and stiff as the blood vessels expand. This facilitates insertion of the penis into the vagina ensuring internal fertilization during copulation.

SEE ALSO **sperm, testis, urethra**

penumbra

The penumbra is the area of blurred or fuzzy shadow around the edges of the umbra. This type of shadow is formed by larger, spread-out sources of light.
- *The **penumbra** is an area where a small amount of light has reached.*

SEE ALSO **eclipse, shadow, umbra**

pepsin

is a protease enzyme secreted into the stomach. It is secreted as the inactive form pepsinogen, which is converted to pepsin by the hydrochloric acid in the stomach.
- *The enzyme **pepsin** helps to break down protein into amino acids.*

SEE ALSO **enzyme, protease, stomach**

peptide link

Peptide links are the -CO-NH- linkage formed between amino acids during protein synthesis. Many of these links form a peptide chain. Peptide chains join with one another to form polypeptides, which again join to form proteins.

SEE ALSO **amino acid, protein**

percentage composition

is the make-up of a chemical compound expressed in terms of each of the elements present, calculated as a percentage by mass. The table shows how to calculate the percentage composition of the elements carbon and hydrogen in various hydrocarbons.

SEE ALSO **compound**

Name of hydrocarbon	Molecular formula	Relative formula mass $A_r(C) = 12$ $A_r(H) = 1$
ethane	C_2H_6	$(2 \times 12) + (6 \times 1) = 30$
ethene	C_2H_4	$(2 \times 12) + (4 \times 1) = 28$
benzene	C_6H_6	$(6 \times 12) + (6 \times 1) = 78$

Name of hydrocarbon	percentage composition % carbon	percentage composition % hydrogen
ethane	$\frac{24}{30} \times 100 = 80\%$	$\frac{6}{30} \times 100 = 20\%$
ethene	$\frac{24}{28} \times 100 = 85.7\%$	$\frac{4}{28} \times 100 = 14.3\%$
benzene	$\frac{72}{78} \times 100 = 92.3\%$	$\frac{6}{78} \times 100 = 7.7\%$

percentage error

is a figure representing the difference between the value determined experimentally and the theoretical value.

$$\text{Percentage error} = \frac{\text{difference between experimental and theoretical}}{\text{theoretical value}} \times 100$$

percentage yield

is the actual mass of product collected in a chemical reaction divided by the maximum mass of product that could have been formed in theory, multiplied by 100.
- ***Percentage yield** is an important factor in the large scale manufacture of chemicals (fertilizers, plastics, drugs, etc.).*

SEE ALSO **chemical equation, chemical reaction, product**

perennial

Perennials are plants that live for a number of years.
- ***Perennial** plants may be herbaceous (non-woody) or woody (shrubs and trees).*

SEE ALSO **herbaceous plant**

period

① (*also* **T**) The period is the time of one oscillation (one complete wave). In periodic motion, the period is the time taken to complete one cycle of motion. For example, the period of rotation of the Earth around the Sun is $365\frac{1}{4}$ days.

$$\text{frequency} = \frac{1}{\text{period}} \qquad f = \frac{1}{T}$$

• *Period is measured in seconds and is the reciprocal of frequency (f).*

SEE ALSO **frequency, oscillation, periodic motion**

② A period is a horizontal row of elements in the periodic table. The first three rows are called 'short periods'. The next four rows, which include the transition metals, are called the 'long periods'. All elements within a period contain the same number of electron shells. As we go across a period, there is a change from reactive metals, through less reactive metals, metalloids, and less reactive non-metals to reactive non-metals. On the extreme right are the noble gases (group VIII or group 0)

SEE ALSO **electron shell, periodic table**

periodicity

is the gradual change of physical properties (melting point, boiling point, etc.) for elements as we go across the periodic table.

• *The graph shows periodicity in the boiling points of the first 50 elements.*

SEE ALSO **periodic table** »

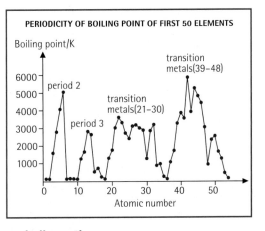

PERIODICITY OF BOILING POINT OF FIRST 50 ELEMENTS

periodic motion

is any motion which is continuous and which repeats itself at regular intervals.

• *Examples of periodic motion are the motion of waves, the swinging action of a pendulum, and other oscillations.*

SEE ALSO **oscillation**

periodic table

The periodic table is an arrangement of elements in order of increasing number of protons (atomic number). Periods and groups place together elements with related electronic configurations.

• *The original form of the modern periodic table was first proposed by Dimitri Mendeleev in 1869.*

SEE ALSO **atomic number, element, group, period**

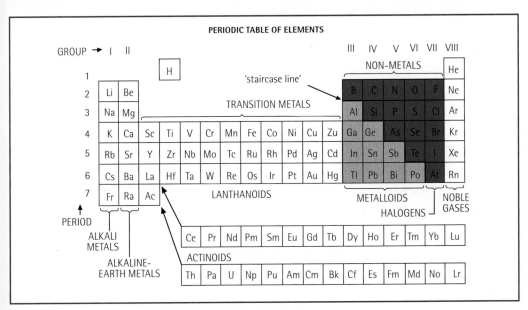

PERIODIC TABLE OF ELEMENTS

peripheral nervous system (*also* PNS)
The peripheral nervous system is that part of the nervous system other than the central nervous system.
• *The peripheral nervous system includes all the nerves outside the brain and spinal cord.*
SEE ALSO **central nervous system, nervous system**

periscope
A periscope is a device for seeing around corners or above the water surface from underwater.
• *A periscope consists of a tube with two angled mirrors to reflect the light through 90°.*
SEE ALSO **reflection of light**

peristalsis
is the wave-like muscular contractions along the oesophagus and intestines which help to move the food through the alimentary canal. Movement of food is helped by the lubricating action of saliva (from the salivary glands) and mucus (from the goblet cells in the intestine wall).
SEE ALSO **alimentary canal, oesophagus, saliva**

permanent hardness *see* hard water

permanent magnet *see* magnetic material

permanent tooth *see* tooth

permeability (*also* magnetic permeability)
is a measure of the ability of a substance to 'conduct' a magnetic field.
• *Soft iron has a higher magnetic permeability than air, so magnetic field lines tend to be concentrated through it (see diagram).*
SEE ALSO **magnetic field, magnetic field line**

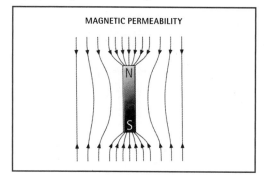

MAGNETIC PERMEABILITY

permeable
describes a material like the membrane around living cells which allows liquids or gases to pass through.
• *Water can pass through a permeable material.*
SEE ALSO **cell membrane, impermeable**

pesticide
Pesticides are chemicals used in agriculture to kill pests (insects, worms) that damage crops. These chemicals can build up in animals that feed on the pests. Birds and mammals (even humans) can be killed if high enough concentrations of pesticides such as DDT build up inside the body, often in fatty tissue.
• *Natural or organic farming does not use pesticides as these can have a negative effect on the local environment.*

petal
A petal is a flower structure which surrounds the reproductive organs (stamens and carpels) of the flower.
• *Petals are often brightly coloured and scented to attract insects.*
SEE ALSO **carpel, corolla, stamen**

petrochemical
Petrochemicals are any of a range of various chemicals derived from petroleum or natural gas.
• *Petrochemicals are organic compounds (like hydrocarbons) and are used to produce a wide variety of materials, including most plastic material.*
SEE ALSO **bitumen, diesel oil, gasoline, kerosene, lubricating oil, refinery gases**

petrol *see* gasoline

petroleum (*also* crude oil, mineral oil)
is a naturally occurring mixture of organic compounds, mainly hydrocarbons, formed underground. Microscopic organisms, which swam around in the oceans and seas around 300 million years ago, died and were buried in silt and mud. The pressure compressed the organic matter in their bodies, which gradually changed into petroleum. This brown/black liquid moved from the source rock to become trapped beneath layers of impermeable (non-porous) rock, floating on a layer of water and held under pressure below a layer of natural gas.
• *Petroleum is the source of petrochemicals which are an important chemical feedstock.*
SEE ALSO **chemical feedstock, hydrocarbon, natural gas**

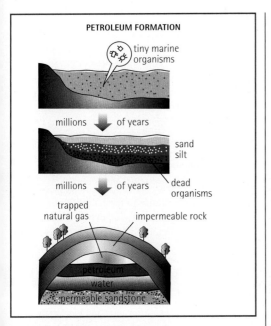

PETROLEUM FORMATION

tiny marine organisms

millions of years

sand
silt

millions of years — dead organisms

trapped natural gas — impermeable rock

petroleum
water
permeable sandstone

pewter *see* **alloy**

pH

pH stands for 'potential of hydrogen'. The pH scale is a logarithmic number scale (0 to 14) for showing the strength of an acid or alkali. As the scale is logarithmic, a change of pH from 4 to 2 means that the substance is 100 times more acidic. Any pH value below 7 represents an acidic solution, and the lower the value the stronger the acid. Any pH value above 7 represents an alkaline solution, and the higher the value the stronger the alkali.

SEE ALSO **acid, alkali, indicator, neutral, soil**

pH value	Colour of universal indicator	Strength
0–3	red	strong acid
4	pink	weak acid
5	orange	weak acid
6	yellow	weak acid
7	green	neutral
8	turquoise	weak alkali
9	blue	weak alkali
10	dark blue	weak alkali
11–14	violet	strong alkali

phage *see* **bacteriophage**

phagocyte (*also* **granulocyte**)

Phagocytes are large white blood cells which 'swallow up' foreign bodies such as bacteria (in a process called phagocytosis). They are made in the bone marrow and travel by amoeboid movement.
• *The cytoplasm of a* **phagocyte** *has tiny granules throughout.*
SEE ALSO **bone marrow, cytoplasm, white blood cell**

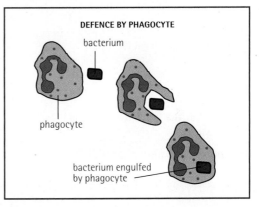

DEFENCE BY PHAGOCYTE

bacterium

phagocyte

bacterium engulfed by phagocyte

phase

A phase is any homogeneous part of a chemical system that is separated from other parts by a definite boundary, e.g. ice mixed with water.
• *Solids, liquids, and gases are the three* **phases** *of matter.*

phase equilibrium

is a type of dynamic equilibrium established between phases or states of matter. At a particular temperature, a liquid will establish an equilibrium with its vapour. At this point, the same number of particles leave from and return to the surface of the liquid (evaporate and condense).
SEE ALSO **dynamic equilibrium, equilibrium, phase**

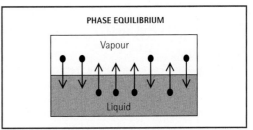

PHASE EQUILIBRIUM

Vapour

Liquid

phases of the Moon *see* **Moon**

phenotype

The phenotype of an organism is its observable characteristics produced by the interaction of its genes.
• *The colour of a person's eyes is determined by their* **phenotype.**
SEE ALSO **allele, gene**

phloem

The phloem is the vascular tissue of plants which moves the products of photosynthesis from the leaves to the storage areas and growing points of a plant (through translocation).
• **Phloem** *tissue consists of long columns of living cells (sieve tubes) which have lost their nuclei and cytoplasm and are connected by porous plates called 'sieve plates'.*
SEE ALSO **photosynthesis, translocation, vascular tissue, xylem**

phosphate (*also* phosphate(V) salt)

Phosphates are ionic compounds containing the phosphate ion PO_4^{3-}. Phosphates are salts of phosphoric acid.
• *Calcium* **phosphate** $Ca_3(PO_4)_2$ *is an important constituent of teeth and bones.*
SEE ALSO **phosphoric acid, salt**

phosphoric(V) oxide (*also* phosphorus pentoxide)

is a white solid P_4O_{10}, made by burning phosphorus in a plentiful supply of air.
• **Phosphoric(V) oxide** *is a dehydrating agent.*

phosphoric acid (*also* phosphoric(V) acid)

is a tribasic acid H_3PO_4, which is a colourless crystalline solid. It may be made by dissolving phosphoric(V) oxide in water.

$$P_4O_{10} \quad + \quad H_2O \quad \rightarrow \quad 4H_3PO_4$$
phosphoric(V) oxide + water → phosphoric acid

• **Phosphoric acid** *is used to form a corrosion-resistant layer on steel.*
SEE ALSO **phosphoric(V) oxide**

phosphorus (*also* P)

is the second element in group V of the periodic table and is a non-metal. It exists as several allotropes. The main one is red phosphorus, which is non-poisonous and not flammable. The other is white (or yellow) phosphorus, which is poisonous, and is kept in water as it is spontaneously flammable in air.
• *White* **phosphorus** *is used in incendiary bombs and in the making of matches.*
SEE ALSO **allotrope, non-metal**

photocell

A photocell is a device that produces an electrical signal in response to exposure to electromagnetic radiation, such as visible light, ultraviolet radiation, infra-red radiation, microwaves, etc.
• **Photocells** *can be used as light sensors, counting devices (for example, to count vehicles travelling on a road as a light beam is interrupted when a vehicle goes past), solar panels (using sunlight to generate electricity), etc.*
SEE ALSO **electromagnetic spectrum**

photoperiodism

is an organism's response to the length of day or night. Often this initiates an important event in the life-cycle of the organism. This event is often linked with reproduction, ensuring that it occurs in the right season, e.g. plants flowering in spring, or birds migrating in winter.

photosynthesis

is the chemical process of separating hydrogen from water (light stage or photolysis) which then combines with carbon dioxide (dark stage) to synthesize simple foodstuffs such as glucose.

$$6CO_2 \quad + 6H_2O \quad \rightarrow \quad C_6H_{12}O_6 \quad + 6O_2$$
carbon dioxide + water → glucose (sugar) + oxygen

It occurs in the chloroplasts of plant cells. The oxygen gas produced is released through the stomata of the leaves of the plant.
• **Photosynthesis** *can be regarded as a 'carbon negative' process as it removes carbon dioxide (greenhouse gas) from the atmosphere.*
SEE ALSO **chlorophyll, chloroplast, leaf, stoma**

➤ **limiting factors of photosynthesis** Limiting factors are the main factors which can affect the rate of photosynthesis: light intensity (and wavelength), carbon dioxide concentration, and temperature. Increasing each of these will increase photosynthesis, up to a certain maximum value. For example, low light intensity limits photosynthesis even if CO_2 concentration is high.

»

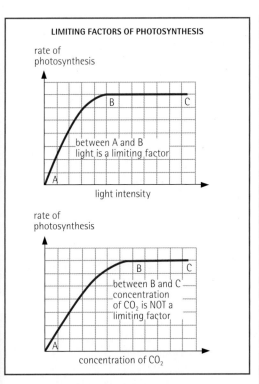

LIMITING FACTORS OF PHOTOSYNTHESIS

rate of photosynthesis

between A and B light is a limiting factor

light intensity

rate of photosynthesis

between B and C concentration of CO_2 is NOT a limiting factor

concentration of CO_2

to ice, and you can separate sugar from ethanol by distillation.
SEE ALSO **chemical change**

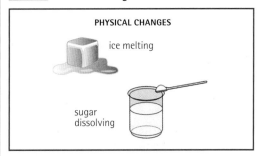

PHYSICAL CHANGES

ice melting

sugar dissolving

physical properties of alkaline–earth metals *see* alkaline–earth metal

physical properties of alkali metals *see* alkali metal

physical properties of halogens *see* halogen

physical property
A physical property of a material is one related to its appearance and its state (solid, liquid, or gas) at room temperature.
• *Among the physical properties of metals are that they are solid, hard, shiny, and good conductors.*
SEE ALSO **chemical property**

physical weathering *see* weathering

physics
is the scientific study of matter and energy, including heat, light, sound, electricity, magnetism, radiation, and motion.

phytoextraction (*also* phytomining)
is a biological extraction method for low-grade metal ores which uses plants. Certain plants are good at absorbing certain metal ions. The absorbed ions then accumulate in their roots, stem, and leaves. The plants are harvested and then burnt to produce an ash with a high metal concentration. The metal can then be extracted as if it was a high-grade metal ore by electrolytic refining.
• *Phytoextraction helps to make profitable the mining of low-grade ores.*
SEE ALSO **electrorefining, ion, ore**

pig iron
is impure iron produced in the blast furnace. It contains about 4% carbon, and is refined to produce steel or cast iron.

»

phototropism (*also* heliotropism)
is the growth response of a plant to light. Most leaves and stems (and some flowers like sunflowers) show this by bending and growing towards the light. It is thought that more auxin gathers on the side of the stem furthest from the light. Therefore that side grows faster, causing the stem to curve over towards the light.
• *Leaves and stems are said to have a positive phototropism but roots have a negative phototropism (grow away from the light).*
SEE ALSO **auxin, tropism**

phyla *see* phylum

phylum (*plural* phyla)
A phylum is a large group of organisms sharing a similar basic structure.
• *A phylum of plants is often called a division.*
SEE ALSO **biological classification**

physical change
A physical change is one which results in no new chemical substance being formed.
• *Ice melting or sugar dissolving in ethanol are both physical changes. Such changes are normally easy to reverse. If you cool the water, it will change back*

• *Pig iron is hard, but very brittle, and melts at about 1,500 K.*
SEE ALSO **blast furnace, cast iron, steel**

pinhole camera

A pinhole camera is the simplest form of camera, consisting of a box with a pinhole at one end and a screen made of tracing paper at the other. An inverted (upside down) real image of an object forms on this screen (see diagram). If the pinhole is made larger, the image becomes brighter but also becomes more blurred. This is because a large pinhole acts like lots of small pinholes, each producing an image in a slightly different position.
SEE ALSO **camera, image**

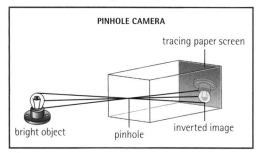

PINHOLE CAMERA

tracing paper screen

bright object
pinhole
inverted image

pipette

A pipette is a graduated glass tube which is filled by suction and used for transferring exact volumes (10 cm^3, 25 cm^3) of liquids.
SEE ALSO **burette, titration**

Pisces see fish

pistil see carpel

pitch

is a property of sound determined by its frequency. High-pitched sounds are associated with high frequencies; low-pitched sounds (deep, low notes) with low frequencies.
SEE ALSO **frequency**

Sound (pitch)	Frequency
upper limit of hearing	20,000 Hz
whistle	10,000 Hz
high note (treble)	1,000 Hz
low note (bass)	100 Hz
drum beat	20 Hz

pituitary gland see brain

pivot

❶ A pivot is the place where a lever turns.
SEE ALSO **lever**
❷ To pivot is to turn on a central point, as a lever does.

placenta

The placenta is an organ in mammals by which the embryo is attached to the uterus by the umbilical cord. Blood capillaries from the mother and the embryo flow into the placenta, and food and oxygen from the mother's blood pass into the embryo's blood by diffusion. Waste material from the embryo also diffuses into the mother's blood.
• *Shortly after birth of the baby the **placenta** is expelled from the uterus through the vagina. This is called the afterbirth.*
SEE ALSO **afterbirth, diffusion, embryo, umbilical cord, uterus**

plane joint see joint

planet

A planet is a major celestial body that orbits the Sun in a slightly elliptical orbit. There is an attractive force of gravity between the Sun and the planet, which acts in a direction towards the centre of gravity of the Sun. Planets orbit the Sun in the same plane and reflect the Sun's light, but do not give out any light themselves. The four inner planets (Mercury, Venus, Earth, Mars) are relatively small, rocky, and volcanic. Scientists call them 'rocky dwarfs'. The outer planets are giant balls of gas. Scientists sometimes call them 'gassy giants'.
• *The further a **planet** is from the Sun, the longer is the period of its orbit (its 'year').*

Planet	Diameter (relative to Earth's diameter)	Distance from Sun (relative to Earth's distance)	Length of year (in Earth years)	Length of day (in Earth days)
Mercury	0.39	0.39	0.24	59
Venus	0.97	0.72	0.61	243
Earth	1	1	1	1
Mars	0.53	1.52	1.88	1.03
Jupiter	11.2	5.2	11.86	0.41
Saturn	9.5	9.53	29.5	0.44
Uranus	3.7	19.2	84	0.67
Neptune	3.5	30	165	unknown

Planet	Force of gravity (compared with Earth)	Number of moons	Average surface temperature (°C)	Atmosphere (main gases)
Mercury	0.38	0	350	none
Venus	0.86	0	460	thick carbon dioxide clouds
Earth	1	1	20	nitrogen and oxygen
Mars	0.38	2	−40	thin carbon dioxide
Jupiter	2.5	16 + 1 ring	−120	hydrogen and helium
Saturn	1.13	18 + 7 ring	−180	hydrogen
Uranus	1.04	15 + 11 ring	−210	helium and ammonia
Neptune	1.4	8 + 4 ring	−220	methane

plankton

are microscopic organisms (plants and animals) that float in the sea or freshwater. Some are so small they can only be seen using a microscope.
• *Plankton are important food sources for many creatures including the largest of all animals, the blue whale.*

plant

A plant is a living organism of the kingdom Plantae. Most plants absorb water and minerals through their roots and manufacture carbohydrates by photosynthesis in their stems and leaves. Plants lack the power of movement that animals have as there is no necessity to search for food.
• *Examples of plants are trees, shrubs, grasses, ferns, and mosses.*
SEE ALSO **photosynthesis, plant kingdom**

plant hormone *see* hormone

plant kingdom (*also* Plantae)

The plant kingdom includes all multicellular organisms which are capable of photosynthesis. Plants are eukaryotes. All plant cells have a distinct nucleus and a cell wall made of cellulose, and contain chlorophyll to absorb the light energy needed for photosynthesis.
• *The plant kingdom is divided into four main groups: bryophytes, ferns, conifers, and angiosperms.*
SEE ALSO **angiosperm, bryophyte, conifer, eukaryote, fern, photosynthesis**

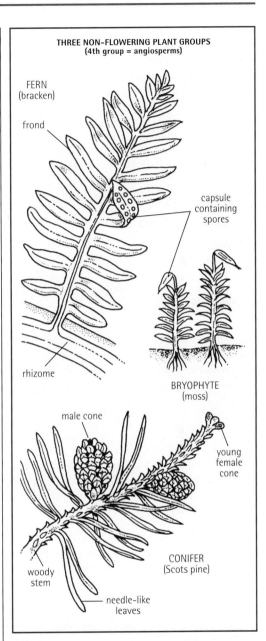

THREE NON-FLOWERING PLANT GROUPS
(4th group = angiosperms)

FERN (bracken)
frond
capsule containing spores
rhizome
BRYOPHYTE (moss)
male cone
young female cone
CONIFER (Scots pine)
woody stem
needle-like leaves

plaque

is a sticky film of food debris, saliva, and bacteria which forms on teeth after meals.
• *If not removed by brushing, plaque hardens to form tartar.*
SEE ALSO **tartar**

plasma

❶ Plasma is the liquid part of the blood, which is about 90% water. Floating in the plasma are the blood cells (red and white) and the platelets. Dissolved in the plasma are food materials for the body cells, waste matter (urea) and carbon dioxide, hormones, and antibodies.

SEE ALSO **blood, platelet**

❷ Plasma is a fourth state of matter (i.e. in addition to solid, liquid, and gas) which can only exist at very high temperatures, e.g. inside the Sun. At such temperatures, matter is broken down into positive ions and electrons.

SEE ALSO **state of matter**

plasmid

A plasmid is a circular strand of bacterial DNA.

• *Plasmids are often used as carriers of genetic information in genetic engineering.*

SEE ALSO **DNA, genetic engineering**

plasmolysis

is an extreme state of wilting where a plant loses water not only by transpiration but also by 'reverse osmosis' caused by extremely dry conditions in the soil.

• *Plasmolysis may cause the death of the plant.*

SEE ALSO **wilting**

plastic

Plastics are a class of materials which, when subjected to heat and pressure, become soft so they can be easily shaped. Most plastics are synthetic polymers, although a few, like cellulose, are natural polymers. Plastics are relatively cheap, lightweight, good insulators, easy to clean, translucent (see-through) or easily coloured, non-corrosive, long lasting, and can be very strong.

• *Plastics are often difficult to dispose of because they are non-biodegradable, and when they burn they often produce toxic fumes.*

SEE ALSO **natural polymer, non-biodegradable, synthetic polymer**

➤ **moulding plastics** Soft or molten plastic can be moulded by compression, injection into a mould, or extrusion. Hollow objects like plastic bottles and dolls can be made by 'blow moulding'.

plastic sulfur *see* **sulfur**

plate boundary

Plate boundaries are areas of volcanic and earthquake activity where tectonic plates meet.

SEE ALSO **tectonic plate**

conservative plate boundary

Conservative plate boundaries occur where plates slide past one another. Earthquakes are common along such boundaries.

• *The San Andreas fault in California is an example of a conservative plate boundary.*

constructive plate boundary
(*also* **divergent plates**)

Constructive plate boundaries occur where plates move apart from each other and new rocks are produced as convection currents bring molten magma to the surface. Volcanoes are common at such boundaries. Rift valleys may form when plates move apart if a central part slips downward when the plates move apart.

• *The Mid-Atlantic Ridge is an example of new crust forming at a constructive boundary.*

destructive plate boundary
(*also* **convergent plates**)

Destructive plate boundaries occur where plates move towards one another so that a more dense plate (oceanic crust) dips below a less dense plate (continental crust) and rejoins the magma underneath (subduction). This can give rise to deep ocean trenches such as the Marianas Trench in the Pacific. If the two plates have similar densities, neither may be subducted, and they crumple to form fold mountains.

• *An example of a destructive plate boundary is the Himalaya range which formed when the Indian and Eurasian plates collided. Mount Everest is getting a few centimetres higher every year as the Indian plate pushes against the Asian plate.*

SEE ALSO **subduction**

»

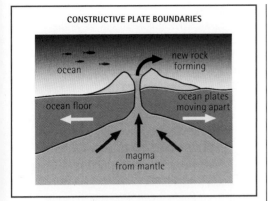

CONSTRUCTIVE PLATE BOUNDARIES

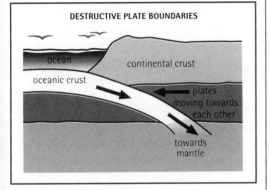

DESTRUCTIVE PLATE BOUNDARIES

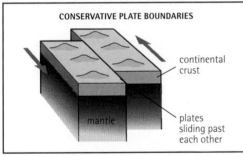

CONSERVATIVE PLATE BOUNDARIES

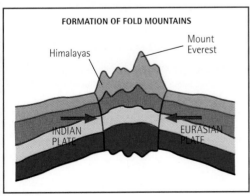

FORMATION OF FOLD MOUNTAINS

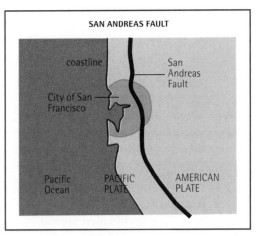

SAN ANDREAS FAULT

platelet (*also* thrombocyte)

Platelets are very small disc-shaped cell fragments found in the blood of mammals which are important in blood clotting.

• *Platelets are formed from larger cells with no nuclei which are made in the bone marrow.*

SEE ALSO **blood clotting, bone marrow**

plate tectonics

is the theory that the crust of the Earth is made of rock plates (tectonic plates) which rest on the mantle and have slowly moved throughout geological time, resulting in continental drift.

SEE ALSO **continental drift, Earth's structure, plate boundary, tectonic plate**

platyhelminth

Platyhelminths are invertebrates which are flatworms with unsegmented bodies. They include planarians, flukes, and tapeworms.

• *Most platyhelminths are hermaphrodite (bisexual).*

SEE ALSO **bisexual, hermaphrodite, invertebrate animal**

pleural membrane (*also* pleura)

The pleural membrane is a double membrane around the lungs filled with fluid which lubricates the lungs as they move against the rib cage.

• *The disease of pleurisy is the inflammation of the pleural membrane, causing pain in breathing.*

a
b
c
d
e
f
g
h
i
j
k
l
m
n
o
p
q
r
s
t
u
v
w
x
y
z

plumule *see* **seed**

plumbago *see* **graphite**

Pluto *see* **dwarf planet**

PM *see* **particulate matter**

pneumonia
is a bacterial disease of the lungs and spreads through airborne droplets from infected people.
• *Pneumonia killed many people before antibiotics were invented.*
SEE ALSO **antibiotic**

PNS *see* **peripheral nervous system**

poikilotherm *see* **cold–blooded animal**

point action
occurs when electric charge becomes so concentrated at a sharp point that it can ionize (remove electrons from) surrounding air molecules. These ions are then repelled by the point, creating an 'electric wind' of air molecules.
SEE ALSO **electric charge, lightning**

polarization
❶ is the separation of the positive and negative charge within a molecule (as in a water molecule).
SEE ALSO **solvent**
❷ is the formation of bubbles of hydrogen gas on the positive plate in a primary cell. These bubbles reduce the electromotive force (emf) of the cell.
SEE ALSO **electromotive force, primary cell**
❸ is the effect of an electromagnetic wave oscillating in one plane only. Only transverse waves can be polarized. Broadcast radio waves are often polarized, so an aerial must be vertically aligned with their electric field to receive them.
SEE ALSO **electromagnetic wave, oscillation, transverse wave**

polar satellite *see* **communication satellite**

polar solvent *see* **solvent**

pollen
is the yellow, dust-like grains which contain the male sex cells (gametes) of a plant.
• *Pollen is a particulate particle which can cause the allergy of hay fever, where the nose, throat, and eyes become irritated.*
SEE ALSO **allergy, gamete, particulate matter, pollination**

pollination
is the transference of pollen from the anther (male reproductive organ) to the stigma (sticky part of female reproductive organ). Pollen can be transferred by insects or by the wind.
SEE ALSO **anther, pollen, stigma**

	Insect pollination (e.g. wallflower)
1.	usually strongly scented
2.	usually have nectaries at base of the flower
3.	large petals, often with 'guide-lines' for insect
4.	anthers and stigma inside the flower so insect has to brush past them to get to the nectar
5.	sticky or spiky pollen to stick to insects
6.	small quantities of pollen

	Wind pollination (e.g. grass)
1.	no scent
2.	no nectaries
3.	small, inconspicuous petals or none at all
4.	anthers and stigma dangle outside flower so pollen can catch wind and stick to large stigma
5.	smooth, light pollen to be blown in the wind (causes hay fever)
6.	large amounts of pollen, as most is lost in the wind

cross–pollination
is when the pollen is transferred from the anther to the stigma of a different flower of the same species. The pollen has to be carried by a pollinating agent such as the wind, insects, birds, water, etc.

self–pollination
occurs when the pollen is transferred from the anther to the stigma of the same flower.

pollutant
A pollutant is any substance released into the environment as a result of human activities which has a harmful effect on living organisms.
• *Pollutants may be either biodegradable or non-biodegradable.*
SEE ALSO **biodegradable, non–biodegradable**

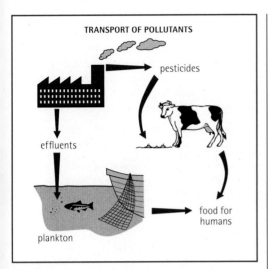

TRANSPORT OF POLLUTANTS

pesticides

effluents

food for humans

plankton

Polymer name	Uses
polyethene (polythene)	1 plastic bags 2 plastic film 3 sheets
polypropene (propathene)	1 crates 2 rope 3 carpet
polychloroethene (polyvinylchloride or PVC)	1 waterproof material 2 insulating wire 3 plastic records 4 guttering
polyphenylethene (polystyrene)	1 packaging material 2 ceiling tiles 3 insulating material
polytetrafluoroethene (PTFE or teflon)	1 coating for bridge bearings 2 non-stick saucepans 3 coating on skis
polymethyl-methacrylate (Perspex)	1 substitute for glass

pollution
is an undesirable change in the environment as a direct result of human activities, both industrial and social.
• *Pollution may affect the atmosphere, the water (rivers, seas, oceans), or the land.*
SEE ALSO **air pollution, land pollution, lead pollution, nitrate pollution, noise pollution, oil pollution, thermal pollution, water pollution**

polyamide *see* nylon

polydactyl
describes a person or animal that has more than five fingers or toes on one or each hand or foot.
• *Polydactyl cats often have more than five toes on their front paws.*

polyester *see* Terylene

polyester–cotton
is a composite made by weaving cotton thread with polyester fibres. The material becomes stronger, cheaper, and easier to wash and dry than pure cotton.
SEE ALSO **composite material**

polyethene *see* polythene

polymer
A polymer is a giant, long-chained molecule made up of a large number of smaller molecules (monomers) joined together.
• *Polymers often contain many thousands of atoms and are called macromolecules.*
SEE ALSO **macromolecule, monomer, natural polymer, synthetic polymer**

polymerization
is the chemical reaction by which monomers are joined together to form a polymer. The number of monomers joining together may vary from 50 to 50,000 or more.
• *Polymerization normally requires a particular range of temperature and pressure, and the presence of a catalyst.*
SEE ALSO **chemical reaction, monomer**

Monomer name		Polymer name	
ethene	H, H $C=C$ H H	polyethene	$\left(\begin{matrix}H & H\\C & C\\H & H\end{matrix}\right)_n$
propene	CH_3, H $C=C$ H H	polypropene	$\left(\begin{matrix}CH_3 & H\\C & C\\H & H\end{matrix}\right)_n$
chloroethene	Cl, H $C=C$ H H	polychloro-ethene	$\left(\begin{matrix}Cl & H\\C & C\\H & H\end{matrix}\right)_n$
phenylethene (styrene)	C_6H_5, H $C=C$ H H	polyphenyl-ethene	$\left(\begin{matrix}C_6H_5 & H\\C & C\\H & H\end{matrix}\right)_n$
tetrafluoro-ethene	F, F $C=C$ F F	polytetra-fluoroethene	$\left(\begin{matrix}F & F\\C & C\\F & F\end{matrix}\right)_n$
methyl metacrylate	$COOCH_3, F$ $C=C$ F F	polymethyl-methacrylate	$\left(\begin{matrix}COOCH_3 & H\\C & C\\H & H\end{matrix}\right)_n$

»

a
b
c
d
e
f
g
h
i
j
k
l
m
n
o
p
q
r
s
t
u
v
w
x
y
z

addition polymerization

is an addition reaction between identical monomers which are unsaturated molecules.
• *Polythene (polyethene) is formed by addition polymerization from unsaturated ethene monomers.*
SEE ALSO addition reaction, polythene, unsaturated molecule

condensation polymerization

is the successive linking together of monomers to form a polymer with the elimination of a simple molecule such as water or hydrogen chloride. A condensation polymer may contain two different kinds of monomer.
• *Nylon and Terylene are examples of polymers formed by condensation polymerization.*
SEE ALSO nylon, Terylene

polysaccharide

Polysaccharides are natural polymers formed by condensation polymerization of simple sugars, often glucose.
• *Starch is a polysaccharide found in plants.*
SEE ALSO glucose, natural polymer, polymerization, starch

polythene (*also* polyethene)

is an addition polymer formed by up to 50,000 ethene molecules joining to form one giant molecule.
SEE ALSO polymerization

H   H   H   H   H   H
 \ /   \ /   \ /
  C=C + C=C + C=C + →
 / \   / \   / \
H   H   H   H   H   H

H H H H H H
| | | | | |
– C–C–C–C–C–C – Part of a polythene molecule
| | | | | |
H H H H H H

poor conductor *see* insulator

pooter

A pooter is a container for collecting small insects or other invertebrates. It has two tubes, one (protected by some gauze) which is sucked and the other up which the insect is drawn.
• *A pooter is very useful when studying ecosystems.*
SEE ALSO ecosystem, insect, invertebrate animal

population

A population is a group of individuals of the same species within a community.
• *The size of a population can vary according to physical factors like drought, and other factors such as the predator-to-prey ratio.*
SEE ALSO predator-to-prey ratio, species

positive charge *see* electric charge

potable water

is water that is suitable for humans to drink as it has sufficiently low levels of microbes and dissolved salts.
• *Potable water is not pure water (distilled water).*
SEE ALSO microorganism, salt

potassium *see* alkali metal

potential difference (*also* p.d.)

is the difference in potential between two charged points. It is equal to the energy associated with the movement of a unit positive charge from one point to the other in an electric field.
• *There is an energy change of one joule if a charge of one coulomb moves through a potential difference of one volt. Electrons always flow from a low to a high potential: that is, from the negative to the positive terminal in a battery.*
SEE ALSO electric potential, volt

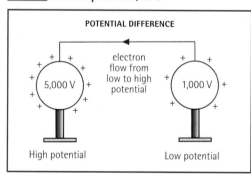

POTENTIAL DIFFERENCE

electron flow from low to high potential

5,000 V   1,000 V

High potential   Low potential

➤ **potential difference of a battery** The potential difference across the terminals of a battery indicates the potential energy given to each coulomb of charge 'pushed' out. There is a p.d. of 1 volt across the battery if each coulomb of charge is given 1 joule of potential energy. This potential difference gradually lessens around the circuit.
• *The sum of all the potential differences around the circuit is equal to the p.d. across the battery.*
SEE ALSO electromotive force

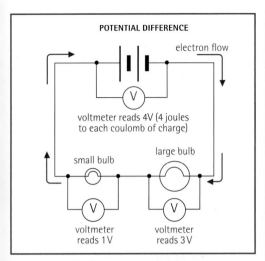

POTENTIAL DIFFERENCE

electron flow

voltmeter reads 4V (4 joules to each coulomb of charge)

small bulb

large bulb

voltmeter reads 1 V

voltmeter reads 3 V

potential divider (*also* **voltage divider**)

A potential divider is a chain of electrical resistors in series (or one continuous long resistor) that can be tapped at one or more points to obtain a known fraction of the total voltage across the chain (see diagram).

SEE ALSO **resistor**

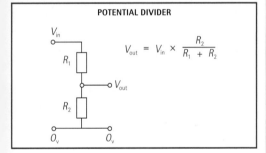

POTENTIAL DIVIDER

$$V_{out} = V_{in} \times \frac{R_2}{R_1 + R_2}$$

potential energy

is energy which is stored in a body or system because of its position, shape, or state.

SEE ALSO **chemical potential energy, elastic potential energy, gravitational potential energy store**

potometer

A potometer is an apparatus which measures transpiration rates under natural or artificial conditions. High temperature, high light intensity (bright sunshine), low humidity, and windy conditions will all increase the rate of transpiration.

SEE ALSO **transpiration**

power (*also* **W**)

is the rate at which work is done or energy is transferred. The power of a person or a machine is the rate at which they change one form of energy into another. Power is measured in watts (joules per second) and can be calculated by the equation:

$$\text{power (W)} = \frac{\text{work done (J)}}{\text{time taken (s)}}$$

• *Both mechanical* **power** *and electrical* **power** *use the same unit.*

SEE ALSO **electrical power, watt**

power cable *see* **electricity cable**

precipitate

A precipitate is an insoluble solid formed when a chemical reaction occurs between two dissolved ionic substances.

• *The clumps of particles in a* **precipitate** *are larger than in a suspension and form a sediment.*

SEE ALSO **suspension**

precipitation

is water that falls through the air towards the ground as rain, hail, sleet, or snow.

• **Precipitation** *occurs when the droplets of water vapour in the cloud become heavy and fall.*

SEE ALSO **water cycle**

predator

Predators are animals that hunt, kill, and eat other animals called their prey.

• *All* **predators** *are carnivores, but not all carnivores are predators.*

SEE ALSO **carnivore, prey**

predator–to–prey ratio

The predator-to-prey ratio is the natural balance between predator and prey, which causes the populations of many species to remain roughly the same size over a period of time.

• *Environmental change as a result of pollution or building, for example, can alter* **predator-to-prey** *ratio.*

SEE ALSO **population**

preferential discharge (*also* **selective discharge**)

occurs because ions which require the least amount of energy are discharged first. Cations (metal ions) higher in the reactivity series are harder to discharge at the cathode than those lower down. There is also an order for ease of discharge for anions (see table).

SEE ALSO **anion, cation, reactivity series**

»

cations	ease of discharge	anions
K^+		SO_4^{2-}
Na^+		NO^{3-}
Ca^{2+}		OH^-
Zn^{2+}		Cl^-
Al^{3+}		Br^-
Fe^{2+}		I^-
Pb^{2+}		
H^+		
Ag^+		

prefix

A prefix is a group of letters placed in front of a word to make a new word which has a different meaning. Prefixes are used as multipliers to the base SI units as shown in the tables.

• *The symbols for **prefixes** are small letters, except for the largest ones.*

Prefix	Symbol	Index notation	Meaning
tera–	T	10^{12}	1,000,000,000,000
giga–	G	10^9	1,000,000,000
mega–	M	10^6	1,000,000
kilo–	K	10^3	1,000
hecto–	h	10^2	100
deca–	da	10	10
deci–	d	10^{-1}	0.1
centi–	c	10^{-2}	0.01
milli–	m	10^{-1}	0.001
micro–	μ	10^{-6}	0.000 001
nano–	n	10^{-9}	0.000 000 001
pico–	p	10^{-12}	0.000 000 000 001

pregnancy (*also* gestation)

is the period between implantation of the embryo and the birth of the fetus. In humans it lasts about 40 weeks. The implanted embryo in the uterine wall becomes surrounded by amniotic fluid. To begin with the embryo obtains the food and oxygen it needs from blood vessels in the uterus. After a few weeks the placenta and umbilical cord develop.

• *The end of the **pregnancy** for the mother is indicated by 'labour pains' from the tightening of the uterine muscles to give birth.*

SEE ALSO **amniotic fluid, embryo, fetus, placenta, umbilical cord**

premolar *see* tooth

preparation of insoluble salts *see* salt

preparation of soluble salts *see* salt

press-on thermometer

A press-on thermometer is a plastic strip containing 'liquid crystals' which change colour with temperature.

• *A **press-on thermometer** is placed on the forehead to take the temperature of small children.*

SEE ALSO **thermometer**

pressure

is a continuous force applied by an object or fluid against a surface, measured as the force acting per unit area of surface. The SI unit of pressure is pascal.

$$\text{pressure} = \frac{\text{force}}{\text{area}}$$

The greater the force and the smaller the area, the larger the pressure.

• *It is because of **pressure** that a sharp knife (small area) cuts better than a blunt knife (large area), and a snow shoe (large area) does not sink into snow like an ordinary shoe (small area).*

SEE ALSO **atmospheric pressure, pascal**

➤ **pressure of a gas** (*also* p)
The pressure of a gas is the result of the continual collision of the molecules of the gas on the walls of the containing vessel.

PRESSURE OF A G

• *The **pressure of a gas** depends upon the temperature and volume of the gas.*

SEE ALSO **Bourdon pressure gauge, Boyle's law, Charles' law, critical pressure, partial pressure, pressure law, temperature of a gas**

➤ **pressure in liquids** Gravity acting on a liquid causes pressure to be exerted on the walls of its container. This, like air pressure, acts equally in all directions but does not depend on the shape of the container. It does depend on the density of the liquid and it increases with depth. The pressure at a point in a liquid is given by:

pressure in liquid at a point	=	height of liquid at a point	×	density of liquid	×	gravitational constant

This is in addition to the atmospheric pressure above the liquid.
• *In water, the* **pressure** *increases by approximately one atmosphere for every 10 m of depth.*

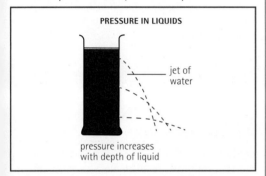

PRESSURE IN LIQUIDS

jet of water

pressure increases with depth of liquid

pressure law (*also* **Charles' law of pressure**)
The pressure law states that the pressure of a fixed mass of gas at constant volume is directly proportional to its temperature (in kelvins):

$$p/T = \text{constant}$$

This law only holds true with an ideal gas at low/medium pressures and temperatures. In terms of kinetic theory: when the temperature of the gas is increased the molecules travel faster with greater kinetic energy; they therefore collide with greater force on the walls of the container, so there is a greater pressure.
SEE ALSO **ideal gas, kinetic theory of gases, pressure of a gas, temperature of a gas**

prevention of corrosion *see* **corrosion**

prevention of heat loss *see* **heat loss**

prey
is an animal that is a source of food for a predator.
• *A* **Prey** *often adapts its appearance (e.g. colouring that blends with its surroundings) to protect itself from predators.*
SEE ALSO **predator**

primary atmosphere *see* **atmosphere**

primary cell (*also* **simple cell**)
A primary cell consists of plates of two different metals separated by an electrolyte such as salt solution or acid solution. A primary cell produces electrons from the metal plate that is the more reactive (negative terminal). These electrons travel towards the metal plate that is less reactive (positive terminal). This movement of electrons produces an electromotive force (emf), but only for a short time because of polarization and local action.
• *All* **primary cells** *have a limited life, as the chemicals inside are used up and cannot be replaced.*
SEE ALSO **electrolyte, electromotive force, local action, polarization, secondary cell**

primary coil *see* **transformer**

primary colour *see* **colour**

primary consumer *see* **consumer**

primate
Primates are the most advanced order of mammal with an enlarged forebrain and well developed cerebral activities, e.g. intelligence, highly developed senses (especially ears and eyes), etc. Primates undergo a long period of growth, development, and learning, with a strong parental influence. All primates have hands and feet with fingernails, and an opposable thumb and forefinger for grasping.
• *The order of* **primates** *includes monkeys, apes, and humans.*
SEE ALSO **mammal**

principal axis (*also* **optical axis**)
The principal axis is an imaginary line which passes through the optical centre at right angles to a lens.
SEE ALSO **lens, optical centre**

principal focus *see* **focal point**

principle of conservation of mass *see* **mass**

principle of flotation
The principle of flotation states that when a body floats, its weight is equal to the upthrust on it. As the upthrust is equal to the weight of displaced fluid (Archimedes' principle), we can restate the principle as 'a floating body displaces its own weight of fluid'.
SEE ALSO **Archimedes' principle, floating, upthrust, weight**

a b c d e f g h i j k l m n o p q r s t u v w x y z

principle of moments *see* **moment**

prism

A prism is a transparent object often triangular in shape.

• *A **prism** is normally used to split white light into the colours of the spectrum.*

SEE ALSO **colour, right-angled prism**

producer

Producers are organisms that can make their own food by autotrophic nutrition and are therefore considered as a source of energy.

• ***Producers** form the beginning of all food chains: the most important are green plants.*

SEE ALSO **consumer, food chain, nutrition**

product

Products are the chemical elements or compounds that are produced during a chemical reaction. The products have different properties from the reactants. Sometimes the products react with each other to re-form the original reactants. These are called reversible reactions.

• *The **products** are placed on the right-hand side in a chemical equation.*

SEE ALSO **chemical equation, chemical reaction, reactant, reversible reaction**

progesterone *see* **hormone**

progressive wave

A progressive wave is one which transports energy (but not matter) away from a source.

• *Sound and electromagnetic waves are **progressive** waves.*

SEE ALSO **electromagnetic wave, longitudinal wave, sound, stationary wave, transverse wave**

prokaryote

A prokaryote is an organism like a bacterium whose cell has a cell membrane and cytoplasm but whose genetic material is not enclosed in a nucleus.

• *A **prokaryote's** genetic material exists as circular loops of DNA called plasmids.*

SEE ALSO **bacteria, plasmid**

promoter (*also* **activator**)

A promoter is a substance which increases the power of a catalyst and thereby speeds up the chemical reaction even more.

SEE ALSO **catalyst, inhibitor**

propane *see* **alkane**

property

A property of a material is a quality or characteristic that it has.

• *Among the **properties** of metals are that they are solid, hard, shiny, good conductors, and react with acids.*

SEE ALSO **chemical property, chemical reaction, physical property**

prostate gland

The prostate gland secretes a fluid into the semen which activates the sperm and prevents them from sticking together.

• *The **prostate gland** produces the fluid in which the sperm swim.*

SEE ALSO **semen, testis**

protease

Proteases are enzymes which break down proteins into polypeptides and amino acids.

• ***Proteases** are found in biological washing powders to help remove food stains on clothes.*

SEE ALSO **enzyme, protein**

protein

Proteins are large organic molecules which are essential for the growth and repair of body tissue. They are natural polymers of amino acids which form all enzymes, and also the main structural materials of animals. Protein can be used as an energy source. Foods rich in protein include meat, fish, eggs, dairy products, beans, whole grains, and nuts. Animals take in proteins and break them down by digestion into amino acids. These are then transported in the blood to body cells where they are reassembled by the cells' ribosomes to make the different proteins the body needs.

• ***Proteins** contain the elements carbon, hydrogen, oxygen, nitrogen, and sulfur. (Fats and carbohydrates only contain carbon, hydrogen, and oxygen.)*

SEE ALSO **amino acid, digestion, natural polymer**

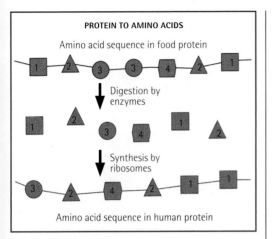

PROTEIN TO AMINO ACIDS

Amino acid sequence in food protein

Digestion by enzymes

Synthesis by ribosomes

Amino acid sequence in human protein

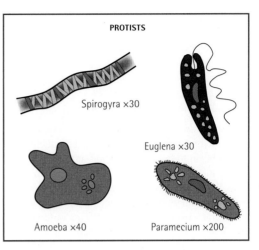

PROTISTS

Spirogyra ×30

Euglena ×30

Amoeba ×40

Paramecium ×200

➤ **hydrolysis of protein** is the chemical reaction of protein molecules with water to produce amino acids. It is important in protein digestion and takes place in the stomach and small intestine.

• *Hydrolysis of proteins should not be confused with denaturing (partial breakdown by heat).*

SEE ALSO **denaturing**

fibrous protein

Fibrous proteins are proteins which are generally insoluble in water and consist of long, coiled strands or flat sheets which give strength and elasticity for structure.

• *Examples of fibrous proteins are actin and myosin in muscle, keratin in skin and hair, and collagen in bone.*

globular protein

Globular proteins are proteins which have compact, rounded molecules and are usually water-soluble.

• *Examples of globular proteins are enzymes, antibodies, haemoglobin, some hormones, and storage proteins such as casein in milk and albumin in egg-white.*

protist (*also* **Protista, Protoctista**)
Protists form a kingdom which includes all unicellular (single-celled) organisms or simple multicellular (many-celled) organisms which possess nuclei but which cannot be classified as either fungi, plants, or animals. This kingdom includes all protozoa and filamented algae such as spirogyra.

• *Nearly all protists live in water.*

SEE ALSO **protozoan**

proton
A proton is a positively charged subatomic particle which is found in the nucleus of an atom. It has a mass equal to that of a neutron but is 1,840 times heavier than an electron.

• *A proton's charge is equal, but opposite, to that of an electron.*

SEE ALSO **electron, neutron, nucleus, subatomic particle**

proton number *see* **atomic number**

protoplasm
is the transparent jelly-like matter found inside living cells.

• *Protoplasm consists of two parts: the cytoplasm and the nucleus.*

SEE ALSO **cytoplasm, nucleus**

protostar
A protostar is a cloud of hot dust and gas (gaseous nebula) collected together under the force of gravity. When it becomes dense enough, nuclear fusion begins and it becomes a star.

SEE ALSO **nuclear fusion**

protozoan *plural* **protozoans, protozoa**
Protozoans are single-celled organisms with a cell membrane and (unlike bacteria) a nucleus.

• *Some protozoans are plant-like and feed by photosynthesis (e.g. euglena). Others are animal-like and feed on other living things (e.g. amoeba, paramecium).*

SEE ALSO **cell membrane, nucleus, protist**

ptyalin (*also* salivary amylase)
is an amylase enzyme which is found in saliva and begins the digestion of starch in the mouth. Digestion is completed in the pancreas by pancreatic amylase.
• *As ptyalin is an enzyme, it breaks down starch best at body temperature (37°C).*
SEE ALSO amylase, enzyme, saliva

puberty (*also* adolescence)
is a stage of development when the reproductive organs begin to function. It begins approximately between the ages of 11 to 15 in girls and 13 to 15 in boys. Puberty is marked by the start of menstruation in females and by the appearance of secondary sex characteristics in both sexes. In males these secondary sex characteristics are controlled by the hormone testosterone. In females the characteristics are controlled by the hormone oestrogen.
SEE ALSO menstruation, sex hormone

Secondary Sex Characteristics		
	Female	
1.	Growth of pubic hair (around sex organs) and hair under arms.	
2.	Hips become wider (which helps with childbirth later on).	
3.	Sex organs enlarge, ovaries produce eggs (ovulation) and menstrual cycle begins.	
4.	Breasts (mammary glands) develop.	
	Male	
1.	Growth of pubic hair and other body hair, especially facial hair.	
2.	Enlargement of larynx (voice box), so voice deepens (voice breaks).	
3.	Sex organs enlarge and testes produce sperm.	
4.	Body becomes more muscular and shoulders broaden.	

pulley
A pulley is a simple machine for raising loads, consisting of one or more wheels with a grooved rim to take a belt, rope or chain. In the diagram with one pulley (assuming the system is frictionless) the effort force F will lift a load of 2F. The mechanical advantage (and velocity ratio) of this pulley is 2. In the diagram with four pulleys, the effort force F will lift a load of 4F, so the mechanical advantage (and velocity ratio) of this frictionless pulley is 4. This pulley arrangement is called a block and tackle.
SEE ALSO mechanical advantage, velocity ratio

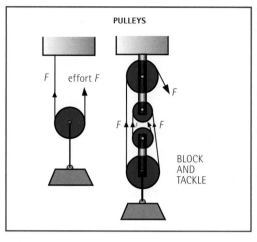
PULLEYS / effort F / F / BLOCK AND TACKLE

pulmonary artery
The pulmonary artery carries deoxygenated blood from the right ventricle of the heart to the lungs (the only artery to carry deoxygenated blood).
SEE ALSO artery, heart, ventricle

pulmonary circulation *see* double circulation

pulp cavity *see* tooth

pulmonary vein
The pulmonary vein carries oxygenated blood from the lungs to the left atrium of the heart (the only vein to carry oxygenated blood).
SEE ALSO atrium, heart, vein

pulsar
A pulsar is a celestial object which emits regular pulses of radio waves (frequency between 0.03 s to 4 s).
• *Pulsars were first discovered in 1968 and since then around 2,000 pulsars have been identified in our own galaxy (Milky Way).*
SEE ALSO quasar

pulse rate *see* heartbeat

pupa (*also* chrysalis)
The pupa is the stage of the life cycle of an arthropod during which the larva is transformed into the adult, and movement and feeding cease.
• *A chrysalis is the pupa formed by a caterpillar changing into a butterfly.*
SEE ALSO arthropod, larva

pupil

In the eye, the pupil is the hole at the centre of the iris which appears as a black circle. It allows light to enter and pass through the lens to the retina.

• *The size of the pupil is controlled by the muscles of the iris.*

SEE ALSO **eye, iris, lens, retina**

pure substance

Pure substances contain only one type of atom or molecule. Elements and compounds are both pure substances as each element or compounds contains only one type of molecule.

• *Pure substances have exact melting and boiling points.*

SEE ALSO **compound, element, mixture**

pyloric sphincter

The pyloric sphincter is a muscular ring between the stomach and the small intestine.

• *When the pyloric sphincter relaxes, it lets the semi-digested food (chyme) through to the duodenum.*

SEE ALSO **chyme, small intestine**

pyramid of biomass

The pyramid of biomass is the biomass of each trophic level represented pictorially as a pyramid. The biomass decreases as we go up the food chain, as the number of organisms at each trophic level decreases.

• *The pyramid of biomass is a more accurate representation of the flow of biomass through the food chain than the pyramid of numbers.*

SEE ALSO **biomass, food chain, pyramid of numbers, trophic level**

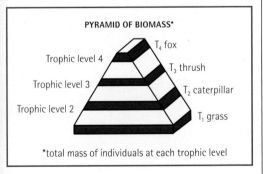

PYRAMID OF BIOMASS*

Trophic level 4 — T₄ fox
Trophic level 3 — T₃ thrush
Trophic level 2 — T₂ caterpillar — T₁ grass

*total mass of individuals at each trophic level

pyramid of numbers

The pyramid of numbers is the number of organisms at each trophic level represented pictorially as a pyramid. The number of organisms at higher trophic levels becomes smaller. This is because at each trophic level the organisms use up most of the biomass they have obtained in respiration to obtain energy. This leaves less biomass (typically around 10%) to pass to higher trophic levels, so higher levels support smaller numbers of organisms.

SEE ALSO **biomass, food chain, pyramid of biomass, trophic level**

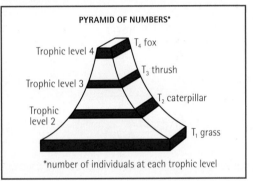

PYRAMID OF NUMBERS*

Trophic level 4 — T₄ fox
Trophic level 3 — T₃ thrush
Trophic level 2 — T₂ caterpillar — T₁ grass

*number of individuals at each trophic level

pyrometer

A pyrometer is an instrument used to measure high temperatures above the range of liquid-in-glass thermometers.

• *Pyrometers are useful to measure the temperature of furnaces, as when manufacturing steel.*

SEE ALSO **liquid–in–glass thermometer, thermocouple thermometer**

pyrosulfuric acid *see* oleum

Qq

Q *see* **electric charge**

quadrat

A quadrat is a square frame (normally with sides of 50 cm) which is used for ecological sampling. The quadrat is randomly placed on the ground and the species inside are counted and recorded. To get an accurate indication of numbers of species, you will need to sample with many quadrats and average your results.

• *A quadrat may also be used to take a sample along a transect.*

SEE ALSO **ecosystem, transect**

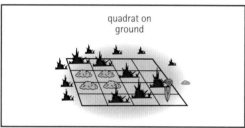

quadrat on ground

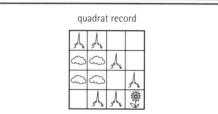

quadrat record

qualitative analysis *see* **chemical analysis**

quality of sound *see* **sound**

quark

A quark is an elementary subatomic particle. However, unlike protons and electrons, quarks have fractions of electronic charge. For example, the 'up quark' has a charge of $+\frac{2}{3}$ but a 'down quark' a charge of $-\frac{1}{3}$. The proton particle consists of three quarks, two ups and one down:

$$+\frac{2}{3} + \frac{2}{3} - \frac{1}{3} = +1 \text{ charge.}$$

However the neutron also consists of three quarks, but this time one up and two down:

$$+\frac{2}{3} - \frac{1}{3} - \frac{1}{3} = 0 \text{ charge.}$$

• *Quarks are one of many different elementary particles found inside atoms (see table).*

Elementary particle	Description
antiparticle	Particle having the same mass as a given particle but opposite electric charge or magnetic effect e.g. positron is antiparticle for electron.
baryon	Heavy particle like a neutron or proton.
hadron	Particle like a baryon or meson.
lepton	Particle like an electron or neutrino.
meson	Particle that binds nucleons together.
muon	An unstable meson.
neutrino	Particle with zero charge and almost zero mass.
nucleon	Particle found in nucleus of atom.
positron	Positively charged electron
quark	Component of elementary particles.

SEE ALSO **electron, neutron, proton**

quartz

is the natural crystalline form of silicon dioxide (silica). It is one of the hardest of common minerals. Quartz is a macromolecule in which each silicon atom is covalently bonded to four oxygen atoms.

• *The tetrahedral arrangement of **quartz** is like that of diamond, and gives quartz a transparent, crystalline structure with a high melting point.*

SEE ALSO **macromolecule, silicon**

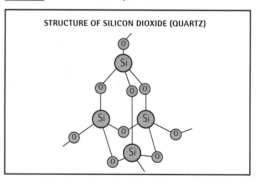

STRUCTURE OF SILICON DIOXIDE (QUARTZ)

quasar

A quasar is an extremely bright and distant celestial object emitting radio waves.

• ***Quasars** were first discovered in 1961 and are thought to be the most luminous objects in the universe.*

SEE ALSO **pulsar**

Rr

radiant heat *see* **radiation**

radiation

❶ is a general term applied to anything that travels outward from its source but which cannot be identified as a type of matter like a solid, liquid, or gas.
• *Radiation applies to forms of energy, electromagnetic waves, and radioactivity.*
❷ (*also* **thermal radiation, radiant heat, infra-red radiation**) is the way in which heat energy is transferred from a hotter to a colder place without a medium such as air or water being present. The heat energy from the Sun travels to Earth through space as radiant heat. Such heat is an electromagnetic wave mainly in the infrared region of the electromagnetic spectrum. When the wave falls on an object, the particles absorb its energy. The particles in the object gain kinetic and potential energy, and the thermal energy and temperature of the object increase.
• *Thermal radiation can pass through a vacuum.*
SEE ALSO **electromagnetic wave, heat transfer, temperature, thermal energy**

➤ **absorption of radiation** is most efficient with dull (matt) black surfaces; shiny silvery surfaces (which reflect thermal radiation) are weak absorbers.

➤ **emission of radiation** is most efficient through dull (matt) black surfaces; shiny silvery surfaces are poor emitters. Heating radiators are misnamed, as they heat mainly by producing convection currents.

❸ (*also* **nuclear radiation**) is the radiation given off from radioactive material by the spontaneous disintegration of unstable atomic nuclei.
• *The three types of nuclear radiation are alpha radiation, beta radiation, and gamma rays.*
SEE ALSO **alpha radiation, beta radiation, gamma ray, radioactivity**

Characteristics of Radiation	
Alpha $^4_2$He	
Nature	helium nucleus (2 protons and 2 neutrons)
Charge	+2
Radio active source (e.g.)	americium-241
Absorbed by	sheet of paper
Ionizing power	strong
Deflection in electric and magnetic field	very small
Hazard	low unless within body
Beta $^0_{-1}$e	
Nature	high energy electron
Charge	−1
Radio active source (e.g.)	strontium-90
Absorbed by	5mm sheet of aluminium
Ionizing power	weak
Deflection in electric and magnetic field	large
Hazard	can damage cells and DNA
Gamma γ	
Nature	high energy electro-magnetic wave
Charge	none
Radio active source (e.g.)	cobalt-60
Absorbed by	25 mm sheet of lead (reduces intensity by half)
Ionizing power	very weak
Deflection in electric and magnetic field	zero
Hazard	dangerous in high intensity

➤ **detecting radiation** Most devices detect and measure radioactivity by detecting the amount of ionization it causes.

WORD BUILD

geiger counter
A Geiger counter is an electronic device which detects the charge produced when a particle causes ionization, and indicates the number of particles detected in the tube per second.

cloud chamber
A small, enclosed chamber is saturated with alcohol vapour and the radioactive source placed inside. Movement of alpha and beta particles causes ionization, which results in condensation tracks.

»

bubble chamber

This is like a cloud chamber, but shows particle tracks as tiny bubbles caused by ionization.

scintillation counter

This detects gamma rays which, when they hit a special crystal, produce flashes called 'scintillae' of light.

dosimeter *also* (film badge)

A dosimeter is a simple device containing photographic film which darkens on exposure to radiation. The larger the dose, the darker the film.

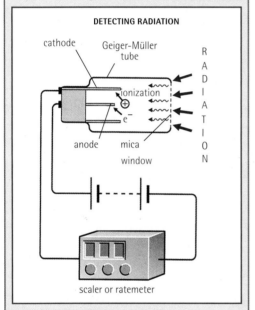

DETECTING RADIATION

cathode

Geiger-Müller tube

ionization

e⁻

anode   mica

window

RADIATION

scaler or ratemeter

radiation sickness

Radiation sickness is illness caused by exposure to large doses of radiation. Such exposure can result in various forms of cancer, especially leukaemia (blood cancer). Gamma rays, especially, can damage cells and cause genetic mutation. Workers using radioisotopes wear protective clothing such as lead-lined aprons, and use tools such as long tweezers.

• *To avoid radiation sickness hazardous radioisotopes must always be handled inside a glove box.*

SEE ALSO gamma ray, glove box, mutation, radiation, radioisotope

radical

A radical is a group of atoms within a compound that maintains its identity throughout a chemical reaction. Common examples of radicals are hydroxide (OH), carbonate (CO_3), nitrate (NO_3), and sulfate (SO_4).

• *Unlike a molecule, a radical cannot exist by itself.*

SEE ALSO radiology, radiotherapy

radioactive contamination

is a measure of possible harm from exposure of the body to radiation produced from the decay of contaminating atoms.

• *Radioactive contamination is measured in grays (Gy) or sieverts (Sv).*

SEE ALSO gray, sievert

radioactive decay

is the spontaneous disintegration of a radioactive nucleus, giving off alpha or beta particles, often together with gamma rays. If the new nucleus formed (daughter nucleus) is also radioactive, then this also undergoes disintegration and a radioactive decay series results.

SEE ALSO half-life, nucleus

alpha decay

is the radioactive decay of a nucleus giving off an alpha particle. The remaining nucleus (new element) has its atomic number decreased by two and its mass number decreased by four.

$$^{235}_{92}U \rightarrow {}^{231}_{90}Th + {}^{4}_{2}He$$

SEE ALSO alpha particle

beta decay

is the radioactive decay of a nucleus by conversion of a neutron into a proton, giving off a beta particle (high-energy electron). The remaining nucleus (new element) has its atomic number increased by one, but its mass number remains the same.

$$^{14}_{6}C \rightarrow {}^{14}_{7}N + {}^{0}_{-1}e$$

SEE ALSO beta particle

radioactive isotope *see* radioisotope

radioactive labelling *see* radioactive tracing

radioactive source

A radioactive source is a quantity of radionuclide which emits ionizing radiation.

• *Radioactive sources typically emit one or more of the radiation types (alpha, beta, or gamma radiation).*

SEE ALSO alpha radiation, beta radiation, gamma ray, radionuclide

➤ **handling radioactive sources** In school laboratories, radioactive sources should have activities of around 3.7 kBq (kilobecquerel) or less. All sources must be handled at arm's length with tweezers, and work should not be undertaken by anyone having a cut, abrasion, or open wound. Outside the body, both beta and gamma sources are dangerous. Inside the body, alpha particles (e.g. from inhaled radioactive gases) also cause tissue damage.
SEE ALSO **becquerel**

radioactive tracing (*also* radioactive labelling)
is a method of following substances by introducing a radioactive isotope, called the tracer. Tracers in underground gas or water pipes can be used to detect leaks. They are used in medicine to follow the movement of body fluids like blood, urine, etc. Such tracers are gamma sources with short half-lives.
SEE ALSO **radioisotope**

radioactive waste *see* nuclear waste

radioactivity
is the spontaneous disintegration of unstable atomic nuclei and is usually accompanied by the emission of radiation. This may be in the form of a stream of alpha particles, beta particles, or gamma rays. Radioactivity is an entirely random process and you cannot predict which nuclei will decay next.

• *Radioactivity is completely unaffected by physical conditions (such as temperature) or chemical conditions (such as bonding).*
SEE ALSO **alpha particle, beta particle, gamma ray, radiation, radioactive source**

SYMBOL FOR RADIOACTIVE HAZARD

radio astronomy
is the study, using radio telescopes, of the radio waves emitted from celestial objects including galaxies and quasars.
• *The telescopes used in radio astronomy often have very large diameter (over 100m) reflecting parabolic dishes which are used to focus the radio waves onto a central amplifier inside the dish.*
SEE ALSO **quasar**

radiography
is the process of producing images of opaque objects on photographic film or fluorescent screen using radiation such as gamma rays or X-rays.
• *Radiography has many medical uses but is also used for flaw detection in industrial products.*

radioisotope (*also* radioactive isotope)
A radioisotope is an isotope of an element that is radioactive. Some radioisotopes are produced by cosmic rays, and others by nuclear fusion.
• *Carbon-14 is a natural radioisotope formed from nitrogen by bombardment with cosmic rays, and present in small proportions among ordinary carbon-12 atoms.*
SEE ALSO **cosmic rays, nuclear fusion**

radiology
is the study of radioactivity, and especially the use of gamma rays and X-rays in medical diagnosis and treatment.
• *Most hospitals have a radiology department.*
SEE ALSO **radiography, radiotherapy**

radionuclide
A radionuclide is a nuclide (atomic nucleus) which is radioactive and decays to give off alpha particles, beta particles, gamma rays, or a combination of these.
SEE ALSO **nuclide**

radiotherapy
is the use of radiation from radioisotopes to treat cancer by killing cancer cells.
• *Radiotherapy is normally carried out in the radiology department of a hospital.*
SEE ALSO **radioisotope, radiology**

radio transmitter *see* transmitter

radio waves
are electromagnetic waves with frequencies between 3 kHz and 300 GHz. Radio waves are chosen as the carrier wave to carry signals (electrical impulses) because they travel fast (speed of light) and are easily reflected and diffracted.
• *Radio waves can be produced by making electrons (electricity) oscillate in an aerial.*
SEE ALSO **aerial, carrier wave, electromagnetic wave, receiver, transmitter**

radius *see* human skeleton

rainbow

A rainbow is an arch of all the colours of a spectrum formed in the sky when the Sun's rays are refracted (by dispersion) through rain or spray. The raindrops act like tiny prisms.

• *Rainbows always appear opposite the Sun.*

SEE ALSO colour, dispersion, prism

rainforest

is a tropical habitat comprising a jungle of tall trees and the plants and animals that live on them.

• *Rainforests cover only 6% of the world's surface but are home to over 50% of the world's plant and animal species.*

SEE ALSO ecosystem, habitat

rare–earth metal *see* lanthanoid

rarefaction *see* sound wave

rare gas *see* noble gas

rate curve

A rate curve is typically a plot of change of mass or volume during a chemical reaction against time. To start with, the gradient of the graph is steep, as the rate of reaction is always fastest at the beginning. As the reactants are used up, the gradient decreases until the reaction has finished and the curve becomes flat.

• *You can use the **rate curve** to calculate the rate of a chemical reaction at a specific time.*

SEE ALSO chemical reaction, rate of reaction

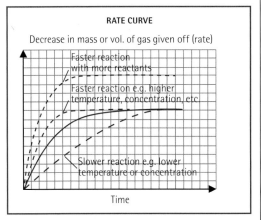

RATE CURVE

Decrease in mass or vol. of gas given off (rate)

Faster reaction with more reactants

Faster reaction e.g. higher temperature, concentration, etc.

Slower reaction e.g. lower temperature or concentration

Time

rate of reaction

is the speed of a chemical reaction, calculated by measuring how quickly reactants (chemicals you start with) change into products (chemicals you produce). The rate of a particular chemical reaction is affected by various factors like the temperature, concentration, and surface area of the reactants, or the presence of a catalyst.

• *Explosive chemical reactions have the highest **rate** of reaction.*

SEE ALSO catalyst, chemical reaction, collision theory, product, rate curve, reactant

➤ measuring rate of reaction

Rate of chemical reaction can be determined by the following relationship:

$$\text{mean rate} = \frac{\text{quantity of reactant used}}{\text{time taken}}$$

$$\text{or} \quad \frac{\text{quantity of product formed}}{\text{time taken}}.$$

However, to measure the rate we need to record some sort of physical change.

	Changes used to indicate the rate of a chemical reaction
1.	when there is a change in mass as a gas is given off (rate = g/s)
2.	when a gas is formed which can be collected (rate = cm³/s)
3.	when there is a temperature change
4.	when there is a colour change
5.	when a precipitate is formed
6.	when there is a change in pH

ray

A ray of light is a very narrow beam of light energy or radiation.

• *In diagrams, light is represented by straight lines called **rays**. An arrow on a ray indicates the direction the light is travelling.*

SEE ALSO beam

reabsorption *see* Bowman's capsule

reactant

Reactants are the chemical elements or compounds that a chemical reaction starts with.

• *The **reactants** are placed on the left-hand side in a chemical equation.*

SEE ALSO chemical equation, chemical reaction, product

reaction of metals with hydrochloric acid *see* reactivity series

reaction of metals with oxygen *see* reactivity series

reaction of metals with water
see **reactivity series**

reaction profile (*also* **energy level diagram**)

A reaction profile is one which shows how the energy changes during a chemical reaction. It is a graph plotting energy change against time.

SEE ALSO **chemical reaction, endothermic reaction, exothermic reaction**

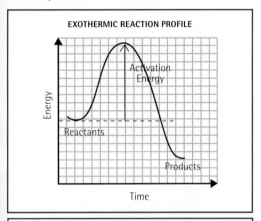

EXOTHERMIC REACTION PROFILE

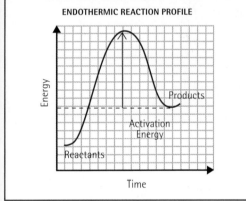

ENDOTHERMIC REACTION PROFILE

reactivity series (*also* **activity series**)

The reactivity series is a list of metals placed in order of their reactivity, as determined by their reaction with air (oxygen), water and dilute acid. The most reactive metals are at the top of the series and the least reactive at the bottom.

• *The element hydrogen is sometimes placed in the reactivity series for comparison. Any element below hydrogen can never displace hydrogen from water or an acid.*

SEE ALSO **chemical reaction, metal compound**

Element	
Potassium (most reactive)	
Sodium	
Calcium	
Magnesium	
Aluminium	
Zinc	
Iron	
Tin	
Lead	
(Hydrogen)	
Copper	
Gold	
Platinum (least reactive)	

➤ **reaction of metals with oxygen** Reactivity of metals with oxygen (air) decreases as we go down the reactivity series. Metals at the top of the series react violently and catch fire. The further down the series the metal is, the slower its reaction. If there is a reaction, the product is always an oxide

SEE ALSO **oxide**

Metal	Reaction with oxygen (air)
Potassium	Violent reaction catching fire and burning with a lilac flame $4K + O_2 \rightarrow 2K_2O$
Sodium	Easily catches fire and burns with a bright yellow flame $4Na + O_2 \rightarrow 2Na_2O$
Magnesium	Can be ignited to burn with a brilliant white light $2Mg + O_2 \rightarrow 2MgO$
Iron	Does not burn but glows brightly and gives off yellow sparks $3Fe + 2O_2 \rightarrow Fe_3O_4$
Copper	Does not burn but the hot metal becomes coated with a black oxide $2Cu + O_2 \rightarrow 2CuO$

➤ **reaction of metals with water** Reactivity of metals with water decreases as we go down the reactivity series. Metals at the top of the series react violently with cold water to produce the alkali and hydrogen. Metals near the middle react with steam to produce the oxide and hydrogen. Metals like copper have no reaction and never displace hydrogen. **»**

Metal	Reaction with water
Potassium	Very violent reaction and metal catches fire $2K + 2H_2O \rightarrow 2KOH + H_2$
Sodium	Violent reaction in cold water $2Na + 2H_2O \rightarrow 2NaOH + H_2$
Calcium	Steady reaction in cold water $Ca + 2H_2O \rightarrow Ca(OH)_2 + H_2$
Magnesium	Reacts very slowly with cold water, but vigorously with steam $Mg + H_2O \rightarrow MgO + H_2$
Zinc	Quite slow reaction with steam $Zn + H_2O \rightarrow ZnO + H_2$
Iron	Very slow reaction with steam $3Fe + 4H_2O \rightarrow Fe_3O_4 + 4H_2$
Copper	No reaction at all

➤ **reaction of metals with hydrochloric acid**

Reactivity of metals with an acid decreases as we go down the reactivity series. Metals at the top of the series (sodium and potassium) should never be reacted with acids, as their reaction is too violent. As we go down the reactivity series, the reaction becomes slower, until with lead we need concentrated hydrochloric acid for any reaction. The reaction produces a salt called a chloride, and hydrogen gas. For metals like copper and those below, there is no reaction with hydrochloric acid and no hydrogen gas evolves. They will react with concentrated sulfuric or nitric acids, but will not produce hydrogen gas.

Metal	Reaction with hydrochloric acid
Magnesium	Violent reaction $Mg + 2HCl \rightarrow MgCl_2 + H_2$
Zinc	Moderate reaction $Zn + 2HCl \rightarrow ZnCl_2 + H_2$
Iron	Slow reaction $Fe + 2HCl \rightarrow FeCl_2 + H_2$
Lead	Reaction only when concentrated acid is used $Pb + 2HCl \rightarrow PbCl_2 + H_2$
Copper	No reaction at all
Gold	No reaction at all

WORD BUILD

displacement reaction (*also* **substitution reaction**)

A displacement reaction is a chemical reaction where a more reactive element (metal higher in the reactivity series) replaces a less reactive element (metal lower in the series) from its compound. For example, if an iron nail is left in blue copper(II) sulfate solution, the iron displaces the copper. The blue colour is replaced by the pale-green colour of iron(II) sulfate solution, and pink copper metal is deposited on the iron nail. This is the chemical reaction

iron + copper(II) sulfate → iron(II) sulfate + copper

$Fe + CuSO_4 \rightarrow FeSO_4 + Cu$

SEE ALSO **chemical reaction, halogen**

stability of metal compounds

Metals high in the reactivity series form stable compounds whereas compounds of metals low down in the series are less stable and are easier to decompose. For example potassium carbonate does not decompose on heating but copper carbonate decomposes to the oxide and gives off carbon dioxide gas.

SEE ALSO **metal compound**

reading error

A reading error is one due to the guesswork involved when a reading lies between two values on a marked scale.

SEE ALSO **analogue reading**

real depth *see* **refraction of light**

real image *see* **image**

receiver

A receiver is an electronic device which converts modulated radio waves into electrical impulses which can be changed into sound, moving images (television), or digital data.

• *Receivers are widely used in television, remote controls, cell phones, and wireless modems.*

SEE ALSO **radio waves**

receptacle

The receptacle is the expanded tip of a flower stalk which bears the sepals, petals, stamens, and carpels.

• *After fertilization the **receptacle** may swell up to form a fleshy false fruit.*

SEE ALSO **carpel, flower, petal, sepal, stamen**

receptor

A receptor is a sense organ like the eyes, ears, nose, skin, taste buds, etc., which can detect information about the surroundings.

• *Information is transmitted from **receptors** by sensory neurones.*

SEE ALSO **neurone, sense organ**

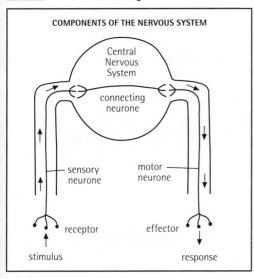

COMPONENTS OF THE NERVOUS SYSTEM

Central Nervous System

connecting neurone

sensory neurone

motor neurone

receptor

effector

stimulus

response

recessive allele *see* allele

rectum *see* large intestine

recycling

is the reprocessing of used material to save money and natural resources, and to improve sustainability. It involves sorting waste material and rubbish into components like metal (tin cans), glass (glass bottles), plastic (recyclable or not) and paper (cardboard, newspaper). The different components are then made into new objects and used again.

• *Recycling is one of the 3Rs (reduce, reuse, recycle) in the sustainability of raw materials.*

SEE ALSO **reduce, reuse, sustainability**

red blood cell (*also* erythrocyte, red corpuscle)

Red blood cells are disc-shaped cells with no nucleus whose main function is to transport oxygen. They are made in the bone marrow (each lasting approximately 120 days) and contain the red pigment haemoglobin. Red blood cells have flexible cell membranes so they can change shape and flow easily through tiny blood capillaries.

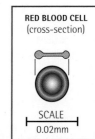

RED BLOOD CELL
(cross-section)

SCALE
0.02mm

• *Red blood cells carry oxygen to all the cells of the body, into which it passes by diffusion.*

SEE ALSO **blood, bone marrow, capillary, haemoglobin, white blood cell**

redox reaction

A redox reaction is a chemical reaction involving simultaneous oxidation and reduction. The two processes always occur together, as when electrons are lost from a substance (oxidation), they must be gained by another substance (reduction).

• *Rusting is a **redox reaction**, as iron loses electrons and oxygen gains them to form iron (III) oxide, which is rust.*

SEE ALSO **chemical reaction, oxidation, reduction**

red shift

The red shift is a lengthening of the wavelength of light from distant stars so that it seems to shift towards the red end of the spectrum.

• *The **red shift** is caused by a form of Doppler effect and demonstrates the expansion of the universe.*

SEE ALSO **Doppler effect, universe**

reduce

can refer to the lowering of usage of a particular material to increase sustainability of the raw materials that are used to make it.

• *Reduce is one of the 3Rs (reduce, reuse, recycle) to achieve sustainability.*

SEE ALSO **recycle, reuse, sustainability**

reducing agent (*also* reductant, electron donor)

A reducing agent is a substance which helps reduction to occur. It removes oxygen and/or donates electrons.

• *Examples of good **reducing agents** are carbon, hydrogen, and carbon monoxide.*

SEE ALSO **reduction**

reduction

is a chemical reaction involving the loss of oxygen (or the gain of hydrogen). Alternatively, reduction can be regarded as a process which involves the gain of electrons by a substance.

A reduction reaction: extraction of iron

$$Fe_2O_3 + 3CO \rightarrow 2Fe + 3CO_2$$

The iron has lost oxygen and gained electrons.

SEE ALSO **chemical reaction, electron, oxidation**

reductive cell division *see* meiosis

refinery gas (*also* fuel gas)

is the petroleum fraction with a boiling point below 40°C. It is made up of a mixture of hydrocarbons with up to four carbon atoms (e.g. methane, ethane, propane, and butane). It is used as a fuel and kept liquefied in bottles as LPG (liquefied petroleum gas).

• *Refinery gas is a chemical feedstock for making other organic chemicals.*

SEE ALSO **chemical feedstock, fraction, fractional distillation**

refining

is the process of converting petroleum into more useful products.

• *Refining typically involves fractional distillation followed by the chemical process of cracking.*

SEE ALSO **cracking, fractional distillation, petroleum**

reflected ray *see* reflection of light

reflection

is the bouncing off of a wave from a barrier. Only the direction of the wave changes.

• *Reflection occurs with sound waves, light waves, and other electromagnetic waves.*

SEE ALSO **diffraction, refraction, wave**

reflection of light

is the change in direction of a light ray after it hits a surface and bounces off. Mirrors are normally used to demonstrate reflection because their shiny flat surfaces produce regular reflection. Uneven rough surfaces produce diffuse reflection. Reflected light always obeys the two laws of reflection.

SEE ALSO **refraction of light, total internal reflection**

	Laws of reflection
1.	The incident ray, the reflected ray and the normal line (at the point of incidence) are all in the same plane.
2.	The angle of incidence is equal to the angle of reflection
3.	A **normal line** is an imaginary line at right angles to a surface where a light ray strikes it.
4.	The **incident ray** is the light ray before reflection.
5.	The **reflected ray** is the light ray after reflection.
6.	The **angle of incidence** is the angle between the incident ray and the normal line.
7.	The **angle of reflection** is the angle between the reflected ray and the normal line.

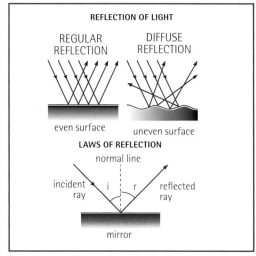

REFLECTION OF LIGHT

REGULAR REFLECTION   DIFFUSE REFLECTION

even surface   uneven surface

LAWS OF REFLECTION

normal line

incident ray   i   r   reflected ray

mirror

reflex action

Reflex actions are special types of involuntary action of which we are aware, like swallowing, coughing, etc. Such actions follow a 'neural short circuit' called a reflex arc.

SEE ALSO **involuntary action**

WORD BUILD

cranial reflex

Cranial reflexes are reflex actions of the head like sneezing and blinking, where the reflex arc goes only through the small section of the brain.

spinal reflex

Spinal reflexes are reflex actions where the reflex arc is through the spine. Sensory information is fed through spinal nerves going into the dorsal

(back) side of the spine. Motor nerves come from the ventral (front) side.
• Often **spinal reflexes** involve withdrawal away from a painful stimulus such as a hot surface (see diagram).

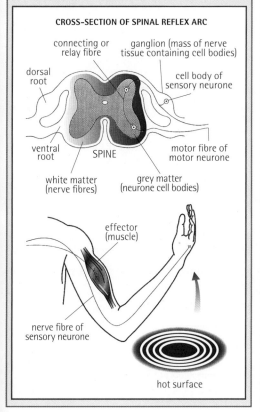

CROSS-SECTION OF SPINAL REFLEX ARC

connecting or relay fibre

ganglion (mass of nerve tissue containing cell bodies)

dorsal root

cell body of sensory neurone

ventral root   SPINE

motor fibre of motor neurone

white matter (nerve fibres)

grey matter (neurone cell bodies)

effector (muscle)

nerve fibre of sensory neurone

hot surface

reforestation

is the replanting of trees on land where forests used to be.

SEE ALSO **afforestation, deforestation**

refraction

is the change in direction of a wave as it passes from one medium to another. During refraction there is a change in speed, direction, and wavelength, but not in frequency.

SEE ALSO **diffraction, reflection, wave**

refraction of light

is the change in direction of a light ray as a result of its change in velocity when it passes from one transparent medium (air, glass, water) to another. If light travels from a less to a more dense medium (air to glass) it is slowed down and the light is refracted (bent) towards the normal line in the second medium.

• *Refraction of light* always obeys the two laws of refraction.

SEE ALSO **reflection of light**

	Laws of refraction
1.	The incident ray and refracted ray are on opposite sides of the normal line and are all in the same plane.
2.	The value of sin i/sin r is a constant for light passing from one medium to anohter (i = angle of incidence, r = angle of refraction).

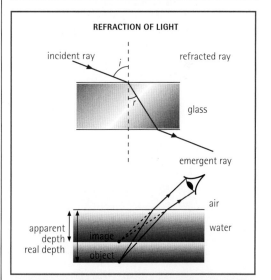

REFRACTION OF LIGHT

incident ray   refracted ray

glass

emergent ray

air

water

apparent depth
real depth

image

object

WORD BUILD

real and apparent depth

The refraction of light can account for a false impression of depth. For example, objects in water can appear closer than they are (the real depth is greater than the apparent depth).

relative atomic mass (*also* A$_r$)

is the average mass of a large number of atoms of a particular element. The relative atomic mass takes into account the percentage abundance of various isotopes of the element that may be present. For example, chlorine gas is 75% chlorine-35 atoms and 25% chlorine-37 atoms.

$$A_r = (\tfrac{75}{100} \times 35) + (\tfrac{25}{100} \times 37)$$
$$= 26.25 + 9.25$$
$$A_r = 35.5 \text{ (chlorine atom)}$$

SEE ALSO **isotope, relative formula mass**

relative density (*also* specific gravity)
is the density of a substance compared with the density of water.

$$\text{relative density} = \frac{\text{density of substance}}{\text{density of water}}$$

$$\text{relative density} = \frac{\text{mass of substance}}{\text{mass of same volume of water}}$$

• *Relative densities* have no units but indicate how much more or less dense a substance is than water.
SEE ALSO density, density bottle

relative formula mass (*also* M$_r$)
is the sum of all the relative atomic masses present in the chemical formula of the substance.
SEE ALSO relative atomic mass

Molecule	Calculation	M$_r$
water (H$_2$O)	H$_2$ + O (2 1) + (1 16) 2 + 16	18
calcium carbonate (CaCO$_3$)	Ca + C + O$_3$ (1×40) + (1×12) + (3×16) 40 + 12 + 48	100
glucose (C$_6$H$_{12}$O$_6$)	C$_6$ + H$_{12}$ + O$_6$ (6×12) + (12×1) + (6×16) 72 + 12 + 96	180
ammonium sulfate ((NH$_4$)$_2$SO$_4$)	N$_2$ + H$_8$ + S + O$_4$ (2×14) + (8×1) + (1×32) + (4×16) 28 + 8 + 32 + 64	132
copper sulfate crystals (CuSO$_4$.5H$_2$O)	Cu + S + O$_4$ + 5H$_2$O (1×63.5) + (1×32) + (4×16) + (5×(2+16)) 63.5 + 32 + 64 + 90	249.5

relay (*also* electrical relay)
A relay is a device which uses a small current in the coil of an electromagnet to switch on a large current in another independent circuit.
• *Relays* are safer than ordinary switches and have a wide range of uses in electrical and electronic circuits.
SEE ALSO electromagnet

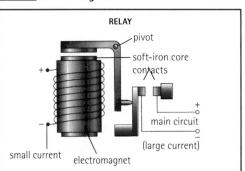

RELAY

pivot
soft-iron core
contacts
main circuit
(large current)
small current   electromagnet

relay neurone *see* neurone

renal artery
The renal artery is the artery that takes blood to the kidneys.
SEE ALSO artery, kidney, urinary system

renal pelvis *see* kidney

renal vein
The renal vein is the vein that takes blood away from the kidneys.
SEE ALSO kidney, urinary system, vein

renewable energy source *see* energy source

renewable resource
Renewable resources include plant and animal products such as food, crops, timber, and wood for fuel, and energy sources such as wind power and solar power.
• *It is important when harvesting renewable resources not to exceed their replacement rate, thus allowing natural restocking to take place.*
SEE ALSO energy source, non-renewable resource

replacement reaction *see* substitution reaction

replenishable energy source *see* energy source

replication (*also* genetic replication)
is the production of identical copies of DNA. The two strands separate, and nucleotides form a new strand by binding to the correct bases on a piece of single-stranded DNA.
SEE ALSO DNA, nucleotide

reproduction
is the process by which living organisms produce offspring.

asexual reproduction
is reproduction that involves only one parent. It occurs in lower animals, microorganisms and plants. Asexual reproduction is faster than sexual reproduction and when conditions are favourable many identical offspring can be produced.
SEE ALSO binary fission, budding, parthenogenesis

sexual reproduction
is a type of reproduction which involves the fusion of specialized male and female sex cells called gametes. This process is called fertilization.

Normally in animals it requires two parents, but in plants both male and female reproductive organs are often on the same parent. Sexual reproduction involves the mixing of genetic material from both parents. This helps to give variation to a species which increases the chances of survival if the environment changes.
SEE ALSO **fertilization, gamete**

vegetative reproduction (*also* vegetative propagation)

is asexual reproduction in plants in which part of the parent plant (called a perennating organ) is able to develop into a new plant. Examples of perennating organs are bulb, corm, rhizome, stolon (runner), and tuber.
SEE ALSO **stem**

reptile (*also* Reptilia)

Reptiles are cold-blooded vertebrates which lay soft-shelled eggs on land. Reptiles were the first class of vertebrate to live entirely on dry land. Their skin is covered by horny scales to prevent water loss. As they live on land, they breathe with lungs. Fertilization is internal and does not require water to transfer the sperm to the egg.
• *The class of reptiles includes snakes, lizards, crocodiles, turtles and tortoises, and the extinct dinosaurs.*
SEE ALSO **vertebrate animal**

residue

is the solid trapped in the filter during filtration. Residue may also describe what remains after other processes have occurred, such as evaporation or combustion.
SEE ALSO **filtrate, filtration**

resistance (*also* electrical resistance)

is the ability of a conductor to resist, or oppose, the flow of an electric current through it. All of the components in an electric circuit have a certain resistance to current. This makes the electrons lose some of the electrical energy which they carry. A bulb has a very high resistance and converts electrical energy into heat and light energy. A conductor's resistance depends on the type of material it is.
• *The resistance of a component decreases if the area of its cross-section is increased, but increases if its length increases.*
SEE ALSO **ohm, Ohm's law**

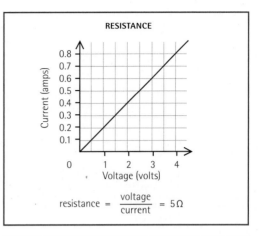

$$resistance = \frac{voltage}{current} = 5\,\Omega$$

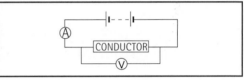

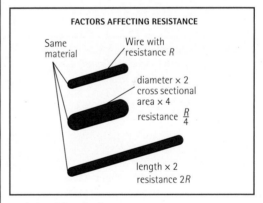

FACTORS AFFECTING RESISTANCE

Same material

Wire with resistance R

diameter × 2
cross sectional area × 4
resistance $\frac{R}{4}$

length × 2
resistance $2R$

resistant bacteria

can be formed when mutations of bacterial pathogens produce new strains. Such bacteria are resistant to antibiotics and so are not killed. They survive and reproduce. This results in more resistant bacteria so that people are not immune to the disease they carry. To reduce the development of antibiotic resistant strains, patients should complete their course of antibiotics so all the bacteria are killed and none mutate to form resistant strains. Also, doctors should not prescribe antibiotics inappropriately, such as treating viral infections or non-serious diseases.
• *Resistant bacteria are called 'super bugs'. MRSA (methicillin-resistant Staphylococcus aureus) is an example of one such super bug.*
SEE ALSO **antibiotic, pathogen**

resistor

A resistor is a component of an electrical circuit that is present because of its electrical resistance.
• *Resistors are often included in circuits to limit the current passing through components and reduce the danger caused by overheating.*
SEE ALSO **electrical circuit, resistance**

➤ **resistors in series** have a total combined resistance (R) which is equal to the sum of all the resistors in the circuit.

$$\underset{\text{(combined resistance)}}{R} = \underset{\text{(individual resistances)}}{R1 + R2 + R3}$$

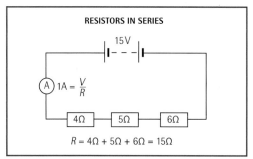

RESISTORS IN SERIES

15V

A $1A = \dfrac{V}{R}$

4Ω   5Ω   6Ω

$R = 4Ω + 5Ω + 6Ω = 15Ω$

➤ **resistors in parallel** have a total combined resistance (R) which can be calculated as follows:
total current = sum of all currents in parallel circuit

$$I = I_1 + I_2 + I_3$$

$$\frac{V}{R} = \frac{V}{R_1} + \frac{V}{R_2} + \frac{V}{R_3}$$

$$\text{so } \frac{1}{R} = \frac{1}{R_1} + \frac{1}{R_2} + \frac{1}{R_3}$$

The reciprocal of the combined resistance is the sum of the reciprocals of the individual resistances.

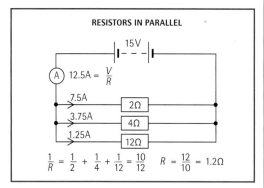

RESISTORS IN PARALLEL

15V

A $12.5A = \dfrac{V}{R}$

7.5A   2Ω

3.75A   4Ω

1.25A   12Ω

$\frac{1}{R} = \frac{1}{2} + \frac{1}{4} + \frac{1}{12} = \frac{10}{12}$ $R = \frac{12}{10} = 1.2Ω$

resolving power *see* **microscope**

resonance

occurs when a system is made to vibrate at its natural frequency by vibrations from another source of the same frequency. A glass can be made to resonate by the effect of sound waves such as a singer's voice at this frequency. When you flick a wine glass with your finger from the outside, it will vibrate and ring at its natural frequency.
• *Resonance can occur in mechanical and electrical systems as well as material objects.*
SEE ALSO **natural frequency**

respiration

is the release of energy in a living organism which occurs when simple products are made from the breaking down of food molecules.
• *Respiration occurs in all living cells all the time (cellular respiration).*
SEE ALSO **aerobic respiration, anaerobic respiration, cellular respiration, gaseous exchange**

respiratory surface

is the part of the respiratory organ through which gaseous exchange takes place. This surface should be thin so that gases can diffuse through quickly, and have a large surface area to speed up the gaseous exchange.
• *The respiratory surface is kept moist to improve diffusion, and has a rich supply of vessels.*
SEE ALSO **gaseous exchange, lung, respiration, stoma**

responsive material *see* **smart material**

retention factor (*also* Rf)

stands for retention factor and is a ratio for paper chromatography. It is calculated by dividing the distance a substance travels up the paper (measured to the centre of the spot) by the distance the solvent travels up the paper. A substance which has a strong attraction for the stationary phase has a low R_f value (wekk below the maximum value of 1).
SEE ALSO **chromatography**

retina

The retina is the layer of light-sensitive (photoreceptive) cells at the back of the eye. There are two types of receptor cell called rods and cones. These send information along the optic nerve to the brain. The brain then interprets the information from each receptor to build up an image.
SEE ALSO **cones, eye, fovea, rods**

reuse
is using an object again, normally after thoroughly cleaning the object. Reusing existing material (glass bottles, tin cans, clothing, etc.) increases sustainability of raw materials.
• *Reuse is one of the 3Rs (reduce, reuse, recycle) to achieve sustainability.*
SEE ALSO **recycle, reduce, sustainability**

reverberation
is the persistence of a sound for a longer period than normal. It occurs when the time taken for an echo to return back to the source is so short that the original and the reflected wave cannot be distinguished.
• *Reverberation in halls is a nuisance, as it makes speech and music indistinct. It can be reduced by using soft materials, such as curtains, carpets, thick cushions or seats, etc., to absorb the sound energy and minimize the echoes.*
SEE ALSO **echo, sound**

reversible process
is a term which commonly applies to physical changes which can be reversed by a change in conditions like temperature and pressure. If the process is a chemical reaction, then it is referred to as a reversible reaction.
• *Reversible processes include melting, boiling, dissolving, etc.*
SEE ALSO **reversible reaction**

reversible reaction
A reversible reaction is a chemical reaction in which the products react with one another to reform the original reactants, which then react to form products, and so on. Eventually a chemical equilibrium is reached.
SEE ALSO **chemical equilibrium, chemical reaction**

reversible sign
The sign ⇌ is used in the formulae of reversible reactions.
SEE ALSO **reversible reaction**

rhesus factor (*also* Rh factor)
The rhesus factor is an antigen which may be present in blood. If blood contains the rhesus antigen, it is rhesus positive (Rh+). If blood does not contain the rhesus antigen, it is rhesus negative (Rh–). Blood transfusions to Rh– people must not use blood which is Rh+.
• *The rhesus factor was first recognized in rhesus monkeys.*
SEE ALSO **antigen, blood group, blood transfusion**

rhizome *see* stem

rhombic sulfur *see* sulfur

rib cage
The human rib cage is made up of 12 pairs of ribs, forming the walls of the thorax or chest area and protecting the heart, lungs, etc. All the ribs are joined at the back to the thoracic vertebrae. The first seven pairs are also joined at the front to the sternum or breastbone, and the next three linked to it by cartilage. The last are small 'floating ribs'.
• *Movement of the rib cage in breathing is controlled by intercostal muscles.*
SEE ALSO **intercostal muscle, thorax, vertebra**

riboflavin *see* vitamin

ribosome *see* organelle

Richter scale
The Richter scale is a logarithmic scale of 1 to 10 used to compare the magnitude of earthquakes.
• *A value of 2 on the Richter scale can just be felt as a tremor. Values of 6 and above can cause damage to buildings.*
SEE ALSO **earthquake**

right-angled prism
Right-angled prisms use total internal reflection to turn the path of light through 90° or 180°.
• *Right-angled prisms are used in binoculars, periscopes, and cameras.*
SEE ALSO **prism, total internal reflection**

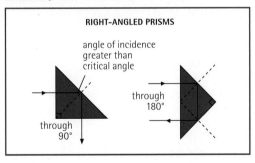

RIGHT-ANGLED PRISMS

ripple tank
A ripple tank is a shallow tank of water with a lamp above which casts shadows on a piece of paper underneath the tank. It is used to study the behaviour of waves. A vibrating bar or ball produces straight waves or circular waves respectively.
SEE ALSO **wave**

»

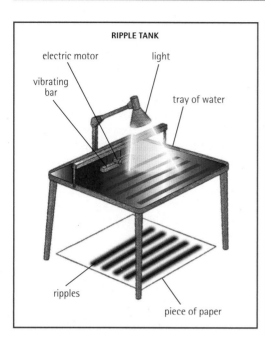

RIPPLE TANK

electric motor

light

vibrating bar

tray of water

ripples

piece of paper

rms value *see* **root mean square value**

RNA

stands for ribonucleic acid. RNA is a single-stranded nucleic acid. Its nucleotides differ from DNA in containing ribose (not deoxyribose), and uracil instead of thymine. Messenger RNA (mRNA) takes part in the copying (transcription) of the genetic code. Transfer RNA (tRNA) and ribosomal RNA (rRNA) take part in protein synthesis.
SEE ALSO **DNA, genetic code, nucleic acid, nucleotide**

rock

A rock is a mixture of mineral particles making up part of the Earth's crust. Rocks may be consolidated (e.g. flint, marble, and slate) or unconsolidated (e.g. sand, gravel, and clay).
• *Rocks can be classified into three main groups: igneous, sedimentary, and metamorphic.*
SEE ALSO **geology, mineral**

igneous rock

is formed when magma (hot molten rock) from the inside of the Earth's crust crystallizes. Such rocks are made up of randomly arranged crystals of a variety of different minerals.
• *The size of the crystals in the igneous rock depends on the rate of cooling of the magma.*
SEE ALSO **magma**

intrusive rock

is igneous rock which has been cooled slowly, usually below the Earth's surface. The rock only comes to the surface when the overlying rock has been removed by erosion.
• *Granite is a typical intrusive rock and has large crystals embedded in it.*
SEE ALSO **erosion**

extrusive rock

is igneous rock which has been cooled quickly on the Earth's surface, perhaps as the magma flowed into the sea. Such rock formed by quick cooling has small crystals embedded in it.
• *Basalt is a common, fine-grained extrusive rock.*
SEE ALSO **magma**

sedimentary rock

begins to form when existing rock is weathered and the fragments of the rock are deposited, often in the sea or a river. These rock sediments are then compressed and the water squeezed out, which causes any salts present to crystallize out. These salts then cement the particles together to form the sedimentary rock. Hardened layers of such rock are called strata. The grains of such rock are usually rounded, due to the past effect of water wearing away the jagged edges, for example sandstone and limestone.
SEE ALSO **crystallization, salt**

metamorphic rock

is rock formed by the action of intense heat (from the Earth's mantle) and pressure (from the rocks above) on sedimentary or igneous rock.
• *Metamorphic rocks are much harder than sedimentary rocks and their grains are usually lined up from the pressure of their formation, for example marble and slate.*
SEE ALSO **Earth's structure**

»

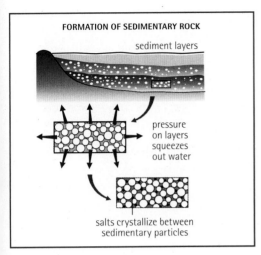

FORMATION OF SEDIMENTARY ROCK

sediment layers

pressure on layers squeezes out water

salts crystallize between sedimentary particles

rock cycle

The rock cycle shows how igneous rock over millions of years forms sedimentary rock or metamorphic rock which may eventually melt and resurface as igneous rock once again.

• *The rock cycle is driven by plate tectonic activity.*

SEE ALSO **plate tectonics, rock**

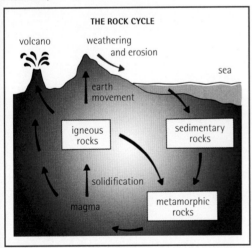

THE ROCK CYCLE

volcano   weathering and erosion   sea

earth movement

igneous rocks   sedimentary rocks

solidification

magma   metamorphic rocks

rock dating

By measuring the amount of radioactive isotope left in a rock sample, and knowing the half-life of the isotope, you can calculate how old the rock is.

• *Rock dating (radiometric dating) can be used to age fossils found in the rocks and help deduce rates of evolutionary change.*

SEE ALSO **carbon dating, radioisotope**

rock salt *see* **sodium chloride**

rods

are light-sensitive cells in the retina which are sensitive to quite dim light but not to colours.

• *Rod cells are more sensitive than cone cells and are almost entirely responsible for night vision.*

SEE ALSO **cones, eye, retina**

room temperature and pressure
(*also* **RTP**)

is the temperature of 25°C (298 K) and a pressure of 1 atmosphere (101,325 pascals).

• *One mole of any gas occupies a volume of 24.0 dm³ at room temperature and pressure.*

SEE ALSO **mole, standard temperature and pressure**

root

Roots are the lowest part of a plant, usually underground, whose functions are anchorage (secure fixing) and uptake of water and mineral salts.

• *Water is taken into the root by osmosis.*

SEE ALSO **osmosis, plant**

➤ **structure of the root** The growing point (meristem) of the root is just behind the root tip. This is protected by a root cap as it grows between the soil particles. In the piliferous (hairy) layer, which is the youngest growth area, there are long outgrowths from the outermost cells, called root hairs.

SEE ALSO **root hair**

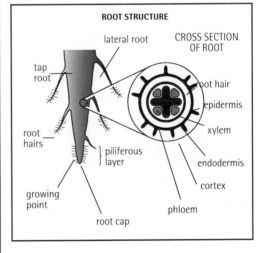

ROOT STRUCTURE

lateral root   CROSS SECTION OF ROOT

tap root   root hair

root hairs   epidermis

piliferous layer   xylem

endodermis

cortex

growing point   phloem

root cap

a
b
c
d
e
f
g
h
i
j
k
l
m
n
o
p
q
r
s
t
u
v
w
x
y
z

root hair

A root hair is an outgrowth from a single cell in the outer layer of a root, in the growth area behind the root tip.

• *Root hairs have a large surface area to volume ratio. They absorb water by osmosis and mineral salts by active transport.*

SEE ALSO **active transport, osmosis**

root mean square value (*also* rms value)

is the value of an alternating current which would give the same electrical power as a similar d.c. value.

SEE ALSO **alternating current**

rose black spot

is a fungal disease where purple or black spots develop on the leaves. The leaves become yellow and drop early, reducing photosynthesis.

• *Rose black spot can be treated using fungicides.*

SEE ALSO **fungus, photosynthesis**

roughage (*also* fibre)

is the part of food that cannot be digested. It is necessary for the proper working of the alimentary canal, and helps prevent appendicitis, constipation, obesity, and cancer of the bowels.

• *Foods rich in roughage include wholemeal cereals, nuts, fruit, and root vegetables.*

SEE ALSO **alimentary canal**

rounding

is the process of reducing the number of digits quoted in a particular reading. We can round up to a certain number of decimal places or of significant figures. The last digit required is increased by one if the digit following it is 5 or more. Too many digits in a value may be misleading if the measurement is not really as accurate as that.

• *9.352 rounded to two significant figures becomes 9.4.*

SEE ALSO **decimal place, significant figure**

round window (*also* fenestra rotunda)

The round window is a membrane-covered opening between the middle and inner ear.

• *Every time the oval window bulges inwards, the round window bulges outwards. This regulates changes in pressure of the liquid inside.*

SEE ALSO **inner ear, middle ear, oval window**

RTP *see* room temperature and pressure

rusting

is the corrosion of iron or steel to form hydrated iron(III) oxide $Fe_2O_3.xH_2O$. For rusting to occur, both air (oxygen) and water must be present.

iron + oxygen + water → hydrated iron (III) oxide

• *Rusting is a redox reaction as the iron loses electrons (oxidation) but the oxygen gains electrons (reduction).*

SEE ALSO **corrosion, oxidation, redox reaction**

Ss

S *see* **sulfur**

sacrificial protection

is a method of protecting a steel structure (bridge, underground pipe, etc.) by fastening to it a more reactive metal such as magnesium or zinc. The protecting metal is more reactive, and in a damp or wet environment loses electrons in preference to the iron. It is therefore used up and periodically has to be replaced. However, the iron does not rust, as it does not release electrons and is not oxidized.

SEE ALSO **corrosion**

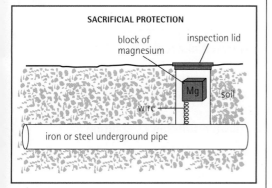

SACRIFICIAL PROTECTION

block of magnesium · inspection lid · Mg · soil · wire · iron or steel underground pipe

saliva

is a watery fluid secreted from the salivary glands in the mouth. Saliva contains mucus and an amylase enzyme (ptyalin) which breaks down starch into maltose.

• *Production of* **saliva** *is stimulated by food in the mouth or by the thought or smell of food.*

SEE ALSO **peristalsis, ptyalin**

salivary amylase *see* **ptyalin**

salmonella

is a bacterial disease spread by bacteria ingested in food or on food prepared in unhygienic conditions. The effects of this infection are vomiting, diarrhoea, and cramps.

• *Salmonella is the main cause of food poisoning.*

SEE ALSO **bacteria**

salt

Salts are chemical compounds formed when the hydrogen of an acid is partially or wholly replaced by a metal or other positive ion.

• *Typically, salts have ionic bonds and are normally formed by the reaction of an acid and base.*

SEE ALSO **acid radical, anhydrous, deliquescence, efflorescence, sodium chloride, water of crystallization**

ACID	+	BASE	→	SALT	+	WATER
sulfuric acid	+	copper oxide	→	copper sulfate	+	water

H_2SO_4 (aq) + CuO(s) → $CuSO_4$ (aq) + H_2O(l)

➤ **nomenclature of salts** If an acid ends in '-ic', then the salt has an ending '-ate' (except with hydrochloric acid), but if the acid has an ending '-ous' (in the old nomenclature), then the salt has an ending '-ite'.

SEE ALSO **acid, radical**

➤ **preparation of soluble salts** There are four ways to prepare soluble salts (see formula).

SEE ALSO **neutralization**

metal	+ acid →	salt + hydrogen
metal oxide	+ acid →	salt + water
metal carbonate	+ acid →	salt + water + carbon dioxide
metal hydroxide	+ acid →	salt + water

➤ **preparation of insoluble salts** involves the reaction between two dissolved ionic substances (e.g. salts or acids) which 'change partners' to form a new insoluble salt (and a soluble salt or acid).

SEE ALSO **double decomposition**

Soluble	Insoluble
all nitrates	(none)
most chlorides	Ag, Pb, Hg chlorides
most sulfides	Ca, Ba, Pb sulfates
Na, K, NH_4 carbonates	most carbonates

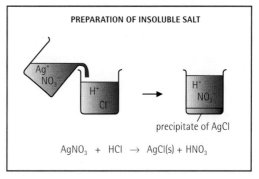

PREPARATION OF INSOLUBLE SALT

Ag^+ NO_3^- · H^+ Cl^- · H^+ NO_3^- · precipitate of AgCl

$AgNO_3$ + HCl → AgCl(s) + HNO_3

sand

is an impure form of quartz derived from the weathering` of quartz-bearing rock. Chemically it is mainly silicon dioxide (SiO_2). Most particles of sand have diameters in the range 0.06–2.00 mm. Sand is often yellow or red in colour due to iron(III) oxide. The element silicon can be extracted from a pure form of sand called 'white sand' by reduction with magnesium.

• *Sand is used in mortar, concrete, and in making glass.*

SEE ALSO **glass, quartz, reduction, silicon**

sandy soil *see* soil

saponification *see* fat

saprophyte (*also* saprotroph)

Saprophytes are organisms such as bacteria or fungi that feed on dead organic (plant or animal) matter. Bacteria help to break down protein and fungi break down cellulose.

• *Saprophytes are important in food chains as they bring about decay and release nutrients for plant growth.*

SEE ALSO **bacteria, decomposer, fungus**

satellite

❶ A satellite is a spacecraft or other artificial body put in orbit around a planet to collect information or transmit signals.

SEE ALSO **artificial satellite, communication satellite**

❷ A natural satellite is a moon or other celestial body orbiting a planet.

SEE ALSO **Moon, planet**

➤ **satellite in orbit** The gravitational pull (weight of satellite) provides the centripetal force needed to keep a satellite in a circular path around the Earth. For a satellite to stay in a particular orbit, it must travel at a certain speed. If it travels at less than this speed, it will spiral inwards towards Earth. If it travels at greater than this speed, it could escape the gravitational pull and go out into space.

• *For a satellite orbiting just above the atmosphere, the orbital speed is 8 km/s. The 'burn time' of the launch vehicle must be carefully controlled to ensure this speed.*

SEE ALSO **centripetal force**

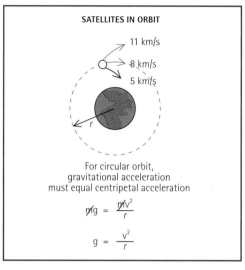

SATELLITES IN ORBIT

11 km/s
8 km/s
5 km/s

For circular orbit, gravitational acceleration must equal centripetal acceleration

$$m g = \frac{m v^2}{r}$$

$$g = \frac{v^2}{r}$$

saturated molecule

Saturated molecules contain only single covalent bonds (e.g. alkanes).

SEE ALSO **alkane, covalent bond, unsaturated molecule**

saturated solution *see* solution

Saturn *see* planet

scalar quantity

A scalar quantity is one which has magnitude (size), but not direction.

• *Examples of a scalar quanity are temperature, mass, density, energy, etc.*

SEE ALSO **vector quantity**

scapula *see* human skeleton

scavenger

A scavenger is an animal that eats dead animals (carrion) that it has not killed itself. Vultures, hyenas, and rats are scavengers.

• *Scavengers play an important role in an ecosystem by consuming dead animals.*

SEE ALSO **ecosystem**

science

is the systematic study of the natural and physical world through observation, experimentation, and analysis.

• *Science is not confined to the laboratory and shows itself in all aspects of our lives.*

SEE ALSO **scientific method**

scientific method (*also* scientific inquiry)
is the way scientists investigate and analyse the natural and physical world. It involves a step-by-step investigation, spilt into five stages.

scientific theory
A scientific theory is a scientific statement which is true under the condition or conditions stated. For example, 'the volume of a fixed mass of gas at constant pressure is directly proportional to its temperature' is Charles' law.

scientific variable
A scientific variable is something you change or control during a scientific experiment. Most experiments involve investigating the effect one scientific variable has on another scientific variable. Common examples of scientific variables are mass, volume, temperature, and time.
• *Scientific variables must be controlled or measured accurately during experiments.*
SEE ALSO **controlled variable, dependent variable, independent variable**

scintillation counter *see* radiation

sclerotic (*also* sclera)
The sclerotic is the tough white outermost layer of the eyeball.
• *The sclerotic encloses the choroid and retina and is continuous with the cornea.*
SEE ALSO **choroid, cornea, eye, retina**

sea salt *see* sodium chloride

season
Seasons are caused by the tilt of the Earth's axis as it orbits the Sun in an anticlockwise direction. The half of the Earth which is tilted towards the Sun will receive a greater concentration of Sun's energy per square metre.
• *On 21st June the northern Hemisphere is tilted towards the Sun, so the season is summer. In the southern Hemisphere on 21st June, the Sun's energy is spread over a larger area, so it is winter. The situation is reversed on 21st December.*
SEE ALSO **Earth's axis**

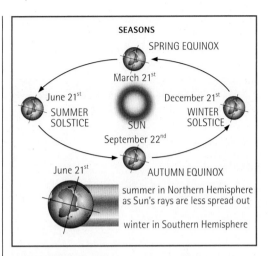

SEASONS
SPRING EQUINOX
March 21st
June 21st — SUMMER SOLSTICE
December 21st — WINTER SOLSTICE
SUN
September 22nd
June 21st — AUTUMN EQUINOX
summer in Northern Hemisphere as Sun's rays are less spread out
winter in Southern Hemisphere

sebaceous gland
The sebaceous gland is a gland alongside the hair follicle which secretes an oily liquid (sebum) to keep the hair and skin soft and supple.
• *Sebaceous glands only occur in the skin of mammals.*
SEE ALSO **hair follicle**

secondary atmosphere *see* atmosphere

secondary cell (*also* accumulator, storage battery)
A secondary cell is a voltaic cell which can be recharged by connecting it to another source of electricity. The chemical reactions taking place in a secondary cell are reversible.
• *Electric vehicle batteries are secondary cells and are typically lithium ion batteries.*
SEE ALSO **alkaline cell, car battery, primary cell, voltaic cell**

secondary coil *see* transformer

secondary colour *see* colour

secondary consumer *see* consumer

sedative *see* drug

sedimentary rock *see* rock

sedimentation *see* sewage

seed
A seed is a fertilized ovule together with its store of food. When the two gametes join together during fertilization, a zygote is formed. This divides by mitosis to form an embryo plant. This embryo and its

»

store of food is the seed. Most seeds have five parts: hilum, testa, cotyledon, plumule, and radicle.

SEE ALSO **embryo, fertilization, germination, mitosis, ovary, ovule, zygote**

WORD BUILD
hilum
A hilum is a scar on the seed showing where the ovule was attached to the ovary.
testa
A testa is a protective seed coat developed from the integuments.
cotyledon (*also* **seed leaf**)
A cotyledon is a store of food (starch and protein) for the developing plant. Cotyledons also contain enzymes.
plumule
A plumule is the primary bud inside the seed that will grow into the shoot of the new plant.
radicle
This develops into the first root of the new plant.

seed dispersal

is the scattering of seeds from a plant over a wide area to avoid overcrowding and competition from other plants. For wind dispersal, seeds need to be small and light, or have shaped fruits to carry them in the wind like the 'wings' of a sycamore or the 'parachute' of the dandelion. Seeds for animal dispersal may have hooked fruits to catch on animal fur, or succulent fruits and berries to be eaten by animals and birds. The seeds have a hard shell so they pass through an animal's digestive system unharmed. Some plants rely on self-dispersal in which the seeds are ejected from the dried seed cases.

• *Seed dispersal is essential for the continued survival of a plant species.*

seismic wave *see* earthquake

selective breeding *see* inbreeding

selective discharge *see* preferential discharge

selectively permeable membrane *see* semipermeable membrane

selective reabsorption *see* reabsorption

self-pollination *see* pollination

semen

is the fluid from the male reproductive organs which consists of sperm from the testes and seminal fluid from the prostate gland and seminal vesicle.

• *Semen also contains enzymes which activate the sperm after copulation.*

SEE ALSO **prostate gland, seminal vesicle, sperm, testis**

semicircular canal *see* inner ear

semiconductor

A semiconductor is a conductor whose electrical resistance decreases as the temperature rises. Semiconductors include metalloids like silicon, germanium, and their compounds (gallium arsenide). Conducting properties of these materials may be altered by introducing impurities ('doping') into their crystal structure.

• *Transistors, diodes, and other electronic components of integrated circuits and microprocessors are made from semiconductors.*

SEE ALSO **conductor, diode, metalloid, silicon chip, transistor**

semilunar valve

The semilunar valves in the heart are valves with crescent-shaped flaps which prevent backflow — one in the aorta, the other in the pulmonary artery.

SEE ALSO **aorta, pulmonary artery**

semimetal *see* metalloid

seminal vesicle

The seminal vesicle is one of a pair of glands close to the prostate gland which secrete a fluid into the semen.

• *The secretion from the seminal vesicle acts as a semipermeable source of energy (contains the sugar fructose) for the sperm.*

SEE ALSO **prostate gland, testis**

semipermeable membrane (*also* selectively permeable membrane)

A semipermeable membrane is a membrane which allows the molecules of water (solvent) to pass through, but not the molecules of most dissolved substances (solutes).

• *Osmosis can only occurs across a semipermeable membrane.*

SEE ALSO **osmosis**

sense organ (*also* sensory organ)

Sense organs allow animals to detect their environment. As well as eyes, ears, and noses, different animals have a variety of sense organs.

WORD BUILD

lateral line

The lateral line is a series of receptor cells along the sides of fish and some amphibians. It is sensitive to pressure changes and so detects sound and water currents.

palps

Palps are jointed sensory organs found by the mouth parts of arthropods which act as smell or taste receptors.

antennae *singular* antenna

Antennae are long, thin sense organs found on the heads of insects and many other arthropods. They are sensitive to touch, temperature, and chemicals.

tentacles

Tentacles are long, flexible body parts in many invertebrate animals, especially coelenterates and molluscs. They are often used to manipulate objects but are also sensitive to touch.

whiskers (*also* vibrissae)

Whiskers are stiff hairs sensitive to touch, found on the noses of many animals, e.g. cats and burrowing animals.
SEE ALSO **ear, eye, nose**

sense organs in the skin *see* skin

sensitivity (*also* irritability)

is the characteristic property of all living organisms to be able to detect, interpret, and respond to changes in their environment. Multicellular animals have specialized sense organs like the ears and eyes, and effector organs like muscles and glands. Simple unicellular organisms like amoeba have no nervous system and the reception and response to a stimulus occur in the same cell.
SEE ALSO **sense organ**

sensory neurone *see* neurone

sepal

A sepal is a small, protective, leaf-like structure found around a flower bud.
• *When the flower opens, the sepals may fall off or remain as a ring underneath the petals.*
SEE ALSO **calyx, flower**

separating funnel

A separating funnel is a funnel with a tap used to separate immiscible liquids such as oil and water. The lighter liquid (oil) collects above the heavier liquid (water). When the tap is opened, the water is run out, but the tap is closed before the oil reaches the bottom. Separation is never entirely complete.
SEE ALSO **immiscible**

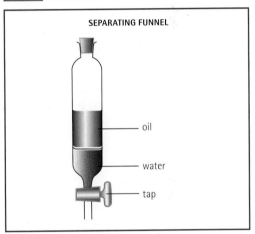

SEPARATING FUNNEL

oil

water

tap

sepsis

is a medical condition in which harmful bacteria are present in a wound.
• *Sepsis is treated with an antiseptic that kills or inhibits the growth of the harmful bacteria.*
SEE ALSO **antiseptic**

series circuit *see* electrical circuit

serum (*also* blood serum)

is blood which has had the cells and clotting substances removed but still contains specific antibodies. Often these serums are derived from non-human mammals.
• *Serum (blood plasma) with a specific antibody or antitoxin may be used in the treatment or prevention of certain infections.*
SEE ALSO **antibody, antitoxin**

sewage

is waste water from homes and factories which contains excretory waste (faeces, urine), used washing water, and surface water. Raw (untreated) sewage is a pollutant and must be treated before being discharged.

• *Sewage treatment involves filtration, sedimentation, digestion, and aeration.*

WORD BUILD

filtration

Filtration of sewage involves passing it through screens to remove floating debris and waste.

sedimentation

Sedimentation of sewage is carried out by leaving it in tanks so that tiny insoluble particles collect at the bottom as sludge.

digestion

Digestion in sewage treatment uses the action of bacteria in a 'sludge digester' to break down organic matter, producing methane gas and solid material ('sludge cake') which can be dried as fertilizer.

aeration

Aeration is the process by which clear water from the top of sedimentation tanks is sprayed over filter beds, where it dissolves oxygen from the air. Harmful anaerobic bacteria are killed, and useful aerobic bacteria multiply. The treated water is then returned to the nearest river or the sea.

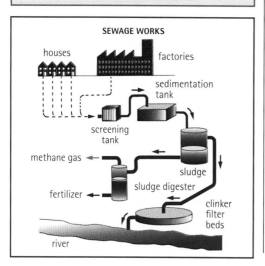

SEWAGE WORKS

houses — factories
sedimentation tank
screening tank
methane gas
sludge
sludge digester
fertilizer
clinker filter beds
river

sex cell *see* gamete

sex chromosome

The sex chromosomes are a pair of chromosomes, found in the nucleus of all cells. These sex chromosomes carry genes which control the development of sex organs and secondary sex characteristics.

• *There are two kinds of sex chromosome, the X-chromosome and Y-chromosome.*

SEE ALSO **chromosome, gamete**

		Male (XY)	
	Gametes	X	Y
Female (XX)	X	XX	XY
	X	XX	XY
		50% Female	50% Male

X-chromosome

X-chromosomes are the larger of the sex chromosomes. A female possesses a pair of these chromosomes (XX).

Y-chromosome

Y-chromosomes are the smaller of the sex chromosomes and cause male characteristics. A male possesses one of each sex chromosome (XY).

sex hormone

Sex hormones are hormones that control sexual development.

SEE ALSO **hormone**

WORD BUILD

androgen

Androgens are male sex hormones such as testosterone.

oestrogen

Oestrogens are female sex hormones such as oestrogen itself and progesterone.

sex linkage

In human males, a recessive gene carried on the X-chromosome will be expressed, because there is no corresponding allele present in the Y-chromosome to mask it (as the Y-chromosome is shorter). In females, the corresponding allele will be present on the other X-chromosome. It is for this reason that females are often carriers of recessive sex-linked disorders, whereas males show the disorder.

SEE ALSO allele, sex chromosome

sexual intercourse *see* copulation

sexually transmitted disease (*also* STD, venereal disease)

Sexually transmitted diseases are diseases that are passed from one individual to another during sexual intercourse. They include bacterial diseases such as gonorrhoea and syphilis, and viral diseases such as genital herpes and AIDS.

• *The transmission of **sexually transmitted diseases** can be reduced by limiting the number of sexual partners and by the use of condoms. Such devices reduce the risk of contact with body fluids (semen, blood, vaginal fluid) that harbour the microorganisms that cause these diseases.*

SEE ALSO AIDS, gonorrhoea, syphilis

sexual reproduction *see* reproduction

sf *see* significant figures

shadow

A shadow is an area of darkness on a surface. It is formed when an opaque object prevents light from a source from falling on that surface.

SEE ALSO opaque, penumbra, umbra

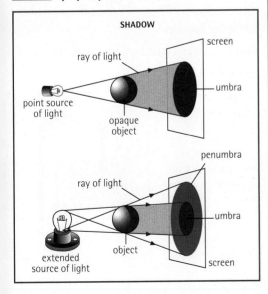

SHADOW

shadow zone *see* earthquake

shooting star *see* meteor

short-sightedness (*also* myopia)

is a vision defect which makes people able to focus clearly only on nearby objects.

• *The solution to **myopia** is to wear glasses or contact lenses with concave (diverging) lenses. These bend the rays outwards so that they focus on the retina and not in front of it.*

SEE ALSO lens, long-sightedness

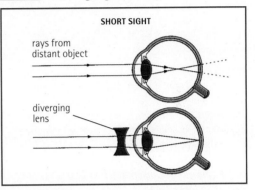

SHORT SIGHT

rays from distant object

diverging lens

shoulder girdle *see* pectoral girdle

Si *see* silicon

sickle cell anaemia

is a genetic disease in which abnormality of the haemoglobin causes red blood cells to become crescent-shaped. These carry little oxygen and get stuck in capillaries, causing blood clots.

• *Sickle cell anaemia* is caused by a recessive allele. If both parents are carriers, there is a 1 in 4 chance for each child that it will develop the disease.

SEE ALSO allele, genetic disease

sievert (*also* Sv)

A sievert is the SI unit for measuring dose equivalent to grays multiplied by a factor depending on the type of radiation and the kind of tissue being irradiated.

• *The sievert is named after the Swedish physicist Rolf Sievert (1896–1966).*

SEE ALSO gray, radioactive contamination

significant figure (*also* sf)

The number of significant figures in a value is the number of digits which express its value to a particular level of accuracy, ignoring any leading or trailing zeros and disregarding the position of the decimal.　　　　　　　　　　　　　　　　**»**

• *For example, the value 0.0012 has two **significant figures**. The zeroes do not add to the accuracy, but just indicate the size of the value.*

SEE ALSO **decimal place, rounding**

number	number of decimal places	number of significant figures
9.3925	4	5
9.393	3	4
9.39	2	3
9.4	1	2
9	0	1

silicate
Silicates are compounds of the elements silicon, oxygen, and a metal. Natural silicates form the main components of most clays and rocks. All silicate minerals are based on one fundamental structural unit - the SiO_4 tetrahedron.
• *Silicate minerals are classified according to how the tetrahedra are linked together and which metal ions are interspersed.*

SEE ALSO **asbestos, clay, glass, kaolin, rock, silicon**

silicon (*also* **Si**)
is the second element in group IV of the periodic table and is the second most abundant element in the Earth's crust (nearly 28%). Silicon is mainly found combined with oxygen in the form of silicon dioxide in quartz and sand. It also occurs in the form of silicates in many rocks and clays. Most compounds of silicon are giant 3D structures. The element silicon is often described as a metalloid, as its properties are intermediate between metals and non-metals. Most of its compounds are covalent.
• *Silicon can exist as a hard, shiny solid which conducts electricity.*

SEE ALSO **covalent bond, metalloid, periodic table, quartz, sand, rock, silicon**

silicon chip (*also* **microchip**)
A silicon chip is a thin wafer of very pure semiconducting silicon which has miniature electronic circuits printed onto it. Silicon chips are extensively used in most electronic systems. They are made by slowly cooling very pure molten silicon. The first crystals to form during this recrystallization process are very pure and are therefore ideal for use as silicon chips.
• *A silicon chip (1 cm in size) can hold hundreds of thousands of electronic circuits.*

SEE ALSO **electronic system**

silicone
Silicones are polymers containing chains of silicon atoms alternating with oxygen atoms, with organic alkyl groups linked to the silicon atoms. Silicone polymers are very water-repellent (like silicon grease) and fire-resistant (unlike normal carbon polymers, they produce no toxic fumes).
• *Smaller silicone molecules are clear, oily liquids and are used in cosmetic creams and paints. Larger molecules form rubbery solids or waxes, some of which are used by surgeons for replacement skin and breast enlargement (silicone implants).*

SEE ALSO **polymer, silicon**

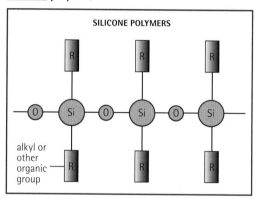

SILICONE POLYMERS

alkyl or other organic group

simple cell *see* **primary cell**

simple distillation *see* **distillation**

sinew *see* **tendon**

single covalent bond *see* **covalent bond**

sinking *see* **floating**

siphon
A siphon is an inverted U-tube with one end longer than the other, which moves a liquid from one place to another place at a lower level.
• *For the **siphon** to work, the tube must be full of liquid before it is placed in position.*

SEE ALSO **pressure**

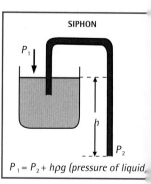

SIPHON

P_1

h

P_2

$P_1 = P_2 + h\rho g$ (pressure of liquid,

SI units (also Système International d'Unités)

are the international system of units recommended for all scientific work. This system of units is derived from the m.k.s. units (metre, kilogram, second) and has now replaced the similar c.g.s. units (centimetre, gram, second) and the imperial units. There are seven base units. There are also two supplementary units and 18 other derived units, each with its own special name.

• *Each SI unit has its own symbol (usually one or two letters). Decimal multiples of the units are indicated by prefixes.*

SEE ALSO **base unit, prefix**

➤ **conventions for units and symbols** The names of units are not written with a capital letter even if they are named after people, but if a symbol is a capital letter it must always be so written. A full stop is not used after a unit symbol (except at the end of a sentence) and there is no plural form of a unit symbol, e.g. 30 N or 40 kg. When writing numbers with SI units the digits are arranged in groups of three, with a space placed between each group, e.g. 657 541.37 m.

Physical quantity	Name of SI unit	symbol	Named after
current	ampere	A	French physicist Andre Ampère (1775–1836)
radioactivity	bequerel	Bq	French physicist Henri Becquerel (1852–1908)
electric charge	coulomb	C	French physicist Charles de Coulomb (1736–1806)
capacitance	farad	F	English scientist Michael Faraday (1791–1867)
frequency	hertz	Hz	German physicist Heinrich Hertz (1857–96)
energy (work)	joule	J	English physicist James Prescott Joule (1818–89)
temperature	kelvin	K	English scientist Lord Kelvin (1824–1907)
force	newton	N	English scientist Sir Isaac Newton (1642–1727)
resistance	ohm	Ω	German physicist Georg Ohm (1787–1854)
pressure	pascal	Pa	French physicist Blaise Pascal (1623–62)
power	watt	W	English engineer James Watt (1736–1819)

➤ **conversion factors to SI units** Although in all science exams SI units will be used, it is sometimes useful to be able to convert other units into SI units.

From	To	Multiply by
inch	metre	2.54×10^{-2}
foot	metre	0.3048
square foot	square metre	2.54×10^{-2}
litre	metre cubed	10^{-3}
gallon	litre	4.54609
miles/hr	metres/second	0.47704
km/hr	metre/second	0.27728
pound	kilogram	0.453592
g/cm^3	kg/m^3	10^3
horsepower	watt	745.7
mm Hg	pascal	133.322
atmosphere	pascal	1.01325×10^5
kW hour	joule	3.6×10^6
calorie	joule	4.1868

skeleton

A skeleton is a structure in an animal that provides support for the body, protection for internal organs, and a framework for anchoring muscles and ligaments.

• *The skeleton of higher vertebrates consists of a system of bones.*

SEE ALSO **endoskeleton, exoskeleton, human skeleton, hydrostatic skeleton**

skin

The skin is the organ which makes up the outermost layer of the body. It is the largest human organ, which in an adult covers about 2 m^2. The skin contains many different structures and has a variety of important functions, as listed in the table.

• *The skin and its blood vessels play a major role in controlling the amount of heat which is lost from the body and maintaining a constant body temperature.*

SEE ALSO **homeostasis**

Function of the skin	
Protection	Outermost layer is tough and waterproof. It protects the body from injury, water loss, and infection.
Sensitivity	Nerve endings in the skin can detect pain, temperature, and pressure.
Homeostasis (water and temperature)	Sweat glands control water loss and help maintain body temperature.

»

| Storage | Fat deposits are stored in the fatty tissue under the skin. |
| Vitamin production | Vitamin D is produced from the action of sunlight on a cholesterol derivative found in the skin. |

➤ **structure of the skin** Human skin is made of two main layers, called the epidermis and dermis.
SEE ALSO **dermis, epidermis**

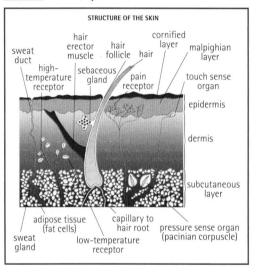

STRUCTURE OF THE SKIN

➤ **sense organs in the skin** There are various nerve endings to different sense organs in all layers of the skin. In the epidermis are pain receptors, in the dermis are high and low temperature receptors, and in the subcutaneous layer are pressure receptors.
SEE ALSO **dermis, epidermis, subcutaneous layer**

skin cancer
can be caused by excessive ultraviolet radiation from the Sun which can damage the DNA in skin cells. This results in cancerous growth (carcinoma) of the skin cells.
• *Melanoma is the most serious type of skin cancer as it is malignant (can spread to other parts of the body).*
SEE ALSO **ultraviolet radiation**

skull
The skull is the skeleton of the head, consisting of the cranium and bones of the face and jaw. Most of the bones in the skull are fused together at immovable joints called sutures. The only bone that can move is the mandible or lower jaw, which is fixed by a hinge joint to the rest of the skull.
SEE ALSO **cranium, human skeleton**

slide projector
A slide projector contains a convex lens which forms a magnified, inverted, real image of a photographic slide (put into the projector upside down) on a screen. The slide must be positioned between the centre of curvature and the focal point of the convex lens.
SEE ALSO **centre of curvature, focal point, image, lens**

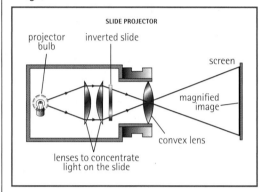

SLIDE PROJECTOR

sliding joint *see* joint

small intestine
The small intestine is the portion of the alimentary canal between the stomach and the large intestine.
• *The small intestine consists of two sections called the duodenum and ileum.*
SEE ALSO **alimentary canal, large intestine**

WORD BUILD
duodenum
The duodenum is the first section of the small intestine and is the main site for the digestion of food. *SEE ALSO* **digestion**
ileum
The ileum is the final section of the small intestine and is the main site of absorption of food through the villi. *SEE ALSO* **absorption, villus**

smart material (*also* **responsive material**)
A smart material is an artificial material which reacts to changes in the environment such as stress, pH, moisture, light, heat, or electric or magnetic fields. The response of smart materials is reversible and can be repeated many times.

• *Smart materials include shape memory alloys, shape memory polymers, packaging (e.g. shrink wrap), and hydrogels.*

SEE ALSO **hydrogel, smart plastic**

smart plastic (*also* smart polymer)

A smart plastic is one that can respond to a particular stimulus such as light, pH, temperature, moisture, etc.

• *Smart plastics are used for biodegradable packaging to help reduce plastic pollution.*

SEE ALSO **biodegradable, plastic, pollution**

smelting

is the process of separating a metal from its ore by heating the ore in a furnace with a suitable reducing agent such as coke (carbon). Usually limestone is added as a fluxing agent to remove impurities such as sand.

SEE ALSO **blast furnace, extraction of metals, reducing agent**

smokeless zone

Smokeless zones are areas of towns and cities where only special smokeless fuels (not coal or wood) are allowed to be burnt, to reduce air pollution.

• *Smokeless zones reduce the particulate matter released into surrounding air.*

SEE ALSO **air pollution, particulate matter**

smoking

There is now definite evidence that smoking cigarettes can seriously damage your health by causing heart disease, high blood pressure, and lung diseases (bronchitis, emphysema, and lung cancer).

The main harmful components of cigarette smoke are nicotine, tar, irritants and carbon monoxide.

SEE ALSO **passive smoking**

WORD BUILD

nicotine

Nicotine is an addictive stimulant which increases blood pressure and makes your heart beat faster.

tar

Tar contains thousands of different chemicals, some of which are carcinogenic (cancer-causing).

irritants

These are chemicals that irritate the lungs and damage the lining of its passages. Irritants also reduce the sense of taste and smell and can cause ulcers in the stomach.

carbon monoxide

Carbon monoxide is a poisonous gas which combines with the haemoglobin in the blood in preference to oxygen. It therefore lowers the oxygen content of the blood and body cells. Smoking during pregnancy increases the possibility that babies will be underweight or stillborn.

smooth muscle *see* muscle

snake

A snake is a vertebrate reptile with no limbs. It is cold-blooded and lays soft-shelled eggs on land.

• *Snakes breathe with lungs and their skin is covered with horny scales to prevent water loss.*

SEE ALSO **reptile**

soapless detergent *see* detergent

socio-economic factors

All industrial processes are influenced by their effects on society, and the economic restrictions needed to make a profit.

• *Socio-economic factors may include the cost of raw materials, the site, and the energy needed; the availability of labour, transport and communication facilities; the percentage yields; the risk of pollution and other environmental effects; and the possibility of recycling.*

sodium (*also* Na)

is a chemical element (symbol Na) in Group I (alkali metals) of the periodic table. It is a soft, silvery-white metal.

• *Sodium is a reactive metal especially with air (oxygen), water and acids.*

SEE ALSO **alkali metal, periodic table, reactivity series**

➤ **uses of sodium** Sodium is the only alkali metal used on a commercial scale: the others are too expensive or too reactive. Sodium is a much better thermal conductor than water and does not boil until 892°C. Molten sodium is therefore a very good liquid coolant (in the absence of air and water). It is used as such in certain types of nuclear reactor. Sodium vapour in street lamps gives them a characteristic yellow colour. Because sodium is so reactive, it can be used in the extraction of less reactive metals from their salts. One such displacement reaction is used to extract titanium metal:
                                                          »

titanium chloride	+	sodium	→	titanium	+	sodium chloride
TiCl4	+	4Na	→	Ti	+	4NaCl

SEE ALSO **reactivity series**

sodium carbonate *see* washing soda

sodium chloride (*also* common salt, table salt, rock salt, sea salt)

is the commonest and most important salt with a chemical formula of NaCl. It is extracted from sea water, which contains about 2.7% by mass, by leaving shallow pools of sea water to evaporate in the sun. It can also be extracted from underground deposits of rock salt by pumping water underground to dissolve the salt. The concentrated salt solution (brine) is then pumped to the surface and left to evaporate.

• *Sodium chloride is used for preserving and seasoning food and for de-icing roads.*

SEE ALSO **brine, metal compound**

soft magnetic material *see* magnetic material

soft water

is water that is easy to lather with soap, as it has few dissolved calcium and magnesium ions. The 'softest' water of all is distilled water and 'deionized water'.

• *Soft water occurs naturally when rainwater falls onto impervious rock.*

SEE ALSO **distilled water, hard water**

soil

is the mixture of tiny rock fragments, minerals, and decomposed organic matter that forms the layer of material in which plants grow.

SEE ALSO **bacteria, bedrock, humus, subsoil, topsoil**

➤ **type of soil** The type of soil depends upon the original bedrock it came from, and the amount of humus and minerals it contains. For healthy plant growth, soils should be rich in humus and minerals. The soil should crumble easily so it can trap air, but it should also be able to hold water. Although no two soils are exactly the same, we can classify soils into three broad categories according to the average size particle they contain: clay soils, sandy soils, and loamy soils.

➤ **pH of the soil** Particular soils have their own pH, depending on the type of parent rock and the amount and condition of the humus. Waterlogged soils such as peat are acidic, as the bacteria cannot

get enough oxygen to decompose the plants properly. Clayey soils are often boggy soils with a pH between 4 and 5.5. Limestone soils are alkaline with a pH of around 8 due to the presence of calcium ions. Most plants grow best in a very slightly acidic pH of 6.5.

SEE ALSO **pH**

clay soil

is heavy soil which contains small particles (less than 0.002 mm in size) which can be packed tightly together. This results in small air spaces (good capillarity) between the particles. There is poor drainage in wet conditions, and the soil easily becomes waterlogged. In dry weather it forms cracks. Clay particles have small electrical charges which attract minerals such as potassium or calcium ions. Clay soils are therefore rich in minerals, as they are attracted to the soil particles and are not easily leached from the soil.

SEE ALSO **capillarity**

loamy soil

is a fertile soil made up of a mixture of sand and clay, with plenty of organic matter or humus. The best loamy soils contain 50% clay, 30% sand, and 20% humus. The balance is ideal for plant growth. It will hold water and minerals but will not become waterlogged too easily.

sandy soil

is light soil which contains large particles (diameters in the range 0.06-2.00 mm) which cannot therefore be packed closely together. This causes large air spaces (poor capillarity) between the particles, which results in good drainage.

SEE ALSO **capillarity**

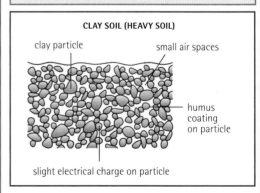

CLAY SOIL (HEAVY SOIL)

clay particle

small air spaces

humus coating on particle

slight electrical charge on particle

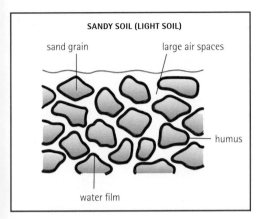

SANDY SOIL (LIGHT SOIL)

sand grain   large air spaces

humus

water film

soil formation
occurs when rocks are broken down by physical or chemical weathering. Physical weathering produces tiny rock fragments of different sizes. Chemical weathering dissolves minerals from the rock fragments to produce clays and soluble mineral salts. Decomposition of organic matter produces humus in the soil.

SEE ALSO **humus, weathering**

soil profile
A soil profile is a vertical section through the soil to show the different layers. Such layers are sometimes called 'horizons'. For example, topsoil is horizon A but bedrock is horizon C.

SEE ALSO **bedrock, subsoil, topsoil**

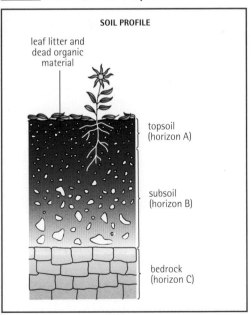

SOIL PROFILE

leaf litter and dead organic material

topsoil (horizon A)

subsoil (horizon B)

bedrock (horizon C)

sol *see* colloid

solar activity
refers to the various disturbances on the Sun's surface and surrounding space. If solar activity increases, it often results in the formation of solar flares and solar winds. A lack of activity on the Sun can result in a localized fall in temperature to create dark areas called sunspots.
• *Solar activity often forms a pattern over an eleven-year cycle.*

SEE ALSO **solar flare, solar wind, Sun, sunspot**

solar eclipse *see* eclipse

solar energy
is energy from the Sun, mainly in the form of light and heat radiation. The Sun's rays may be used directly to heat water in a solar panel, or focused by a curved mirror to a single point in a solar furnace.
• *Photocells (solar cells) can be used to change solar energy (sunlight) into electrical energy.*

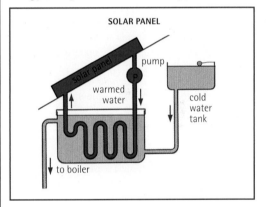

SOLAR PANEL

solar panel

pump

warmed water

cold water tank

to boiler

solar flare
A solar flare is a burst of hot material that shoots out from the Sun into space. Some solar flares are 400,000 km in length.
• *Solar flares affect radio communication on Earth.*

solar storm
A solar storm is when activity on the Sun interferes with the Earth's magnetic field. Such activity on the Sun can result in solar flares and a massive burst of solar wind.
• *Solar storms can affect communications and power infrastructure on Earth.*

SEE ALSO **Earth's magnetic field, solar flare, solar wind, Sun**

a b c d e f g h i j k l m n o p q r s t u v w x y z

solar system

The solar system is our Sun and the eight major planets that orbit around it: Mercury, Venus, Earth, Mars, Jupiter, Saturn, Uranus, and Neptune. The solar system also includes moons of planets, and also asteroids and comets.

• *The Sun accounts for over 99% of the mass of the solar system, and Jupiter for more than half of the rest.*

solar wind

The solar wind consists of charged particles that stream out from the Sun all the time but whose intensity varies with the month or time of year.

• *As the solar wind sweeps past the Earth, it distorts magnetic fields and causes radio interference. It also causes the aurora.*

SEE ALSO aurora

solder *see* alloy

solenoid

A solenoid is a long cylindrical coil of insulated wire. A current flowing through a solenoid produces a magnetic field which is similar to that produced by a bar magnet. The position of the poles depends on the direction of the current.

• *The magnetic field of a solenoid can be increased by increasing the current and/or the number of turns of conducting wire.*

SEE ALSO coil, electromagnet

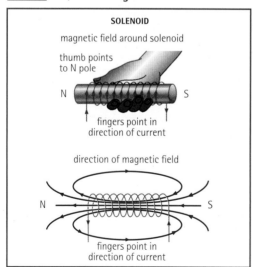

SOLENOID

magnetic field around solenoid

thumb points to N pole

N   S

fingers point in direction of current

direction of magnetic field

N   S

fingers point in direction of current

solid

A solid is the physical state of matter in which the particles are close together and vibrating about a fixed position.

• *A solid is a basic state of matter (along with liquid and gas) with both melting point and boiling point above room temperature.*

SEE ALSO melting point, state of matter

solstice

A solstice is the time of year when either the day or the night are at their longest. In the Northern Hemisphere the summer solstice occurs on June 21st and the winter solstice on December 21st. The dates are reversed for the Southern Hemisphere.

SEE ALSO equinox

solubility

The solubility of a solute in water, at a particular temperature, is the maximum amount that will dissolve in a given volume of water at that temperature.

• *Normally the volume of water is 100 cm³ (100 g), so the units of solubility are g/100 g of water.*

SEE ALSO solute

➤ **solubility of gases** The solubility of gases normally decreases as the temperature increases. When a liquid boils, all dissolved gases are expelled.

solubility curve

A solubility curve is a graph to show how the solubility of a solute changes with temperature. With most solid solutes, the solubility increases with temperature, although with some, like sodium chloride, there is little change. If there is a noticeable increase in solubility with temperature, then hot solutions can be made to crystallize out their solute on cooling.

SEE ALSO solute

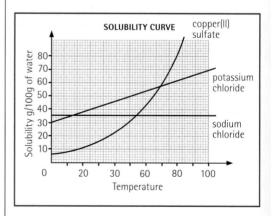

SOLUBILITY CURVE   copper(II) sulfate

potassium chloride

sodium chloride

Solubility g/100g of water: 80, 70, 60, 50, 40, 30, 20, 10

Temperature: 0, 20, 30, 60, 80, 100

soluble

describes a substance (solute) that will dissolve in a liquid (solvent) to form a solution.

• *The particles of the soluble substance are spread about and surrounded by solvent particles, therefore becoming invisible to the human eye.*

SEE ALSO **insoluble, solute, solvent**

solute

A solute is a substance which dissolves in a solvent to form a solution.

• *Salt water has water as the solvent and common salt as the solute.*

SEE ALSO **solvent**

solution

A solution is a homogeneous mixture in which the particles of solute and solvent are evenly spread out.

solution = solute + solvent

SEE ALSO **buffer solution, mixture, molar solution, solute, solvent**

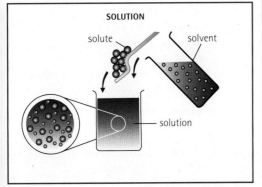

SOLUTION

solute

solvent

solution

aqueous solution

An aqueous solution is one where the solvent is water.

• *In chemical equations aqueous solutions are marked (aq).*

saturated solution

A saturated solution is one which will not dissolve any more solute at a particular temperature.

Solvay process

The Solvay process is used for the industrial manufacture of sodium hydrogen carbonate and sodium carbonate by bubbling ammonia and carbon dioxide gases through concentrated salt water.

$NaCl + H_2O + NH_3 + CO2 \rightarrow \quad NH_4CL + NaHCO_3$

salt water $\rightarrow$ sodium hydrogen carbonate

solvent

A solvent is a substance, normally a liquid, which is used to dissolve other substances (solutes).

• *The resulting mixture of solvent and solute is called a solution.*

SEE ALSO **solute, solution**

polar solvent

A polar solvent is a liquid (e.g. water) which has polar molecules. In water, the oxygen atom in the molecule is better at attracting electrons from the covalent bonds than the hydrogen atoms. The oxygen side therefore becomes negatively charged, whereas the hydrogen side becomes positively charged.

• *Polar solvents normally dissolve ionic compounds such as common salt.*

SEE ALSO **ionic bond, polarization**

non-polar solvent

A non-polar solvent is a liquid which has non-polar molecules.

• *Non-polar solvents normally dissolve covalent compounds and are often organic liquids such as hexane and tetrachloromethane.*

SEE ALSO **covalent bond**

WATER IS A POLAR SOLVENT

slight negative charge of oxygen atoms is attracted to positive charge on the rod

stream of water attracted to charged rod

solvent abuse

is the inhaling of volatile solvents found in aerosols, sprays, glues, cleaning fluids, nail-varnish removers, etc. These solvents can make the users become intoxicated. They are addictive, and regular

»

inhalation can cause brain damage and kidney and liver failure.

• *Solvent abuse in young people is becoming a serious social problem.*

sonar

stands for **SO**und **NA**vigation **R**anging. Sonar is a system which uses ultrasound for echolocation to detect underwater objects or to determine the depth of the water.

SEE ALSO **echolocation, ultrasound**

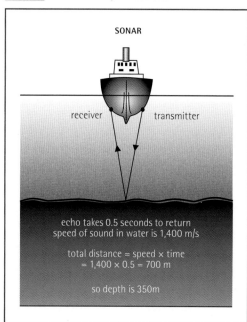

SONAR

receiver   transmitter

echo takes 0.5 seconds to return
speed of sound in water is 1,400 m/s

total distance = speed × time
= 1,400 × 0.5 = 700 m

so depth is 350m

sonic boom

A sonic boom is the loud bang caused by the shock wave produced by an aircraft travelling at supersonic speeds. At supersonic speeds the aircraft overtakes its own sound waves. This causes a build-up of pressure on the front of the aircraft which is unable to escape. This is the shock wave which a listener hears as a sudden loud sonic boom. The loudness depends on the speed and altitude.

• *Aircraft flying over land must not travel faster than the speed of sound (subsonic) so produce no* **sonic boom.**

SEE ALSO **supersonic**

sonometer

A sonometer is an apparatus for investigating stretched wires or strings as sources of sound.

SEE ALSO **sound**

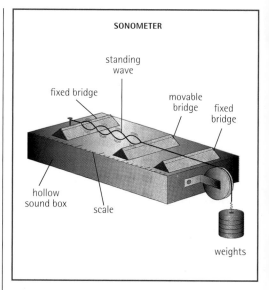

SONOMETER

standing wave

fixed bridge

movable bridge   fixed bridge

hollow sound box   scale

weights

sonorous *see* **metal**

soot *see* **carbon black**

sound

is a progressive longitudinal wave caused by the vibration of an elastic medium such as air.

SEE ALSO **longitudinal wave, loudness, medium, pitch, progressive wave, sound wave**

➤ **quality of sound** (*also* **timbre**) The quality or 'timbre' of a sound is a result of the harmonics which are present. Middle C played on a piano has a different sound to Middle C played on a guitar because of the different harmonics.

SEE ALSO **harmonic**

➤ **speed of sound** The speed of sound depends upon the density and temperature of the medium. Sound waves cannot travel in a vacuum because there is no material (medium) to vibrate. In general, sound travels fastest in solids, slower in liquids, and slowest in gases. This is because the particles in solids are closest together, so the vibrations of the sound are passed on more rapidly. The speed of sound in air increases with temperature, but is unaffected by pressure.

• *The speed of sound is about a million times slower than the speed of light, which is why you see lightning before you hear thunder.*

SEE ALSO **density, medium**

Medium	Density (g cm^{-3})	Speed of sound (at 0°C)
air	0.001	330 m/s
water	1	1,400 m/s
brick	3.6	3,700 m/s
concrete	7.8	5,000 m/s

sound wave

Sound waves consist of compressions and rarefactions caused in a medium when it is disturbed by a vibrating object. They are normally drawn as a series of wavefronts which mark the regions of compression of the wave. The distance between each wavefront is the wavelength of the sound.

SEE ALSO **wavelength**

WORD BUILD

compression

is the squashing together of particles in a medium as a longitudinal wave (like sound) passes through.

SEE ALSO **longitudinal wave**

rarefaction

is the spreading apart of particles in a medium as a longitudinal wave (like sound) passes through.

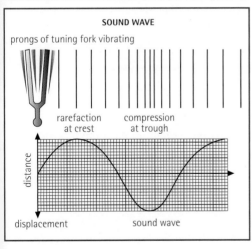

SOUND WAVE

prongs of tuning fork vibrating

rarefaction at crest   compression at trough

distance

displacement   sound wave

southern lights *see* **aurora**

south pole *see* **magnetic pole**

south-seeking pole *see* **magnetic pole**

space

is everything outside of the Earth's atmosphere. Most of space is a vacuum.

• *Space probes have left our solar system and are exploring* **space** *between the stars.*

SEE ALSO **vacuum**

species

A species is a group containing living organisms of the same kind. Members of a species may breed with one another, but normally cannot breed with members of another species. The table shows the approximate number of different species of invertebrate animals there are.

• *Rarely, very closely related* **species** *interbreed to produce a hybrid.*

SEE ALSO **binomial classification, biological classification, genus, hybrid**

Invertebrate animal	Number of species
protozoans	30,000
cnidarians	10,000
platyhelminths	25,000
annelids	14,000
arachnids	60,000
crustaceans	39,000
myriapods	13,000
insects	1,000,000
molluscs	100,000
vertebrates	46,000

specific gravity *see* **relative density**

specific heat capacity (*also* c)

is the heat energy absorbed or released when 1 kg of a substance changes its temperature by 1 K. The SI unit of specific heat capacity is joule per kilogram per kelvin or J/(kg.K).

• *Water has a* **specific heat capacity** *of 4,200 J/(kg.K). To raise the temperature of 1 kg of water by 1 K (1°C) requires 4,200 J (4.2 kJ) to be gained.*

SEE ALSO **heat capacity, heat energy**

»

Material	Specific heat capacity (Jkg^{-1}K^{-1})
water	4,200
meths	2,500
ice	2,100
concrete	800
glass	700
steel	500
copper	400
mercury	150

specific latent heat of fusion
see **latent heat**

specific latent heat of vaporization
see **latent heat**

spectral colours see **colour**

speed
is the rate at which an object moves, expressed as distance travelled in a certain time.

$$\text{speed (m/s)} = \frac{\text{distance (m)}}{\text{time (s)}}$$

• *Speed is a scalar quantity as it has size but no direction.*

SEE ALSO **scalar quantity, velocity**

speed of light see **light**

speed of sound see **sound**

sperm (also **spermatozoon**) plural spermatozoa
is the male gamete of animals. It consists of a head containing the genetic material and a tail (flagellum) for movement.

• *In male mammals **sperm** is produced in the testis.*

SEE ALSO **gamete, testis**

spherical aberration
is the production of an optical image which is not sharp because the edges of the lens focus in slightly different positions from the centre of the lens.

• *When taking pictures with a camera **spherical aberration** must be minimized.*

SEE ALSO **chromatic aberration, lens**

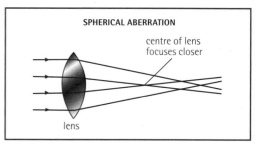

SPHERICAL ABERRATION

centre of lens focuses closer

lens

spider
A spider is an arachnid as it is an eight-limbed invertebrate with two parts to its body.

• *Spiders cannot sting but have poisonous fangs to kill their prey.*

SEE ALSO **arachnid**

spinal column see **vertebral column**

spinal cord
The spinal cord is that part of the central nervous system which runs down from the brain and is enclosed within the vertebral column (spine). It consists of nervous tissue which is connected to receptors and effectors in the other parts of the body.

• *The **spinal cord** is involved in reflex or involuntary actions.*

SEE ALSO **central nervous system, effector, involuntary action, receptor, reflex action, vertebral column**

spinal reflex see **reflex action**

spine see **vertebral column**

spirillum see **bacteria**

spongy bone see **bone**

spongy mesophyll see **mesophyll layer**

sporangium
A sporangium is the reproductive structure in a fungus which produces spores.

SEE ALSO **fungus, spore**

spore
A spore is a tiny reproductive cell of plants such as fungi, bacteria, ferns, and mosses.

• *Spores, because of their small size, are normally dispersed by the wind.*

SEE ALSO **fungus**

spring tide see **tide**

stability *see* **equilibrium**

stability of metal compounds
see **reactivity series**

stable equilibrium *see* **equilibrium**

stainless steel
is an alloy of iron 74%, chromium 18%, and nickel 8%, which is resistant to corrosion.
• *Stainless steel is commonly used in making cutlery, chemical plant equipment, and surgical instruments.*
SEE ALSO **alloy**

stalactite
A stalactite is a downward projection from the ceiling of the roof of a limestone cave. It is formed from dripping water containing dissolved calcium hydrogen carbonate. The water evaporates, leaving a deposit of calcium carbonate.
• *Stalactites may take thousands of years to grow and can eventually join with a stalagmite to form a column.*
SEE ALSO **stalagmite**

stalagmite
A stalagmite is an upward projection of calcium carbonate from the floor of a limestone cave.
• *Stalagmites tend to be broader at their base than stalactites.*
SEE ALSO **stalactite**

stamen
A stamen is the male reproductive organ of a flower.
• *Typically each stamen has a filament with an anther at its tip.*
SEE ALSO **anther, filament, flower**

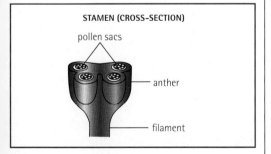
STAMEN (CROSS-SECTION)
pollen sacs
anther
filament

standard temperature and pressure (*also* **STP**)
is the temperature of 0°C (273 K) and a pressure of 1 atmosphere (101,325 pascals).
• *One mole of any gas occupies a volume of 22.4 dm³ at standard temperature and pressure.*
SEE ALSO **mole, room temperature and pressure**

standing wave *see* **stationary wave**

stapes *see* **ossicle**

star
A star is a celestial body that generates its own light and heat from nuclear fusion within its core.
• *Stars are not distributed uniformly throughout the universe, but are collected together in galaxies.*
SEE ALSO **constellation, galaxy, nuclear fusion**

starch
is a polysaccharide found in plants, especially in the roots, tubers, seeds, and fruit. It is formed by the condensation polymerization of around 3,000 glucose units.
• *Starch is an important carbohydrate energy source.*
SEE ALSO **carbohydrate, glucose, polymerization, polysaccharide**

WORD BUILD
starch hydrolysis
is the hydrolysis of starch into smaller molecules, and eventually into glucose. It is important in the digestion of starchy foods.
enzyme hydrolysis
is starch hydrolysis by the enzyme amylase, found in saliva in the mouth. It breaks the starch down into the disaccharide maltose $C_{12}H_{22}O_{11}$, which contains two glucose units minus a water molecule.
acid hydrolysis
is starch hydrolysis by an acid and takes place in the stomach of mammals. Acid hydrolysis is slow, but eventually the starch is broken down into glucose $C_6H_{12}O_6$, which is the monomer and will not undergo further hydrolysis. *SEE ALSO* **amylase, glucose, hydrolysis**

state of matter
States of matter are the three common physical forms or phases in which matter exists: **solid, liquid,** and **gas.** Substances can change between these states, usually when heated or cooled, as the kinetic energy (indicated by the velocity of the particles) increases or decreases respectively.
SEE ALSO **kinetic theory, plasma**

a
b
c
d
e
f
g
h
i
j
k
l
m
n
o
p
q
r
s
t
u
v
w
x
y
z

static see static electricity

static electricity (also frictional electricity, static)

is the accumulation of electric charge on an object which is a poor conductor of electricity or is insulated in some way. It is caused by the removal of electrons from atoms by friction. Friction does not create charge: it just separates out existing charges.
SEE ALSO electric charge

	uses of static electricity
1.	Electrostatic smoke and dust precipitators are used in chimneys to attract tiny particles of smoke and dust.
2.	Many photocopiers use static to form the image of a document on a charged drum. The charged areas of the drum attract graphite particles which stick to a resin coating. When paper is pressed against the heated drum, the resin and carbon particles are forced on to the paper fibres.
3.	Electrostatic spraying is used to apply a very even coat of charged paint droplets to an object (such as a car body) which is oppositely charged.

➤ **static and safety** Whenever poor conductors are rubbed together in a dry atmosphere, static electricity can build up, causing a spark, and if a poor conductor is close to something flammable, there is a risk of explosion. Examples are the build-up of static on the plastic of petrol pipes, the chutes into grain containers (silos), and the rollers in a paper mill. It is important that such material is earthed in some way.

static equilibrium

is a type of equilibrium where a balance is reached so there is no movement of material.
• *Two people balanced on a see-saw provide an example of static equilibrium.*
SEE ALSO dynamic equilibrium, equilibrium

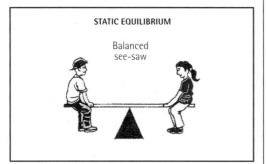

STATIC EQUILIBRIUM

Balanced
see-saw

static frictional force see friction

stationary phase see chromatography

stationary wave (also standing wave)

A stationary wave is one which does not transport energy away from a source.
• *Stationary waves are caused by interference.*
SEE ALSO interference, progressive wave

STD see sexually transmitted disease

steady-state theory

The steady-state theory proposed that the universe has always existed in a steady state with no beginning, and will have no end. It suggests that matter is being created as the universe expands.
• *The steady-state theory has lost favour to the big-bang theory, as it has failed to account for the evidence of evolution in the universe.*
SEE ALSO big-bang theory, universe

steam evaporation see evaporation

steam reforming

is an industrial method of preparation of hydrogen gas. The raw materials are methane gas (natural gas) and steam, mixed together and passed over a mixture of nickel and iron(III) oxide catalysts at 1,200°C and 50 atmospheres pressure.

methane + steam → carbon dioxide + hydrogen

$$CH_4 + 2H_2O \rightarrow CO_2 + 4H_2$$

SEE ALSO catalyst, hydrogen gas

steel

is an alloy of iron containing small (0.1–1.5%) but controlled quantities of carbon.
• *Most steel is manufactured by the basic oxygen process.*
SEE ALSO alloy, basic oxygen process

stellar evolution (also life of a star)

This consists of a series of changes that occur to a star during its lifetime, from birth to extinction. There are two types of stellar evolution, depending on the size of the protostar (see diagram).
SEE ALSO protostar

»

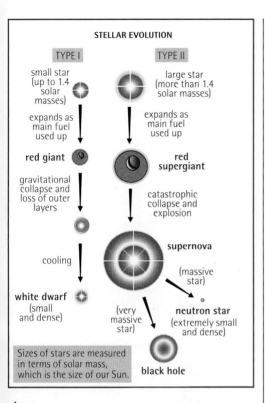

STELLAR EVOLUTION

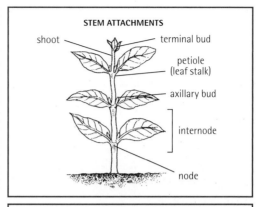

STEM ATTACHMENTS

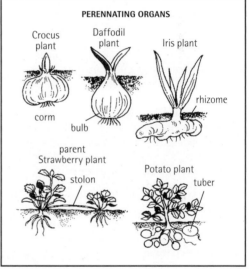

PERENNATING ORGANS

stem

A stem is the part of a plant which usually grows vertically upward towards the light. Water and food travel up and down the stem through vascular bundles and it supports the leaves, buds, and flowers. Some plant species have organs formed from modified stems which are important in vegetative reproduction:
- a bulb which is a short, thick underground stem with scaly leaves containing stored food (e.g. daffodil, onion)
- a corm which is a short, thick stem like a bulb, but food is stored in the stem itself (e.g. crocus)
- a rhizome which is a thick stem that grows horizontally underground and is used for food storage (e.g. lily, fern, iris)
- a stolon (or runner) which is a stem that grows horizontally from the bulb of a plant and forms roots for new plants where it touches the ground (e.g. strawberry)
- a tuber which is a swollen underground stem or root that acts as a food storage organ and produces buds for new plants (e.g. potato, dahlia).

SEE ALSO reproduction, vascular bundle

stem cell

A stem cell is a cell (like bone marrow cells or human embryo cells) that can divide to form more stem cells or differentiate to form other specialist type of cells (like lymphocytes which produce antibodies to fight disease).
• *Stem cells may be able to help conditions like diabetes and paralysis.*
SEE ALSO antibody, cell, diabetes, embryo, lymphocyte

step-down transformer *see* **transformer**

step-up transformer *see* **transformer**

sterilization *see* **irradiation**

sternum *see* **human skeleton**

stethoscope
A stethoscope is a medical instrument used to hear the sounds inside the bodies of people and animals. The sound travels up two hollow tubes to the ears.
• *A stethoscope is used by a doctor to hear sound inside the lungs and the heart.*

stigma
In a flower, the stigma is the uppermost part of the carpel.
• *During pollination the stigma secretes a sticky substance so that pollen attaches to it.*
SEE ALSO carpel, pollination

stimulant *see* drug

stolon *see* stem

stoma *plural* stomata
A stoma is a pore found on the lower epidermis of a leaf, surrounded by a pair of guard cells. These cells are responsible for opening and closing the stoma. The stoma opens when the guard cells become turgid and closes when they become flaccid.
• *Stomata are responsible for letting gases in and out of the leaf during photosynthesis, and water vapour out by evaporation during transpiration.*
SEE ALSO flaccid, leaf, photosynthesis, transpiration, turgid

stomach
The stomach is a large muscular sac where gastric juice is secreted to begin digestion. Hydrochloric acid is also secreted in the stomach, as the enzyme pepsin (which begins the digestion of protein) prefers acid conditions.
• *The stomach is part of the abdomen region of the body.*
SEE ALSO abdomen, digestion, gastric juice, pepsin

stopping distance *see* braking distance

storage battery *see* secondary cell

STP *see* standard temperature and pressure

stratosphere *see* atmosphere

strength of acids *see* acid

striated muscle *see* muscle

stroke *see* high blood pressure

strong electrolyte *see* electrolyte

structural formula *see* chemical formula

structural isomerism *see* isomerism

structure of the human ear *see* ear

structure of the kidney *see* kidney

structure of the root *see* root

structure of the skin *see* skin

style
In a flower, the style is the part of the carpel between the stigma and the ovary. The length of the style varies with the species of flower.
• *The pollen tube grows through the style after pollination.*
SEE ALSO carpel, pollination

subatomic particle
Subatomic particles are particles which are smaller than, or form part of, an atom.
• *There are three subatomic particles which make up most atoms: protons, neutrons, and electrons.*
SEE ALSO atom, electron, neutron, proton

Particle	Approximate radius
Atom	10^{-10} m
Nucleus	10^{-14} m
Electron	10^{-15} m

subcutaneous layer (*also* adipose tissue)
The subcutaneous layer is the layer of fatty tissue underneath the skin. It contains fat deposits which act as an insulating layer and helps keep body heat in.
• *The subcutaneous layer is also a store of food.*
SEE ALSO skin, sweat gland

subduction
is the dipping of one plate below another at a destructive plate boundary
SEE ALSO plate boundary

sublimation
is the direct change of state from a solid to a gas (or vapour) on heating, or from a gas to a solid on cooling.
• *Iodine, solid carbon dioxide (dry ice), and some ammonium salts undergo sublimation.*

subsoil
is the lighter coloured layer of soil between the topsoil and bedrock. It contains coarser rock particles, no humus, and few living organisms.
• *The roots of many trees do penetrate the subsoil, as it contains useful mineral salts.*
SEE ALSO bedrock, mineral salt, topsoil

subsonic
describes a speed below the speed of sound in the same medium.
• *Subsonic speed is less than mach one (speed of sound).*
SEE ALSO **mach number, supersonic**

substitution reaction (*also* replacement reaction)
A substitution reaction is a chemical reaction in which an atom or molecule is replaced by another atom or molecule.
• *Saturated molecules like alkanes undergo substitution reactions.*

methane + chlorine → chloromethane + hydrogen chloride

$$CH_4 \quad + \quad Cl_2 \quad \rightarrow \quad CH_3Cl \quad + \quad HCl$$

SEE ALSO **addition reaction, alkane, saturated molecule**

substrate
A substrate is a molecule on which an enzyme acts in a biochemical reaction. The enzyme amylase catalyses the breakdown of starch into sugar by the reaction of water (hydrolysis). The substrate in this reaction is the starch molecule.
SEE ALSO **amylase, starch**

subtractive mixing
is colour mixing by adding together paints, dyes, or pigments, which have colour because they absorb some components of white light and reflect the rest. It is called subtractive mixing because the colour you see is the colour left after you have subtracted from white light all the wavelengths that have been absorbed.
• *Subtractive mixing is the basis of the colour printing process used in colour photography and the mixing of paints.*
SEE ALSO **additive mixing**

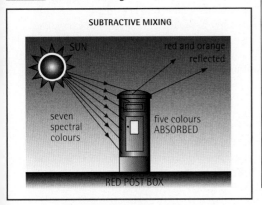

SUBTRACTIVE MIXING

SUN
red and orange reflected
seven spectral colours
five colours ABSORBED
RED POST BOX

sulfate (*also* sulfate(VI) salt)
Sulfates are ionic compounds containing the sulfate ion SO_4^{2-} e.g. sodium sulfate Na_2SO_4.
• *Sulfate is classed as a radical group of atoms as it cannot exist by itself.*
SEE ALSO **radical**

sulfide
Sulfides are binary compounds (made of two elements), one of which is sulfur: e.g. iron(II) sulfide FeS.
• *Many sulphides are ores.*
SEE ALSO **hydrogen sulfide, ore, sulfur**

Acid	Anion in salts
hydrogen sulfide H_2S	sulfide S^{2-}
sulfurous acid H_2SO_3	sulfite SO_3^{2-}
sulfuric acid H_2SO_4	sulfate SO_4^{2-}

sulfite (*also* sulfate(IV) salt)
Sulfites are ionic compounds containing the sulfite ion SO_3^{2-} e.g. sodium sulfite Na_2SO_3.
• *Sulfite is classed as a radical group of atoms as it cannot exist by itself.*
SEE ALSO **radical**

sulfur (*also* S)
is a yellow, non-metallic element found in group VI of the periodic table.
• *Sulfur is an element which forms allotropes.*
SEE ALSO **allotrope**

rhombic sulfur (*also* alpha sulfur, orthorhombic sulfur)
is a pale yellow, crystalline allotrope of sulfur which is stable at room temperature.
SEE ALSO **allotrope**

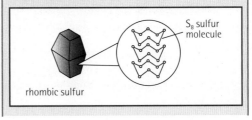

S_8 sulfur molecule

rhombic sulfur

»

monoclinic sulfur (*also* beta sulfur)

is a yellow, crystalline allotrope of sulfur which is stable at temperatures above 96°C.

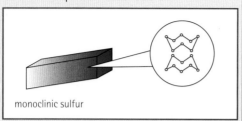

monoclinic sulfur

plastic sulfur

is an amorphous (non-crystalline) form of sulfur formed when molten sulfur (m.p. 113°C) is poured into cold water. It forms into long fibres which can be stretched and pulled like plastic. It is not stable and eventually crystallizes to S_8 molecules.
SEE ALSO amorphous

flowers of sulfur

is an amorphous form of sulfur formed when sulfur vapour (b.p. 445°C) is cooled quickly. It is used as a plant fungicide.

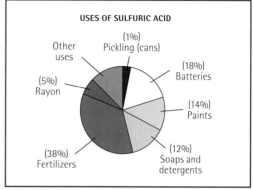

USES OF SULFURIC ACID

Other uses
Pickling (cans) (1%)
(5%) Rayon
(18%) Batteries
(14%) Paints
(12%) Soaps and detergents
(38%) Fertilizers

	uses of sulphuric electricity
1.	manufacture of fertilizers such as ammonium sulfate and calcium superphosphate
2.	manufacture of non-soapy detergents by sulfonating organic molecules with concentrated sulfuric acid
3.	as an electrolyte in car batteries
4.	Other uses include the manufacture of drugs (sulfanilamide drugs), paints (lead sulfate), and rayon (artificial silk).

sulfur dioxide (*also* sulfur(IV) oxide)

is a pungent smelling gas, SO_2, formed when sulfur burns in air. It is a reducing agent and dissolves in water to form sulfurous acid. It is used in bleaching, as a fumigant, and in food preserving.
• *Large quantities of sulfur dioxide are used in the contact process.*
SEE ALSO contact process, reducing agent, sulfurous acid

sulfuric acid (*also* sulfuric(VI) acid)

is an oily, very corrosive mineral acid, H_2SO_4, formed when sulfur trioxide reacts with water. When concentrated, it is a dehydrating agent and oxidizing agent.
• *Commercially sulfuric acid is very important and is made on a large scale by the contact process.*
SEE ALSO acid, contact process, oxidizing agent, sulfur trioxide

sulfurous acid (*also* sulfuric(IV) acid)

is a colourless, weak acid, H_2SO_3, formed when sulfur dioxide dissolves in water.
• *Sulfurous acid forms salts called sulfites.*
SEE ALSO sulfite, sulfur dioxide

sulfur trioxide (*also* sulfur(VI) oxide)

is a white, crystalline solid, SO_3, which is formed in the contact process.
• *Sulfur trioxide is very volatile (m.p. 17°C) and reacts violently with water to form sulfuric acid.*
SEE ALSO contact process, sulfuric acid

Sun

The Sun is a star at the centre of our solar system. It is about 149,600,000 km from Earth and its diameter is about 110 times that of Earth. The temperature inside is about 15 million°C and on the surface is about 6,000°C. The core is so hot that atoms are broken down into ions and electrons (plasma). The Sun is about 75% hydrogen and 25% helium, with less than 1% heavier elements. Light from the Sun takes around 8 minutes to reach Earth.
• *Like all stars, the Sun emits a wide spectrum of electromagnetic radiation, not just visible light.*
SEE ALSO plasma, solar activity, star

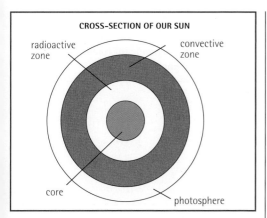

CROSS-SECTION OF OUR SUN

radioactive zone

convective zone

core

photosphere

sunspot

A sunspot is a dark patch on the Sun's surface, resulting from a localized fall in temperature to about 4,000°C. Sunspots tend to occur in clusters and last about two weeks.

• *The number of sunspots changes over an eleven-year cycle.*

SEE ALSO solar activity

superconductivity

is the absence of electrical resistance at temperatures close to absolute zero (zero Kelvin).

• *Only certain metals show superconductivity, as the flow of current often heats up the metal so that it cannot reach very low temperatures.*

SEE ALSO absolute zero, resistance

superior vena cava

The superior vena cava is a main vein which carries deoxygenated blood from the upper body to the heart.

SEE ALSO inferior vena cava, vein

supernova

A supernova is an explosive brightening of a star which results when an old and very massive star uses up most of its fuel for nuclear fusion and collapses under the force of its own gravity.

• *A supernova takes several years to fade and during that time illuminates the whole galaxy in which it lies.*

SEE ALSO nuclear fusion

supersonic

describes a speed greater than the speed of sound in the same medium.

• *Supersonic speed is greater than mach one (speed of sound).*

SEE ALSO mach number, sonic boom, sound, subsonic

surface catalyst

A surface catalyst holds reactant particles on its surface for long enough for them to react with each other to form products.

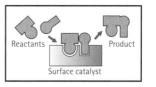

Reactants

Product

Surface catalyst

• *Many surface catalysts are transition metals which speed up the reaction between gases.*

SEE ALSO catalyst, product, reactant, transition metal

susceptibility

is a measure of the ability of a substance to become magnetized.

• *Magnetic materials have high susceptibility.*

SEE ALSO magnetic material

suspension

A suspension is a mixture of insoluble small solid particles in a gas or liquid. The particles often stay in clusters and are spread through the liquid by molecular collisions.

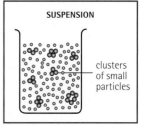

SUSPENSION

clusters of small particles

If the clusters become large, they may sink to the bottom and form a sediment.

SEE ALSO colloid, solution

sustainability

is an indication of the availability of raw materials required and energy needed to make a manufactured product. In order to conserve valuable resources and thereby increase sustainability we need to practise the 3Rs (recycle, reduce, reuse).

• *Sustainability, if it is increased, helps towards a 'greener' chemical industry.*

SEE ALSO recycling, reduce, reuse

Sv see sievert

sweat

is a watery fluid with small amounts of salt and urea.

• *Perspiration is producing sweat and an average person perspires up to 6 litres (1.5 gallons) of sweat per day.*

SEE ALSO sweat gland

a
b
c
d
e
f
g
h
i
j
k
l
m
n
o
p
q
r
s
t
u
v
w
x
y
z

sweat gland

A sweat gland is a small exocrine gland in the subcutaneous layer which secretes sweat. Sweat passes along a narrow tube (sweat duct) to the surface of the skin. It cools the body by evaporation.

SEE ALSO **exocrine gland, skin, subcutaneous layer, sweat**

switch

A switch is a safety device placed on the live wire to switch electrical circuits off when not in use.

SEE ALSO **electricity cable**

symbiosis see **mutualism**

synapse

A synapse is the junction between two adjacent neurones.

• Across the **synapse** chemicals (neurotransmitters) are released.

SEE ALSO **neurone, neurotransmitter**

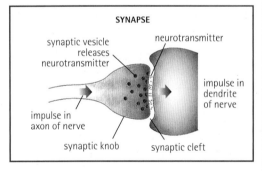

SYNAPSE

synaptic vesicle releases neurotransmitter — neurotransmitter — impulse in dendrite of nerve — impulse in axon of nerve — synaptic knob — synaptic cleft

synovial fluid

is a liquid secreted by the synovial membrane which lubricates a joint and reduces friction between the bones when they are moving.

SEE ALSO **joint, synovial membrane**

synovial membrane

The synovial membrane is the lining of the sac which surrounds a movable joint.

• The **synovial membrane** secretes the synovial fluid.

SEE ALSO **joint, synovial fluid**

synthesis

is a chemical change by which a compound is built up from its elements or from simpler compounds. For example, ammonia gas can be built up from its elements (as in the Haber process).

$$\text{nitrogen} + \text{hydrogen} \rightarrow \text{ammonia gas}$$
$$N_2 + 3H_2 \rightarrow 2NH_3$$

SEE ALSO **chemical change, decomposition, Haber process, photosynthesis**

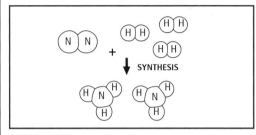

synthetic detergent
see **detergent**

synthetic fertilizer
see **fertilizer**

synthetic polymer

Synthetic polymers are substances such as plastics, and man-made fibres such as nylon and Terylene.

• **Synthetic polymers** are a major contributor to landfill.

SEE ALSO **landfill, nylon, plastic, polymer, Terylene**

syphilis

is the disease caused by a bacterium (*Treponema pallidum*) transmitted during sexual intercourse. The symptoms of the initial stages of the disease are sores and rashes. If untreated, the later stages are deformed joints, paralysis, insanity, and eventual death. As with gonorrhoea, an infected woman can pass the disease to her baby at birth.

SEE ALSO **gonorrhoea, sexually transmitted disease**

Système International d'Unités see **SI units**

systemic circulation see **double circulation**

systole see **heartbeat**

Tt

T *see* **period, temperature**

T$\frac{1}{2}$ *see* **half–life**

table salt *see* **sodium chloride**

tactic movement *see* **taxis**

tarsal *see* **human skeleton**

tartar (*also* **calculus**)
is a form of hardened dental plaque formed on the teeth that cannot be removed by brushing.
• *Tartar can be removed with ultrasonic tools or dental hand instruments.*
SEE ALSO **plaque**

taste bud
A taste bud is a small sense organ on the tongue. It contains chemoreceptors which are sensitive to four types of taste: sweet, sour, salt, and bitter. Taste buds for each taste are concentrated in certain areas of the tongue.
• *Nervous impulses from the taste buds are interpreted by the brain as taste sensations.*
SEE ALSO **tongue**

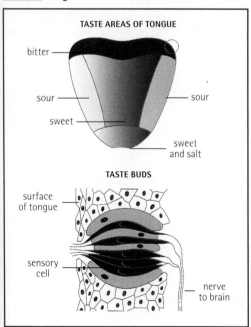

TASTE AREAS OF TONGUE

bitter

sour — sour

sweet

sweet
and salt

TASTE BUDS

surface
of tongue

sensory
cell

nerve
to brain

taxis (*also* **tactic movement**)
is the movement of an organism with respect to a stimulus from a specific direction. This stimulus may be chemical (chemo**taxis**), light (photo **taxis**), gravity (geo**taxis**), etc. For example, woodlice show negative phototaxis (move to avoid light).
• *Taxis is restricted to organisms capable of movement.*

taxonomy
is the study of the theory, practice, and rules of classification of living and extinct organisms. These organisms are put into groups based on similarities in structure and appearance as well as genome analysis (DNA sequencing).
SEE ALSO **genome**

tectonic plate
Tectonic plates are huge sections of the Earth's crust which move across the underlying mantle.
• *There are six major **tectonic plates** (Eurasian, American, African, Pacific, Indian, and Antarctic) together with a number of smaller ones.*
SEE ALSO **continental drift, Earth's structure, plate boundary, plate tectonics**

teeth *see* **tooth**

telecommunications
involves sending information over long distances either by wires or by electromagnetic radiation (radio, light, microwave, etc.). The message must be:
  – sent by a transmitter
  – placed on a carrier wave
  – detected by a receiver.
SEE ALSO **carrier wave, receiver, transmitter**

temperature (*also* **T**)
is the degree of hotness or coldness of something.
• *Temperature is a measure of the average kinetic energy of its particles.*
SEE ALSO **heat, kinetic energy store**

temperature of a gas (*also* **T**)
The temperature of a gas is a measure of the average kinetic energy of the molecules of the gas.
• *The **temperature of a gas** is measured in degrees centigrade or kelvin but for calculations using the ideal gas equation it must be measured on the absolute scale in kelvin.*
SEE ALSO **absolute scale, Boyle's law, Charles' law, critical temperature, ideal gas equation, pressure law, pressure of a gas, volume of a gas**

temporary hardness *see* hard water

temporary magnet *see* magnetic material

tendon (*also* sinew)
is tough connective tissue that connects a muscle to a bone. Tendons consist of collagen fibres which are non-elastic, and therefore transmit the contraction or relaxation of the muscle to the bone.

SEE ALSO **connective tissue**

tendril
A tendril is a slender extension of a stem or leaf found in many climbing plants which shows thigmotropism.

SEE ALSO **leaf, stem, thigmotropism**

tension forces *see* force

terminal velocity
is the constant velocity reached by an object falling through a fluid (liquid or gas) when its gravitational force (weight) is equal to the frictional forces acting on it. Overall the net resultant force on an object travelling at terminal velocity is zero.

• *All free-falling objects will reach a* **terminal velocity**. *The size of this terminal velocity depends on their shape and area.*

SEE ALSO **friction, gravitational force, velocity**

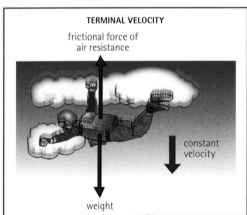

TERMINAL VELOCITY

frictional force of air resistance

constant velocity

weight

tertiary consumer *see* consumer

Terylene (*also* polyester)
is a synthetic polymer made by condensation polymerization of a diol monomer with a dicarboxylic acid chloride monomer.

• *Terylene (more correctly referred to as polyethene terephthalate or PET polyester) is used in making clothing and plastic bottles.*

SEE ALSO **polymerization, synthetic polymer**

testis *plural* testes
The testes are the pair of male sex organs which are responsible for the production of sperm and androgens (male hormones). The testes lie in a sac called the scrotum which hangs outside the body. This allows the testes to be at a temperature slightly below body temperature, which is ideal for sperm production. Sperm are stored temporarily in a coiled tube (epididymis) and are then carried away in the sperm duct (vas deferens) towards the urethra. Where the sperm duct joins the urethra, there are glands called the prostate gland and seminal vesicle.

SEE ALSO **male reproductive organ system, sex hormone, sperm, urethra**

testosterone *see* hormone, sex hormone

test-tube baby
is an informal term for a baby conceived by in vitro fertilization.

• *The first* **test-tube** *baby was born in Britain in 1978.*

SEE ALSO **in vitro fertilization**

thermal capacity *see* heat capacity

thermal conduction *see* conduction

thermal conductivity
is a measure of the ability of a substance to conduct heat. Good conductors have a high thermal conductivity, poor conductors (insulators) have a low thermal conductivity.

• *The SI unit of* **thermal conductivity** *is watt per metre-kelvin or w/(m.K).*

SEE ALSO **conductor, insulator**

Conductor	Insulator
silver	sulfur
copper	carbon
aluminium	water
iron	glass
brass (alloy)	plastic
graphite	wood
gold	rubber
silicon	air

thermal cracking *see* cracking

thermal energy (*also* internal energy)

is the energy an object possesses because of the kinetic and potential energy of its particles. When an object has heat energy, its particles move and therefore have kinetic energy. They also have potential energy because their movements keep them separated. When an object absorbs heat energy, its thermal energy increases. When an object loses heat energy, its thermal energy decreases.

Heat and temperature are not the same. Heat is the sum of the total energies of all the particles, whereas temperature is a measure of the average energy of the particles.

• *There is more* **thermal energy** *in an iceberg than in a cup of boiling water, even though its temperature is lower, because the total energy of the particles in the iceberg is greater.*

SEE ALSO **heat energy, kinetic energy store, potential energy**

thermal pollution

is caused by warm water released from power stations and factories into rivers. Warm water contains less dissolved oxygen and so is harmful to aquatic life.
• *Thermal pollution decreases the biodiversity of a river.*

SEE ALSO **biodiversity**

thermal radiation *see* radiation

thermistor

A thermistor is a resistor made from a semiconductor whose resistance falls sharply when its temperature rises above room temperature.

THERMISTOR

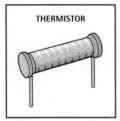

• *Thermistors can be used as temperature switches which switch on devices when they have 'warmed up'.*

SEE ALSO **resistor, semiconductor**

thermocouple thermometer

A thermocouple thermometer depends on the temperature difference between two junctions made up of two different metals such as copper and iron. The greater the temperature difference between the hot and cold junction, the greater the emf which is produced. Thermocouples are suitable over a wide range of temperatures from about –200°C to 1,600°C.
• *Thermocouples can be used in pyrometers.*

SEE ALSO **pyrometer, thermometer**

THERMOCOUPLE THERMOMETER

iron wire

meter scale marked in °C

hot junction

cold junction (inside meter)

copper wire

thermodynamic temperature scale
see **absolute scale**

thermogram

A thermogram is a pictorial representation of the temperature variation of different objects in the form of a photograph taken with a thermographic camera.
• *Thermograms can be used to identify heat loss from buildings and thereby improve possible heat insulation.*

SEE ALSO **heat loss, insulator, temperature**

thermometer

A thermometer is an instrument which is used to measure temperature.
• *There are many types of* **thermometer**, *but all measure how a particular property such as volume, resistance, or emf changes with temperature.*

SEE ALSO **clinical thermometer, liquid-in-glass thermometer, maximum–and–minimum thermometer, thermocouple, thermometer**

thermometric liquid

Thermometric liquids expand uniformly with temperature and can be used in liquid-in-glass thermometers.
• *The table compares two common* **thermometric liquids**, *mercury and alcohol.*

SEE ALSO **liquid-in-glass thermometer**

	For	Against
mercury	– does not wet sides of tube – good conductor so responds quickly	– freezes at –39°C – poisionous – expensive
alcohol	– freezes at –115°C – expansion greater than mercury	– has to be coloured to be visible – thread has tendency to break – clings to side of tube

thermoplastic *see* **thermosoftening**

thermoregulation

is the control of body temperature in warm-blooded animals. Heat gain results from metabolic activity. Heat loss occurs mainly through the skin. The hypothalamus at the base of the brain continually monitors blood temperature and controls thermoregulation. If the body temperature is too low, it sends instructions (by hormones or through the nervous system) to produce more heat by increasing metabolic activity, and to reduce heat loss through the skin. If the body temperature is too high, the reverse happens.

SEE ALSO **brain, homeostasis, skin**

thermosetting

describes a type of plastic (polymer) which, on heating, becomes permanently hard, as strong cross linking develops between the polymer chains.

• *Thermosetting plastics include formica and bakelite as well as polyester and epoxy resins. Thermosetting plastics are non-biodegradable and therefore cause land pollution.*

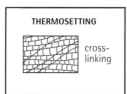

THERMOSETTING

cross-linking

SEE ALSO **land pollution, plastic**

thermosoftening (*also* **thermoplastic**)

describes a type of plastic (polymer) which can be softened on heating. Thermosoftening plastics include polythene, polypropylene, and polystyrene, which can be easily moulded and shaped. This is because there are only weak forces between the polymer chains.

• *Many thermosoftening plastics contribute to landfill, such as polythene bottles, polypropylene food containers, and polystyrene insulating and packaging materials.*

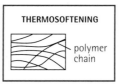

THERMOSOFTENING

polymer chain

SEE ALSO **landfill, plastic**

thermostat

A thermostat is a device for automatically controlling the temperature of an appliance such as an oven or central heating system.

• *The thermostat switches off the current when the appliance is hot enough. It is then switched back on when the temperature falls.*

SEE ALSO **bimetallic strip**

thigmotropism

is the growth response of a plant to touch or contact. For example, the tendrils of a pea plant curl around stems and other supports.

SEE ALSO **insectivorous plant, tendril**

thin-layer chromatography *see* **chromatography**

thorax

The thorax is the chest region between the skull and the stomach which contains the heart and the lungs.

• *The thorax is protected by the rib cage.*

SEE ALSO **rib cage, skull**

thrombocyte *see* **platelet**

thrombosis *see* **high blood pressure**

thunder

is the sound made when lightning flashes from clouds. The sound is caused by the rapid expansion of the air around the flash of lightning which causes a sonic (sound) shock wave, often referred to as a 'thunderclap' or 'peal of thunder'.

• *We hear the sound of **thunder** after we see the lightning as sound travels much more slowly than the flash of light of the lightning.*

SEE ALSO **lightning, sound**

thyroid gland

The thyroid gland is an endocrine gland at the base of the neck which produces thyroxine under the influence of thyroid stimulating hormone, and controls the metabolic rate.

• *Thyroxine production requires iodine, and iodine deficiency causes the **thyroid gland** to swell and form a goitre (neck swelling).*

SEE ALSO **endocrine gland, hormone, metabolic rate**

thyroxine *see* **hormone**

tibia *see* **human skeleton**

ticker-timer

A ticker-timer is a device which is used to study motion. The moving object (trolley) is attached to a paper tape which is pulled through a timer that prints a dot on the tape every $\frac{1}{50}$th of a second. The distance between the dots on the tape indicates the speed at which the object is moving. If the dots are equally spaced, then the object is moving at constant speed. If the distance between the dots increases, the object is accelerating; if the distance decreases, the object is decelerating.

tidal energy

is produced by the use of tidal barrages to trap water at high tide, which is then allowed to flow through turbines set in a concrete wall. These turbines drive a generator to produce electricity.

• *Tidal energy is a renewable energy source.*

SEE ALSO **energy source, wave energy**

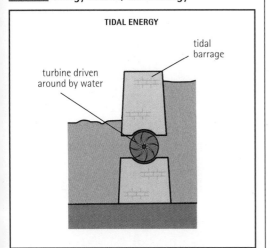

TIDAL ENERGY

tidal barrage

turbine driven around by water

tide

Tides are the regular rise and fall of the water level in the Earth's oceans as a result of the gravitational forces between the Earth, Moon, and Sun. The size of the gravitational force depends on both the distance and mass of the celestial body. Although the Moon is very much smaller than the Sun, it is comparatively close. As a result, the Moon is approximately twice as effective as the Sun in causing tides.

SEE ALSO **gravitational force**

neap tide

Neap tides are the relatively small tides caused when the Sun and Moon's gravitational forces are acting at right angles to one another, decreasing the overall gravitational force.

spring tide

Spring tides are extra high or extra low tides caused when both the Moon and the Sun are aligned with one another, increasing the gravitational force on the Earth's oceans.

timbre *see* **sound**

timeline

A timeline is a graphical representation of events which shows the order in which they occurred.

• *A timeline of evolution is shown below.*

tin plating

is electroplating a thin layer of tin metal on both sides of a sheet of mild steel to make tinplate.

• *Tin plating is used in the canning industry for 'tin cans' for fruit, vegetables, baked beans, etc., because tin is unreactive and non-toxic.*

SEE ALSO **electroplating**

TIR *see* **total internal reflection**

tissue

is a collection of cells which perform a specific function.

• *Examples of **tissue** are muscle tissue, nerve tissue, skin tissue, and leaf tissue.*

tissue culture

is the growth of tissue or cells in an artificial medium, separate from the organism. It is often used for plants, placing plant cells (normally meristem tissue) in a suitable culture medium containing growth hormones. Growth is very rapid and can produce disease-free plants all year round. However, the plants are clones, whose lack of genetic variation make them vulnerable to new diseases.

SEE ALSO **clone, meristem**

tissue fluid

is plasma which has leaked from the capillaries and is returned to the blood through the lymphatic system.

SEE ALSO **lymphatic system, plasma**

titration

is a technique which can be used for neutralization of an acid and an alkali. The alkali is accurately measured using a pipette and placed in a conical flask with an indicator. The acid is then added slowly from a burette.

• *In a **titration**, when the indicator changes colour, the neutral point has been reached.*

SEE ALSO **burette, indicator, neutralization, pipette**   **»**

a b c d e f g h i j k l m n o p q r s t u v w x y z

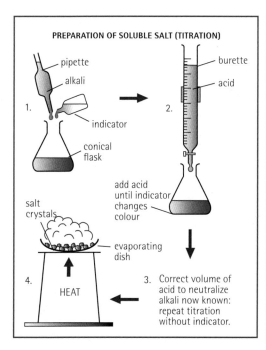

PREPARATION OF SOLUBLE SALT (TITRATION)

➤ **titration curve** A titration curve shows the effect on pH of changing the hydrogen ion concentration during a neutralization reaction. For example, the curve below shows how the pH changes when increasing the volume of acid added to an alkali in a titration reaction.

SEE ALSO **neutralization, pH**

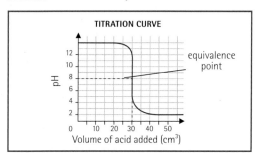

TITRATION CURVE

tobacco mosaic virus (*also* **TMV**)
is a widespread plant pathogen affecting many species of plants including tomatoes.
• *Tobacco mosaic virus decolourizes the leaves of the plant which affects plant's growth due to lack of photosynthesis.*

SEE ALSO **pathogen, photosynthesis, virus**

tongue
The tongue is the muscular organ of taste which is attached to the floor of the mouth. It is also used in manipulating food during chewing and swallowing, and in humans is involved in speech.
• *The surface of the tongue is covered with taste receptors called taste buds.*

SEE ALSO **taste bud**

tooth *plural* **teeth**
A tooth is a hard, bone-like structure in a vertebrate, which is mainly used for biting, chewing, and grinding food.

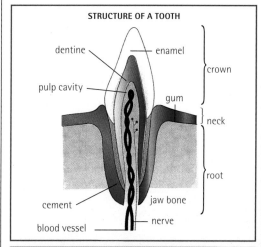

STRUCTURE OF A TOOTH

WORD BUILD

canine (*also* **cuspid, eye-tooth**)

Canines are sharp, cone-shaped teeth used to tear food.
• *Carnivores, like dogs, have highly developed canine teeth. Herbivores, like rabbits, do not have canine teeth.*

deciduous tooth (*also* **milk tooth**)

Deciduous or milk teeth are the first of two sets of teeth in a mammal.
• *In a child there are 20 milk teeth. At around 7 years of age, these deciduous teeth begin to fall out and are replaced by permanent teeth.*

incisor

Incisors are sharp, chisel-shaped teeth at the front of the mouth used for biting and cutting.

permanent tooth

Permanent teeth are the second and final set of teeth in a mammal.
• *An adult human normally has 32 permanent teeth consisting of incisors, canines, premolars, and molars.*

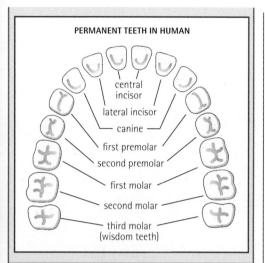

PERMANENT TEETH IN HUMAN

central incisor

lateral incisor

canine

first premolar

second premolar

first molar

second molar

third molar
(wisdom teeth)

premolar (*also* **bicuspid**)

Premolars are blunt, broad, ridged teeth in front of the molars, used for grinding and chewing food.

wisdom tooth

Wisdom teeth are the four molars which appear last of all, sometimes into middle age – hence their name.

molar (*also* **tricuspid**)

Molars are blunt, broad, ridged teeth (like premolars) but with a larger surface area and at the rear of the mouth.

tooth decay (*also* **dental caries**)

is caused by bacteria in plaque. If you eat sweet foods, the plaque absorbs the sugar like a sponge. Bacteria in the plaque then feed on this sugar and convert it to acid. This dissolves away the protective enamel layer of the tooth, making a hole. If untreated, the acid gradually works its way into the dentine and pulp cavity of the tooth, causing infection and the death of the tooth.

• *Tooth decay may be reduced by regular cleaning and flossing (using soft medical thread pulled between the teeth).*

SEE ALSO **gum disease, plaque, tooth**

topsoil

is the fertile top layer of dark soil, usually less than 20 cm deep. It is the part of the soil where most of the living organisms exist.

• *Topsoil contains humus, minerals, air, and water.*

SEE ALSO **humus, soil, soil profile**

tornado

A tornado is a rotating column of air which travels in a narrow path (10m–100m diameter) with the appearance of a funnel-shaped cloud above.

total internal reflection (*also* **TIR**)

is the complete reflection of light at a boundary between two media.

• *In total internal relection light must travel from more to less dense media and must be incident at the boundary at an angle greater than the critical angle.*

SEE ALSO **critical angle, optical fibre, right-angled prism**

toxin

A toxin is a poisonous substance produced by a living organism, especially microorganisms like bacteria.

• *Toxins, although harmful in the human body, act as an antigen because they stimulate the production of antibodies.*

SEE ALSO **antibody, antigen, bacteria, microorganism**

trace element

Trace elements are elements which are only needed in small amounts but are still essential for healthy plant growth.

• *Trace elements include calcium, magnesium, sodium, and sulfur, as well as very small amounts of iron, copper, zinc, molybdenum, and cobalt.*

trachea (*also* **windpipe**)

The trachea is a tube through which air is drawn into the lungs.

SEE ALSO **bronchus, epiglottis, larynx, lung**

transducer

A transducer is a device which converts electricity into different energy forms (sound, light, mechanical, etc.) or vice versa.

• *The transducer in a receiver circuit is usually a loudspeaker or earpiece.*

SEE ALSO **receiver**

Transducer	Main energy conversion
battery	chemical → electrical
light bulb	electrical → light
earpiece	electrical → sound

»

thermocouple	heat → electrical
solar cell	light → electrical
loudspeaker	electrical → sound
microphone	sound → electrical
dynamo	mechanical → electrical
motor	electrical → mechanical

transect

A transect is a straight line across a field or habitat along which ecological measurements are made. You can use a long tape measure and, perhaps every 50 cm, record which plant species touch the tape.
• *Transects are particularly useful where one kind of habitat changes into another.*
SEE ALSO **ecosystem, habitat, quadrat**

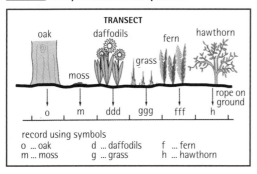

TRANSECT

oak   daffodils   fern   hawthorn
           grass
    moss   rope on
                                ground
    o   m   ddd   ggg   fff   h

record using symbols
o ... oak   d ... daffodils   f ... fern
m ... moss   g ... grass   h ... hawthorn

transformer

A transformer is a device for changing the voltage of an alternating current without changing its frequency. It consists of two coils of wire wound on to the same soft-iron core. The current in the primary coil causes an alternating magnetic field in the iron core. This induces a current in the secondary coil. The two coils are not connected and the power (voltage x current) in each coil is the same.

$$\text{primary voltage } (V_p) \times \text{primary current } (I_p) = \text{secondary voltage } (V_s) \times \text{secondary current } (I_s)$$

SEE ALSO **alternating current, coil, core, mutual induction**

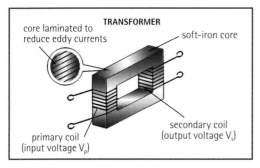

TRANSFORMER

core laminated to reduce eddy currents
soft-iron core
primary coil (input voltage V_p)
secondary coil (output voltage V_s)

step-down transformer

A step-down transformer is one in which the number of turns of the secondary coil is less than the primary coil, so the secondary voltage (V_s) is less than the primary voltage (V_p). The turns ratio is greater than one.

step-up transformer

A step-up transformer is one in which the number of turns on the secondary coil is greater than the primary coil, so the secondary voltage (V_s) is greater than the primary voltage (V_p). The turns ratio is less than one.

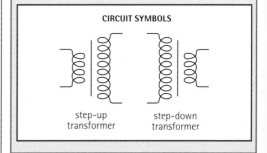

CIRCUIT SYMBOLS

step-up transformer   step-down transformer

WORD BUILD

primary coil

The primary coil is the input coil in a transformer.

secondary coil

The secondary coil is the output coil in a transformer.

turns ratio

The turns ratio is the ratio of the number of turns on the primary and secondary coils of a transformer. It is equal to the ratio between the voltages of each coil.

$$\frac{\text{primary number of turns } (n_p)}{\text{secondary number of turns } (n_s)} = \frac{\text{primary voltage } (V_p)}{\text{secondary voltage } (V_s)}$$

transistor

A transistor is an electronic device which is commonly used as a switch or an amplifier. Transistors are connected into electronic circuits at three points called the base, collector, and emitter. When a small current (about 5 mA) flows to the base, the resistance between the collector and emitter changes from very high to very low and the transistor is switched on.

• *By varying the size of this current to the base, we can control when the **transistor** switches on, and therefore when the electronic switch is activated.*
SEE ALSO **electronic switch**

transition metal
Transition metals are the block of metallic elements in the middle of the periodic table. They have partly filled inner electron shells, which gives them distinctive properties. They are typical metals. They are strong and hard, good conductors of heat and electricity, and have high melting points.
• *Many of the **transition metals** (Cr, Mn, Fe, Co, Cu) have variable valency and coloured compounds, and act as catalysts.*
SEE ALSO **catalyst, periodic table, variable valency**

translocation
is the transport of minerals and products of photosynthesis within a plant. Minerals travel in solution through the xylem vessels, and sugars travel in solution through the phloem vessels.
SEE ALSO **phloem, xylem**

translucent
describes objects that transmit light but diffuse (scatter) the light as it passes through.
• *You cannot see clearly through a **translucent** material such as plastic or obscure glass.*
SEE ALSO **opaque, transparent**

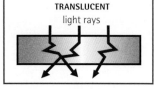

TRANSLUCENT
light rays

transmitter (*also* **radio transmitter**)
A transmitter is a device which converts electrical impulses into modulated radio waves.
SEE ALSO **radio waves, telecommunications**

transparent
describes objects that transmit light with little or no diffusion or scattering of light.
• *You can see clearly through a **transparent** material such as water or glass.*
SEE ALSO **opaque, translucent**

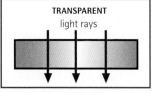

TRANSPARENT
light rays

transpiration
is the process in which water is lost by evaporation from the leaves of a plant through the stomata. The flow of water and mineral salts through the plant from the roots to the leaves is maintained by 'root pressure' (action of osmosis and active transport) and by the pull through the xylem vessels caused by water being evaporated from the leaves.
• *Transpiration can result in a large oak tree evaporating over 1,000 litres of water each day.*
SEE ALSO **active transport, leaf, osmosis, potometer, wilting**

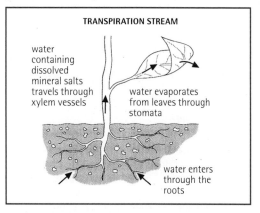

TRANSPIRATION STREAM

water containing dissolved mineral salts travels through xylem vessels

water evaporates from leaves through stomata

water enters through the roots

transponder
A transponder is a device that, upon receiving a signal, automatically emits a different signal in response.
• *Transponders are very important in telecommunications.*
SEE ALSO **telecommunications, transducer, transmitter**

transverse wave
A transverse wave is a progressive wave in which the oscillation or vibration is at right angles to the direction in which the wave is travelling (direction of energy movement). Only transverse waves can undergo polarization.
• *Examples of **transverse waves** are water waves (oscillation of water molecules) and electromagnetic waves (oscillation of electric and magnetic fields).*
SEE ALSO **electromagnetic wave, polarization, progressive wave**

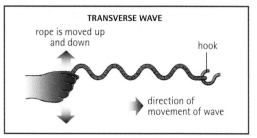

TRANSVERSE WAVE

rope is moved up and down

hook

direction of movement of wave

triatomic molecule

A triatomic molecule is formed from three atoms chemically bonded together.

• *Examples of **triatomic molecules** are ozone O_3, water H_2O, and carbon dioxide CO_2.*

SEE ALSO **chemical bond, diatomic molecule, molecule**

triceps

is the extensor muscle in the upper arm which straightens the forearm.

• *The **triceps** forms an antagonistic pair of muscles with the biceps to raise and lower the forearm.*

SEE ALSO **antagonistic pairs, biceps, muscle**

tricuspid *see* tooth

tricuspid valve

The tricuspid valve in the heart consists of three flaps and prevents blood from flowing back into the right atrium.

• *The **tricuspid valve** opens to allow blood to flow from the right atrium to the right ventricle.*

SEE ALSO **atrium, bicuspid valve, ventricle**

triple covalent bond *see* covalent bond

tritium (*also* ^{3}H)

is an isotope of hydrogen with two neutrons in the nucleus of its atom.

• ***Tritium** is radioactive, and is made artificially for use in radioactive tracing.*

SEE ALSO **hydrogen, isotope, radioactive tracing**

trophic level (*also* feeding level)

A trophic level is the position an organism occupies in a food chain.

• *Producers make up the first **trophic level**, and consumers make up the second and third levels.*

SEE ALSO **biomass, consumer, food chain, producer**

tropism

A tropism is a growth or movement in plants that occurs due to a specific stimulus.

• *Positive **tropism** occurs towards the stimulus. Negative **tropism** occurs away from the stimulus.*

SEE ALSO **gravitropism, hydrotropism, phototropism, thigmotropism**

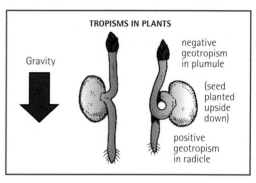

TROPISMS IN PLANTS

Gravity

negative geotropism in plumule

(seed planted upside down)

positive geotropism in radicle

troposphere *see* atmosphere

trypsin

is a protease secreted into the duodenum in the pancreatic juice. It is secreted as the inactive form trypsinogen, which is converted to trypsin by another enzyme.

• ***Trypsin** plays an important role in the digestion of proteins in the small intestine.*

SEE ALSO **pancreas, protease, small intestine**

tsunami

A tsunami is a long high sea wave caused by an underwater earthquake (seaquake).

• ***Tsunamis** can be very destructive when they reach land.*

SEE ALSO **earthquake**

tuber *see* stem

Tullgren funnel

A Tullgren funnel is a special funnel used to collect small animals (insects, beetles, etc.) from soil samples of leaf litter.

• *A **Tullgren funnel** is often used to extract arthropods from a sample of soil.*

tumour

A tumour is a growth of abnormal cells which are contained within one area, usually with a membrane. Malignant tumour cells are cancers. They invade neighbouring tissue and spread to different parts of the body where they form 'secondary tumours'.

• ***Tumours** are benign if they do not invade other parts of the body and are not classed as cancers.*

SEE ALSO **cancer, cell**

turgid

describes the state of a cell which has full turgor.

• *A **turgid** cell will not allow any more water (from osmosis) to enter the cell.*

SEE ALSO **flaccid, turgor**

turgor

is inflation of a plant cell to a rigid state brought about by osmosis. Healthy plant cells will take in no more water because the outward pressure (turgor pressure) equals the inward pressure of the cell wall.
• *A decrease in* **turgor** *inside the plant cells results in the plant wilting.*

SEE ALSO **osmosis, wilting**

turning force

A turning force is a force applied to an object which is fixed at a point around which it may rotate. The size of the turning force is its moment, which can be increased by increasing the force, or increasing the distance from the pivot, or both.

SEE ALSO **couple, moment, pivot**

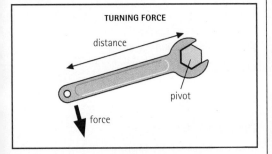

TURNING FORCE

distance

pivot

force

turns ratio *see* **transformer**

twin

A twin is an individual born at the same time as another individual to the same mother.
• *Twins can develop from the same egg (identical twins) or from two separately fertilized eggs (non-identical twins)*

SEE ALSO **identical twin, non–identical twin**

tympanic membrane *see* **outer ear**

tympanum *see* **outer ear**

typhoon

A typhoon is a tropical cyclone or hurricane which occurs over the Pacific Ocean and brings strong winds and rain to parts of south east Asia.
• *Typhoons can cause terrible destruction to buildings, trees, and crops.*

Uu

ulna *see* **human skeleton**

ultrasound

is sound above the human hearing range, around 20,000 Hz. Such sounds can be detected by animals such as bats and dogs. Ultrasound travels as waves with frequencies between 20 kHz and 10 MHz. Such waves have a wide range of uses.

WORD BUILD

ultrasound scanning

is used during pregnancy to check the development of unborn babies. It is painless, and safer than X-rays. The detector can be tuned to pick up only frequencies reflected from one particular source such as bone or fat or muscle, which reflect ultrasonic waves at particular speeds. It can therefore distinguish between these tissues. The reflected signals are processed by a computer, which produces an image (scan) of the baby inside the womb.

ultrasonic cleaning

uses the high-frequency vibrations of ultrasound to shake the dirt from clothing or other materials, and may be used by dentists to clean the coating of tartar off your teeth.

ultrasonic stress detection

uses ultrasound to detect internal cracks in metal parts such as aircraft bodies and wings. These cracks are stress fractures caused by continuous flexing.

SEE ALSO **human hearing range, sonar**

ultraviolet radiation (*also* UV radiation)

is produced from objects at very high temperatures, like the Sun. Such radiation from the Sun is used by your skin to produce vitamin D and will also give you a sun tan. However, excess exposure to ultraviolet radiation can cause skin cancer and could also damage the retina of your eye.
• *Ultraviolet radiation is an invisible electromagnetic wave but it can cause some chemicals to fluoresce (produce light) when they absorb this radiation, hence the use of such chemicals in washing powders.*

SEE ALSO **electromagnetic wave, ozone** ·

a
b
c
d
e
f
g
h
i
j
k
l
m
n
o
p
q
r
s
t
u
v
w
x
y
z

umbilical cord

The umbilical cord is a flexible tube that connects the embryo to the placenta in mammals.

• *Inside the **umbilical cord** is an artery which takes blood from the embryo into the placenta and a vein which returns blood to the embryo.*

SEE ALSO **embryo, placenta**

umbra

The umbra is the area of total or sharp shadow behind an opaque object where no light has reached. This type of shadow is formed by point sources and has a clearly defined outline.

SEE ALSO **eclipse, penumbra, shadow**

unicellular

describes living organisms which are made up of only one single cell, such as bacteria and protozoans.

SEE ALSO **bacteria, multicellular, protozoan**

unintentional enrichment *see* eutrophication

universal indicator *see* indicator

universe

The universe is all the matter, energy, and space that exists.

• *It is estimated that our **universe** contains 10^{41} kg of mass collected into 10^9 (a billion) galaxies.*

SEE ALSO **big–bang theory, steady–state theory**

➤ **expansion of the universe** The universe appears to be expanding because all the galaxies are getting further apart from each other. This expansion is a result of the universe stretching outwards as the number of objects (planets, stars, galaxies) embedded in space stays the same.

• *Evidence of the **expansion of the universe** comes from the red shift of light from distant galaxies before it reaches Earth.*

SEE ALSO **red shift**

unsaturated molecule

Unsaturated molecules contain double covalent bonds (alkenes) or triple covalent bonds (alkynes).

SEE ALSO **alkene, alkyne, covalent bond, saturated molecule**

unstable equilibrium *see* equilibrium

upthrust

is the upward force on an object which is immersed in a fluid.

• *If the **upthrust** is equal to or greater than the weight of the object, then the object will float in the fluid.*

SEE ALSO **Archimedes' principle, buoyancy, principle of flotation**

Uranus *see* planet

urea

is a toxic compound produced when proteins are broken down. It is a soluble, colourless compound found in urine.

• *Urea is also manufactured industrially for use in making plastics (thermosetting resins) and as a nitrogen fertilizer.*

SEE ALSO **urine**

ureter

The ureters are two tubes which carry urine from the kidneys to the bladder.

SEE ALSO **bladder, kidney, urine**

urethra

The urethra is the tube through which urine is discharged from the bladder to the exterior (urination).

SEE ALSO **bladder, urine**

urinary bladder *see* bladder

urinary system

The urinary system is the main system in the body concerned with the removal of waste material from the blood (excretion) and with water regulation (osmoregulation).

• *In mammals the **urinary system** consists of two kidneys, each linked to the bladder by a ureter.*

SEE ALSO **bladder, excretion, kidney, osmoregulation, ureter**

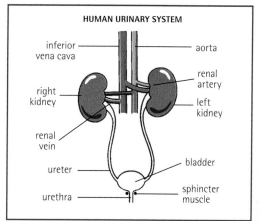

HUMAN URINARY SYSTEM

inferior vena cava — aorta — right kidney — renal artery — left kidney — renal vein — ureter — bladder — urethra — sphincter muscle

urine
is a liquid produced in the kidneys and stored in the bladder. It is an aqueous liquid containing nitrogenous waste materials such as urea, uric acid, and ammonia.
• *Urination is the release of **urine** from the bladder through the urethra to outside of the body.*
SEE ALSO **bladder, kidney, urea, urethra**

uterus (*also* womb)
The uterus is a hollow, muscular organ in which a fertilized egg develops into a fetus prior to birth.
• *The lining of the **uterus** shows cyclical changes during the menstrual cycle.*
SEE ALSO **female reproductive organ system, menstrual cycle**

UV radiation *see* ultraviolet radiation

uvula
The uvula is a small fleshy extension at the back of the mouth which hangs above the throat.
• *The **uvula** helps you to swallow (produces thin saliva) and helps in the production of certain sounds.*

V *see* **volt, voltage, volume**

v *see* **velocity**

vaccine
A vaccine is a liquid preparation of treated disease-producing microorganisms which can stimulate the immune system to produce antibodies in the blood.
• *Vaccines take the form of dead or weakened bacteria or viruses that can still act as antigens, but cannot reproduce.*
SEE ALSO **antibody, antigen, inoculation, microorganism**

vacuole
A vacuole is a fluid-filled sac found in the cytoplasm of cells.
• *Vacuoles are small and temporary in animal cells. Plant cells have one large permanent **vacuole** which is filled with cell sap.*
SEE ALSO **cell, cell sap, cytoplasm**

vacuum
A vacuum is a space in which there is no matter.
• *A perfect **vacuum** would contain no atoms or molecules. However, this is impossible to achieve as the surrounding material containing the vacuum would have a vapour pressure.*
SEE ALSO **vapour pressure**

vacuum flask
A vacuum flask is a container designed to minimize heat transfer. It is used to keep hot liquids hot, or cold liquids cold. It is made of a double-walled glass bottle, silvered on the inside and with a vacuum between its walls. The bottle has a cork or plastic stopper and is supported by cork blocks in an outer protective case. The vacuum prevents heat loss by conduction or convection, as there is no matter

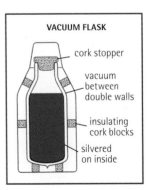

VACUUM FLASK

cork stopper

vacuum between double walls

insulating cork blocks

silvered on inside

»

a
b
c
d
e
f
g
h
i
j
k
l
m
n
o
p
q
r
s
t
u
v
w
x
y
z

to vibrate or move. The silvered walls of the flask minimize radiation loss by reflecting the heat back into the flask.

SEE ALSO conduction, convection, radiation

vagina

The vagina is a muscular tube leading from the uterus which holds the penis during mating or copulation.

• *The fully developed fetus is born through the vagina.*

SEE ALSO female reproductive organ system

valence electron

A valence electron is an electron found in the outermost electron shell of an atom. The number of valence electrons determines which group in the periodic table the element belongs to.

• *Valence electrons* are important in bonding of atoms.

SEE ALSO chemical bond, electron, group, periodic table

valency (*also* valence)

is the combining power of an atom or radical. In ionic compounds the valency is equivalent to the charge on the ion. In covalent compounds it is equal to the number of bonds formed.

SEE ALSO atom, covalent bond, ionic bond, radical, variable valency

Valency of Ionic Compounds		
Element	Ion	Valency
hydride	H^-	1
chloride	Cl^-	1
bromide	Br^-	1
iodide	I^-	1
oxide	O^{2-}	2
sulfide	S^{2-}	2
nitride	N^{3-}	3
phosphide	P^{3-}	3

Radical	Ion	Valency
ammonium	NH_4^+	1
hydroxide	OH^-	1
hydrogen carbonate	HCO_3^-	1
hydrogen sulfate	HSO_4^-	1
nitrate	NO_3^-	1
sulfate	SO_4^{2-}	1
sulfite	SO_3^{2-}	2
carbonate	CO_3^{2-}	2
phosphate	PO_4^{2-}	3

Valency of Ionic Compounds		
Element	Ion	Valency
sodium	Na^+	1
potassium	K^+	1
silver	Ag^+	1
hydrogen	H^+	1
lead(II)	Pb^{2+}	2
copper(II)	Cu^{2+}	2
magnesium	Mg^{2+}	2
calcium	Ca^{2+}	2
zinc	Zn^{2+}	2
barium	Ba^{2+}	2
iron(II)	Fe^{2+}	2
iron(III)	Fe^{3+}	3
aluminium	Al^{3+}	3

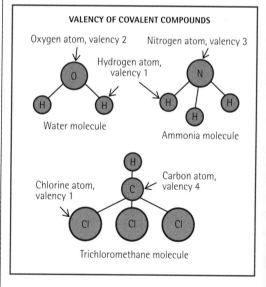

VALENCY OF COVALENT COMPOUNDS

Oxygen atom, valency 2   Nitrogen atom, valency 3

Hydrogen atom, valency 1

Water molecule

Ammonia molecule

Chlorine atom, valency 1

Carbon atom, valency 4

Trichloromethane molecule

Van de Graaff generator
A Van de Graaff generator is a machine used to produce electric charge from the mechanical movement of a rubber conveyor belt. The moving belt has electrons rubbed off it, so it becomes positively charged. This positive charge is transferred to a large metal dome mounted on a hollow insulating support. The region around the charged metal dome is its electric field. If a tuft of hair is inserted in the charged dome, the hair stands on end. This is due to the repulsive forces of like charges between each strand. The hair has electric potential.
SEE ALSO **electric charge, electric field, electric potential**

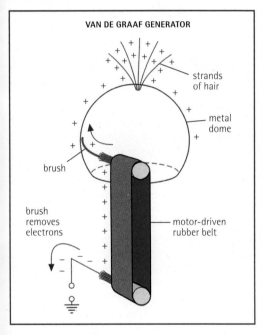

van der Waals forces
are intermolecular forces caused by induced dipoles (separation of positive and negative charge) brought about by the movement of electrons.
• *Van der Waals forces are weak attractive forces between atoms or molecules and typically measure around 10 kJ mol^{-1} (compared to the 1,000 kJ mol^{-1} of the attractive forces inside the molecules).*
SEE ALSO **intermolecular force**

vapour
A vapour is a gas which is below its critical temperature and can be liquefied by pressure alone.

• *Substances described as a **vapour**, like water vapour, have a boiling point above room temperature.*
SEE ALSO **critical temperature, evaporation**

vapour pressure
is the pressure of the vapour which is suspended above the surface of a liquid (or solid) at a particular temperature. The liquid and the vapour are in a phase equilibrium with each other.
• *When the temperature of a liquid increases so does the **vapour pressure** above the liquid.*
SEE ALSO **boiling point, phase equilibrium, volatile liquid**

variable valency
is the combining power of an element which can combine with other elements in different proportions. Many transition metal ions can have a variable valency. To distinguish the ions, we use roman numerals. For example, compounds containing Cu^+ are called copper(I) compounds to distinguish them from copper(II) compounds containing Cu^{2+}. Compounds containing Fe^{2+} and Fe^{3+} ions are distinguished as iron(II) and iron(III) compounds.
SEE ALSO **element, transition metal, valency**

Roman numeral	Old name
Cu(I)	cuprous
Cu(II)	cupric
Fe(II)	ferrous
Fe(III)	ferric

variation
is the range of differences between members of the same species. Only differences which are genetic in origin can be inherited and so acted on by natural selection.
SEE ALSO **natural selection**

continuous variation
shows a range of values between two extremes. Height, weight, hair colour, skin colour, IQ all show continuous variation. A graph showing such a variation is usually a normal distribution curve. Most of the population come in the middle of the range with few at the lower and upper ends.
• *Continuous variation is usually controlled by many different genes.*

»

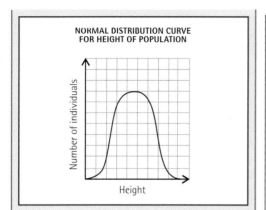

NORMAL DISTRIBUTION CURVE
FOR HEIGHT OF POPULATION

discontinuous variation

consists of specific characteristics or values
with nothing in between. Blood groups show
discontinuous variation. You are either A, B, O,
or AB. Other examples: garden peas are either
wrinkled or smooth; people have earlobes either
attached or unattached.

• *Discontinuous variations are often controlled
by one particular gene.*

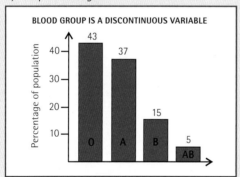

BLOOD GROUP IS A DISCONTINUOUS VARIABLE

environmental variation

is due to acquired characteristics such as diet,
upbringing, surroundings (food, water, shelter,
light), etc. Many characteristics are affected by
the environment, but not all. For example, blood
group, eye colour, hair colour, and inherited
diseases are due to genetic variation.

SEE ALSO **acquired characteristic**

genetic variation

is the variation in the genotype between
different individuals. During meiosis there is
an exchange of genes between homologous
chromosomes, by a process of 'crossing over'.

The gametes formed are never exactly the same.
When these gametes fuse during fertilization,
the possible combination of genes which may
be produced in the new zygote is large. Sexual
reproduction normally produces new vigour in
a species by mixing genetic material to produce
genetically varied offspring. It achieves the
greatest variation when the parents are drawn
from the widest population possible.

SEE ALSO **chromosome, fertilization,
meiosis, zygote**

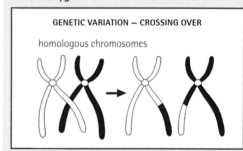

GENETIC VARIATION – CROSSING OVER

homologous chromosomes

vascular bundle

Vascular bundles (in seed plants) are regions of
vascular tissue (called conducting tissue) which are
responsible for the movement of water, mineral
salts, and food from the leaves to the storage and
growth organs. Vascular bundles normally consist
of xylem and phloem tissue separated by a living
cambium layer.

• *Roots often have a central **vascular bundle**,
whereas stems have vascular bundles arranged in a
ring near the outside edge.*

SEE ALSO **cambium, phloem, vascular tissue, xylem**

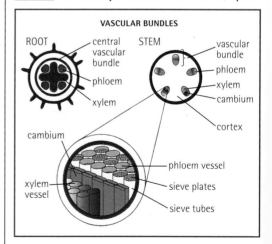

VASCULAR BUNDLES

vascular tissue

is the fluid-conducting tissue in the plant and consists of two types: xylem and phloem. In the roots of most flowering plants, the xylem vascular tissue is arranged in an X-shaped mass and the phloem vascular is found between the arms of the X.
• *In the stem of most plants the vascular tissue is in rings near the outside edge.*
SEE ALSO **phloem, vascular bundle, xylem**

vasoconstriction

is the closing of the dermal capillaries so that less blood flows and less heat is lost through the skin. This occurs when the body is cold.
• *Vasoconstriction results in an increase in blood pressure.*
SEE ALSO **blood pressure, capillary, dermis, skin**

vasodilation

is the opening of the capillaries in the dermis layer so that more blood flows and more heat is lost through the skin.
• *Vasodilation results in a decrease in blood pressure.*
SEE ALSO **capillary, dermis, skin**

vector

A vector is an agent (organism) responsible for carrying pathogens from one organism to another.
• *An example of a vector is the mosquito which transmits malarial pathogen.*
SEE ALSO **malaria, pathogen**

vector quantity

A vector quantity is one which has both magnitude and direction. When a value is given to a vector quantity, the direction must also be shown, normally by an arrow. The length of this arrow indicates the magnitude of the vector quantity.
• *Examples of a vector quantity are displacement, velocity, acceleration, force, etc.*
SEE ALSO **scalar quantity**

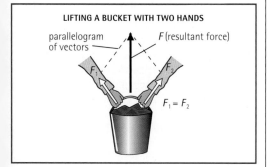

LIFTING A BUCKET WITH TWO HANDS

parallelogram of vectors

F (resultant force)

F_1 F_2

$F_1 = F_2$

vegan

A vegan is a person who does not eat or use animal products at all. A vegan's diet will not include fish, eggs, cheese, butter, or milk but does includes pulses, seeds, and nuts to provide protein.
• *Vegans do not wear leather, silk, or wool as these are animal products.*
SEE ALSO **vegetarian**

vegetarian

A vegetarian is a person who does not eat animals, including fish.
• *A vegetarian's diet includes milk and egg products, as well as nuts, seeds, and pulses, to provide protein.*
SEE ALSO **vegan**

vegetative propagation *see* reproduction

vegetative reproduction *see* reproduction

vein

A vein is a blood vessel that carries blood towards the heart and away from the body tissue. Veins contain valves to stop the blood from flowing backwards due to gravity. This is because the blood inside is at low pressure.
• *With the exception of the pulmonary vein, veins carry blood rich in carbon dioxide (deoxygenated blood) and waste products.*
SEE ALSO **artery, blood vessel, pulmonary vein, renal vein**

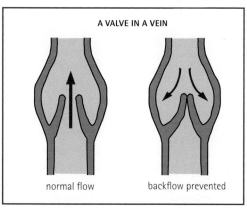

A VALVE IN A VEIN

normal flow   backflow prevented

velocity (*also* v)

❶ is the rate at which an object moves in a particular direction, expressed as the displacement of an object in a certain time.
• *Unlike speed, velocity is a vector quantity, as it has both size and direction. However, it is measured in the same units.*
SEE ALSO **speed, vector quantity**   »

❷ is the distance travelled by a wave in one second.

• *Velocity is calculated by multiplying the number of complete waves made in one second (frequency) by the length of each wave (wavelength).*

SEE ALSO **frequency, wave equation, wavelength**

velocity ratio (*also* V. R., distance ratio)

The velocity ratio for a simple machine is the distance moved by the effort (input force) divided by the distance moved by the load (output force) in the same time.

$$\text{velocity ratio} = \frac{\text{the distance moved by the effort}}{\text{distance moved by the load}}$$

• *A velocity ratio greater than one means that the effort moves further than the load.*

SEE ALSO **efficiency, machine, mechanical advantage**

velocity–time graph *see* graph

venereal disease *see* sexually transmitted disease

ventilation *see* breathing

ventricle

The ventricles are the two lowermost chambers of the heart which pump blood either to the lungs (right ventricle) or around the body (left ventricle).

SEE ALSO **heart**

venule

A venule is a small vein that receives blood from the capillaries.

SEE ALSO **capillary, vein**

Venus *see* planet

vermiform appendix *see* large intestine

vernier caliper

A vernier caliper is a measuring device which uses a vernier scale to measure to the nearest 0.1 mm. This permits more accurate readings than a simple calibrated scale. It is a small, movable scale graduated in intervals that are $\frac{9}{10}$ of those on the main scale. If this main scale reads to 1 mm, then the vernier reads to 0.1 mm.

SEE ALSO **micrometer screw gauge**

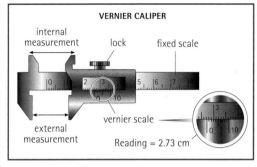

VERNIER CALIPER
internal measurement — lock — fixed scale
external measurement — vernier scale
Reading = 2.73 cm

verruca

A verruca is a painful wart (plantar wart) on the sole of the foot. Verrucas are a highly contagious viral lesion and can be caught when the skin is exposed with a cut or scrape. The virus is spread in communal areas such as swimming pools, showers, and sports facilities.

• *Verrucas range in size from 1 mm to 1 cm and have a small black dot on their surface.*

SEE ALSO **wart**

vertebra *plural* vertebrae

Vertebrae are the bones that make up the vertebral column. They generally have a thick body (centrum), a canal for the spinal cord, and projections for attachment of muscles.

• *There are 33 vertebrae (7 cervical, 12 thoracic, 5 lumbar, 5 sacral, 4 coccogeal) in the human backbone.*

SEE ALSO **vertebral column**

vertebral column (*also* backbone, spinal column, spine)

The vertebral column is a flexible series of small bones called vertebrae.

• *The vertebral column supports the skull, protects the spinal cord, and provides points of attachment for the pelvic and pectoral girdles.*

SEE ALSO **human skeleton, pectoral girdle, pelvic girdle, spinal cord, vertebra**

vertebrate (*also* craniate)

Vertebrates belong to a major subphylum of Chordata which contains all those animals with a vertebral column. Vertebrates are characterized by having a flexible endoskeleton made of bone and cartilage. They also have a complex nervous system and a well developed brain.

• *There are five classes of vertebrates: fishes, amphibians, reptiles, birds, and mammals.*

SEE ALSO **chordate, endoskeleton, nervous system, vertebral column**

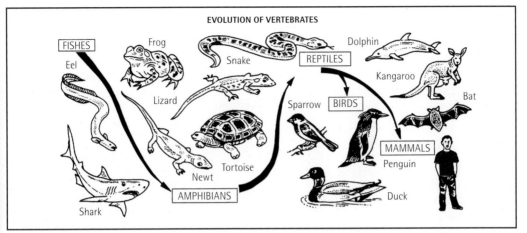

EVOLUTION OF VERTEBRATES

vestigial structure

Vestigial structures are reduced structures in a plant or animal which serve no function but have been 'left over' after the evolutionary process.

• *Examples of vestigial structures are the appendix in humans, the wings of flightless birds such as the ostrich, and the limb girdles of snakes.*

SEE ALSO homologous structure, large intestine

vibrating string

Vibrating strings produce sound waves when stretched and made to vibrate (e.g. in a piano or guitar). If the vibrating length of a string is halved, then the frequency of the note doubles and increases by one octave. If the tension in the string is increased, the frequency increases, but if its thickness increases, then the frequency decreases.

SEE ALSO harmonic, octave, sonometer

vibrio see bacteria

villus plural villi

A villus is one of the finger-like projections which line the wall of the small intestine. Inside the villus is a network of blood capillaries for absorption of soluble food material.

• *Each villus has a large surface area to increase absorption.*

SEE ALSO absorption, lacteal, small intestine

WORD BUILD

microvillus

A microvillus is one of a number of minute hair-like projections on the surface of the villus which increases surface area.

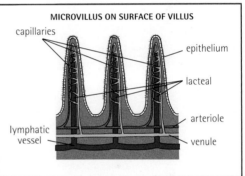

MICROVILLUS ON SURFACE OF VILLUS

capillaries — epithelium — lacteal — arteriole — lymphatic vessel — venule

virtual image see image

virus

Viruses are microorganisms which consists of a core of nucleic acid (DNA or RNA) surrounded by a protein coat. Viruses are about 100 times smaller than bacteria. Viruses are totally parasitic and infect plants, animals, and some bacteria (see bacteriophage). Outside their host organisms,

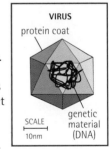

VIRUS
protein coat
genetic material (DNA)
SCALE
10nm

viruses are inactive. Only when attached to or inside the host cell can the virus start to multiply. It interferes with the cell's normal metabolism, and the viral DNA directs the host cell to make protein coats and nucleic acid for new viruses.

• *Many viruses are pathogens causing common diseases like the common cold or the flu (influenza).*

SEE ALSO bacteriophage, microorganism, nucleic acid, pathogen

viscous

describes a fluid (gas or liquid) which does not flow very easily.

• *A viscous substance is thick and sticky, like treacle.*

SEE ALSO fluid

visible light spectrum *see* colour

vitamin

Vitamins are organic compounds required by animals in small amounts to maintain health (see table). There are two major groups, those that are water soluble (e.g. vitamins B and C) and those that are fat soluble (e.g. vitamins A, D, E, and K).

• *Many vitamins are destroyed by cooking.*

SEE ALSO nutrient

Vitamin	Food sources
A (retinol)	carrots, milk
B_1 (thiamine)	yeast, beans
B_2 (riboflavin)	yeast, liver
C (ascorbic acid)	citrus fruit
D (calciferol)	cod liver oil, eggs
E (tocopherol)	cereal, green vegetables
K	egg yolk, green vegetables

Vitamin	Deficiency disease
A (retinol)	weakens vision (night blindness)
B_1 (thiamine)	beri-beri
B_2 (riboflavin)	mouth sores
C (ascorbic acid)	scurvy
D (calciferol)	rickets (soft bones)
E (tocopherol)	infertility
K	poor blood clotting

vitreous humour

is a jelly-like material which fills the rear cavity of the eye.

• *The vitreous humour exerts outward pressure to maintain the shape of the eyeball, and helps to refract (bend) the light.*

SEE ALSO eye

voice box *see* larynx

volatile liquid

A volatile liquid is one which has a low boiling point and changes easily into a vapour (high vapour pressure).

• *Perfumes and aftershaves contain volatile liquids, thereby producing pleasant aromas (vapours).*

SEE ALSO vapour, vapour pressure

volt (*also* V)

One volt is the p.d. between two points when one coulomb of electricity passes between these points and produces one joule of work.

$$\text{voltage (V)} = \frac{\text{electric energy (J)}}{\text{electric charge (C)}}$$

• *A volt is the SI unit of potential difference or electromotive force.*

SEE ALSO electromotive force, potential difference

voltage (*also* V)

is the potential difference or a measured value of this in volts.

SEE ALSO electromotive force, potential difference

voltage divider *see* potential divider

voltaic cell (*also* galvanic cell)

A voltaic cell is any device that produces an electromotive force (emf) by converting chemical to electrical energy.

• *The first voltaic cell was devised by Alessandro Volta (1745–1827).*

SEE ALSO electromotive force

voltmeter

A voltmeter is an instrument used to measure the potential difference (voltage) between any two points in an electrical circuit.

• *A voltmeter must be connected in parallel across the component whose potential difference it is measuring.*

SEE ALSO electrical circuit, electromotive force, potential difference

volume (*also* V)

The volume of a substance is the amount of space it occupies and is normally measured in cubic units (cm^3, m^3), or litres.

➤ **measurement of volume** depends on the physical state of the substance (solid, liquid, or gas). Volumes of gases can be measured using a gas syringe. Volumes of liquids can be measured approximately using a beaker, or more accurately using a measuring cylinder, burette, or pipette. Volumes of irregular shaped solids can be measured using a eureka can.

SEE ALSO burette, eureka can, pipette

➤ **volume of a gas** (*also* **V**) The volume of a gas is the amount of space the gas occupies, at a particular pressure and temperature.
• *The **volume of a gas** at different temperatures and pressures can be calculated by the ideal gas equation.*
SEE ALSO **Boyle's law, temperature of a gas**

voluntary action
Voluntary actions are actions which are controlled by conscious activity of the brain. Most voluntary actions involve voluntary muscles as effectors, often called skeletal muscles as they are attached to the skeleton. Information from the brain is carried to such muscles by motor neurones.
• *Examples of **voluntary actions** are movement of the neck, arms, legs etc.*
SEE ALSO **effector, involuntary action, muscle, neurone**

voluntary muscle *see* **muscle**

V. R. *see* **velocity ratio**

vulva
The vulva are the external parts of the female genitals in mammals.
• *The **vulva** consists of folds of tissue (labia), the clitoris and the vaginal opening.*
SEE ALSO **clitoris, female reproductive organ system, vagina**

Ww

W *see* **watt**

warm-blooded animal (*also* endotherm, homoiotherm)
Warm-blooded animals include all birds and mammals which can generate and maintain their body temperature no matter what the temperature of their environment. Such animals normally have feathers or fur (hair) to help to keep their body temperature constant (36–38°C in mammals and 38–40°C in birds). High internal body temperature allows fast action of muscles and nerves. As a result such animals can be highly active even in cold climates.
• *Some **warm-blooded animals**, including mammals (like bats) and birds (like owls), are active at night (nocturnal).*
SEE ALSO **cold-blooded animal**

wart
A wart is a small rough lump on the skin. It is caused by a virus, which causes a reaction in the skin. Warts can occur anywhere on the body but are most commonly found on the hands and feet. They do not cause any harm but some people find them itchy or embarrassing.
• *A **wart** can be treated with cream, spray, or plaster.*
SEE ALSO **skin, verruca, virus**

washing soda (*also* sodium carbonate)
acts as a water softener and is a cheap method of removing all hardness. It does this by chemical reaction to precipitate out the calcium and magnesium ions as carbonates.
• *Washing soda ($Na_2CO_3.10H_2O$) is a decahydrate as the hydrated crystals have ten water molecules associated with each molecule.*
SEE ALSO **soft water, water of crystallization**

waste management
involves classifying matter (garden waste, recyclable or non-recyclable waste) so that it can be recycled when possible. An increase in the standard of living and the rapid growth in human population means that more resources are used and much more waste is produced. Most waste will end up in landfill sites. Practice of the 3Rs (reduce, reuse, recycle) will help to reduce the vast quantities of waste that are produced. »

a
b
c
d
e
f
g
h
i
j
k
l
m
n
o
p
q
r
s
t
u
v
w
x
y
z

• *Waste management has become increasingly important due to the massive increase in quantities of waste throughout the world.*

SEE ALSO **landfill, land pollution**

water

is a colourless, tasteless, transparent liquid with highly unusual properties, and is essential to life. It boils at exactly 100°C when pure, and freezes at 0°C to form ice which is (unusually) less dense than the liquid form.

• *Water can be identified in the laboratory by adding it to anhydrous copper sulfate (which turns white to blue) or anhydrous cobalt chloride (which turns blue to pink).*

water cycle (*also* **hydrological cycle**)

The water cycle is the constant circulation of water between the atmosphere, the land, and the oceans. Evaporation from oceans, lakes, and vegetation produces water vapour, which forms clouds in the atmosphere. The water in the clouds then falls to the ground by precipitation (rain, snow, hail). Some percolates through the soil as groundwater to underground streams. Some drains off the surface directly into streams and rivers. All this water eventually drains back into the seas and oceans for the cycle to begin again. Some water on the ground is taken in by plants and animals. This is returned to the atmosphere as water vapour by respiration in animals and plants, and by transpiration in plants.

SEE ALSO **evaporation, precipitation, respiration, transpiration**

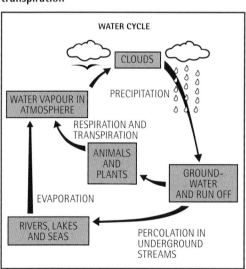

WATER CYCLE

water of crystallization

is water that is present in definite proportions in a crystal, which is normally a salt. Such salts are called hydrated salts, and the chemical formula shows the number of molecules of water of crystallization associated with each molecule of the hydrate: e.g. hydrated copper(II) sulphate $CuSO_4.5H_2O$.

• *Water of crystallization can usually be removed by heating.*

SEE ALSO **anhydrous, efflorescence, salt**

water pollution

results from human activities such as farming, industry, etc., causing various pollutants to dissolve in streams, rivers, and the sea. Fertilizers used by farmers are washed from the soil into streams (leaching) and cause eutrophication. Other water pollutants include agricultural waste (slurry), effluent and sewage, and oil from refineries and tankers.

SEE ALSO **effluent, eutrophication, leaching, oil pollution, sewage**

Water pollutant	Source
fertilizers	added to soil by farmers and leached from the soil by rainwater
effluent	industrial waste material including chemicals, solvents, detergents discharged from factories
sewage	human waste from washing and using the toilet. All sewage must be treated before being discharged into rivers or the sea
oil	from oil refineries or accidents at sea with oil tankers. Also many oil tankers wash out their holds after delivery

watt (*also* **W**)

A watt is the SI unit of power which is equal to 1 joule per second. It is a measure of how quickly energy is being transferred and can be linked with brightness (100W or 60W bulbs) or amount of heat (1 kW or 2 kW electric fires). With electrical power 1 watt is equivalent to 1 amp flowing under a potential difference of 1 volt.

• *The **watt** was named after a British engineer, James Watt (1736–1819).*

wave

A wave is a regular periodic disturbance in a medium or space. When an object disturbs the medium or

space around it, the disturbance travels away from the object or source in the form of waves.
SEE ALSO **carrier wave, electromagnetic wave, longitudinal wave, medium, progressive wave, sound wave, stationary wave, transverse wave**

wave energy
is the movement of the waves which can be used to rock large floats backwards and forwards. This movement can then be used to drive a generator to produce electricity.
• *Wave energy is pollution-free and is not a finite energy source.*
SEE ALSO **tidal energy**

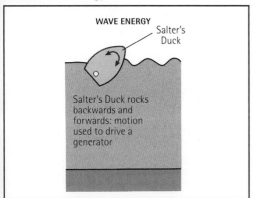

WAVE ENERGY
Salter's Duck

Salter's Duck rocks backwards and forwards: motion used to drive a generator

wave equation
The wave equation relates velocity (v), frequency (f), and wavelength (λ):

$$v = f \times \lambda$$

SEE ALSO **frequency, velocity, wavelength**

wave intensity
is a measurement of the energy carried by a wave.
• *Wave intensity depends on both the amplitude and frequency of the particular wave.*
SEE ALSO **amplitude, frequency**

wavelength (*also* λ)
is the distance between two identical points on the wave, e.g. two adjacent peaks or two adjacent troughs.
SEE ALSO **frequency, velocity, wave**

weak electrolyte *see* electrolyte

weathering
is the wearing down of rocks by the environment.
• *Weathering of rock is important as it allows minerals from the rock into the surrounding soil, which can then be absorbed by plants.*
SEE ALSO **erosion, rock**

chemical weathering
is the dissolving and breakdown of rock by chemical reactions. Rainwater is a weak acid, as it contains dissolved carbon dioxide gas. This can dissolve certain types of rock such as limestone or chalk.
• *Chemical weathering has been increased by the action of acid rain.*
SEE ALSO **acid rain**

physical weathering
is weathering caused by the sea, wind, ice, temperature changes, etc. Sea waves continuously pounding the rocks of a cliff, or wind carrying tiny particles of grit, can wear away even the hardest rocks. Ice forming in rock crevices can split rocks, as water expands when it freezes. Great changes in temperature (especially in desert regions) can shatter rock. Plant roots can grow into crevices and break off rock fragments (biological weathering).

weight
is the gravitational force exerted on an object by the Earth (or another planet).
• *The weight of an object on the Moon is one sixth of that on Earth, as the gravitational force of the Moon is one sixth that of the Earth.*
SEE ALSO **gravitational force, mass**

wet cell
A wet cell is a voltaic cell which has a liquid electrolyte.
• *A common example of a wet cell is the car battery.*
SEE ALSO **car battery, electrolyte, voltaic cell**

white blood cell (*also* leucocyte, white corpuscle)
White blood cells are colourless blood cells with a nucleus which are important in defence against disease.
• *There are two main types of white blood cell, called lymphocytes and phagocytes.*
SEE ALSO **lymphocyte, phagocyte, red blood cell**

white dwarf
A white dwarf is a small dense star about the size of a planet, formed as the end product of the stellar evolution of a star of relatively low mass.
SEE ALSO **stellar evolution**

a
b
c
d
e
f
g
h
i
j
k
l
m
n
o
p
q
r
s
t
u
v
w
x
y
z

whooping cough *see* **childhood illness**

wilting
is a state in which the plant is losing more water by transpiration than it can replace by osmosis, so that its cells become flaccid.
• *If* **wilting** *continues the plant will die through lack of nutrients and minerals.*
SEE ALSO **flaccid, osmosis, plasmolysis, transpiration**

windpipe *see* **trachea**

wind power
is the use of the motion of the Earth's atmosphere to drive machinery or generators to produce electricity. Wind has been used as a source of power in windmills, sailing ships, etc. since early times.
• *Wind power* *is a renewable source of energy and is pollution-free.*

wisdom tooth *see* **tooth**

womb *see* **uterus**

wood charcoal *see* **charcoal**

work (*also* **J**)
is the energy transfer that occurs when a force causes an object to move a certain distance in the direction of the force.

work done (J) = force (N) × distance moved in the direction of the force (m)

$W = F \times d$

Work can only be done if a force moves something. Energy can be used up without work being done if the object does not move. For example, work is done when a crate is lifted. However, if the crate is too heavy to lift, then no work is done, but energy is still used up in trying to lift the crate.
• *Work* *is measured in joules (J).*
SEE ALSO **energy, joule**

wrought iron
is a purer form of iron than pig iron or cast iron, with 1–3% impurities.
• *Wrought iron* *is easy to weld and work (malleable) and is used for chains, hooks, gates, etc.*
SEE ALSO **cast iron, pig iron**

Xx

X-chromosome *see* **sex chromosome**

xenon *see* **noble gas**

X-ray
An X-ray is given off when fast-moving electrons are suddenly stopped so that they lose their energy very quickly. They are very high frequency electromagnetic waves and can penetrate solid material. X-rays are used in CT scans (computed tomography) in hospitals to produce virtual image 'slices' throughout the body. They are also used to examine bone fractures and to identify dental problems.
• *Overexposure to X-rays is very dangerous because their ionizing effect damages living cells.*
SEE ALSO **electromagnetic wave**

xylem
The xylem is the vascular tissue of plants which allows water and dissolved mineral salts to move from the roots through the stem to the leaves. The cells of the xylem are strengthened by a rigid substance called lignin in their cell walls.
• *Xylem* *vessels form the woody part of a plant and do not contain living cytoplasm.*
SEE ALSO **phloem, vascular tissue**

Yy

Y-chromosome *see* **sex chromosome**

year
A year is the time it takes for the planet Earth to complete one orbit of the Sun. A year is 365¼ days.
• *Every four years we have a leap year, with an extra day (February 29th) to add the 'four quarters of a day' missed with the normal 365 day year.*
SEE ALSO **planet**

yeast
Yeasts are a group of unicellular fungi which carry out the biochemical process used in baking and brewing. They are saprophytes which secrete enzymes to convert sugars into other substances.
• *One of the substances produced from sugars by the yeast is ethanol (alcohol). In brewing the alcohol is used in drinks but in baking the alcohol is evaporated away inside the oven.*
SEE ALSO **baking, brewing, fermentation, fungus, saprophyte**

Zz

Z *see* **atomic number**

zero error
A zero error is one caused when a measuring instrument does not start from exactly zero.
• *The zero error here is shown for a vernier caliper.*
SEE ALSO **vernier caliper**

ZERO ERROR

Vernier caliper is closed and should read 0.0 mm. However, it reads 0.3 mm, so the caliper has a zero error of 0.3 mm

Vernier caliper reads 4.34 cm, but 0.3 mm must be subtracted from this reading to give a true reading of 4.31 cm

zinc (*also* **Zn**)
is a white metallic element which is moderately reactive with oxygen, steam acids etc.
• *Zinc is used in alloys to coat iron and steel (galvanizing) as a protection against corrosion.*
SEE ALSO **galvanizing, metal, reactivity series**

zoology
is the scientific study of animals and animal life.

zooplankton
are microscopic animals that float in the sea or fresh water. They are a food source for many creatures but unlike plant plankton (phytoplankton) they cannot photosynthesize their own food.
• *Near the surface of the sea there may be many thousands of zooplankton per cubic metre.*
SEE ALSO **plankton, photosynthesis**

zygote
A zygote is a fertilized egg produced by the fusion of the nucleus of the male and female sex cells.
• *A zygote is a single cell, but rapidly divides by mitosis to form the embryo.*
SEE ALSO **conception, embryo, mitosis**

zymase
is an enzyme found in yeast that causes the breakdown of glucose and some other sugars.
• *The enzyme zymase is important in the fermentation of sugars to make alcohol.*
SEE ALSO **enzyme, fermentation, glucose, yeast**

a
b
c
d
e
f
g
h
i
j
k
l
m
n
o
p
q
r
s
t
u
v
w
x
y
z

What have customers been saying about the *Oxford Student's Science Dictionary?*

Choose Oxford Science for revision support that counts

Browse our range of Revision Guides, Homework Books, and Exam Practice Workbooks at

www.oxfordsecondary.com/revision

ISBN: 978-1-38-200484-8

ISBN: 978-1-38-200485-5

ISBN: 978-1-38-200487-9

ISBN: 978-1-38-200488-6